IN INDIAN MEXICO

AMS PRESS
NEW YORK

The Music at Cancuc

IN INDIAN MEXICO

A NARRATIVE OF TRAVEL AND LABOR

BY

FREDERICK STARR

CHICAGO
FORBES & COMPANY
1908

Library of Congress Cataloging in Publication Data

Starr, Frederick, 1858-1933.
In Indian Mexico.

Reprint of the ed. published by Forbes, Chicago.
1. Indians of Mexico. 2. Mexico—Description and travel. 3. Starr, Frederick, 1858-1933. I. Title.
F1220.S78 1978 972'.004'97 74-9025
ISBN 0-404-11903-4

First AMS edition published in 1978.

Reprinted from the edition of 1908, Chicago. [Trim size of the original has been slightly altered in this edition. Original trim size: 15.5 × 23.7 cm. Text area of the original has been maintained in this edition.]

MANUFACTURED
IN THE UNITED STATES OF AMERICA

IN INDIAN MEXICO

IS AFFECTIONATELY DEDICATED TO

A. A. ROBINSON

TO WHOM ALL MY WORK IN MEXICO IS DUE

AND

WHOSE INTEREST HAS BEEN CONTINUOUS

AND UNFAILING

PREFACE

The reading public may well ask, Why another travel book on Mexico? Few countries have been so frequently written up by the traveler. Many books, good, bad, and indifferent, but chiefly bad, have been perpetrated. Most of these books, however, cover the same ground, and ground which has been traversed by many people. Indian Mexico is practically unknown. The only travel-book regarding it, in English, is Lumholtz's "Unknown Mexico." The indians among whom Lumholtz worked lived in northwestern Mexico; those among whom I have studied are in southern Mexico. The only district where his work and mine overlap is the Tarascan area. In fact, then, I write upon an almost unknown and untouched subject. Lumholtz studied life and customs; my study has been the physical type of south Mexican indians. Within the area covered by Lumholtz, the physical characteristics of the tribes have been studied by Hrdlička. His studies and my own are practically the only investigations within the field.

There are two Mexicos. Northern Mexico to the latitude of the capital city is a *mestizo* country; the indians of pure blood within that area occupy limited and circumscribed regions. Southern Mexico is indian country; there are large regions, where the *mestizos*, not the indians, are the exception. From the time of my first contact with Mexican indians, I was impressed with the notable differences between tribes, and desired to make a serious study of their types. In 1895, the accidental meeting with a priest from Guatemala led to my making a journey to Central America. It was on that journey that I saw how the work in question might be done. While the government of Mexico is modeled upon the same pattern as our own, it is far more paternal in its nature. The Republic is a confederation of sovereign states, each of which has its elected governor. The states are subdivided into districts somewhat corresponding to our counties, over each of which is a *jefe politico* appointed by the governor; he has no responsibility to those below him, but is directly responsible to the man who names him, and who can at will remove him; he is not expected to trouble the state government unnecessarily, and as long as he turns over the taxes which are due the state he is given a free hand. Within the districts are the cities and towns, each with its local, independent, elected town government.

The work I planned to do among these indian towns was threefold: 1. The measurement of one hundred men and twenty-five women in each population, fourteen measurements being taken upon each subject; 2. The making of pictures,— portraits, dress, occupations, customs, buildings, and landscapes; 3. The making of plaster busts of five individuals in each tribe. To do such work, of course, involved difficulty, as the indians of Mexico are ignorant, timid, and suspicious. Much time would be necessary, in each village, if one depended upon establishing friendly and personal relations with the people. But with government assistance, all might be done promptly and easily. Such assistance was readily secured. Before starting upon any given journey, I secured letters from the Department of Fomento, one of the Executive Departments of the Federal Government. These letters were directed to the governors of the states; they were courteously worded introductions. From the governors, I received letters of a more vigorous character to the *jefes* of the districts to be visited. From the *jefes*, I received stringent orders upon the local governments; these orders entered into no detail, but stated that I had come, recommended by the superior authorities, for scientific investigations; that the local authorities should furnish the necessaries of life at just prices, and that they should supply such help as was necessary for my investigations. In addition to the orders from the *jefes* to the town authorities, I carried a general letter from the governor of the state to officials of every grade within its limits. This was done in case I should at any time reach towns in districts where I had been unable to see the *jefe politico*. It was desirable, when possible, that the *jefe* should be seen before serious work was undertaken. As Governor Gonzales of Oaxaca once remarked, when furnishing me a general letter: "You should always see the *jefe politico* of the district first. These indians know nothing of me, and often will not recognize my name; but the *jefe* of their district they know, and his orders they will obey." In using these official orders, I adopted whatever methods were best calculated to gain my ends; success depended largely on my taking matters into my own hands. Each official practically unloaded me upon the next below him, with the expectation that I should gain my ends, if possible, but at the same time he felt, and I knew, that his responsibility had ended. In case of serious difficulty, I could not actually count upon the backing of any one above the official with whom I then was dealing.

Upon the Guatemala expedition, which took place in January – March, 1896, my only companion was Mr. Ernst Lux, whose knowledge of the language, the country, and the people was of the utmost value. As the result of that journey, my vacations through a period of four years were devoted to this field of research. The first field expedition covered the period from November, 1897, to the end of March, 1898; the plan of work included the visiting of a dozen or more tribes, with interpreter, photographer, and plaster-worker; the success of the plan depended upon others. Dr. W. D. Powell was to serve as interpreter, Mr. Bedros Tatarian as photographer; at the last moment the plans regarding the plaster-worker failed; arrived in the field, Dr. Powell was unable to carry out his contract; the photographic work disintegrated, and failure stared us in the face. Reorganization took place. Rev. D. A. Wilson was secured as interpreter, two Mexican plaster-workers, Anselmo Pacheco of Puebla and Ramon Godinez of Guadalajara, were discovered, and work was actually carried through upon four tribes. The second field expedition covered the period of January-March, 1899; eight tribes were visited, and a most successful season's work was done; Charles B. Lang was photographer, Anselmo Pacheco plaster-worker, and Manuel Gonzales general helper. The third field season, January-March, 1900, was in every way successful, six populations being visited; my force consisted of Louis Grabic photographer, Ramon Godinez plaster-worker, and Manuel Gonzales general assistant. The work was brought to a conclusion in January-March, 1901, during which period six tribes were visited; the party was the same as the preceding year.

"In Indian Mexico" claims to be only a narrative of travel and of work. It is intended for the general public. The scientific results of our expeditions have been published under the following titles:

1. The Indians of Southern Mexico: an Ethnographic Album. Chicago, 1899. Cloth; oblong 4to; pp. 32. 141 full-page plates.

2. Notes upon the Ethnography of Southern Mexico. 1900. 8vo, pp. 98. 72 cuts, maps, etc. Proc. Dav. Acad. Nat. Sci., Vol. VIII.

3. Notes on the Ethnography of Southern Mexico, Part II. 1902. 8vo, pp. 109. 52 cuts, map, etc. Proc. Dav. Acad. Nat. Sci., Vol. IX.

4. The Physical Characters of the Indians of Southern Mexico. 4to, 59 pp. Sketch map, color diagram, and 30 double cuts. Decennial Publications, University of Chicago, 1902.

5. The Mapa de Cuauhtlantzinco or Codice Campos. 1898. 8vo, pp. 38. 46 engravings. University of Chicago Press.

6. Recent Mexican Study of the Native Languages of Mexico. 1900. 8vo, pp. 19. 7 portraits.

7. Picture of Otomi woman beating bark paper. Printed on sheet of the original paper; mounted.

8. The Mapa of Huilotepec. Reproduction; single sheet, mounted.

9. The Mapa of Huauhtla. Reproduction; single sheet, mounted.

10. Survivals of Paganism in Mexico. The Open Court. 1899.

11. Mexican Paper. American Antiquarian. 1900.

12. The Sacral Spot in Maya Indians. Science. 1903.

Naturally, in a work of such extent we have been under obligation to many parties. It is impossible to acknowledge, in detail, such obligations. We must, however, express our indebtedness, for assistance rendered, to the Mexican Central Railroad, the Mexican Railway, the Mexican National Railroad, the Tehuantepec Railroad, the Mexican Southern Railroad, and the Interoceanic Railroad; also to the Ward Line of steamers. Among individuals, it is no unfair discrimination to express especial thanks to Mr. A. A. Robinson and Mr. A. L. Van Antwerp. President Diaz has ever shown a friendly interest in my plans of work and the results obtained. Señor Manuel Fernandez Leal,

Minister of the Department of Fomento, more than any other official, lent us every aid and assistance in his power; his successor, Señor Leandro Fernandez, continued the kindness shown by Minister Leal. And to all the governors of the states and to the *jefes* of the districts we are under many obligations, and express to each and all our appreciation of their kind assistance. Those personal friends who have been helpful in this specific work in Indian Mexico are mentioned in the appropriate places in the text. To those companions and assistants who accompanied us upon the journeys a large part of the results of this work are due.

CHICAGO, January, 1908.

CONTENTS

IN INDIAN MEXICO

CHAPTER I

PRIESTLY ARCHÆOLOGY

(1895)

WHILE we stood in the Puebla station, waiting for the train to be made ready, we noticed a priest, who was buying his ticket at the office. On boarding the train, we saw nothing of him, as he had entered another car. Soon after we started, Herman made his usual trip of inspection through the train, and on his return told me that a learned priest was in the second-class coach, and that I ought to know him. As I paid no great attention to his suggestion, he soon deserted me for his priestly friend, but presently returned and renewed his advice. He told me this priest was no common man; that he was an ardent archæologist; that he not only collected relics, but made full notes and diagrams of all his investigations; that he cared for live indians also, and had made a great collection of dress, weapons, and tools, among Guatemalan tribes. When I even yet showed no intention of hurrying in to visit his new acquaintance, the boy said: "You must come in to see him, for I promised him you would, and you ought not to prove me to be a liar."

This appeal proved effectual and I soon called upon the priestly archæologist in the other car. He was an interesting man. By birth a German, he spoke excellent English; born of Protestant parents and reared in their faith, in early manhood be became a Catholic; renounced by his parents and left without support, he was befriended by Jesuits and determined to become a priest. Entering the ministry at twenty-nine years of age, he was sent as mission priest to foreign lands. He had lived in California, Utah, and Nevada; he had labored in Ecuador, Panama, and Guatemala. His interest in archæology, kindled in the Southwest, continued in his later fields of labor. Waxing confidential he said: "I am a priest first, because I must live, but it does not interfere much with my archæology." For years past the padre has lived in Guatemala, where he had charge of one of the largest parishes in that Republic, with some eighteen thousand full-blood indians in his charge. Like most Germans a linguist, the padre spoke German, French, Spanish, English, and Quiche, the most important indian speech of Guatemala. In his parish, he so arranged his work as to leave most of his time free for investigation. Twice a week he had baptisms, on Thursday and Sunday; these duties on Thursday took but a couple of hours, leaving the rest of the day free; Sundays, of course, were lost, but not completely, for the indians often then told him of new localities, where diggings might be undertaken. Always when digging into ancient mounds and graves, he had his horse near by ready for mounting, and his oil and other necessaries at hand, in case he should be summoned to the bedside of the dying. As the indians always knew where to look for him, no time was lost.

Not only was the padre an archæologist: he also gathered plants, birds, and insects. When he was leaving Germany, his nephew, the ten-year-old child of his sister, wished to accompany him. The parents refused their permission, but the uncle gave the boy some money, and they met each other in Frankfort and started on their journey. They have been together ever since. The padre depends completely on the younger man, whom he has fashioned to his mind. The plants, birdskins, and insects have supplied a steady income. The plants cost labor; insects were easier to get. All the indian boys in the parish were supplied with poison-bottles and set to work; a stock of prints of saints, beads, medals, and crucifixes was doled out to the little collectors, according to the value of their trophies. To allay the suspicions of his parishioners, the padre announced that he used the insects in making medicines. One Sunday a pious old indian woman brought to church a great beetle, which she had caught in her corn field four days before; during that time it had been tied by a string to her bed's leg; she received a medal. One day a man brought a bag containing some five hundred living insects; on opening it, they all escaped into the house, causing a lively time for their recapture.

The nephew, Ernst, had made a collection of eleven hundred skins of Guatemalan birds. The padre and he have supplied specimens to many of the great museums of the world, but the choicest things have never been permitted to leave their hands.

The padre is a great success at getting into trouble. He fled from Ecuador on account of political difficulties; his stay in Guatemala is the longest he has ever made in one place. During his eight years there he was successful; but he finally antagonized the government, was arrested, and thrown into jail. He succeeded in escaping, fled to Salvador, and from there made his way to the United States, where, for a little time, he worked, unhappily, at San Antonio, Texas. A short time since, the Archbishop of Oaxaca was in Texas, met the padre, and promised him an appointment in his diocese. The padre was now on his way to Oaxaca to see the prelate and receive his charge.

He was full of hope for a happy future. When he learned that we were bound for the ruins of Mitla, he was fired with a desire to accompany us. At Oaxaca we separated, going to different hotels. My party was counting upon the company of Mr. Lucius Smith, as interpreter and companion, to the ruins, but we were behind our appointment and he had gone upon another expedition. This delighted the padre, who saw a new light upon the path of duty. The archbishop had received him cordially, and had given him a parish, although less than a day had passed since his arrival. When the padre knew of our disappointment, he hastened to his prelate, told him that an eminent American archæologist, with a party of four, wished to visit Mitla, but had no interpreter; might he not accompany these worthy gentlemen, in some way serving mother church by doing so? So strong was his appeal, that he was deputed to say mass at Mitla Sunday, starting for his new parish of Chila on the Monday following.

In the heavy, lumbering coach we left next morning, Saturday, for Mitla. The road, usually deep with dust, was in fair condition on account of recent rains. We arrived in the early afternoon and at once betook ourselves to the ruins. At the curacy, we presented the archbishop's letter to the indian cura, who turned it over once or twice, then asked the padre to read it, as his eyes were bad. While the reading proceeded, the old man listened with wonder, and then exclaimed, "What a learned man you are to read like that!" As we left, the padre expressed his feelings at the comeliness of the old priest's indian housekeeper, at the number of her children, at the suspicious wideness of his bed, and at his ignorance, in wearing a ring, for all the world just like a bishop's. But he soon forgot his pious irritation amid those marvelous ruins of past grandeur. In our early ramble he lost no opportunity to tell the indians that he would repeat mass on the morrow at seven, and that they should make a special effort to be present.

WITH THE PADRE IN MITLA RUINS

THE PADRE, ERNST AND THE DOGS

But as we wandered from one to another of the ancient buildings, the thought of the morrow's duty lost its sweetness. He several times remarked that it was a great pity to lose any of our precious morning hours in saying mass, when there were ruins of such interest to be seen. These complaints gained in force and frequency as evening approached, until finally, as we sat at supper, he announced his decision to say mass before daybreak; he would call me at five o'clock, we would go directly to the church, we would be through service before six, would take our morning's coffee immediately after, and then would have quite a piece of the morning left for the ruins, before the coach should leave for Oaxaca.

The plan was carried out in detail. At five we were called from our beds by the anxious padre. Herman and I were the only members of the party who were sufficiently devout to care to hear mass so early. With the padre, we stumbled in the darkness up to the church, where we roused the old woman who kept the key and the boy who rang the bell. The vestments were produced, the padre hastily robed, and the bell rung; the padre was evidently irritated at the absence of a congregation, as he showed by the rapid and careless way in which he repeated the first part of the service. When, however, at the *Credo*, he turned and saw that several poor indians had quietly crept in, a change came over him; his tone became fuller, his manner more dignified, and the service itself more impressive and decorous. Still, we were through long before six, and throwing off his vestments, which he left the boy to put away, the padre seized me by the arm, and we hastened down the hill to our morning's coffee. On the way we met a number of indians on their way to mass, whom the padre sternly rebuked for their laziness and want of devotion. Immediately after coffee, we were among the ruins.

The padre had kindly arranged for my presentation to his Grace, Archbishop Gillow. Reaching Oaxaca late on Sunday afternoon, we called at the Palace. His Grace is a man of good presence, with a face of some strength and a courteous and gracious manner. He appeared to be about fifty-five years of age. After the padre had knelt and kissed the ring, the archbishop invited us to be seated, expressed an interest in our trip to Mitla, hoping that it had proved successful. He then spoke at some length in regard to his diocese. He emphasized its diversity in climate and productions, the wide range of its plant life, the great number of indian tribes which occupied it, the Babel of tongues within it, its vast mineral wealth. A Mexican by birth, the archbishop is, in part, of English blood and was educated, as a boy, in England. He speaks English easily and well. He showed us many curious and interesting things. Among these was a cylindrical, box-like figure of a rain-god, which was found by a priest upon his arrival at the Mixe Indian village of Mixistlan.* It was in the village church, at the high altar where it shared worship with the virgin and the crucifix. The archbishop himself, in his description of the incident, used the word *latria*. We were also shown a little cross, which stood upon the archbishop's writing-table, made in part from a fragment of that miraculous cross, which was found by Sir Francis Drake, upon the west coast. That "terrible fanatic" tried to destroy it, according to a well-known story. The cross was found standing when the Spaniards first arrived and is commonly attributed to St. Thomas. Sir Francis upon seeing this emblem of a hated faith, first gave orders to hew it down with axes; but axes were not sharp enough to harm it. Fires were then kindled to burn it, but had no effect. Ropes were attached to it and many men were set to drag it from

* Survivals of Paganism in Mexico. The Open Court. 1899.

the sand; but all their efforts could not move it. So it was left standing, and from that time became an object of especial veneration. Time, however, destroys all things. People were constantly breaking off bits of the sacred emblem for relics until so little was left of the trunk near the ground that it was deemed necessary to remove the cross. The diggers were surprised to find that it had never set more than a foot into the sand. This shows the greatness of the miracle.

The padre had been assigned to the parish of Chila, a great indian town, near Tehuacan. Early the next morning he left for his new home.

* * * * *

Not only did the padre, while in Oaxaca, urge us to call upon him in his new parish; after he was settled, he renewed his invitation. So we started for Chila. We had been in the *tierra caliente*, at Cordoba. From there we went by rail to Esperanza, from which uninteresting town we took a street-car line, forty-two miles long, to Tehuacan. This saved us time, distance, and money, and gave us a brand-new experience. There were three coaches on our train, first-, second-, and third-class. When buying tickets we struck acquaintance with a Syrian peddler. Three of these were travelling together; one of them spoke a little English, being proficient in profanity. He likes the United States, *per se*, and does not like Mexico; but he says the latter is the better for trade. "In the United States, you sell maybe fifteen, twenty-five, fifty cents a day; here ten, fifteen, twenty-five dollars." The trip lasted three hours and involved three changes of mules at stations, where we found all the excitement and bustle of a true railroad station.

The country was, at first, rolling, with a sparse growth of yuccas, many of which were exceptionally large and fine. On the hills were occasional *haciendas*. This broken district was succeeded by a genuine desert, covered with fine dust, which rose, as we rode, in suffocating clouds. Here the valley began to close in upon us and its slopes were sprinkled with great cushion cactuses in strange and grotesque forms. After this desert gorge, we came out into a more open and more fertile district extending to Tehuacan. Even this, however, was dry and sunburned.

Our party numbered four. We had written and telegraphed to the padre and expected that he, or Ernst, would meet us in Tehuacan. Neither was there. No one seemed to know just how far it was to Chila. Replies to our inquiries ranged from five to ten leagues.* Looking for some mode of conveyance, we refused a coach, offered at fifteen pesos, as the price seemed high. Hunting horses, we found four, which with a foot *mozo* to bring them back, would cost twenty pesos. Telling the owner that we were not buying horses, but merely renting, we returned to the proprietor of the coach and stated that we would take it, though his price was high, and that he should send it without delay to the railroad station, where our companions were waiting. Upon this the owner of the coach pretended that he had not understood that there were four of us (though we had plainly so informed him); his price was for two. If we were four, he must have forty pesos. A fair price here might be eight pesos for the coach, or four for horses. So we told the coach owner that we would walk to Chila, rather than submit to such extortion. This amused him greatly and he made some facetious observations, which determined me to actually perform the trip on foot. Returning to the railroad station, where two of the party were waiting, I announced my intention of walking to Chila; as the way was long and the sand heavy and the padre's silence and non-appearance boded no great hospi-

* The Mexican league is 2.7 miles.

tality in welcome, I directed the rest to remain comfortably at Tehuacan until my return on the next day. Herman, however, refused the proposition; my scheme was dangerous; for me to go alone, at night, over a strange road, to Chila was foolhardy; he should accompany me to protect me. Consenting that he should accompany, we began to seek a *mozo*, as guide to Chila. With difficulty, and some loss of time, one was found who would undertake the business for two pesos. In vain a Jew peddler standing by and the station agent remonstrated with the man; two pesos was a full week's wages; it was ridiculous to demand such a price for guiding two foot travellers to Chila. He admitted that two pesos might be a week's wages; but he did not have to go to Chila and if we wanted him to do so we must pay his price. We capitulated, the station agent loaned us a revolver, we left our friends behind us and started on our journey. It was now dark. In a mysterious voice, our guide said we must go first to his house; there he secured his *serape* and a heavy club. As we left his house he feared we must be hungry and indicated a bread-shop; we purchased and all three ate as we walked; a moment later he suggested that we would need *cigarros* of course, and a stock of these were added, at our expense. Then, at last, we came down to business.

Plainly our guide did not enjoy his task. Shortly after we started, the moon rose and, from its shining full on the light sand, it was almost as bright as day. We were in single file, our guide, Herman, and I. At sight of every bush or indistinct object, our guide clutched his club and crossed himself, as he mumbled a prayer. When we met anyone, we kept strictly to our side of the road, they to theirs, and, in passing, barely exchanged a word of greeting. The timidity and terror of our guide increased as we advanced, until I concluded to be prepared for any emergency and carried the revolver in my hand, instead of in my pocket. Mile after mile we trudged along through the heavy sand, into which we sunk so far that our low shoes repeatedly became filled and we had to stop to take them off and empty them. We passed through San Pablo, left the Hacienda of San Andres to one hand, and, finally, at 10:10 found ourselves in the great indian town of San Gabriel de Chila. It was much larger than we had anticipated and almost purely indian. We walked through a considerable portion of the town before we reached the plaza, the church, and the *curato*. Our journey had probably been one of fifteen miles. All was dark at the *curato;* an indian was sleeping in the corridor, but he was a traveller and gave us no information on being awakened. At our third or fourth pounding upon the door, Ernst appeared at the window; on learning who we were he hastened to let us in. He reported trouble in the camp; the padre had gone hastily to Oaxaca to see the archbishop; our telegram had not been received; our letter came that morning. We found that things were packed ready for removal. A good supper was soon ready, but while it was being prepared we took a cool bath, by moonlight, in the trough bath-tub out in the *patio*.

In the morning we heard the full story. Formerly there was here a priest, who devoted his whole life to this parish, growing old in its service; in his old age he was pensioned, with sixty pesos monthly from the parish receipts. The priest who succeeded him, coming something over three years ago, was a much younger man. During his three years of service, he was continually grumbling; the work was hard, his health was bad at Chila, the heat was intolerable; he wished another parish. The archbishop finally took him at his word; without warning he transferred him to another parish, and sent our friend, the archæologist here, in his place. This did not suit the man relieved; Chila itself was much to his liking; what he really wanted was to be relieved from the support of his superannuated predecessor. No sooner was he transferred than he began to look with longing on his former charge and to make a vigorous effort to regain it. Accusations were hurried to Oaxaca; the new priest was pursuing agriculture as a means of profit; he had not paid the dues to the aged priest; he had himself admitted to parishioners that his object in coming to Chila was more to study antiquities and natural history than to preach the gospel. It is claimed that, immediately on receiving this communication, the archbishop sent a peremptory letter to the padre demanding an explanation; this letter, Ernst said, never was delivered, hence no explanation was sent. The prelate acted promptly; orders were sent to our friend to give up the parish to the former priest, who appeared on the scene to receive his charge. Then, and then only, it is said the delayed letter came to light. The padre had left, at once, for Oaxaca and his archbishop. From there he sent messages by telegraph: "Pack up, and come to Tehuacan;" "Wait until you hear further." A third came the morning we were there: "Pack up; meet me at Tehuacan, ready to go to a new parish."

It was really sad to look about the new home, to which he had come with such buoyant hopes and of which he had been so soon dispossessed. When he arrived, the place was neglected and filthy; two whole days were necessary to clean it. It had contained practically no furniture; he had made it look like a place in which to live. He had improved and beautified its surroundings. He had planted a little corn and set out some young banana trees; he had gathered many species of cactus from the neighboring hills and had built up a fine bed of the strange plants in his *patio*.

Passionately fond of pets, he had two magnificent greyhounds and a pug — all brought from Guatemala — a black collie, doves, hens and turkeys on the place. And now, he was again without a home and his time, money, and labor were lost.

Ernst accompanied us to Tehuacan. We rented three horses and a man on foot went with us to bring them back to the village. And for the whole we paid the regular price of eighty-seven centavos — twenty-five each for the animals, and twelve centavos for the man — something less than the twenty pesos demanded the day before at Tehuacan.

CHAPTER II

WE START FOR GUATEMALA

(1896)

THE evening we were at Mitla, Señor Quiero came hurrying to our room and urged us to step out to the corridor before the house to see some Mixes. It was our first glimpse of representatives of this little known mountain people. Some thirty of them, men and women, loaded with fruit, coffee, and charcoal, were on their way to the great fair and market, at Tlacolula. They had now stopped for the night and had piled their burdens against the wall. Wrapping themselves in their tattered and dirty blankets, they laid themselves down on the stone floor, so close together that they reminded me of sardines in a box. With a blazing splinter of fat pine for torch, we made our inspection. Their broad dark faces, wide flat noses, thick lips and projecting jaws, their coarse clothing, their filthiness, their harsh and guttural speech, profoundly impressed me and I resolved to penetrate into their country and see them in their homes, at the first opportunity.

Our friend the padre never tired of telling how much more interesting Guatemala was than Mexico; he could not understand why any man of sense should waste his time in Mexico, a land so large that a dozen students could not begin to solve its problems, while Guatemala, full of interesting ruins and crowded with attractive indians, was of such size that one man's lifetime could count for something. His tales of indian towns, life, dress, customs, kindled enthusiasm; but it was only after thinking over the Mixes, that I decided to make a journey to Guatemala. The padre, himself, could not accompany me, being a political refugee, but he had told me Ernst should go with me. After three months' consideration my plan was made. We would start from Oaxaca overland via the Mixes country; we would everywhere keep in the mountains; in Chiapas we would completely avoid the usual highway, hot and dusty, near the coast; in Guatemala itself, we would go by Nenton, Huehuetenango and Nibaj. This did not suit the padre: he had had in mind a journey all rail and steamer; and friends, long resident in Mexico, shook their heads and spoke of fatigues and dangers. But I was adamant; the Mixes drew me; we would go overland, on horse, or not at all.

When the Padre left Chila, he took a letter of recommendation from the Archbishop of Oaxaca to the Bishop of Vera Cruz at Jalapa. By him, the padre was located at Medellin, a few miles from Vera Cruz itself. Thither I journeyed to join Ernst and make the final preparations for the journey. Ernst met me at the station at 6:30 in the evening and we stayed the night in the hot, mosquito-tortured, plague-stricken city. Leaving at eight o'clock in the morning we were at Medellin in an hour. Our journey was through low, swampy ground on which the chief growth was of palm. The padre, whom we had not seen since we parted at Oaxaca, met us at the station and took us at once to his house. The town is small, the population a miserable mixture of black, white, and indian elements. Few of the couples living there have been legally married. The parish is one of the worst in the whole diocese. The bishop warned the padre that it was an undesirable field, but it was the only one then unoccupied. But the padre was working wonders and the church was then undergoing repairs and decorations. The actual *curato* was long ago

The Padre's House; Medellin

The Church; Medellin

seized by the government and is now used as a schoolhouse. The priest lived in a rented house close by the river bank. The house is a double one and the priest occupied but half of it; those in the other half were hostile to him and he was anxious to rent the whole place. His neighbors, however, did not care to leave and threatened vengeance; they were behind a mass of accusations filed against him with the bishop. His friends rallied to his support, sent in a strong endorsement, and he remained. The padre had been industrious while here. Behind his house is the little river, with a bath-house built over it; crossing in a dugout canoe we found his garden flourishing, filled with fresh vegetables. The family of pets had grown; Baldur, Freia, Votan, Doxil — the dogs — were here as at Chila, but he also had fantail and capuchin pigeons, hens and chicks, ducks and geese, canary birds, and native birds in cages. Here also were archæological relics, plants, beetles and birds for gathering. And here too, for the first time, I had the opportunity of examining his great collection of Ecuadorean humming-birds and a magnificent lot of Guatemalan quetzal skins, among them probably the finest ever collected.

We left Medellin on January 8th; went by rail to Puebla, then to Oaxaca. Here we found our friend Doctor Hyde, of Silao, who was nursing Lucius Smith, in what proved to be a final illness. He aided us in finding animals and completing preparations for our journey. We secured a large bay horse for myself, a roan for Ernst, a little mule for baggage. For my own part, I dislike mules; Ernst and the doctor, however, were loud in their praise of such a beast; both asserted that a good mule should sell for double its cost on our arrival at Guatemala City. When, finally, after inspecting a variety of animals we found one lively, young one, the doctor was delighted. Taking me to one side, he informed me that such an opportunity was unlikely to occur again. I yielded and the little mule was ours. We named the three animals Mixe, Zapotec, and Chontal, from three tribes through whose country we expected to pass.

The doctor's helpfulness was not confined to advice regarding mules. He insisted upon our buying various supplies, such as boxes of sardines, sago, coffee, etc., the utility of which appeared neither at the time nor later. Also at his suggestion a quart of whiskey was purchased and carefully divided into two flasks, one for each saddlebag. Most useful of all the doctor's suggestions, and one for which we had reason many times to thank him, was the securing from the governor of a letter to all local authorities in the state, directing them to supply us with the necessities of life, at just prices.

We had hoped to start from Oaxaca in the early morning, but it was well on in the afternoon before all arrangements were completed. The doctor and his Mexican friend rode with us to Tule to see us well started. It was out over the old road to Mitla. The afternoon was hot, dust was deep, and a heavy wind blew it up into our faces in clouds. The sun was already setting when we rode into Santa Maria Tule, and we went at once to see the famous cypress tree, which no one in the party, save myself, had seen. It seems now to be a single tree, but was perhaps, originally, three; at present it displays a single, vast trunk, buttressed with heavy irregular projecting columns. So irregular is this enormous mass that no two persons taking its girth exactly agree. We measured it four feet above the ground and made the circumference one hundred and sixty feet. The mass of delicate green foliage above was compact, vigorous, and beautiful. Many years ago Humboldt cut a rectangular piece of bark from the old trunk and on the smooth surface thus exposed carved an inscription with his name.

The Rain-god; from the Church at Mixistlan

The Great Tree at Tule

Bark has since grown over the sides and corners of this tablet, but much of the inscription may still be read. Since Humboldt's visit many lesser men have gashed the old tree to leave their mark.

As it was now darkening we hurried to the *meson* of the village. The old lady in charge received us with suspicion; she could not feed us and refused to receive us into the house for the night; she would permit us to sleep outside, in the corridor — which we might have done without asking permission. At this moment, the doctor's friend remembered that he knew a man here and went out to reconnoitre; he soon returned and led us to his friend's house, where we were well received. A supper of eggs, *tortillas*, and chocolate was soon served. Before we had finished the moon had risen and by its light the doctor and his friend started on their return to town. We slept on beds, made of boards laid upon sawhorses, in a grain storeroom, where rats were running around all night long.

The next day, we were again at Mitla. It was a festival day, that of the Conversion of St. Paul the Apostle. In the evening there were rockets, the band played, and a company of drummers and *chirimiya* blowers went through the town. Señor Quiero had fires of blazing pine knots at the door. When the procession passed we noted its elements. In front was the band of ten boys; men with curious standards mounted on poles followed. The first of these standards was a figure, in strips of white and pink tissue paper, of a long-legged, long-necked, long-billed bird, perhaps a heron; next stars of colored paper, with lights inside; then were large globes, also illuminated, three of white paper and three in the national colors — red, white, and green. Grandest of all, however, was a globular banner of cloth on which was painted a startling picture of the saint's conversion. All of these were carried high in the air and kept rotating.

Behind the standard bearers came a drummer and the player on the shrill pipe or *pito—chirimiya.* The procession stopped at Señor Quiero's *tienda,* and the old man opened both his heart and his bottles; spirits flowed freely to all who could crowd into the little shop and bottles and packs of *cigarros* were sent out to the standard-bearers. As a result we were given a vigorous explosion of rockets, and several pieces by the band, the drummer, and the *pitero.*

Beyond Mitla the valley narrows and the road rises onto a gently sloping terrace; when it strikes the mountains it soon becomes a bridle-path zigzagging up the cliffside. As we mounted by it, the valley behind expanded magnificently under our view. We passed through a belt of little oak trees, the foliage of which was purple-red, like the autumnal coloring of our own forests. Higher up we reached the pine timber. As soon as we reached the summit, the lovely valley view was lost and we plunged downward, even more abruptly than we had mounted, along the side of a rapidly deepening gorge. At the very mouth of this, on a pretty terrace, we came abruptly on the little town of San Lorenzo with palm-thatched huts of brush or cane and well grown hedges of *organo* cactus. Here we ate *tortillas* and fried-eggs with chili. Immediately on setting out from here we rode over hills, the rock of which was deeply stained with rust and streaked with veins of quartz, up to a crest of limestone covered with a crust of stalagmite.

The road up to this summit was not good, but that down the other side was *bad.* The irregular, great blocks of limestone, covered with the smooth, dry, slippery coating, caused constant stumbling to our poor animals. From this valley we rose onto a yet grander range. Here we had our first Mixe experience. At the very summit, where the road became for a little time level, before plunging down into the profound valley beyond, we met two indians,

The Start from Oaxaca

The Celebration at Mitla

plainly Mixes. Both were bareheaded, and both wore the usual dirty garments — a cotton shirt over a pair of cotton trousers, the legs of which were rolled up to the knees or higher. The younger of the men bore a double load, as he had relieved his companion. The old man's face was scratched and torn, his hands were smeared with blood and blood stained his shirt. We cried an "*adios*" and the old man kissed my hand, while the younger, pointing to his friend said "*Sangre*, *Señor*, *sangre*" (Blood, sir, blood.) Vigorously they told the story of the old man's misfortune, but in incomprehensible Spanish. While they spoke three others like them, each bent under his burden came up onto the ridge. These kissed my hand and then, excitedly pointing to the old man, all talking at once, tried to tell his story. Having expressed our sympathy, we left the five looking after us, the old man, with his torn and bleeding face, being well in the foreground.

Down in the valley, across a little stream, we struck into a pleasant meadow road leading to the Hacienda of San Bartolo. Suddenly, before us, in the road, we saw a man lying. We thought he was dead. He was a young man, an indian in the usual dress, apparently a Zapotec. His face was bloody and his shirt was soaked in front with blood, which had trickled down upon the ground forming a pool in which he lay. We could see no deep wound, but, as he lay upon his side, there may have been such. Near him in the road there lay a knife, the blade covered with blood. The man lay perfectly still, but we fancied we could see a slight movement of the chest. In Mexico, it is best not to investigate too closely, because the last to touch a murdered man may be held responsible for his death. So we hurried on toward the *hacienda* but, before reaching it, met two girls about nineteen years of age and a little lad, all Zapotecs. We told them what we had seen and bade them notify the authorities. One of the girls cried, "*Si, Señor, es mi hermano*" ("Yes, sir, it is my brother"), and they ran down the road. As for us, we hurried onward, without stopping at the *hacienda*, in order not to be delayed or held as witnesses.

There is no love between the Zapotecs and Mixes. We never learned the actual story, but imagined it somewhat as follows. The old Mixe, carrying his burden, had probably encountered the young Zapotec and had words with him. Probably there had been blows, and the old man was having the worst of it when his companions came along and turned the tide of battle.

The road, after passing the *hacienda*, ascended almost constantly for many miles. We passed clumps of yuccas. As we mounted we faced a strong and cutting wind, and were glad when any turn in the road gave us a moment's relief. The final ascent was sharp and difficult, up a hill of red or purple slate, which splintered into bits that were both slippery and sharp to the feet of our poor animals. Just as the sun was setting and dusk fell, we reached the miserable pueblo of Santa Maria Albarradas. It was situated on a terrace or shelf, and its little houses were made of red or purple adobe bricks, and thatched with grass. Little garden patches and groups of cultivated trees surrounded the houses. The church was little larger than the dwellings, and was constructed of the same clay, thatched with the same grass. Near it was the town-house. We summoned the *presidente*, and while we waited for him, the men, women, and children of the town thronged around us and watched our every movement, commenting the while on our actions and words. When the *presidente* came, we made known our wants and soon had supper for ourselves, food for our animals, a shelter for the night, and a *mozo* as guide for the morrow. The town-house was put at our disposition; it was sadly in need of repairs, and consisted of two rooms, one larger than the other. In the larger room there was a long and heavy table, a bench or two, and some wooden chairs. We slept upon the ground, and long before we rolled ourselves up in our blankets the wind was blowing squarely from the north. The sky was half covered with a heavy black cloud; as the night advanced, it became colder and colder, the wind cutting like a knife, and while we shivered in our blankets, it seemed as if we had been born to freeze there in the tropics.

CHAPTER III

THE LAND OF THE MIXES

(1896)

SANTA MARIA was the last Zapotec town; we were on the border of the country of the Mixes. Starting at seven next morning, we followed a dizzy trail up the mountain side to the summit. Beyond that the road went down and up many a slope. A norther was on; cold wind swept over the crest, penetrating and piercing; cloud masses hung upon the higher summits; and now and again sheets of fine, thin mist were swept down upon us by the wind; this mist was too thin to darken the air, but on the surface of the driving sheets rainbows floated. The ridge, which for a time we followed, was covered with a thicket of purple-leaved oaks, which were completely overgrown with bromelias and other air-plants. From here, we passed into a mountain country that beggars description. I know and love the Carolina mountains — their graceful forms, their sparkling streams and springs, the lovely sky stretched above them; but the millionaires are welcome to their "land of the sky"; we have our land of the Mixes, and to it they will never come. The mountains here are like those of Carolina, but far grander and bolder; here the sky is more amply extended. There, the slopes are clad with rhododendrons and azaleas, with the flowering shrub, with strawberries gleaming amid grass; here we have rhododendrons also, in clusters that scent the air with the odor of cloves, and display sheets of pink and purple bloom; here we have magnificent tree-ferns, with trunks that rise twenty feet into the air and unroll from their summits fronds ten feet in length; fifty kinds of delicate terrestrial ferns display themselves in a single morning ride; here are palms with graceful foliage; here are orchids stretching forth sprays — three or four feet long — toward the hand for plucking; here are pine-trees covering slopes with fragrant fallen needles. A striking feature is the different flora on the different slopes of a single ridge. Here, too, are bubbling springs, purling brooks, dashing cascades, the equals of any in the world. And hither the tourist, with his destroying touch, will never come.

We had thought to find our wild Mixes living in miserable huts among the rocks, dressed in scanty native garb, leading half wild lives. We found good clearings on the hillside; fair fields of maize and peas, gourds and calabashes; cattle grazed in the meadows; fowls and turkeys were kept; the homes were log-houses, substantially built, in good condition, in neat enclosures; men and women, the latter in European dress, were busied with the duties of their little farms. Clearing after clearing in the forest told the same story of industry, thrift, and moderate comfort.

After more than five hours of hard travel we reached the Mixe town of Ayutla, and rode at once to the *curato*. The priest was not at home. It was market-day, and people were in town from all the country round. The men, surprised at sight of strangers, crowded about us; some gazed at us with angry glances, others eyed us with dark suspicion, some examined us with curious and even friendly interest. Many of them spoke little or no Spanish. Thronging about us they felt our clothing, touched our skins, saddles, baggage, and exhibited childish curiosity. The women at the *curato* spoke Spanish, of course; we told them we should stay there for a day or two, and sent out for the *presidente*. On his coming, we explained to him our business and asked leave to occupy the *curato* in the absence of the priest.

Ayutla is situated on a high terrace, before which opens a lovely valley and behind which rises a fine mountain slope. The village church, while large, is roofless; the town-house lies below the village, and by it are two jails for men and women. The houses of the village are small, rectangular structures of a red-brown-ochre adobe brick; the roofs slope from in front backward, and are covered with red tiles they project in front so as to cover a little space before the house.

By evening most of the indians in the town were drunk. At sunset a miserable procession started from the church, passed through the village, and then returned to the church; composed mostly of women, it was preceded by a band of music and the men who carried the *santito*. Later, we heard most disconsolate strains, and, on examination, found four musicians playing in front of the old church; three of them had curious, extremely long, old-fashioned horns of brass, while the fourth had a drum or *tambour*. The *tambour* was continuously played, while the other instruments were alternated in the most curious fashion. The music was strange and wierd, unlike any that we had ever heard before. However, we became thoroughly familiar with it before we had traversed the whole Mixe country, as we heard it twice daily, at sunrise and after sunset. It was the music of the Candelaria, played during the nine days preceding February 2d. As we sat listening to the music the *presidente* of the town appeared. His Spanish, at no time adequate, was now at its worst, as he was sadly intoxicated. We tried to carry on a conversation with him, but soon seeing that naught but disaster could be expected, if we continued, we discreetly withdrew to our room.

A Street in San Lorenzo

Ayutla

There we found the *fiscal*, and I have rarely seen so drunk an official. When drunk, he is violent and abusive, and it was plain that the women at the *curato* were afraid of him. More than one hundred and fifty years ago Padre Quintana, who was the mission priest at Juquila, translated the *Doctrina* into Mixe and wrote a *Gramatica* of the language, both of which were then printed. We wished to secure copies of these old and rare books, and asked the *fiscal* if there were any here. He promptly replied that he had one at his house, and invited us to go there with him to see it. We at once started, and on our way had to pass the drunken *presidente* and the musicians. As we drew near them the *presidente*, with drunken dignity, rose and said: "Where are you going, Señores?" The *fiscal* was for going directly onward without giving answer; we hesitated and began a reply. Our delay was fatal; staggering up to us, his Honor said: "I shall not permit you to go; this man is drunk; he will be dangerous. I am responsible for your safety." The *fiscal*, standing at a little distance, cried: "Señores! shall we go?" We started toward him; the *presidente* interfered: "No, Señores, you shall not go to-night; the man is drunk; return to your house." "*Vamonos*," (Let us go) hiccoughed the *fiscal*. "*Manana*," (to-morrow) hiccoughed the *presidente*. The *fiscal* stormed; the *presidente* threatened him with jail, ordered him home, and with a body-guard for our protection led us to our room. Scarcely able to totter, the *presidente* assured us that drunken men were dangerous and ought not to be trusted; at the same time he produced his bottle and offered us a drop to warm us. It required tact and time to get rid of him and his corps of protectors. Early the next morning both of these worthy officials, *presidente* and *fiscal*, still drunk, called upon us with the book — a *Doctrina* of 1729. With the *presidente* were two stalwart fellows, intended, as he whispered to us audibly, to handle the *fiscal* in case he became dangerous. The audience ended, and the party dismissed, the *presidente* stood in the road until the *fiscal* had started for home, when he left for the town-house. The *fiscal's* home-going, however, was mere pretense. No sooner was the *presidente* gone than he came staggering into the *patio* of the *curato*. The women ran into our room, in terror: "The *fiscal* comes; bar the door; do not let him in." A moment later a feeble rap at the door, a call and a mournful request for admission; the barricaded door gave no encouragement. At intervals through the morning there came the flying maids: "He comes! don't let him in." Again and again the barricade; again and again, the vain appeal for entrance. We left Ayutla at noon. We had scarcely well started when we heard some one calling behind us. Turning, we saw the *fiscal*, running unsteadily toward us. We waited; he came up out of breath. "*Ya se va?*" (Now you are leaving?) "*Si, señor,*" (Yes, sir.) With a look of despair he removed his hat, and fumbling in its depths produced two cigarettes; presenting one to each of us, he waved his hand as we rode away and cried: "*Adios! señores.*"

For some distance our road led up a cañon. Reaching its head, we gained the pass at two o'clock. A wonderful sight here presented itself. Above us was a brilliant blue sky — cloudless; every detail of the rock crest upon which we stood was clear. Forested to its summit, the ridge formed the half of a magnificent amphitheatre, whose slopes had been vertically furrowed at a hundred points by torrents; to the left a spur projected, the crest of which sloped gently downward, forming an enclosing wall upon that side. Before us, beyond the valley, was a boundary line of mountain masses, sharply outlined against the sky. Lower ridges, nearer to us, paralleled this distant rampart. The only apparent outlet from this valley was around the spur to our left. Looking down upon this magnificent valley, we saw it occupied by a sea of clouds, the level surface of which looked like a lake of water flecked here and there with white-caps. The higher hills within the valley rose like islands from the water; to the left a mighty river seemed to flow around the spur, out into a boundless sea of cloud beyond. The level surface of this lake, river, and sea of clouds was hundreds of feet below us.

From this summit, our trail plunged downward into this sea of mists. When we reached its upper surface, which was plainly defined, little wisps of mist or cloud were streaming up along the furrowed channels of the mountain walls. As we entered the lake of cloud the sunlight became fainter, uprushes of cold mists struck us, gloom settled, denser and denser grew the fog, drops of condensed vapor dripped from the trees under which we passed. At the bottom of the valley, we could scarcely see a dozen yards in any direction. We were passing along meadows, like those of New England, with brakes, sunflowers, and huckle-berries; here and there were little fields of wheat or peas. The fog was too dense for us to know whether we lost fine scenery. We saw nothing of the little villages through which we passed. On and on we plunged along the trail, until it began an ascent of a ridge, almost like a knife-edge, with steep slopes on both sides. When we had reached the summit of this ridge, we found the trail level, through a growth of oak trees which were loaded with bromelias and orchids. Though still dim, the light had brightened as we rose to higher levels. Graceful ferns and sprays of terres-trial orchids overhung our trail at every cutting or slope. One spray, which I plucked as I rode under it, was more than a yard in length, and its curiously colored brown and yellow flowers were strangely like insects in form. At one level summit of our ridge, we came upon a little white-washed building of adobe, dome-topped, with no windows and but one little door. Pushing this open, I entered through a doorway so narrow that I had to remove my hat, and so low that I was forced to bend, and found myself in a little shrine with a cross and pictures of two or three saints, before which were plain vases filled with fresh flowers, the offerings of travelers. We added our spray of orchids before we resumed our journey.

For three hours, during which no distant view had delighted our eyes, we had traveled in the mists; we had almost forgotten that the sun could shine. At the end of a long, narrow ridge, where it joined the greater mountain mass, we found a rest-house. Here the trail turned abruptly onto the larger ridge, mounted sharply through a dugway, and then to our complete surprise emerged into the fair sunlight. The clear, blue sky was over us, and directly below us, at our horses' feet, was the flat top of the sea of clouds. A moment more and we rose to a point of view from which the grandest view of a lifetime burst upon our vision. Opposite, the evening sun was nearing the horizon, before and below us lay the valley; we were upon the very edge of a great mountain slope. To our right lay the cloud mass, which was all in movement, precipitating itself down the slope into the profound valley. It was a river of vapors, more than two miles, perhaps, in width, plunging, perhaps, two thousand feet into the abyss. Niagara, which I have often seen, is a pigmy cataract in comparison. The cloud mass tossed and heaved, whirled and poured in one enormous sheet over the precipice, breaking into spray as it struck against projecting rock masses. Every movement of whirling and plunging water was there; the rapid above the fall, the plunge, the whirlpool, the wild rush of whirlpool rapids, all were there, but all silent, fear-

Cloud Cataract; Near Juquila

Dancers in the Danza de la Conquista; Juquila

fully and impressively silent. We could have stood there gazing for hours, but night was coming and a stretch of unknown road still lay before us. At the other end of the valley, in the dusk of early evening, we saw a second cataract pouring in. From both ends the cloud rivers were rushing in to fill the valley, along the edge of which we crept. And presently we plunged down again into the mists; night fell; our trail was barely visible, and we had to trust to our horses to find it; the air was cold and penetrating. Long after dark, we rode into Juquila.

The *cura* had gone to bed; the *meson* had no room for us and no food for our horses; our case seemed desperate. We heard, however, noisy laughter and the loud voices of men drinking. So I begged Ernst to seek the *presidente* and tell him our needs while I looked after the animals. The official was at the *tienda*, drinking with his friends. Ernst made known our wishes, producing our letter from the governor. At this, the *presidente* became furious: "Who is this with orders from the governor? Let me kill him," and with that he drew his *machete* and made at Ernst. Some of his less-intoxicated friends restrained him, and Ernst, concluding that the moment was not propitious, returned to me. After other fruitless efforts to get food for ourselves and animals we resigned ourselves to our fate, and lay down upon the stone floor of the corridor outside the *meson*, with a crowd of sleeping indians as companions.

Very early in the morning, all the town officials, except the *presidente*, came to apologize for the occurrence of the night. They announced that the *presidente*, realizing what he had done, had taken to the mountains, and asked what they could do for us. We ordered fodder for our hungry beasts, food for ourselves, and a place of shelter. The town-house was offered to us, and we were moved into those quarters with due ceremony.

Although we stayed several days at Juquila, the *presidente* did not return, during our presence, to resume his duties of office. We were, however, well treated. The *cura* aided us with advice, information, and helpers. While we were in the village the *danza de la Conquista* took place. It is a popular play, with much dancing and music, and little action or dialogue, which celebrates the Conquest of Mexico by Cortez. It was rendered in the shade of a great tree near the church. In the first act, nine men and two girls took part; in the second act, there were many others. The nine men and two girls represented indians; they wore crowns with plumes of snow-white down; in their hands they carried a rattle, made from the fruit of a tree and a wand of white down, with which they beat time. One man, representing Montezuma, had a crown of brilliantly colored plumes. The other eight men were warriors; the two girls were "*Malinches*." The first act consisted of a series of dances, including a very pretty maypole dance. The play lasted about three hours, and represented the life of the indians before the Conquest — Montezuma in his court, with the amusements celebrated for his entertainment. Hearing of the arrival of the Spaniards, he is filled with sad forebodings, which the amusements fail to dispel. In the second act, Hernando Cortes appears, with soldiers. While the costumes of the indians were gay, and more or less attractive, those of these European warriors were ludicruously mongrel and unbecoming. The newcomers demanded that Montezuma acknowledge the authority of the King of Spain and the cross of Christ. Conversations, demands, replies, tableaus, sword-dances, etc., ensued. Finally, Montezuma and his warriors yielded, and kissed the crucifix.

While this drama was being enacted under the shade-tree, another amusement, in connection with the *fiesta of*

Road Approaching Quezaltepec

San Marcos, was in progress in front of the church. The musicians with the long horns made doleful music; a dozen gayly-costumed dancers took part. They wore dark trousers slitted up the sides; bright kerchiefs, with the point hanging down in front, were tied about the waists; crowns of plumes were on the heads; red vests and kerchiefs, crossed at the neck, completed the costume. One player, who seemed to be a leader, carried a tri-colored flag; another represented a man on horseback, by creeping into a frame of sticks, covered with cloth, in the shape of a horse. They danced in the full sunlight for hours; their movements were varied and pretty, quite different, too, from the figures in the *danza de la Conquista*. Two outside characters played the clown. One of these was a little lad dressed in a garment representing a tiger-skin, while over his face he wore a heavy, old wooden mask, imitating an animal's head. The other was older, dressed in a leather suit, with a wooden mask like a vacant-looking human face. These two were very popular, and indulged in many acts that bordered on the obscene. We got no satisfactory explanation of this whole performance. The *cura* said that it represented the conflict between Christ and the Jews; this we greatly doubted.

Mixe roads avoid no mountains, and usually go straight up one slope and down the other. The Mixe villages are set upon the very crests, or upon little terraces a few hundred feet below the crest, or the summit of some spur that juts out from the great mountain mass, of a long and narrow ridge. The road from Juquila, by Ocotepec to Quezaltepec was beautiful and typical. The ascent, just before Quezaltepec, was magnificent. We had a letter of introduction from the *cura* at Juquila to the schoolteacher at Quezaltepec, and therefore rode directly to the school. The four boys who were in attendance were promptly dismissed and the *maestro* was at our disposition. He was a *mestizo*, and possessed the art of lying in a fine degree, like so many of his kind. This man set us an excellent supper, having asked us beforehand what we would like. We replied that we would be glad to have fresh meat, if there was any to be had. He replied, "There is always fresh meat here; someone kills every day." It really appeared in the dinner, but, as we ate it, our host remarked — "Gentlemen, it is indeed lucky that you arrived here just now, because to-night we have fresh meat, and like enough a month will pass before anyone in town kills again." Our teacher friend fully appreciated his opportunity, and we paid a large price for our meal, with its fresh meat, our beds on the school benches, and the fodder supplied our horses. The next day being Saturday, the *maestro* offered to accompany us to Ixcuintepec, where his half-brother, the local teacher, would welcome our coming and arrange for our entertainment.

Passing Camotlan, we entered a magnificent gorge, along one side of which we climbed, passing in front of lovely cascades and having magnificent outlooks. While we were on this trail, we encountered the *maestro* from Ixcuintepec, who was on his way to Quezaltepec to spend his holiday. A whispered word with his half-brother, our companion, quickly changed his plan, and he accompanied us. Upon this trail we found our first swinging foot-bridges made of *lianas*, or vines, hanging from trees. These are, of course, only suitable for foot-travellers, but are a great convenience, where streams are likely to be swollen. Two or three long and slender vines, laid side by side and lashed together, form the footway, which is swung from one tree to another; other *lianas* are stretched across as side rails, smaller vines being twined in between and around them to hold them in place; long vines, pend-

Tree Fern in Tropical Forest; Quezaltepec

Cascade, Near Quezaltepec

ant from the high branches of the supporting trees, are fastened to the upper rails to steady and anchor these frail bridges, which swing and yield with every weight.

Ixcuintepec is upon one of the most abrupt ridges of this whole district. We went first to the schoolhouse, where our animals were to be guarded in a little open space before it; then we walked over to the *curato* which was being prepared for us. We had ordered *zacate* (fodder) for our animals and had divided it suitably between them. We ate our own meal, took a turn around the town, and were about to go to our quarters for the night, when Ernst noticed that the fodder, for which we had paid an outrageous price, had completely disappeared from before the two horses, although the pile before the mule had diminished but little. No doubt the two school teachers could have explained this mysterious disappearance; we could not, however, tax them with theft, but we made so much fuss over the matter that the officials brought a new supply. While I went to our room to write up my notes, Ernst sat in the gathering darkness watching the animals, as they ate, to prevent further robbery. I was busily writing, listening now and then to the fierce gusts of a gale that was blowing without, when the door burst open and Ernst, greatly excited, called me to follow, and we hastened to the place where our animals were tied. There we found that the great tree under which Chontal, the little mule, had been feeding, had been torn by the tempest and half of it had fallen upon the animal, bearing it to the ground. The crash had come without a moment's warning. Fortunately, the mule was unhurt, though it could not move until the branches which had crushed it to the earth had been cut away with axes. When we had released the beast and were retiring to our quarters, we saw a sight never to be forgotten. Looking down from our crest into the valley and across upon the other ridges and mountains beyond, we saw that the camp-fires of charcoal-burners and wayfarers had been fanned by the winds and spread into the forest until a dozen great lines of blazing trees lit up the landscape in every direction.

Our leaving Ixcuintepec in the early morning was not agreeable. The teachers were irritated over the affair of the *zacate*; the town authorities were dissatisfied with our refusal to pay for two lots of it. There was grumbling, and many dark looks followed us. We were rather glad to get away from the town without a serious outbreak. We were now on the road to the last of the Mixe towns we should visit, Coatlan. The road seemed endless, the ascent interminable; the town itself impressed us as exceptionally mean and squalid, and we stopped only long enough to eat a miserable dinner of eggs with chili and *tortillas*. The women here wore native dress. Several were clad as the Zapotec women from here to Tehuantepec, but a few were dressed in striking *huipilis* of native weaving, with embroidered patterns, and had their black hair done up in great rings around their heads, bright strips of cloth or ribbon being intermingled in the braiding. Literally and figuratively shaking the dust of the Mixe towns from our feet, we now descended into the Zapotec country. We were oppressed by a cramped, smothered feeling as we descended from the land of forested mountains and beautiful streams. At evening we reached San Miguel, the first Zapotec settlement, a little group of houses amid coffee plantings.

At the first indian house, we asked if we might have shelter for the night. The owner cordially answered, "*Como no? señores*," (Why not? sirs). He explained, however, that there was nought to eat. After eating elsewhere, we made our way back to our lodging-place, a typical Zapotec hut, a single room, with dirt-floor, walls of canes or

Fiesta of San Marcos; Juquila

Bridge of Vines, Near Ixcuintepec

poles, and thatch of grass. The house contained a hammock and two beds of poles, comforts we had not known for days. I threw myself into the hammock; Ernst lay down upon one of the beds; the man and woman, squatting, were husking corn for our horses; a little girl was feeding a fire of pine splints, built upon the floor, which served for light. As they worked and we rested the man asked that question which ever seems of supreme importance to Mexican indians, "*Como se llama Ud. señor?*" (What is your name, sir?). "Ernst," replied our spokesman, to whom the question was addressed. "*Y el otro?*" (And the other?), pointing to me. I replied for myself, "*Federico.*" The man seemed not to catch the word and badly repeated it after me. "*No, no,*" said the much quicker woman, "*Federico! Federico! si, señor, nosotros tenemos un Federico, tambien,*" (Yes, sir, and we have a Frederick, also). "Ah, and where is he?" "He will come, sir; we have four boys, Luca and Pedrito, Castolo and Federico; Federico is the baby; the little girl, here, is between him and Castolo; they are working in the coffee-field, but they will soon be here." At nine o'clock the little fellows appeared. They lined up in the order of age, placed their hands behind them, and waited to be addressed. Castolo, then about ten years of age, most pleased me, and I asked him, among other things, whether he could read and write. His father answered for him, that he could not read or write; that the opportunities were not good; but that he believed Castolo *could* learn, that he had a good mind. At this point the mother spoke to her husband in Zapotec. Some argument ensued, in which at last she triumphed. Turning to me, the man said: "She says you may have Castolo; you may take him to your country and there he can learn to read and write and whatever else you wish." It was not altogether easy to refuse this gift; finally I replied that we had a long journey ahead and that Castolo would weary on the road; that he had better wait until some later time.

It was now time for the family to dispose of itself for the night. I was already in the hammock and Ernst had one of the pole-beds; the man, his wife, and little Federico occupied the other bed; the little girl and the three older boys climbed, by a notched log, up to a loft constructed of poles or canes on which they laid themselves down. After all were located, the woman barred the door and we were soon asleep.

All rose early. Not only did we wish to make an early start, but the boys, too, were to make a journey. Our friends had agreed to make us some coffee and *tortillas*. We had made our preparations for starting and were waiting for our breakfast, when a shriveled and wrinkled old woman tottered up to beg the strangers to visit her sick son and prescribe some *remedio*. On our consenting to go with her, she caught up a stick of fat pine, lighted it in the fire, and with this blazing torch to light the way, preceded us to her house. Her son had been a strong and robust young man, but four months of lying upon his pole-bed had sadly reduced him. He was thin and pale, coughed sadly, and suffered with fever, chills, and dreadful headaches. He was taking medicines brought from Tehuantepec, but these seemed to have no effect and we were begged to suggest treatment. We advised continuance of the remedy she had been using, but also prescribed hot water taken in the morning and at night, hot water applications for the headaches, quinine for the chills and fever, and a digestive for the stomach trouble, and furnished these remedies from our own supplies. Having lighted us back to our lodging-place the old lady asked our charge. When we refused to receive payment from the poor creature, we noted an increased activity on the part of our host and hostess; a bit of cheese

Santiago Guevea

was promptly found and added to the waiting coffee and *tortillas*, and when we called for our own reckoning, we received the hearty response — "*Nada, señor, nada;*" (nothing, sir, nothing) "and when you come this way again, come straight to us, our door is always open to you."

We were now ready and found that the three boys, Luca, Pedrito, and Castolo, were waiting to accompany us as far as our roads were the same. They were to go on foot, five leagues, into the mountains to bring back some mules from a camp; they expected to reach their destination that day, to sleep on the mountain, and to bring in the animals the next day. The little fellows, from thirteen to nine or ten years old, seemed to find nothing extraordinary in their undertaking; each carried his little carrying-net, with food, drinking-gourd, and an extra garment for the chilly night, upon his back; Pedrito buckled to his belt the great *machete*, which men here regularly carry for clearing the path, cutting firewood, or protection against animals. They were very happy at accompanying us for a distance. We soon rose from the low, malarial, coffee *fincas* onto a fine mountain, which was the last of its kind that we saw for many days; it was like the mountains of the Mixes, with its abundant vegetation of ferns, begonias, and trees loaded with bromelias and orchids. Our bodyguard kept up with us bravely until we had made one-half of the ascent, where they fell behind and we saw them no more. Reaching the summit, we saw before us a distant line of blue, interrupted here and there by some hill or mountain,— the great Pacific. From here on, the beauty of the road disappeared. We descended and then mounted along dry slopes to Santiago Guevea, then hot and dusty. Our friends of San Miguel really live in Guevea and are at San Miguel only when the coffee needs attention. From Guevea the road was hard and dry and dusty to Santa

Maria. The mountain mass over which we passed was a peak, the summit of which was covered with masses of chalcedony of brilliant colors, which broke into innumerable splinters, which were lovely to see but hard upon the feet of horses; the surface of this part also gave out a glare or reflection that was almost intolerable. We descended over granite which presented typical spheroidal weathering. We went onward, up and down many little hills, reaching Santa Maria at noonday. The village sweltered; the air scorched and blistered; there was no sign of life, save a few naked children playing in the shade or rolling upon the hot sand. It was so hot and dusty that we hated to resume our journey and tarried so long that we had to ride after nightfall before we reached the *rancho* of Los Cocos, where we lay in the corridor and all night long heard the grinding of sugar-cane at the mill close by.

We had just such another hard, hot, and dusty ride the next day, on through Auyuga and Tlacotepec, where we stopped for noon, until Tehuantepec, where we arrived at evening.

CHAPTER IV

THROUGH CHIAPAS

(1896)

TEHUANTEPEC is meanly built; it is hot and dusty, and the almost constant winds drive the dust in clouds through the streets. But its picturesque market is a redeeming feature. Every morning it is crowded and presents a brilliant and lively spectacle. All the trade is in the hands of women, and the Tehuantepec women have the reputation of being the handsomest in the world. They are large, finely-built, and in their movements exhibit an indescribable freedom and grace. Their natural attractions are set off by a characteristic and becoming costume. The *huipilili* is a little sleeveless waist, loose at the neck and arms, and so short that it rarely reaches to the waist-line, to which, of course, it is supposed to extend; it is of bright cotton — red, brown, purple, with stripes or spots of white — and is stitched at the neck with yellow silk. The *enagua*, or skirt, is a strip of heavy cotton cloth, less than a yard wide, which is simply wrapped around the figure and hangs from the waist, being held in place by a brightly colored belt or girdle. The *enagua* is usually a rich red, but it is sometimes a fine violet purple. It reaches but little below the knees. It generally fails to meet the *huipilili* above, so that a broader or narrower band of fine, dark brown separates the two garments. Nothing is worn on the feet, which are exposed, as are also the finely shaped and beautifully developed arms. But the most striking article in the Tehuantepec woman's costume is her *huipil*, which travellers usually describe as a head-dress, although it is nothing of the kind. It is in reality a waist-garment with sleeves. It is made of lace or cotton, or linen, and is bordered at the neck, the sleeves, and the lower margin with broad ruffs of pleated lace. Only at church or on some important or ceremonial occasion is the *huipil* worn as it was meant to be. Usually at church the wearer draws the garment over her upper body, but does not put her arms into the sleeves, nor her head through the neck-opening, simply fitting her face into this in such a way that it appears to be framed in a broad, oval, well-starched border of pleated lace. Usually, however, the garment is not even worn in this manner, but is turned upside down and carelessly hung upon the head so that the broad lower fringe of lace falls back upon the hair, while the upper part of the garment, with the sleeves, the collar, and cuff-ruffs, hangs down upon the back. The whole effect is that of a fine crest rising from the head, coursing down the back, and moving with the breeze as the woman walks. These Zapotec women are fond of decoration, but particularly prize gold coins. In the past, when Tehuantepec was more important than now, it was no uncommon thing to see a woman in this market with several hundred dollars in gold coins hanging to her neck chain. In these later days of little trade and harder times, these once prized decorations have been spent, and it is rare to see any woman wearing more than twenty to fifty dollars as display.

Resuming our journey, we struck out upon the highway which parallels the coast. Almost immediately, the road changed from a fair country cart-road to a road remarkable at once for its straightness, breadth and levelness. It was, however, dreadfully hot and dusty, and was bordered on both sides with a tiresome and monotonous growth of low, thorn-bearing trees, with occasional clumps

Ready for Church; Tehuantepec

The Wide Road; Tehuantepec to Juchitan

of palms. We ate dinner at Juchitan, in a little eating-house conducted by a *Japanese!* A little beyond that important indian centre, we saw a puma pace forth from the thicket; with indescribably graceful and slow tread it crossed the dusty road and disappeared in the thicket. In the morning we had startled flocks of parrots, which rose with harsh cries, hovered while we passed, and then resettled on the same trees where they had been before. In the evening we saw pairs of macaws flying high, and as they flew over our heads they looked like black crosses sharp against the evening sky. At evening we reached Guviño, a dreadful town, in the population of which there seems to be a negro strain. We stopped with the *presidente*, in whose veins flowed Spanish, indian, and negro blood. In his one-roomed house besides ourselves there slept the owner, his wife, two daughters, one with a six-weeks baby, a son, and two young men — friends of the family.

Turning north the next day, onto the Niltepec road, we wandered from our trail, losing five leagues of space and more than three hours of time. The country through which we passed was terribly dry; there were no running streams. We crossed the bed of one dried river after another — streaks of sand and pebbles. The people in the villages near these dried river-beds dug holes a foot or two deep into this sand and gravel and thus got water. At the place where we camped for the night, Suspiro Ranch, a new house was being palm-thatched. All the men and boys of the neighborhood were helping; the labor was carefully divided; some were bringing in great bundles of the palm leaves; others pitched these up to the thatchers, who were skilfully fitting them under and over the poles of the roof framework and then beating them firmly home. Many of the helpers had come considerable distances and spent the night, so that we shared our room with quite a dozen men and boys, while the women and children slept in another house.

Passing through Zanatepec, we stopped for Sunday at Tanatepec. Here we found ourselves again upon the low coast road. It was, however, our last point of low altitude, as from there we struck inland over a higher, cooler, and more interesting mountain road. At Zanatepec we first saw the *marimba* played. This musical instrument, unquestionably African in name and origin, is hardly found north of Chiapas, but is extremely common through Central America. It consists of a wooden frame supporting keys made of wood and metal, each of which gives forth its own note when struck with small hammers. Below the keys of lowest tone are hung tubes, pipes, or gourds, as sounding boxes to increase the sound produced by striking the key. Usually four players perform at one time, each using two or more little hammers. The music is rapid and brilliant, somewhat resembling that of the piano. The instrument usually has some fanciful name, which is painted upon it. The one at Tanatepec was *La Azteca* (The Aztec Lady), while our next one was *La reina de las flores* (The queen of the flowers). At Zanatepec, *La Azteca* was an advertising part of a traveling circus. The troupe consisted of three men and three women, the latter of whom seemed to be mulattos. The men were ridiculously garbed and painted to represent wild indians. The real, live indians, who followed these clowns in delighted crowds, enjoyed thrills of terror at their whoops, fierce glances, and wild antics, and assured us that these actors were, if not the real thing, at least wonderfully accurate impersonations of the natives of the *Estados unidos* (United States) — the land of the "Apaches."

From Tanatepec we were in Chiapas, the southernmost

state of the republic. We struck out over a fine mountain road, *passable for carts* all the way to Tuxtla Gutierrez, the capital of the state. Our first ascent was over a magnificent mountain mass of syenite, which at some places seemed to be as fine as our own Quincy stone. The road, with many short zigzags, made a remarkably abrupt ascent, and, having reached the crest, wound like a vast serpent along the summit. As we descended into the following valley, we encountered a beautiful deer, which stood in the middle of the road, eyeing us with curiosity, until we were almost upon it, when it dashed into the thicket and then stopped to again eye us. Upon attaining the second summit we were amid pines. All day we had had a wind in our faces, cold and so strong as to almost blow us from the narrow ridge, yet the sky was cloudless. Looking back from our summit, a magnificent view to the ocean was spread before us. Below us were the mountains over which we had come, then a valley broken with mountains of a lesser size; beyond, was the dry, coastal plain, and yet beyond it, the sea. The dark green pines, the blue sky, the brown hills, the gray plain, the stretch of blue-green waters, made a wonderful color combination.

The next two days were most uninteresting. We were often reminded of the recent threat of war between Mexico and Guatemala, the disputed border-line between which we were now nearing. We met marching bands of soldiers who were returning to Juchitan. Officers were on horses, common soldiers on foot, pack-mules were laden with luggage, the women (accompanying their husbands) were weighed down with coffee-pots, bundles of clothes, and babies, all strapped on their backs together. They were a motley crew. At Jiquipilas a company was encamped in the plaza. Our mule, Chontal, took particular delight in running into such bands of marching soldiers as we encountered, causing no end of trouble. On one occasion, as a group approached us, he ran forward at a lively pace into their midst and tangled himself up with a party of prisoners,— apparently soldiers in disgrace, — who, tied together with ropes, were under guard. As we rode up to capture him, I felt a hand at that coat pocket which contained our money-bag and, turning suddenly, found one of the guard trying to draw the bag of money from my pocket. I struck at him with my whip and he slunk away.

The last day of travel before reaching Tuxtla Gutierrez, we passed one of the few pretty places on this dreary road, Agua Bendita. At this point the road makes a great curve, almost like a horseshoe; at the middle of this curve there rises to the right of the road a wall of limestone rock the plainly defined strata of which are thrown into a gentle anticlinal fold. The upper layers of this arch were covered with shrubs, clinging to its face, while the lower layers were tapestried with a curtain of delicate ferns, which hung down over the open arch below, under which the road passed. Water trickled through this limestone mass and dripped and collected in little basins, which had been excavated in the ledge close by the roadside. Some grateful passer had set up little crosses by the water pools, and they were gay that day with purple orchids plucked from a nearby tree. In this tree, amid the brilliant clumps of yet unplucked blossoms of the orchids, were a number of toucans with their enormous, brightly colored bills — the *picos de canoa* (canoe beaks) of the people.

Tuxtla Gutierrez is a town of some thousands population, with a central plaza where the local band plays almost every evening, and a market place of exceptional interest. Here, as nowhere else, we saw crowds of the purest indians in native dress. Chiapas is the home of at least thirteen tribes, each with its own language. Among the most interesting indians we saw in the market were the Tzotzils, from Chamula, who wore heavy, black woolen garments. The indians of the town and its immediate vicinity are Zoques.

Few Mexican governors possess the breadth of view and the intelligent enterprise of Governor Leon, whom we encountered here. A man of middle age, of fair stature though slight in build, with dark complexion, iron-gray hair, beard and whiskers carefully trimmed after the French fashion, his appearance creates a favorable impression. He did everything in his power for our comfort and assistance, and supplied us with letters to the *jefes politicos* of the districts through which we were to pass. We congratulated him upon the cart-road over which we had come from Zanatepec, an important public work for this part of the world; he told us he began it three years ago with a force of but nine men; that it would be extended to San Cristobal and San Bartolome; that he was no engineer, but that he could tell quite well when a road was passable for a cart. We found him greatly interested in a congress which he had called of persons interested in labor questions. Among the questions which he hoped to see considered was the abolition of the system of *peonage*, which still exists in full development in the state.

Less than three leagues from Tuxtla Gutierrez is Chiapa, famous for the brightly painted gourds and calabash vessels there manufactured and sent out to all parts of the republic. Toys, rattles, cups, and great bowl-basins are among the forms produced. We visited a house where five women were making pretty rattles from little crook-necked gourds. The workers sat upon the floor, with their materials and tools before them. The first one rubbed the body of the dry gourds over with an oil paint. These paints are bought in bulk and mixed upon a flat slab, with a fine-grained, smooth, hard pebble as a grinder, with *aje* and a white earth dug near the road between Chiapa and Tuxtla Gutierrez. The *aje* is a yellow, putty-like mass which gives a brilliant, lacquer-like lustre; the white earth causes the color to adhere to the surface to which it is applied. The second woman rubbed the neck of the gourd with green paint; the third painted the line of junction of the two colors with white, using a brush; the fourth brought out the lustre of the before dull object by rubbing it upon a pad of cotton cloth upon her knee, giving a final touch by careful rubbing with a tuft of cotton-wool; with a brush, the final worker rapidly painted on the lustrous surface delicate floral or geometric decoration. Though representing so much delicate and ingenious labor, these pretty toys were sold at the price of two for a *medio* (three cents in United States currency).

The *aje* which gives the brilliant lustre to this work deserves more than a passing notice. It is made chiefly at San Bartolome and is secured from an insect, a sort of plant-louse, which lives upon the blackthorn and related trees. The insect is found only in the wet season, is small, though growing rapidly, and is of a fiery-red color, though it coats itself over with a white secretion. It lives in swarms, which form conspicuous masses. These are gathered in vessels, washed to remove the white secretion, boiled, crushed, and strained through a cloth; an oily matter, mixed with blood (?) and water passes out, which is boiled to drive off the water and to concentrate the oily mass. This is then washed in trays, to rid it of the blood, and made up into balls, which are sold at ten or twelve *centavos* (five or six cents) a pound. It is a putty-like substance, with a handsome yellow color. We have already stated that it is ground up with dry paints to be rubbed on the object which is to be adorned, and that the brilliant lustre is developed by gentle and rapid friction.

Zapotec Woman; San Blas

Case of White Pinto; Tuxita Gutierrez

Pinto, a spotting or discoloring of the skin, is a common disease in many parts of Mexico. Three varieties are recognized — white, red, and blue or purple. The disease is particularly frequent in the states of Guerrero and Chiapas, and we had heard that it was very common in Chiapa. Perhaps twenty per cent of the population really has the disease; at San Bartolome perhaps seventy-five per cent are affected; in some towns an even larger proportion is reported. The white form appears the commonest. One subject examined at Tuxtla Gutierrez was a woman some sixty years of age. At birth she showed no symptom of the trouble, but spots began to appear when she was seven or eight years old. She was naturally dark, and the white spots were in notable contrast to her normal color; the spots increased in number and in size until her face and arms looked as if they had been white and become brown-spotted, instead of *vice versa*. After she was forty years of age her spots varied but little. The cause of this disease is still obscure, although several treatises have been written upon it. Authorities do not even agree as to the sequence of the forms of the disease, if there be such sequence. Some assert that the white form is the early stage and that the disease may never progress beyond it; others assert that the white spots are merely the permanent scars, left after the disappearance of the disease itself. Maps of distribution seem to show a distinct relation of the disease to altitude and character of water-supply. The common herd attribute it to an insect sting, to drinking of certain water, or to bathing in certain pools. Usually, there is no pain or danger connected with the trouble, except in the red form, but if the person affected changes residence, itching and some discomfort may temporarily ensue. The *presidente* at Chiapa took us to the jail, where the prisoners were filed before us and made to hold out hands and feet for our inspection. Such cases of *pinto* as were found were somewhat carefully examined. All we encountered there were of the white variety. Later, at private houses, we saw some dreadful cases of the purple form. Very often, those whose faces were purple-blotched had white-spotted hands and feet.

We had not planned to stop at Acala, but after a hard ride over a dreary road and a ferrying across a wide and deep river in a great dug-out canoe thirty feet or more in length — our animals swimming alongside — we found our beasts too tired for further progress. And it was a sad town. How strange, that beautifully clear and sparkling mountain water often produces actual misery among an ignorant population! Scarcely had we dismounted at our lodging place, when a man of forty, an idiot and goitrous, came to the door and with sadly imperfectly co-ordinated movements, gestured a message which he could not speak. Almost as soon as he had gone a deaf-mute boy passed. As we sat at our doorway, we saw a half-witted child at play before the next house. Goitre, deaf-mutism, and imbecility, all are fearfully common, and all are relatedly due to the drinking water.

To us, sitting at the door near dusk, a song was borne upon the evening breeze. Nearer and nearer it came, until we saw a group of twelve or fifteen persons, women in front, men and children behind, who sang as they walked. Some aided themselves with long staves; all carried burdens of clothing, food, utensils; all were wearied and footsore with the long journey, but full of joy and enthusiasm, as they were nearing their destination — a famous shrine. Passing us, they journeyed onward to an open space at the end of town, where, with many others who had reached there sooner, they camped for the night. The next day we constantly passed such parties of pilgrims; coming or going

River Between Chiapa and Acala

The Indian Government at San Bartolome

to this shrine which lay a little off the road between Acala and San Bartolome. In one group, we counted ninety pilgrims.

We had been told that San Bartolome was full of goitre, and we really found no lack of cases. It is said that forty years ago it was far more common than now, and that the decrease has followed the selection of a new water source and the careful piping of the water to the town. In the population of two thousand, it was estimated that there might be two hundred cases, fifty of which were notable. None, however, was so extraordinary as that of which several told us, the late *secretario* of the town, who had a goitre of such size that, when he sat at the table to write, he had to lift the swelling with both hands and place it on the table before he began work. The former prevalence of the disease is abundantly suggested by the frequency of deaf-mutes, a score or more of whom live here — all children of goitrous parents. Bad as was San Bartolome, it seemed to us surpassed by San Antonio, where we found the disease in an aggravated form, while at Nenton, our first point in Guatemala, every one appeared affected, although we saw no dreadful cases.

San Bartolome is an almost purely indian town, where for the first time our attention was called to the two sets of town officials — indian and *ladino*. The indian town government consisted of four indians of pure blood, who wore the native costume. This, here, is characteristic, both for men and women. The men wore wide-legged trousers of native woven cotton, and an upper jacket-shirt, square at the bottom, made of the same stuff, with designs — rosettes, flowers, geometrical figures, birds, animals, or men — wrought in them in red, green, or yellow wools; about the waist was a handsome brilliant native belt, while a bright kerchief was twisted about the head. The men were well-built, but the *alcalde* was a white *pinto*. Women wore *huipilis*, waist-garments, sometimes thick and heavy, at others thin and open, in texture, but in both cases decorated with lines of brightly colored designs. Their *enaguas*, skirts, were of heavy indigo-blue stuff or of plain white cotton, of two narrow pieces sewed together and quite plain except for a line of bright stitching along the line of juncture. As among other indian tribes, this cloth was simply wrapped around the figure and held in place by a belt. The town is famous for its weaving and dyeing; the loom is the simple, primitive device used all through Mexico long before the Conquest. We were surprised to find that the designs in colored wools are not embroidered upon the finished fabric, but are worked in with bits of worsted during the weaving.

From San Bartolome to Comitan, the road passes over a curious lime deposit, apparently formed by ancient hot waters; it is a porous tufa which gave back a hollow sound under the hoofs of our horses. It contains moss, leaves, and branches, crusted with lime, and often forms basin terraces, which, while beautiful to see, were peculiarly harsh and rough for our animals. But the hard, and far more ancient, limestone, onto which we then passed, was quite as bad. At the very summit of one hill of this we found a cave close by the road; entering it, we penetrated to a distance of perhaps seventy-five feet, finding the roof hung with stalactites and the walls sheeted with stalagmite. Just after leaving this cave, we met a tramp on foot, ragged, weary, and dusty, and with a little bundle slung upon a stick over his shoulder. He accosted me in Spanish, asking whence we had come; on my reply, probably catching my foreign accent, he winked and said in plain English, — "Yes? And where are you going, pard?"

After a hard day's ride, over a shut-in road, destitute of

fine views, we reached the crest overlooking Comitan. The descent was almost precipitous. The town, better built and more compact than most, was situated near the foot of the hill; near it, on a terrace, was the cemetery. On the level road, stretching to a long distance from the town, we saw lines of hundreds of pack-mules, dwarfed by distance. South from the town stretched a grassy plain, bordered here and there with pine trees. Back of this plain rose round-topped hills, and beyond them were again the blue mountains; far in the distance, behind these, towered the mighty crests of the Guatemalan Sierra Madre.

The town was crowded, as the annual *feria* (fair) was in progress, and it was with difficulty that we found a room to sleep in, going for our meals to one of the many temporary eating-places in the plaza. Comitan is the last town of consequence in Mexico, and has wide fame on account of its spirits, known at *comiteco*. This drink, of enormous strength, distilled from coarse, brown sugar (*panela*), is a favorite in Guatemala, and its smuggling across the border, though risky, is a lucrative business. There are scores of little distilleries in the town, many of them belonging to and conducted by women.

Mexican paper money is useless between Tuxtla Gutierrez and Comitan. At the latter city it may be exchanged for silver, but with difficulty. From here on we found no copper in circulation, and before reaching Comitan we had begun to receive Guatemalan silver in our change. Fully thirty leagues from the border we ceased to receive Mexican silver from anyone. This notable displacement of Mexican currency seems curious, because Guatemalan money is at a heavy discount in comparison with it. At San Bartolome we sent a soldier-police to buy *zacate*, giving him Mexican money. He brought back two Guatemalan pieces in change, and on our objecting to receive it, assured me, not only that the money was good, but also that here the people were Guatemalans. "Here," said he, "not Mexico: here we are all Carrera's people." This, of course, was sheer treason. Carrera, the pure-blood indian who in the stirring days of 1839 seized the power in Guatemala, a strange and wild being who had a real love for his country, has left a profound impression. At times an exile, he had lived at Comitan, where his name was familiar to all the indians around. His coins are much prized by the indians for necklaces and earrings, and even at Tehuantepec we had seen women wearing his little gold pieces in their ears.

It should have been an easy matter to go from Comitan to Nenton (in Guatemala) in a single day. As it was, we made it with great difficulty in two, our mule Chontal apparently being completely worn out. We crossed the *llano*, passed through patches of pines, and then came out upon a terrible country of limestone hills. In our last day's journey we had to coax, threaten, beat, drag, and push that mule until our voices were gone and our arms were tired. Immediately on passing the line into Guatemala, we found the telegraph wires cut and poles down, a result of the late unpleasantness with Mexico. The mountain mass before us, which had been in view for two days past, loomed up frightfully before us. Would our little mule be able to pass it? We remembered what an American tramp, whom we had met at Tuxtla Gutierrez and who had walked on foot from Guatemala City, had said: "Between Nenton and Huehuetenango you will pass over a mountain that will make your heart sick; may God help you." Just at dusk we looked down upon Nenton in a little valley, with a fine stream crossed by a pretty bridge, where mountains rose steeply on every side. Having been registered by the custom officials, we slept that night, our first in the new republic, in the municipal house.

Next morning we started bravely, the whole town having assembled to see us off. We safely reached the foot of the mountain, where the mule stopped and braced himself. We spoke kindly, coaxed, dragged, but all to no effect. Finally he started, but three times within the next few minutes, he and we went through the same procedure. Patience had ceased to be a virtue; we held a serious consultation. Ernst asserted that by placing the rope over the nostrils of the animal and then leading, he must move. We tried the experiment. The beast gave a snort, a groan, lurched, fell over, kicked convulsively, closed his eyes, and lay to all appearance dead. The town below, which had been watching progress, came running up. We removed the halter; the animal lay quiet. The pity of the bystanders was maddening; their remarks exasperating. "Poor little mule, he dies;" they pointed to his rubbed sides, — "Ah, poor creature! What a heavy load! How thin he is." It is certain that the best mule in the town was in far worse condition, and as for food, Chontal had eaten more the night before than our two horses put together. Having exhausted their vocabulary of sympathy, our friends left us, as the "poor little animal" showed signs of coming to. We concluded to engage a man on foot to carry the burden across the mountains and to lead Chontal. After some delay a man was found, who readily agreed to carry the burden and pack-saddle, but when he found he was to lead the mule besides, he defied the town authorities and refused to go. Unfortunately, he was a carpenter and, by law, could not be made to go against his will. Hours passed, while another carrier was sought. Declaring that I would not return to town, I waited on the road with the mule, while Ernst rode back and forth. As soon as he had left, the beast began to mend; he coughed, raised his head, and, opening one eye, gravely winked. Taking his halter and encouraging him to rise, I led him a few yards up the hill, when he again braced himself and I desisted. There he ate *zacate*. Presently we took another turn, mounted a little higher up the hill, where he stopped again. A little later we made another journey, and again halted. Just then I heard an indian boy of fourteen years calling from the cliff above me in great excitement, "*Señor*, *un animal*" (An animal, sir). Clambering over rocks, I came up to the boy, with his *machete* in his hand, standing at the foot of a tree upon the leafless branches of which was a fine iguana (lizard) two feet or more in length. Visions of iguana steak, which I had long desired to try, rose in fancy. The boy was disgusted when he found I had no pistol with which to shoot his animal, but grunted, "If we but had a cord." I directed him where to find a cord among our luggage and on his return he made a slip-noose, cut a long and slender pole to which he tied his snare, then handing me his *machete* he raised his pole and tried to slip the noose over the lizard's head. The iguana gave a leap, and as it shot by me I struck at it with the *machete*, which hit it and threw it on the rocks below. However, before we could reach it, it had made good its escape.

Returning to the mule I found it eating grass contentedly by the roadside. It was three o'clock in the afternoon when our human beast of burden finally arrived, took up his burden and was ready to start. Then, suddenly, I took a new resolve. Before us rose the appalling mass of the Sierra Madre; to get that mule across it would wear us out in mind and body; I regretted that he had not died, and determined to have no further trouble with him. Quickly, we sent back word to Nenton that a mule and saddle were for sale; the crowd gathered. We demanded fifteen dollars for the mule, ten for the saddle; and were offered ten and five respectively. But we declared we would kill the mule and burn the saddle before we would take less; we triumphed. Our account stood:

Cost of mule	$45.00	
Cost of saddle	6.00	
		$51.00
Selling price of mule	15.00	
Selling price of saddle	10.00	
		$25.00
Loss — paid for experience in mules		$26.00

CHAPTER V

AT HUIXQUILUCAN

(1897)

OUR serious work was to begin with one of the most conservative and reserved of Mexican indian populations. If we could do what we planned to do with the Otomis, we were likely to have but little greater trouble with any tribe. In ancient times the name of Otomi was synonymous with stupidity. When an Aztec was particularly stupid or clumsy, his fellows in derision called him an Otomi. They still are ignorant, suspicious, and unprogressive.

Huixquilucan, which we had chosen as our field for labor, is situated on a high ridge within sight of the National Railroad, at a distance of perhaps a mile and a half from the station of Dos Rios. A crowd of indian women and children are always at the station when trains pass, to sell *tortillas*, *chalupas*, and *pulque* to passengers; few travellers from the United States, passing over this road, have failed to notice the dark and ugly faces of these sellers, and have received their first impression of the indians of Mexico from seeing them. Our party, three in number, reached Dos Rios in the morning and began work at the station with the women who were selling there. Dr. Powell, as our interpreter, undertook the personal dealings, and our material, as was to be expected, was chiefly women. When we came to record the names of our subjects, we found that every woman's first name was Maria, the differentiation between them being first found in the middle name. They were

Otomi Indian Girls; Huixquilucan

The Moon-stone, at Dos Rios Station

little creatures, scarcely larger than well grown girls of eleven or twelve among ourselves. Some old women, with grey hair and wrinkled faces who piously kissed our hands when they met us, were among the smallest. Now and then some young woman or girl was attractive, but usually their faces were suspicious, sad, and old before their time. The skin was a rich brown; the eyebrows heavily haired, often meeting above the nose; the hair grew low upon the forehead, and in young women the forehead itself was covered with a fine downy black growth. The nose was flat, broad, and depressed at the roots, while its tip was flat and wide. The eyes were dark brown and the hair was black and coarse. If we were to judge the population by the women only, we might call the Otomis true pygmies. The average stature of 28 subjects was 1,435 millimeters — while Sir William Flower's limit for pygmy peoples is 1,500 millimeters.

Many of the women whom we measured and photographed carried babies; the disposition of the children while the mothers were being examined was something of a problem. When given to another woman they usually cried lustily, and so conducted themselves as to distract the attention of their mothers and interfere seriously with our work. In the crowd of lookers-on there chanced to be a little girl, surely not more than ten years old, who seemed to be a born caretaker. Upon her back, supported by her *ayate*, she carried her own baby brother. We quickly found that really refractory babies were best committed to her charge. No matter how loudly they might have been crying beforehand, when transferred to the arms of this little creature they became instantly quiet. The poor little thing was kept busily employed the greater part of the afternoon with the two babies, one upon her back, the other in her arms.

Almost all the women wear the ancient costume, which consists of the *huipil*, *enagua*, *faja*, and *ayate*. The *huipil* is a cotton blanket, with a slit through which the head passes. On each side of the slit are bands of patterns embroidered in bright colors. Much of the remaining surface of the garment may be similarly decorated; sometimes it becomes one mass of designs. The patterns are usually geometrical figures, but may be representations of animals, birds, or human beings. They may be regularly arranged, or jumbled together haphazard. The *enagua*, skirt, consists of two strips of cloth of different kinds and colors, sewn together side by side and then wrapped horizontally about the body. The strips of cloth are native spun, native dyed, and native woven. The favorite colors are dark blue, brownish purple, or indian red, horizontally banded with narrow black stripes. The two strips are usually joined by a line of colored stitching. The *enagua* is simply wrapped about the body, sometimes thrown into pleatings in front, and held in place by a broad cotton belt of bright color, into which are woven birds, animals, human figures, and geometrical forms. These belts are called by the Spanish name, *faja*. Both men and women carry *ayates*. These are square or rectangular blankets made of *ixtli*, the strong fibre of the maguey. Like the *enaguas*, they usually consist of two pieces, side by side, stitched together with some bright color. The fibre, which is gotten from the leaves partly by maceration, partly by beating, is spun in a primitive fashion. Almost every woman one meets upon the road, no matter what burden of babies or goods she carries, has a hank of the fibre thrown over her shoulder, and keeps her little spindle whirling, spinning the strong thread as she walks. Her spindle consists of a slender stick thrust through a whorl of baked pottery. Such whorls are no longer made, but the ancient ones, called by the Aztec name *malacates*, are picked up in the fields and reapplied to their old use. Usually the *ixtli* thread is left of its original grey or white color, but sometimes the fibre is dyed, a fine shade of orange being favored. The *ixtli* thread is woven into *ayates*, which are used for carrying burdens. Vegetables, charcoal, babies — anything — are put into them. Two ends are tied together to hold the burden in place, and the other two are passed across the breast and tied in front. These blankets are astonishingly strong and unyielding.

At evening, after a fair day's work, we made our way on foot across the valley and up the long slope to the summit of the ridge on which lay Huixquilucan, the official centre of a municipality of 11,000 persons. Of these, 3,000 live in the village, while the remainder are clustered together in hamlets like San Bartolito, San Francisco, Agua Bendita, or are scattered in single-house settlements over the mountains. Of the 11,000 persons, more than three-fourths claim to be full Otomis. There are no truly poor in the whole town. Every family has its field, its house, its bit of woodland. All the people still speak the native tongue, and many speak no other. The town is picturesquely situated upon the crest and flank of a long, narrow ridge, which is enclosed by a grand sweeping curve of lofty mountains. The flanks of the enclosed ridge and the whole slope of the surrounding mountains are occupied by the little fields of the indians, long narrow patches separated by lines of *maguey* or century-plants. The houses are built of adobe bricks with thick and solid walls, which are usually plastered on the outside and tinted white or pink. The roofs are pitched, but with a gentle slope. They consist of frameworks of poles upon which long narrow shingles are laid, and pegged in place with wooden pegs which project both above and below for several inches in a formidable, bristling way. Sometimes the shingles, instead of being pegged in place, are held by stones, which in some cases weigh several pounds, and are laid in regular horizontal lines.

When we were there, great stacks of corn-husks were to be seen in almost every yard; these were placed on floorings, raised by posts some distance above the ground to keep them from animals. A long ladder usually leaned against one side of the stack and a light cross of sticks stuck into the top of the stack kept off evil influences. Sometimes this cross was cut in relief on the smooth, carefully trimmed end of the stack itself. More striking than these stacks, and quite characteristic of the Otomi country, were the queer corn-bins or granaries called by the Aztec name *cincalote*. They rose in all directions like great square columns. The floor of boards was slightly raised from the ground by stones, and measured some 4 or 5 feet on a side; from its corners rose 4 poles, sometimes to the height of 20 feet; these were connected at the top and held firm by ropes. The sides of the bin were built up of a cob-work of slender staves laid horizontally. The vertical bin thus formed was filled with ears of corn roofed about with a light thatch or shingled roof. Later in the season, as the corn was taken from these bins, the sides would have been removed piecemeal to keep progress with the diminishing hoard. When the time of planting should be near, the whole structure but the floor and upright poles would have disappeared.

Next to maize the chief culture among the Otomis is *maguey*. This forms division lines between the corn-fields and the village yards, and is sometimes, though not commonly here, planted in fields. The *maguey* is an agave very close to the century-plant. Manifold are its uses, but to the Otomi its value is chiefly in two directions. It furnishes *ixtli* fibre for *ayates*, and it yields *pulque*. For a dozen years the *maguey* plant stores away starchy food in its long, thick, sharp-pointed leaves. It is the intended nourishment for a great shaft of flowers. Finally, the flower-bud forms amid the cluster of leaves. Left to itself the plant now sends all its reserve of food into this bud, and the great flower-stalk shoots upward at the rate of several inches daily; then the great pyramid of flowers develops. But man interferes. The flower-bud is cut out, and a neat, deep cup is fashioned amid the bases of the cluster of leaves. The sap which should produce that wonderful growth is poured into this cup. The *pulque* gatherer, with his long gourd collecting-tube, and skin carrying-bottle, goes from plant to plant and gathers the *agua miel* — honey-water. Fermented, it becomes the whitish, dirty, ropy, sour-tasting, bad-smelling stuff so dear to the indians. And the Otomi are fond of *pulque*. We were compelled to do our work in the mornings; in the afternoons everyone was drunk and limp and useless in the operator's hands.

We slept and ate at the house of the *presidente*, an old *mestizo* of rather forbidding manners but kindly spirit. Our cases came rather slowly and a deal of coaxing, argument, and bribes were necessary to secure them. Here we gave a trifle, a few *centavos*, to each subject. The policy was bad, and we abandoned it with reference to all subsequent populations. Naturally the natives were hostile to our work. They thought that we were measuring them for their coffins; that they would be forced into the army; that disease would result; that an uncanny influence was laid upon them; that witchcraft might be worked against them. After having had a lot of trouble with many of our subjects, we were surprised one day to have the oldest man of the village, Antonio Calistro, born in 1813, still so hale and hearty that he works his own fields, come in for measurement and photographing. He still wears the old style of dress: a loose jacket with wide sleeves made of dark blue woolen cloth, gathered around the waist by a closely-woven cotton belt; short, wide-legged trousers of buckskin. He is the only man left in the village who wears his hair after the old fashion; that on top of his head in front was combed together and braided into a little tail, while that on the sides and back of the head was made into a longer braid. When we asked him how it was that he was not afraid to undergo our measurement and photographing, we learned that someone had told him that the purport of the work was to send information to the Pope in Rome as to how his Otomi children looked, and from respect for the Holy Father the old man of eighty years had walked in from his distant farm to be measured and photographed.

A curious fact in respect to the Otomis resulted from our study. The men, apparently of pure blood, presented two quite different types. There are many who are as little as the women; these present almost the type already given as that of the women, but are a little lighter in color. The second type is tall, sometimes over 1,700 millimeters. It is lighter in color, presenting at times a light brownish-yellow shade. Some indians of this large type have white skins, blotched with disagreeable red or purple. The eyes of these large men are usually widely-spaced, and the face appears rounder than in their smaller brethren. All the Otomis of both types, men and women, have astonishingly big heads, and many dwarfish individuals would require a 7¼ hat.

One night during our stay we had a grand illumination. It was St. Martin's Eve. During the afternoon the men and boys planted dead trees in the plaza and streets, and filled the branches with bunches of dry brush. At

THE CHURCH; HUIXQUILUCAN

OTOMI INDIAN; HUIXQUILUCAN

dusk we walked up to the crest before the church. All through the valley the men and boys had been busy, and as darkness settled down, blaze after blaze sprung forth until every hillside was dotted with flaming heaps. On every church and farm-house of large size, straight lines of little bonfires were built along the edges of the roof. There must have been many hundreds of fires in sight at once. Meanwhile, all the churches of the little hamlets around clanged their bells discordantly. Then the church close by us burst into illumination, and its bells joined in the clangor as we started down the hill. The villagers were putting torches to the piles, and children were dancing in the glare, shooting off their little rockets and adding their full share to the general confusion.

In the olden time Huixquilucan had a bad reputation for highway robberies. A great hill overlooking the town is called the hill of crosses, and here a cross by the wayside usually signifies a place of murder. Many a traveller in the not distant past found his way from here as best he could to the capital city minus burden and money, minus hat and shoes, and sometimes minus clothing. They used to say that from Toluca to the city a man was robbed three times; the first time they took his money, the second his watch and valuables, the third, his clothes. We were told that the church here, the chief church of our Otomi friends, is called "the church of the thieves," and that it was even lately a favorite resort of *ladrones*, who prayed for blessing upon their thieving expeditions and for release in case they should be taken captive. And not so long ago, among the little silver votive offerings,— eyes, legs, arms, hands,— all given in fulfillment of promises for the cure of ailing members,— one might see little chains and manacles, visible evidence that saint or Virgin had kindly released some fellow, taken in his misdeeds, from a well deserved punishment, in answer to his pious prayers.

Below the station of Dos Rios a little ravine borders the main valley. There, within sight of the track on one side of the ravine lies the stone which long ago "fell from the moon." It is a great boulder, with flat lower surface, and round upper surface, sufficiently large for a considerable party to camp on. The earth is washed away somewhat from below it, and on its under side are rude figures painted in imitation of suns and circles and symbolic designs. It is said that the indians throughout the country around respect this rock, making prayers and offerings to it.

One of Huixquilucan's pretty hamlets is Agua Bendita, — blessed water,— near the upper, narrowing end of the valley. A dozen or so houses compose the settlement. Near it, upon a little side gorge, two lovely springs burst forth from the rock. From them a babbling stream of sparkling water flows, in which, in the bright sunshine, women wash clothes, and lay them out on bushes or grassy banks to dry; little naked children play about while the mothers labor; hither dusky maidens come to perform their toilets; here women fill their *ollas* with water; here *pulque*-gatherers wash and scrape their skin bottles. In the little tank below, where the water lies so clear that everything is visible upon its bottom, one may see axolotls creeping. They are water-salamanders, but they have a strange history. Like frogs, they pass through a series of changes, and the larval is very different from the adult form. In some Mexican lakes of genial temperature, the little creature goes through its full history from the larva to the adult; but in cold mountain lakes, the adult form is never attained, and the larva (elsewhere immature) lays eggs that hatch its like.

Our last evening at Huixquilucan, I went out to purchase native garments. We rode from house to house, and were quite away from the town in a district where houses were few and far between. It was nearly dusk and our search must end. We were at the last house on a slope near the bottom of a valley, on whose opposite slope were but a few houses. The people were primitive in appearance, dress and language. They could not understand all we said, but were anxious to please the "*padrecito*," whose hand they kissed. Having no clothing to sell us, they tried to help us procure some. Orders were given to a shy and wild girl, with deep-set, shining jet-black eyes, raven hair and dark brown skin, dressed in rags. Stepping to a little out-jutting mass of rock, she gave a wild cry, looking across the valley to the nearest house on the opposite slope, fully half a mile away. We could see the people of the house turn out to hear. Then, in a high, clear voice, strangely penetrating, but without harshness or a break or pause for breath, with rising and falling intonation, she cried her message. There was a moment's pause, and then we saw the answering crier take her place, and in the same clear, penetrating, unbroken, up-and-down voice, came back the reply. It was not favorable, and the old man apologized for the failure, as he kissed the *padrecito's* hand in parting.

* * * * * * *

Some weeks later we were again at Huixquilucan, this time to secure some busts. Having reached the house of the *presidente*, we sent out our drunken friend Augustin, who had been useful to us during our measuring experiences, to find subjects. He finally appeared with a man who agreed to submit to the operation for one *peso*. Everything went well until the moulds were removed; it is true that in the removal a good deal of hair was pulled out, but no serious damage was done. When the *peso* agreed upon was offered, the subject indignantly refused to receive it, demanding five. I replied that he well understood our agreement: there was his *peso*; if he cared to take it, good; if not, I would keep it; but that to pay five *pesos* was out of the question. He thereupon grew angry and boisterously demanded the increased sum. Several of his friends gathered and backed him in his demand. The noise they made attracted a still greater crowd until at last we were surrounded by forty or fifty angry indians. The man continued to demand his five *pesos*, the other crying, "Pay him five *pesos*." I was firm, declaring that the man should receive no more than had been promised. Again the *peso* was offered, again to be rejected. At that moment some brilliant genius cried, "If you do not pay five *pesos* we will break your moulds." And the cry was caught up by the angry crowd: "Yes, we will break the moulds unless you pay five *pesos*." At this threat I told my two companions to stand back out of the way, and then, speaking to him who had suggested the breaking of the moulds, said, pointing to them, "Yes, break the moulds." His ardor cooled. Turning to another, I said to him, "Come, break the moulds." He began to back away. Turning to the cause of the disturbance, who had joined in the cry about destroying the moulds, I said to him, "Come, come, we are waiting for you to break the moulds." No one made a move toward destroying our plaster-work, so I said, "No, you know quite well you will not break the moulds; if you did, you know what would happen; I should take you all as prisoners to Toluca." At that moment, catching sight of the old *presidente* who was passing on the road, I clapped my hands and beckoned him. When the old man came I laid the matter fairly before him, telling him the agreement that had been made, the time taken for the work, and the fact I had offered the man the *peso* promised; that he now demanded five *pesos*, refusing to take the proffered money. The old man looked a moment at me, then at the angry indian; then at me, and again at the indian; then, stepping up to him, he patted him on the back as a father might a spoiled child, saying, "Come, come, son; don't be a fool; three good days' wages for an hour's time; take your *peso* and be gone." We had feared the incident would cast a damper on our work and hinder other subjects. Far from it. We were supplied as rapidly as our men could work at the same price we paid our first subject.

CHAPTER VI

LAKE PATZCUARO

(1897)

MEXICO has few large lakes, the largest, Chapala, having an area of only 1,685 square kilometers. Patzcuaro is much smaller, but far more picturesque. The form is something like a fat horseshoe; fine hills rise around it on all sides, behind which are mountain heights, with jagged outlines; pretty islands dot its waters, and twenty-two villages or towns of Tarascan indians are situated on its borders. The indians of these villages rarely use the land roads in going from town to town, commonly journeying by canoes, of a somewhat peculiar type. These are "dug outs," made from single tree trunks, and range in size from those intended for a single hunter to those which will carry ten or twelve persons. At the stern they are cut almost squarely across; at the bow they are trimmed to a slope; they are flat-bottomed and considerably wider at at the bottom than above; they are dug out in such fashion that the walls are thin and almost vertical on the inner side. Buttressing pieces are left at the bottom, at two or three places, extending across the canoe and no doubt strengthening the sides; they also serve as squatting places for the passengers. The prow narrows as well as slopes upward, and a buttressing piece left in it serves as a foot-rest for the steersman, who sits in the bow, instead of in the stern. He steers by means of a long-handled paddle thrust through a loop of wood fastened to one side of the canoe. The paddles used for propulsion have handles three or

Santa Fe de la Laguna

four feet long, with round blades. The paddlers sometimes make their stroke on but one side of the canoe, sometimes on both. When they paddle over one side only, the stroke of the oar through the water is oblique, maintaining a steady course.

In such canoes the Tarascans of the lake villages go from place to place; in such a canoe, we started one morning before six o'clock, for Sante Fé de la Laguna. Our force consisted of three persons, an old man named Felipe, his wife, and a young man. All three had paddles, but only two really paddled, the third one steering. The sun rose shortly after we started, and the light effects of early morning on the water and surrounding mountains were fine. Though we had made an early start, many had started earlier, and in the first part of our journey we met scores of canoes, the paddlers of which were on their way to Patzcuaro. It was a beautiful sight to see six or eight paddlers in some great canoe keeping exact time in their movements, singing as they went. Sometimes two canoes were raced, and laughter and excited cries accompanied the contest. Here and there along the shores we saw little huts of fishermen, with nets hung out to dry, or groups of men seining or dropping dip-nets; upon many slopes were little terrace garden spots, where modest crops were cultivated; here and there were mats lately finished or heaps of fresh-cut rushes for their fabrication. Five hours of good paddling brought us to Santa Fe de la Laguna, just opposite the far more famous Tzintzuntzan, and but a little distance from the much larger town, Quiroga. Santa Fe is quite a town, stretching for a considerable distance along a terrace, but little elevated above the water level. The houses are built of rather large, dark-brown, adobe bricks; the walls are usually white plastered; the roofs of all the houses are tiled, and the supporting rafters of the roof extend out far beyond the front wall of the house, so that the passer on the footpath is sheltered against rain and the noonday sun. The outer ends of these rafters are cut to give an ornamental effect. All the houses are surrounded by fruit trees — orange, lemon, lime, *ahuacate* and *chirimoya*. Each little property is surrounded by a stone wall of some height; the gateway through this, giving entrance to the yard, is surmounted by a pretty little double-pitched roofing of thatch.

A crowd of pure indians had gathered at the landing, by the time we were unloaded. Forty or fifty men and women of medium stature, dark-brown skin and broad, expressionless faces, watched our every movement with curiosity, but none was ready to assist us in carrying our luggage to the *curato*. Taking it ourselves, as best we could, we found a boy to direct us and made our way to the house. The *cura* had gone to Quiroga and his suspicious household would not receive us until his return, although permitting us to leave our goods. Going to the *plaza*, we succeeded in getting bread and cheese at a *tienda*, and after eating loitered until, at half-past-two, the Padre Ponce made his appearance. We showed him our letters and asked his interest and aid. He at once made us at home in his house, summoned the officials, read the governor's letter aloud to them, and told them it was their duty to assist us in every way. We at once began our work, and before nightfall had measured and photographed a number of cases.

The next morning, Saturday, all started merrily. After breakfast, however, Padre Ponce left us, going to Quiroga for celebrating Christmas. The moment he was gone, work slackened, and it was with difficulty that we could procure subjects. Early the next morning the *padre* appeared to say mass, after which he stirred up the people and we were again at work. But as soon as he left for Quiroga, once more, the interest diminished. Finally, as no one

Los Viejos; Santa Fe de la Laguna

came and the officials had disappeared, we started out upon a tour of investigation. We found the whole town drunk; the *juez*, the chief of police, the *mayores*, all were too drunk for measurement. We experimented upon two or three subjects, but soon gave up in despair.

Padre Ponce need not have gone to Quiroga for Christmas celebrations; we had them also. For example, we had *Los Viejos*. One afternoon, we saw a band of half-a-dozen persons singing in the street. All but one of them were men or boys dressed in long robes of brilliant red, purple or green, which were buttoned down the front; their heads were covered with white cloth, over which were fitted little masks of clay. The last one in the company was a woman, dressed quite in the usual fashion, but barefoot and with her *rebozo* covering her face and a man's *sombrero* on her head. Two of the party had guitars of local manufacture. This company strolled through the streets, singing and dancing; some of the dancing was clog-dance, some the *jarabe*, a man and woman taking part. Having noticed this group, we saw that the whole town seemed in movement toward the *corral* connected with the shrine behind the church. Following with the crowd, we found the *corral* already filled with people. The men were seated on benches or squatting against the walls; women and children were sitting on the ground. We noticed that all the women brought burdens, which proved to be pots full of hot *atole*, bundles of large *tortillas*, trays heaped high with *tamales*, or sacks full of little cups. Various bands of dancers made their way around, delighting the crowd with their performances. The group we had already seen was the least interesting. Those that really represented *los viejos* (the old men) were the best. These wore large, comic, wooden masks, many of which showed signs of long-continued use; one represented a long, warty, bearded face and was painted purple; others were painted red or brown, but most of them were of the natural color of the wood; great wigs of corn-husk or of matting were worn over the back of the head; the clothing was ragged and dirty, and in some cases was really of ancient style; some wore roughly made garments of the skin of the *tigre*. Each band had its leader, and each tried to outdo the others in the oddity of performance, vigor of dancing and coarseness of jest. Much fun and laughter were caused by their antics. Meantime, boys and young women were busied as waiters. Cups of steaming *atole*, delicious *tortillas*, hot *tamales* were distributed until everyone, including the strangers, were supplied. No one ate until the whole company had been served, when the town officials set the example and all fell to feasting. Dancing, music, laughter and fun followed, and were kept up until some time after nightfall.

On the second day after Christmas a strolling band of *pastores*, from San Geronimo, passed from house to house singing their Christmas songs. The company consisted of two or three musicians, a carrier — who was an indian boy about fifteen years old — and half a dozen other youngsters, wearing new palm hats and carrying long staves ending above in a loop from which streamed strips of brilliantly colored tissue paper. The carrier bore a cushion, upon which was stretched a figure of the infant Christ. At each house, he passed before the spectators, allowing them to kiss the figure and to deposit gifts of flowers or of money for the little church at San Geronimo; the music then struck up, the leader began to sing, and the little shepherds (*pastores*) marched around and around singing in chorus.

We lost quite two days on account of the drunkenness of the town. When it was past, by a vigorous indulgence in wheedling and threatening, we got the work again under way, and were just finishing with our one-hundredth man,

Churchyard and Bells; Tzintzuntzan

View at Janicho; Lake Patzauaro

when Padre Ponce returned for good and all. We had nearly starved during his absence; his old housekeeper had done her best with the poor materials which we were able to secure, but the best was bad. With Padre Ponce came another priest, Padre Torres of Patzcuaro, who used to be located at Santa Fe and was much loved by the natives. With the assistance of the two Padres we were able to secure and deal with our female subjects in less than a day, and were ready to bid adieu to the *padrecitos* and leave for Tzintzuntzan.

All the tourist world that goes to Patzcuaro visits Tzintzuntzan to see the Titian. Padre Ponce was anxious to have us see the famous picture and photograph it. It was late when we reached the town, which consists in large part of *mestizos* and indians who speak little but native Tarascan. We found the *cura* was not in town, but were taken to the *curato*; arrived there, we discovered that the good man had taken his keys with him. We arranged, with some difficulty, for something to eat, and, after supper, were shown into an open room, with an unfinished roof, without a door, and with no hint of bed. Here we shared a lumber pile with two or three young men and suffered frightfully from cold all night. We were up early, as sleep was impossible, and filled our time as best we could, until it was light enough to photograph the picture.

We had our letter from Padre Ponce to the *cura*, in which he recommended the priest to have us photograph the painting. This letter and the governor's letter we had shown the town officials the night before, telling them that we should make the picture. They replied that they could not give permission to do so during the *padre's* absence. After we had breakfasted, and the light had become sufficient, we made our way to the old church, in front of which are some beautifully gnarled and irregular ancient olive trees, amid which the old bells are quaintly hung. Entering the church, we soon found the Titian, a descent from the cross. The figures are boldly painted and skillfully grouped; the action and lighting concentrate upon the figure of the Christ. Padre Ponce had told us that the proper place from which to photograph was the pulpit, and he was right. The sacristan was looking on with doubt: when he saw us making preparations for the picture, he hurried to us and said it was against all rule for anyone to take a photograph when the *cura* was not present. We told him our time was short; that we must return to Patzcuaro that day to arrange our farther journey; we showed the governor's order and Padre Ponce's letter, but all in vain. We must wait until the *cura* came. With this I put some *centavos* in his hand and told him I was certain his duties called him outside the church and that we would not detain him; that we should stay awhile to gaze upon the picture, which deserved close and pious examination. He at once withdrew, locking the door behind him. The instrument was quickly placed in the pulpit and the picture taken. Curiously, the sacristal duties ended just as we were ready to leave the church and the door opened as if we had said "Open sesame."

By ten-thirty we had secured a canoe and boatmen, two young and vigorous pure-blood indians. Though a wind was blowing squarely against us, we made good time. We stopped at the picturesque fishing-village of Janicho, on its rock island. Its houses cluster on a little terrace near the bottom of the hill, which rises behind it as a fine background. Steps of rock lead up the stony slope from the water's edge to the houses. In every yard mattings are laid, upon which little white fish are drying. As they walk through the streets or stand talking together, the men are ever tatting at nets; long lines of net-cord are

Tarascan Fishermen; Janicho

reeled out for many yards along the wayside; hundreds of feet of seines are hung out in the sun to dry. The houses, with their pretty red tiling, are irregularly clustered along narrow winding streets. The people are purely indian, and wear the characteristic dress.

No town in all the region makes so much use of the *tsupakua*, or spear-thrower, a wooden stick cut to fit the hand and support the shaft of a spear or long dart, the end of which rests against a peg near the tip of the thrower. By means of this instrument, the long, light, darts of cane with iron points are thrown more directly and forcibly than by the hand alone. These spears are used in hunting ducks. Anciently a spear-throwing stick was widely used through Mexico; to-day it lingers in few places, the best known of which is here on Lake Patzcuaro.

CHAPTER VII

TO URUAPAN BEFORE THE RAILROAD

(1898)

WE easily arranged at Patzcuaro to leave for Uruapan the next morning. Although delayed beyond our proposed hour of starting, we were off at six. It was early enough, indeed, for the morning air was cold; heavy frost coated the leaves and grass and lay upon the soil; in spite of our heavy blankets, wrapped closely about us, we shivered as we rode along upon our horses.

The ride, however, was a lovely one. At first we seemed to leave the lake behind us; mounting for some time we reached a summit from which it again broke upon our view; descending, we constantly caught glimpses of it, with its sinuous shores, its lovely mountain backgrounds, its islands, and its pretty indian towns. Finally, we again left it and rose into a magnificent mountain region, covered chiefly with pines. Passing through Ajuno, which lies upon a steep slope, we overtook a party of police, mounted on horses, taking a group of prisoners to Uruapan. At Escondidas, itself a miserable village, we were impressed by the mercantile spirit of these indians. In all these villages the houses are constructed of heavy logs or timbers, closely and neatly joined; the roofs are shingled with long and narrow shingles, and are abruptly four-sloped. At every house there was something for sale — food, drink, or *cigarros*. All these houses were built close to the edge of the road, and in the middle of the front was a little square window, in which the goods were shown. When no trade

Tarascan Women; Janicho

was solicited, these windows were closed with solid wooden shutters. Not only, however, was every house a store, but on the highway between towns, we passed many places where, beneath brush shelters, women offered fruit, food, or drink for sale. Usually several such shelters would be near together, and the venders had gay times, chatting, laughing and singing. Such houses and roadside-selling are common through the whole Tarascan region.

Soon after passing Escondidas, we began a descent, which seemed absolutely endless. Time after time we thought we had reached the bottom, only to find that we were on a terrace from which another drop led us still further down. On and on into this bottomless pit we descended to Ziracuaretaro, a striking town. Banana plantings surrounded the houses; orange-trees covered with their golden spheres reared themselves to the unusual height of thirty feet or more; *mameys*, with their strange nut-brown fruits, and coffee-trees, loaded to breaking, were abundant. Amid this luxuriant mass of tropical vegetation, houses were almost invisible until we were directly in front of them. Notwithstanding the enormous descent we had made, it appeared to us, when we crossed the stream and began the ascent, that we had not really been to the bottom of the great valley. For a long distance we mounted through a district of sugar-canes; then passed a little settlement of rude huts spread out over a reddish space; then, by a gentle but circuitous ascent, to a rugged trail which brought us to the summit and the edge of the great slope to Uruapan. At the further side of the valley and to our left, in a mass of green, we saw smoke rising from the factories of Uruapan. Crossing one of the characteristic bridges of the district, with a pretty shingled roof — four-sloped like those of the houses — over it, and with benches at the sides, where passers can sit and rest, while looking at the dashing, gurgling, foaming, water below,—we followed a level road between blackberries, wild roses, and other shrubs, to Uruapan.

No town in Mexico is more beautiful. Perpetual spring reigns. Although several thousand feet above sea level, it is so situated, with reference to mountain slopes and funnel valleys, that it has a genial climate, where plants flourish which are usually found only at lower altitudes. Its fruits and "the finest coffee in the world" have rendered the town long famous. The houses, bowered in dense groves of green, are of the picturesque Tarascan type. The four-sloped roofs, now covered with long, narrow shingles, now with the dull red tiles, suggest the prettiest pictures in Japanese towns. The streets are clean. Through the centre of the town dashes a mountain stream of clearest water, with the hue of sapphire. This pretty stream furnishes power for mills, factories and lighting-plant, and is crossed several times by picturesque, roofed bridges, in the shelter of which one may spend hours in watching the dashing water, foaming cascades, curious potholes worn in the rocky banks, and the passing indians. Most Mexican towns are contented with one *plaza*; this one has three, following each other closely, separated only by single lines of narrow buildings. They are neatly planted, and supplied with bandstand and monuments. The town is electric-lighted and several hotels had been lately put in readiness to receive the crowd of visitors expected with the completion of the railroad, a matter of a few months later.

The *prefecto* of Uruapan and *jefe politico* of the district is the son-in-law of Governor Mercado, and to him we bore a special letter from his father-in-law. The old gentleman had been insistent that we should return by Capacuaro and Cheran, indian towns. He said that at the former we should find a *mogote* (mound or heap of stones and dirt)

Indian Spear-Thrower; Lake Patzcuaro

which every traveler should see, while at the latter Lumholtz had secured some skulls of exceptional interest, and that we should do the same. As our time was short, we asked the *prefecto* to send a messenger to Cheran with orders to dig some skulls and have them ready against the time of our arrival. That official expressed delight in doing our bidding, and we saw the messenger summoned and the order placed in his hands, with full direction as to its delivery.

Meantime, there were objects of interest for us in Uruapan itself. The town is famous for its lacquer work, made with *aje*, like that of Chiapa. Gourds are ornamented, fruit-forms are colored after nature, bowls made from fruit shells are elaborately decorated, all quite like the Chiapa work. What is characteristic of Uruapan are the placques and table-tops of wood, decorated with floral designs in brilliant colors, upon a background of dark-green, pink, blue, yellow, or black. This art is in the hands of a few persons, some pure indians. Visiting them, we found the wooden placques and table-tops are brought from one of the mountain villages of the Tarascans; they are first covered thickly with the background color; upon this the pattern is pencilled and then cut out in the lacquered surface; the color, mixed with oil and *aje*, as with other substances, is then applied with the finger-tips to fill the cut patterns; the lustre is then brought out by careful rubbing. The work is striking, and is prized throughout the Republic.

In the same quarter of the town, where this local industry is carried on, are many goitrous persons. The disease seems to be confined to the one district, but there perhaps one-half the people have it, most of them to but a slight degree. Occasionally the swelling is notable, and in the families affected we find, as usual, deaf-mutism.

On the morning of New Year's day, we left for Capacuaro and Cheran. As we rode out from the city, we were more than ever impressed with its verdant beauty and picturesqueness. The road to Capacuaro was unexpectedly level and good, and we reached the town, which is purely indian, by nine o'clock. Women, almost without exception, wore the native dress. Goitres were common, and some, among the men, were really enormous. Riding through the long town, we drew up before the house of the *jefe de policia* (chief of police), and summoned the village officials. On their appearance we found that all but the *jefe* himself, were drunk, the *secretario* in particular being almost useless. When we handed him the letter from the *prefecto* he was quite unable to make aught of its grandiloquence. Having looked it through in a dazed way, he declared that we were "gringos," "like the one who was here last year" (presumably Lumholtz). With some severity, I told him he did wrong to call visitors to the town by the opprobrious name of *gringos*, and ordered him to read the letter and make known its contents to the *jefe*. He made another effort and then helplessly said —"Who can make anything of such a letter? It is in their *idioma*." Sternly pointing to the signature I said — "The letter is from your *prefecto* and written in his *idioma*; you see the *firma*." Helplessly shaking his head, he said, "Oh, yes, the *firma* is that of Silvano Martinez, but the letter is in your *idioma*." Seeing that he was of no earthly use, I took the letter from him, and, turning to the crowd which had gathered, rebuked them for their drunkenness, asserting that it was disgraceful for a whole town government to be intoxicated at the same time; that some one ought always to be sober enough to attend to business; that we had been insulted by being called *gringos*, and that our order had not been read to them because the *secretario* was too drunk to do his business; that there were two ways

Houses at Uruapan

of dealing with such town governments, and that, unless something was done promptly, we would see how they would like to go back with us to Uruapan, whence we had come. The *jefe*, who was really not drunk, thereupon begged to know what we desired, and the drunken *secretario* was somewhat frightened; the remainder of the official body expressed a wish to do only what we wanted. I then read the *prefecto's* letter in my best manner and added that we had come to Capacuaro only at the desire of the governor himself, to visit their *mogote*, and that we ought to wait no longer for guidance. At once all was commotion and bustle. Bidding the disgraced *secretario* go to his house and stay there, the *jefe de policia* summoned the rest of his company about him, seized his staff of office, buckled on his great *machete*, and took the lead; three policemen, with their *machetes*, followed; two others, unarmed, followed, and, with this escort, we started to hunt our ruins on the mountain. They proved to be two heaps of rubbish, from constructions of stone. Had we had time for serious investigation they might have proved of interest; as it was, we spent but a few minutes in their inspection, and then, bidding our drunken escort good-bye, we continued our journey. We had planned to go first to Nehuatzen, thence to Parracho, and, after visiting Cheran, back again to Nehuatzen. At the *mogote*, however, we were already near the Parracho highway and at once struck into it. Our journey led through forests, chiefly of pine, with open glades, at intervals; on many of the trees we saw great bunches of a parasite that bore honeysuckle-like, yellow flowers. Parracho we found lying at the base of mountains at the very end of a long stretch of level. It is an unattractive town, our only reason for visiting which was to see something of the manufacture of its famous *rebozos*, which differ from others in the wide border of white and azure blue silk, which is attached to a netted foundation to form decorative patterns, representing birds and animals, or geometric figures. The work is curious, and I am inclined to see in it a surviving imitation of the ancient feather-work for which the ancient Tarascans were famous. From Parracho our road led through Aranza to Cheran. Just beyond Aranza we passed over the astonishing wash from some summer torrent. During the wet season a single rain may fill the gorges, sheet the mountain slopes with water, tear great trees from their hold, break off mighty rock fragments and carry them onward, like wooden blocks, with hundreds of tons of finer gravel. At this season there was not a sign of water; not a trickling thread was visible in any of the gorges; but from their now dried mouths there spread fan-shaped deposits many rods in length and breadth, containing quantities of blocks of rock that measured from four to ten feet in diameter, trunks of trees up to two feet in thickness, all in the greatest confusion and at places completely covering our road to a depth of several feet. We could trace the tailing out of the fans of deposit, from their thicker, heavier part at the base of the torrent, to their margin on the plain; from heavy rock masses weighing tons, through smaller masses, into sand and gravel.

The way to Cheran seemed endless, but at last we reached that interesting, great indian town, when the afternoon was nearly spent. It was the New Year, and the street celebration of *los negritos* (the negroes — or the little negroes) was in progress. As we rode through the streets, however, we attracted much attention and the performance was neglected. We rode directly to the town-house, entered and asked for the *presidente.* He was slow in appearing and long before he arrived scores of people were crowding around the doors and windows to see us and know our business. When he arrived, we greeted him in a most friendly way and told him that we had come for the skulls. He looked aghast. "The skulls, what skulls, sir?" "The skulls the *prefecto* ordered you to dig for us." By this time, the crowd outside, which had increased with every minute, showed uneasiness. The *presidente* declared he knew nothing of any skulls. After we had explained the matter more fully, he assured us that no messenger had come from the *prefecto*; this, which at first we thought to be a lie, was no doubt true. He was plainly scared. He begged us to be careful lest the people, who were ignorant, should overhear us. He told us that a year before Don Carlos (Lumholtz) had been there; that he, too, had wanted skulls, and that the town officials had given him permission to dig some from the graveyard; that this caused so much excitement and so many threats that the permission had to be revoked. He feared the people had already heard our wishes and were even then in an ugly mood — a thing which seemed likely from an inspection of the faces in the doorway and windows. He said, however, that Don Carlos afterward secured some skulls from an ancient burial-place not distant from the village, and, if we pleased to wait in Cheran through the morrow, as it was now too late, five in the evening, to do aught, he would gladly show us the burial place of the ancients, where no doubt abundant skulls could be secured. Not yet certain that the man was telling truth, we spoke to him severely, saying that we should report him to the governor for not having obeyed the order of the *prefecto*. At the same time we demanded an official document signed by himself as *presidente*, and by the *secretario*, and duly sealed, stating that no messenger had come to him from the *prefecto*. To our surprise this document was promptly furnished, good evidence that the *prefecto* had played us false, only pretending to despatch the messenger whom we had seen started.

With profuse apologies and expressions of regret from the officials, we left Cheran, hurrying on to Nehuatzen for the night. Our chief reason for doing so was that everyone who knew of our intention to visit Cheran had shaken their heads, remarking "Ah! there the nights are always cold." Certainly, if it is colder there than at Nehuatzen, we would prefer the frigid zone outright. Nehuatzen is famous as the town where the canoes for Lake Patzcuaro are made. We had difficulty in securing food and a place to sleep. The room in which we were expected to slumber was hung with an extensive wardrobe of female garments. These we added to the blankets we carried with us, but suffered all night long from the penetrating cold. The two indian boys, who accompanied us as guides and carriers, slept in the corridor outside our door and when day broke they were so cramped and numbed and stiff with cold, that they lighted matches and thrust their cold hands into the flames, before they could move their finger-joints. We had planned to leave at five, but it was too cold to ride until the sun should be an hour high, so finally we left at seven. There was heavy frost on everything; curved frost crystals protruded from the soil, and we broke ice a half inch thick in water-troughs, unfinished canoes, by the roadside.

For ten hours we rode, without even stopping for lunch, through Sabina and Pichataro, San Juan Tumbio and Ajuno, back to comfortable Patzcuaro.

CHAPTER VIII

TLAXCALA

(1898)

WE have always loved the State of Tlaxcala and its quaint little capital city of the same name. For more than a dozen years its governor has been Prospero Cahuantzi, a pure-blood indian, whose native language is Aztec. He is a large, well built man, with full face and little black eyes that are sunken deeply into the flesh. He is a man of some force and energy. The population of his little state, the most densely populated in the Republic, is almost entirely indian, and it at once fears, hates, and respects him. Having made several previous visits to the city, and having always been graciously received by Don Prospero, we thought it hardly necessary to carry with us our usual letters of recommendation from the Federal authorities.

Just before we were ready to visit Tlaxcala, while we were in the City of Mexico, we learned that Governor Cahuantzi was there, on business. We thought it best to call upon him, explaining our proposed work and asking his interest. So to the Hotel Sanz, where he always stops when in the Capital, we went. We called twice without finding him and our third call appeared to be as unsuccessful, but just as we were leaving, resolved not to try again, we met the governor alighting from his carriage at the door. Intercepting him, we asked a moment's interview, which was granted, though with ill grace. It was plain that he was sadly out of humor. Apologizing to him for our intrusion at so late an hour and so immediately after his return to his hotel, we told him of our projected visit, described the measurements, photographs and other data we were gathering, reminding him that two years earlier he had heard our plans and promised his assistance. In a somewhat gentler mood, he told us we might visit Tlaxcala and that he would aid us, but he must have a little time "for preparing the soil;" that all his people were indians, and that our work would necessarily be considered with suspicion. Upon our asking him how much time would be needed "to prepare the soil," we received no definite reply. He, himself, planned to leave for home the following morning, Friday; so we suggested that we would go first to Puebla, and reach his capital on Monday. He plainly considered this somewhat hasty, but grunted his assent, and we left him, somewhat surprised at his unusual gruffness and lack of interest.

Early Monday morning, we appeared upon the scene. After breakfast we betook ourselves to the state palace; the governor was already in his reception room, but, instead of being ushered promptly into his presence, as had always happened in our previous visits, we were left to sit two hours in the outer office. Finally, on our displaying some impatience, a message was again taken to his Excellency, and a few minutes later, the *jefe politico* of the district bustled past us into the carefully guarded reception chamber. He did not long remain there, and, on coming out into the office where we were waiting, brusquely asked, "Are you the persons who want to measure heads? Well, they are waiting for you out there in the corridor; why don't you go to work?" Seizing our instruments, blanks and camera, we hurried to the corridor and began operations. Three or four were measured in quick succession; then, when I cried, "*Otro*" (another), the *jefe's* eyes began to bulge. That one measured, and another called for, he seemed half-distracted; desperation seized him; as he faintly repeated "*Otro*," he looked wildly around in search of subjects and it was plain that he had not begun to realize what demands we planned to make upon him. Before the noonday rest, we had measured fourteen subjects, but the *jefe's* personal interest had ceased, and he had completely disappeared from the scene of action. When we returned at three o'clock to resume work, only the guards were there to help us. One and another subject, invited to be measured, showed no interest in advancing science. So, Mr. Wilson went to see the *jefe* in his office; the old man was furious and actually ran out, with the statement that he had plenty of his own work to do. When this scene had been reported, it in no wise increased the readiness of subjects to undergo the operation. Finding that we were accomplishing nothing, we decided upon desperate measures. Going to the office of the governor's private secretary, we insisted on his telling the chief executive that we were losing time, that no one was assisting us, that subjects were obdurate and stubborn, and that something must be promptly done. We waited but a few minutes. The fiat went forth; the *jefe politico* appeared, puffing and blowing, and wildly excited. He was closeted a moment with the governor. On his reappearance, we greeted him cordially, and told him that the people present would not be measured and indicated one particularly stubborn subject, who was dealt with, promptly, and without gloves. The *jefe* remained long enough to reestablish order, though, under his breath, he muttered curses and threats, and expressed his feeling to any official, who chanced to pass. He said the business was driving him clean crazy; that he was doing what he did, not for love of us, but from respect to the orders of his chief. Having set the ball to rolling, he left us and there were no more delays.

When the labor of the day was over, we stopped at the *jefe's* office to inform him that we should continue work the following day, and emphasized the fact that we wished one hundred cases, and, as yet, had less than half that number. We suggested that systematic arrangements would not only facilitate *our* labor, but would lessen his own task. The result was evident; on the following day delegations, ordered by the *jefe*, and consisting of from six to a dozen persons each, began to come in from the outlying villages. This made our work easy, indeed. In one respect, Tlaxcala differs from all the other Mexican states with which we are acquainted. Most of the people live in very little towns, which cluster around the larger places. Thus, around the capital city, Tlaxcala, there are some seventeen of these small pueblos.

Working at the palace, we had secured almost no women for measurement. Asking the advice of the *cura* in the matter, he recommended that we should go to some one of the neighboring indian villages; that he would give us a letter to the *juez* and that, thus, we would secure our subjects easily. He suggested San Estevan and wrote the promised letter to the *juez* of that village. San Estevan is a pretty village, near the summit of some low gray hills of tufa, behind which rises a background of higher hills of the same material. The slope is terraced for the houses, which are all built of adobe bricks and have flat roofs. The "three part house," of the ancient Aztec type — godhouse, kitchen, and granary — is better shown in this state than almost any other part of the Republic. The granary, or *cuezcomate*, is particularly characteristic. It is built of clay, in the form of a great vase or urn, open at the top, above which is built a little thatch to shed rain and to protect the contents. The *cuezcomate* is often ten feet high. One or more of them is found in connection with every house.

House and Cuezcomate; Los Reyes

The *juez* lived in a comfortable house of two rooms, half of which is used at present for the boy's school, of which his son is teacher. He received us graciously, and was pleased to receive a letter from the *padre*, though he stated it was not a government order and carried no actual authority; that if the women cared to be measured, well and good, but if not, no force could be employed. The appearance of the camera, however, interested him; plainly, he desired to have a family group photographed; he hinted at this so broadly that, taking him to one side, I whispered that it was, of course, impossible to take family groups for everyone, but if we secured the twenty-five women without delay, notwithstanding the fact that we had no more authoritative document than a *cura's* letter, the group should be taken. The effect was immediate. The police were summoned and sent through the village to bring in women for measurement and naught was said about their right of refusal.

When, toward evening, we returned from San Estevan, tired but quite satisfied with the day's work, we found a delegation of more than a dozen men waiting for us in the *plaza*. We did not need so large a number to complete our work, and it was nearly dark; we would gladly have dismissed them and run our chances of securing others the next day. But neither they nor the *jefe politico* were to be bluffed. So we marched into the corridor, lighted candles and got to work. When those lacking to make our full hundred had been measured, we proposed to let the others go, but they were not to be thus got rid of, and insisted on being measured as such were the orders of the governor. We were not through until long after dark, and we were ravenously hungry.

This delegation was one of the most attractive, clean, and intelligent with whom we had dealt. It was from Los

Reyes, a little town at a distance of about half a league. It was headed by the village *juez*. After we had completed the measuring, they stood, shifting their *sombreros* from hand to hand and plainly wishing to say something further; finally, mustering courage, the *juez* and *secretario* advanced and stated that it was the town's desire to have a picture taken of the church, with the saint and people of the village before the door. Would it be possible for us to make the picture and on what conditions? We replied that time was precious and that the trip, if it involved a loss of time, was quite impossible; but if they supplied carriers to take the instruments to and from their village, and had all ready before seven in the morning, we would make it. Delighted, the officials then inquired what we would wish for breakfast; we answered French bread and red wine. When we looked out of our window, a little before seven, we saw our party ready and waiting. The *juez*, the *secretario*, and two others made the company. A basket, carefully carried by one, was suspected to contain our breakfast. The burdens were shouldered, and we started out in the cool, fresh morning air, for the village, where we arrived in about half an hour. It is a town of less than one hundred people, situated upon a little mountain, hidden, to one looking from Tlaxcala, by intervening hills. We were received in the townhouse, which is a portion of the old church building; mass was in progress, and we told those who received us, that we had no wish to interfere with their religious duties; that those who wished, might go to service. Most went, but two or three were left as a committee of entertainment. They took us to a view-point from which there was a magnificent valley to be seen. And, here, we found one of the finest echoes possible. Rockets were exploded and the noise was echoed from hill to hill around the great amphitheatre; it was like a long reverberation of thunder, but

The Village and its Saint; Los Reyes

Cuezcomate, or Granary; San Nicolas Panotla

it sank and swelled, sank and swelled, repeatedly, until it seemed that it would never stop. Service over, the procession formed, and the *santito* was brought out before the church. The townspeople were arranged and the view taken. We were then invited in to breakfast, which was fine. There were plenty of French rolls and the red wine brought from town, and a great heap of *enchiladas*, fresh lettuce and eggs. After eating, we expressed a wish to hear the village drum, a great *huehuetl*. This musical instrument is a reminder of the olden times; it is not found everywhere, but a number of indian towns possess one, which is kept to be played on festal occasions. The one as Los Reyes was some three feet or so in height, a hollow cylinder of wood with a membrane stretched across the upper end; it was painted blue. A chair of state was placed for me in the little *patio*. After I was seated the three musicians took their places,— one played the great *huehuetl*, a second beat the *tambour* or ordinary drum, the third performed upon the *chirimiya*, a shrill wooden pipe. It was the first time we had really heard a *huehuetl*. The player used two sticks with padded heads, beating with great force in excellent time. The booming of the instruments was audible to a great distance. The whole village had gathered, and in a mometary lull in the music, I told the people of the ancient use of the *huehuetl*; that Bernal Diaz, in his history of the Conquest of Mexico, tells us what feelings filled the hearts of the Spaniards, when they heard the great *huehuetl*, in the temple of the ancient city of Tenochtitlan; then it was chiefly beaten when human victims were being sacrificed to the gods, and the soldiers knew that some fellow-countryman, or a Tlaxcalan ally, was dying. Never have I given a public lecture, that was listened to with more attention or greater appreciation.

The day we measured women at San Estevan, we found

an indian mason there at work, whom we had measured at Tlaxcala, and with whom, on one occasion, we had some conversation. He was disgusted at the conduct of the women while undergoing measurement, and at evening said, "Sir, it is a pity for you to waste your time in a town like this; these people are little better than animals; in my town there is great enthusiasm over your work, and by going there you might do your will and find people with minds, not beasts." There was really no work left to be done, but we desired to see a town where there was great enthusiasm over our investigations. Hence, we arranged with Ignacio Cempoalteca to visit his pueblo of San Nicolas Panotla. Accordingly, on the afternoon of the day when we visited Los Reyes, we went across the valley to Panotla, Ignacio and an older brother, Jose, met us at the hotel, where — excusing himself on account of the mason-work at San Estevan, which could not wait — Ignacio left us, assuring us that Jose would do everything for us. This was quite true, and we found Panotla all that it had been painted.

Jose led us directly to their home. The walls were well built of stone set in adobe mortar; they were smoothly coated with a snowy plaster; the supporting walls of the little terrace on which the house was built were also well constructed and it was with some pride that Jose told us that the work had all been done by himself and Ignacio. Jose is married and has a wife and three children; Ignacio is a bachelor; a younger brother, Carmen, is also unmarried — he has taught himself free-hand and architectural drawing and showed us examples of his work. The old father and mother own the home and received us hospitably. Jose guided us through the village, where we photographed whatever took our fancy, entered houses, examined all that interested us, and really found enthusiasm for our work

The Ancient Drum—Huehuetl; Los Reyes

Fiesta at Cholula; Day of San Antonio Abad

everywhere. Before the churchyard stands a quaint old cross of stone, dated 1728, upon which are represented all the symbols of Christ's passion; a long inscription in Aztec is cut into the base. Close by the church, we visited the boy's school, where we found some forty dark-skinned, black-eyed, youngsters, whose mother-speech is Aztec. We proposed to photograph them, so they were grouped outside the schoolhouse, but not until a pair of national flags and the portrait of the governor, Prospero Cahuantzi, were fixed upon the background wall.

After the picture had been taken, we told the *maestro* we would like to hear the boys sing. It was plain he did not consider singing their strong forte, but our wishes were met. One boy, standing, wielded the baton, beating time. When the singing was done with, the *maestro* said he would like us to see the class in arithmetic, if we had time. Accordingly fourteen or fifteen boys, from ten to fourteen years of age, stepped out upon the dirt floor; we were told that they could work examples in percentage, interest, bonds and mortgages, discount, alligation — which did we prefer? Truth to say, it was so long since we had studied alligation, that we had really forgotten what it was, and so expressed a preference for it. "Very good, sir," said the *maestro*. "Will you not propound a problem?" From this quandary we escaped by stating that we could not think of doing so; that we had every confidence in his fairness and that he had better give it, as the boys were more accustomed to him. We have visited many classes of the same grade and age in the United States and have never seen one that would surpass them in quickness, accuracy, and clearness of explanation. After our trip through San Nicolas Panotla, Jose took us back to his house, where, meantime, a dinner had been made ready.

* * * * * * *

Weeks later, we learned the probable reason of the governor's gruffness, which was in such marked contrast to his previous treatment, that it puzzled us considerably. At about the time of our visit, a number of wealthy *haciendaderos*, of the State of Tlaxcala, had been arrested for counterfeiting silver money. They were men whose *maguey* fields brought them enormous incomes; one would suppose their legitimate sources of wealth would have contented them! But such was not the case, and they had gone into wholesale counterfeiting. The fraudulent coin had long been known and diligent efforts were made to find the criminals, efforts at last crowned with success. The guilt was fixed without a doubt, the parties were arrested, tried, and sentenced. Every attempt was made to secure their pardon, in vain. Governor Cahuantzi is an old friend of President Diaz, believed to have great influence with him. Men of wealth, interested in the release and pardon of the criminals, promised Cahuantzi ten thousand dollars in case of his successful intercession with the President in the matter. These details, not generally known, we received from a source respectable and trustworthy, and we believe them true. Anxious to gain the reward, and probably feeling certain of his influence with Diaz, the old man made the journey to Mexico. It was the very time when we called upon him. When we had our interview, he had just seen the President, and it is hinted that, not only did Don Porfirio refuse to pardon the counterfeiters, but showed a dangerous inclination to investigate the reason of the indian governor's intervention. No wonder that the old man was gruff and surly to his visitors, after the loss of ten thousand dollars which he had looked upon as certain, and with uncertainty as to the final outcome of his unlucky business.

Tlaxcalan Schoolboys; San Nicolas Panotla

CHAPTER IX

ZAMORA AND THE ONCE PUEBLOS

(1898)

THE morning train from Guadalajara brought us to Negrete at about two in the afternoon, and we had soon mounted to the top of the clumsy old coach, which was dragged by six horses. The road to Zamora runs through a rich farming district. For the greater part of the distance the road is level and passes amidst great *haciendas*. The corn crop had been abundant and carts were constantly coming and going from and to the fields. These carts were rectangular, with side walls some four or five feet in height, made of cornstalks set close together and upright. All were drawn by oxen. Most of the carts had a light cross, made of cornstalks, set at the front end, to protect the load from adverse influences. Great numbers of men, dressed in leather trousers drawn over their cotton drawers, in single file lined past us, with great baskets full of corn strapped on their backs. Here and there, in the cornfields, groups of such men were cutting the ripened ears from the plants.

We now and then met groups of men bringing great timbers from the mountains fifty or sixty miles away. These timbers were many feet in length and trimmed to a foot square; from four to six made a load. The cart upon which they were carried consisted of a pair of wheels and an axle; one end of the timbers was attached to this, and the other was fastened to the yoke of oxen. It was rare that we met with a single timber cart, as four or five usually went together. The drivers who were in charge of them were pure Tarascans.

For a considerable distance a fine slope rose to our left, strewn with loose rock masses, and covered with a growth which was chiefly *pitahaya*, some of the plants attaining the size of grown trees. Many of them presented an appearance which we had not seen elsewhere — the tips and upper part of the upright branches being as white as if intentionally whitewashed; the simple explanation of this strange appearance was that the branches in question had served as buzzards' roosts. Our journey of twenty-five miles was made with two relays of horses. After perhaps three hours' riding, we reached the Zamora River, which we followed for some distance. From the time when we began to follow this stream, our road was almost a dead level. At many places along the river, we saw a peculiar style of irrigation machine, a great wooden scoop or spoon with long handle swung between supporting poles. The instrument was worked by a single man and scooped up water from the river, throwing it upon the higher land and into canals which carried it through the fields. Sometimes two of these scoops were supported side by side upon a single frame, and were worked in unison by two persons. At the only town of any consequence upon the road, we found numbers of interesting hot springs which might really be called geysers. They were scattered at intervals over the flat mud plain for a distance of a half mile or more. We could see jets of steam of more or less vigor rising from a score or so at a time. At some of these the water really boiled, and we saw it bubbling and tossing to a height of a foot or so above the margin of the spring. Groups of women, laughing and talking or singing snatches of songs, were washing clothes at several of these hot springs, and the garments were spread out over the bushes and trees to dry.

At one little geyser, bubbling up in the very middle of the road, as we passed we saw a boy pelting the water with stones and mud in order to make it mad and see it spout. The plain was sprinkled here and there with thickets of acacia and mesquite. In the early evening the breeze came loaded with the fragrance of the golden balls of the acacia. There was bright moonlight, and we could see the country, even after sunset. The latter portion of the journey was through low swampy ground, much of the time over causeways.

There are few towns in central Mexico, not on a railroad, to be compared with Zamora. It is large, clean, well built, and presents an air of unusual comfort. The main *plaza* is large, and finely planted with palms, orange-trees, roses and flowering shrubs. The orange-trees were in full bloom and the air was heavy with their odor. The town is electric-lighted and has a good system of waterworks. The great church, with two slender towers, fills up the whole of one side of the *plaza*, while the other three are ocupied with business houses. The amount of life in the town at night surprised us. Even after ten o'clock, many were on the streets, and the *dulce* stands, *cafe* tables and *loto* hall were doing a large business. Few towns in Mexico are so completely under priestly influence, but few again appear as prosperous, progressive, and well-behaved. Two distinct types of houses predominate, the older and the newer. The old style house is such as is characteristic of many other Tarascan towns, but is here more picturesquely developed than in most places. The low-sloped, heavily-tiled roof projects far over the street and is supported below by projecting timbers, which are trimmed at the end to give a pleasing finish. So far do these roofs project over the sidewalk that the water is thrown into the middle of the street and the footpath below is well sheltered. The new style of house, which is required by the recent laws, has an almost flat roof which ends squarely at the sidewalk, and from which long tin pipes project to throw the water into the streets. Here, as so frequently, the old fashion is at once more comfortable and more artistic.

We spent the morning in efforts to secure horses, but finally secured a man, Don Nabor, who agreed to accompany us with five animals. The party consisted of myself, my interpreter, my plaster-worker, and Don Nabor. Each of us was mounted, and a fifth horse carried the plaster and other luggage. Leaving at noon, we took the long road past Jacona, a little town famous for its fruit. Having passed there, after a long journey, we looked down from the height almost directly upon the place whence we had started. The scene was of unusual beauty — the wide-spreading, flat valley, with its fields of wheat and clustered trees, presented a mass of rich green coloring, in the midst of which stood the pretty city. After a long climb, we descended into a valley in which lies Tangancicuaro, a large town with a *plaza* full of fine, great trees, where we ate at a quaint little *meson.* From here we pushed on to Chilchota, the head town of the Once Pueblos. From the crest, just above the town, we looked down upon a level valley, green with new wheat. Entering the town a little after five, we rode up to the *meson* of San Francisco, near the little *plaza.* It was with difficulty that we secured a room containing a single bed, with mattress, and two mats. There was nothing at all to eat at the *meson*, but on strolling out to the *plaza* we found some indian women selling *atole* and bread. With this we were compelled to be content until morning, paying seven *centavos* for our four suppers. Hunting up the *presidente* of the town, we found him sitting, with his court, on benches in the *plaza.* He was a pleasant, rather dressy young man, but at once took interest in our work, and told us that

Huancito was the best town for our bust work, as the population there is primitive and purely indian.

The Once Pueblos — eleven towns — are famous through this portion of the Republic. Several of them are purely indian; Chilchota is largely *mestizo.* The towns lie in a long line on the side of the little valley, at the foot of the bordering hills. Between some, spaces of considerable extent intervene; others are so close together that, in riding through them, one sees no line of separation. All consist of adobe houses, of a rich brown color, roofed with tiles. Some of the churches are of considerable size, but are also built of brown adobe. The Once Pueblos are famous for their pottery, and in some of them almost every house has its little kiln or oven. Fruit is cultivated, and the houses are frequently embowered in trees; in many yards are bee-hives. The valley is abundantly watered with little streams of perfect clearness.

The *presidente* had insisted that the school teacher at Huancito would prove invaluable. He gave us a letter of introduction to him, and an order upon the authorities. We were at once given possession of the schoolhouse for our work, and I started out to find a subject. Almost the first person encountered was a young man of twenty-three years, who presented the pure Tarascan type. I at once told him that he was the very man we wanted; that we planned to make a picture of him in plaster; at the same time, I described the method of work, and while talking, holding him by the arm, drew him over toward the schoolhouse. Almost before be realized it, we were ready for the task. As he removed his shirt and prepared for the operation of oiling and the application of the plaster, he looked somewhat sombre. After seeing the work well begun, I stepped outside and sat in the portico until it should be done. The first piece of plaster had been applied, the subject had been turned, and was lying ready for the second application. At this moment, an indian maiden, with dishevelled hair, came rapidly running across the *plaza* toward the school-house. Rushing past me, she entered the school-room, and seeing the subject lying on the floor clasped her hands and cried, "Florencito! My Florencito, why wait here? Stay not with these cruel men; flee with me!" Seizing him by the hand, they dislodged the plaster from his shoulders and started for the door, but catching sight of me, cast a glance around, saw the open window, and leaping through it, dashed off home. Up to this time the local authorities had shown an interest in our work and a willingness to aid. Calling the chief of police, I bade him and the teacher seek our subject and bring him back for the completion of the operation. "But, sir," said the chief of police, "suppose he does not wish to come?" "Why are you chief of police?" was my reply. The teacher, who is himself a *mestizo* and despises the poor indians in his charge, was loud in his complaints. He vigorously declared that what these people needed was a second Cortez, that they had never been properly conquered, and, with the chief of police, he started out for the new conquest. After an hour or more of waiting, we saw them reappear with Florencito. But humanity is ever loath to admit defeat. As he passed us, he grumbled that he saw no good reason for such a fuss, as he had simply gone to eat his breakfast.

Having completed the work with this subject, we suggested that others should be brought, but met with a prompt refusal. The judge and the chief of police both declared that the people did not wish to have busts made, and that they would bring no more. In vain I suggested that a meeting of the townspeople should be called together in order that we might address them and explain the purpose of our visit. It was impossible to move the officials. Finally I told the judge that I should send a mounted messenger, who had accompanied us from the *presidente*, to Chilchota to report the failure of the town officials to do their duty. He promptly declared that he was going to Chilchota himself to see the *presidente* in the matter. Sure enough, when my messsenger was ready, he had made his preparations, and the two departed together to present the different sides of the question. Neither returned until we were through for the day. During the afternoon we secured two more subjects, and by nightfall had three good busts as the result of the day's labor. Then we faced new difficulties. Carriers could not be had for love nor money. What was wanted were three men, one to carry each bust back to Chilchota, where we planned to spend the night. Finally, after loss of time and temper, each of us shouldered a bust and rode back on horseback with our trophies.

We soon discovered that the eleven towns were in a ferment of excitement. Most dreadful tales were rife with regard to us and our work. Some asserted that we cut off heads and hung them up to dry; that in drying, they turned white. Others reported that with knives, made for the purpose, we sliced off the ears of unfortunate indians, close to their heads. Still others reported that we had a frightful instrument which was fitted into the nose, and by means of which we tore strips of flesh and skin from the face of the subject. It was said, and quite likely truly, that they were arming in all the houses; that *machetes*, guns, pistols, and clubs were laid convenient to hand.

The next day was Sunday, and we made no attempt to continue work. It was market-day, and indians from all the pueblos had gathered in the *plaza* to buy and sell. All were pure in blood and spoke Tarascan. Fruits, sugar-cane, corn, *tortillas*, *atole*, coffee, were the chief staples. Stocks of pottery were attractively displayed. Two characteristic wares are both pretty. Most typical, perhaps, is the black and green ware which is made into bowls, plates, mugs, and pitchers. The clay of which it is baked is local and dark brown in color; a white earth applied to this, on baking, gives rise to a rich metallic green glaze. Designs are painted upon this in black. This black and green ware goes far and wide, and everywhere is recognized as coming from the Once Pueblos. At Huancito and some other pueblos, they make little *canteras* with a red ground and decorative designs in black and white. One thing, offered in the market, was new to us, dishes full of *ucuares* — long, irregular, swollen, dry, brown objects that looked like stewed worms with thick and fleshy skins. One *centavo* bought far more than any person would be likely to eat; even after having been stewed in sugar, they were bitter, and had a foul smell that was most unpleasant; they appeared to be roots or tubers of some plant.

Naturally, our work had attracted much attention in Chilchota. No one of the many dozen visitors who came to see us at the *meson* was so profoundly impressed as a boy of fourteen, named Ignacio. Appearing early in the morning, he remained with us almost all the hours of the twenty-four. Thinking that the effect on the villagers might be good, I decided to ride in the afternoon through the pueblos. When the *presidente* discovered my intention, he insisted upon supplying a mounted and armed escort, and at the same time gave me a general letter to the eleven towns, in which strict orders were given that my wishes should be respected, and dire threats made in case any one should show me aught but the greatest consideration. Ignacio accompanied me. Riding through the towns, we passed far enough beyond Huancito to see the most remote of the eleven pueblos. They are separated somewhat from the rest, and lie rather higher up in a bend of the valley. Everywhere I took some pains to talk with the people, to visit their houses, to examine their pottery, their bees and their growing crops, as I felt that such an interest would help us in our work. On our return, Ignacio told me that he should stay to dinner with us, as he much preferred to do so to going home. He also told me that it would be a great pity to lose the theatre, which was to take place that evening. Accordingly, after dinner was over, we went to see the play. I expected that at that season of the year it would be a *pastorela* — and in fact it had been so announced. It was, however, a true drama, and one of the funniest — unintentionally — imaginable. The stage was set in the middle of the *patio* of a large house. The boy insisted that we would be late, and so we went at 7:15, although the bill announced the hour as 8. The spectators brought their own chairs with them. Except a few youngsters, no one arrived before 9, and the curtain at last rose at a quarter before eleven. Among the last to arrive was the *presidente* and his party. He was resplendent in a cape of crimson velvet with brilliant yellow facings. Hardly was his party seated, when we were politely invited to sit with them. Three acts were rendered, and while waiting for the fourth, one of the party declared that there would be eleven more. This gave the *presidente* an opportunity to relate an experience of his own. On one occasion, after watching a play from seven in the evening until four in the morning, the stage broke down; the management appeared and apologized regarding the accident, particularly, since some twenty acts were still to have been rendered. Our play, however, turned out to have had but eight acts, and one of these was omitted. When it should have been given, the whole troupe appeared upon the platform; the manager announced the reason why the act would not be given, but promised that on the following Sunday, in another play, an extra act should be inserted, in order that all might receive the full value of their money. Our play ended at one, when the audience dispersed.

Needing but two more subjects, we looked about Chilchota the next day, hoping to find indians from the more remote villages, who might permit their busts to be made. Two excellent cases were found. The last was a man from Carapan, the most remote of the eleven towns. He was a man of forty years, whose father accompanied him, and both were for a long time dubious about the operation. Finally, however, consent was given and the bust was made. As he arose and dressed to go, I said, "Did I tell you the truth? Did the operation hurt you, or did it not? Was there a reason why you should not have your bust made?" He promptly answered, "Sir, you told me truth; the operation did not hurt me and there surely is no harm in it; but, sir, you can hardly believe what an excitement this work has caused in our town. Yesterday, in the market-place at Chilchota, there were more than twenty men from Carapan who carried weapons in their clothing. We had selected leaders and arranged signals, and at the first sign of an attack from your party, we were prepared to sell our lives dearly."

It was a work of time to fill the moulds and pack the busts. Before we were ready to start upon our journey, it was half-past four in the afternoon. True wisdom would have suggested waiting until morning. Time, however, was precious, and I hoped to make Cheran that night; consequently, though against the advice of many, we started out, with eight leagues to go, over a road with a bad reputation, and at some points difficult to traverse. For a little distance, we followed the familiar trail down through the pueblos, but at Tanaquillo we turned up into the mountain. The ascent was steady until we reached the pass, through which an icy wind drove down upon us. We could hope to make the distance in six hours. At first we met many persons, all of whom warned us that we would be late in arriving, and recommended that we should stop at Rancho Seco. We had no intention of so doing, but knew that we must turn at that point into a new road. Between sunset and bright moonlight, there was an interval of darkness, and in that interval we must have passed the turning which led to Rancho Seco. At all events, we presently found ourselves entirely at a loss, wandering over a rocky hill covered with brush, amid which the trail had entirely disappeared. Retracing, as well as we could, our road, we finally found ourselves upon another trail which we followed until 9:30, when we met a little band of indians, the first whom we had seen for a long time. From them we found that we were not upon the road for Cheran, but at the edge of a slope at the bottom of which was a little indian town, Tanaco. Descending to it, we found a house where they agreed to shelter us for the night, and in the *tienda* near by we bought hard bread and old cheese. We were sheltered in a substantially built room, into which the cold air did not penetrate. The indians with whom we were staying were unusually intelligent; a number of books, including a large dictionary, lay upon the table, and the men, who crowded in upon us, were anxious to learn the English words for common things. This was an experience which rarely happened to us in indian Mexico. The people, however, were not quite sure of our intentions, and Nabor said that when he went to water the horses, a committee of village folk waited upon him, asking whether we were the party of white men who had been skinning live indians over in the Once Pueblos.

There were four leagues between us and Cheran, and many more beyond it to Patzcuaro, where we hoped to arrive the next night. Accordingly, we made an early start. Our host agreed to pilot us over the indistinct and tortuous bridle-path to the highroad. Many little mountains, almost artificially regular, arose in the otherwise plain country. As we rode along the trail we saw the church of Parracho far behind us in the distance. The latter part of the road, after Cheran was once in sight, seemed hopelessly long, but a little before ten o'clock we pulled up at the *meson*. We at once made arangements for food for ourselves and the horses, and determined to rest until noon. Our reputation had preceded us. I asked a child at the *meson* to bring me a mug of water. When he brought it, I noticed that the mug was of the characteristic black and green ware of the Once Pueblos, but asked the boy where it was made. With a cunning look, he answered, "O yes, that comes from where you people have been,— up at the Once Pueblos." And yet we had not come over the road from the Once Pueblos, but by the main highway from Parracho.

Rested and refreshed, we started at 12:30 for the long fourteen leagues of journey. We passed Pichataro, where the round paddles for Patzcuaro canoes are made, and where the applewood, so prized as material for spear-throwers, is procured. We passed Sabina, where the canoes themselves are hollowed out, miles from their launching place, to which they must be carried over mountains. Each town we passed made me more and more uneasy, as I knew that Nabor contemplated revolt. He did not like the idea of too long a journey for his horses. He wished to stop long before the goal that I had fixed. When we left the last of the important towns behind us, I felt for the first time secure. It was now dark, and we found the roads far worse than we remembered them. They were worn into deep gullies, into which our horses fell and over which they stumbled. Long before reaching Ajuno I felt convinced that we had missed the road, but we floundered on, and never was sight more welcome than the light of fires shining through the cane walls of the wretched huts of that miserable town. Here there was a final council regarding resting for the night. The whole party, except myself, considered Ajuno as a capital resting-place. All yielded, however, and we continued on our way. It was almost midnight when we rode up to the hotel, upon the *plaza* in quaint old Patzcuaro. All were cross and tired; neither crossness nor weariness were helped when we were told that there was no room for us at the inn. We made such vigorous representations, however, that the doors were finally thrown open. An old store-house was cleaned out and supplied with decent beds, and a good supper was served.

CHAPTER X

THE BOY WITH THE SMILE

(1898)

IT is doubtful whether the common people of any country are so rarely surprised, or taken unaware, as those of Mexico. At a moment's notice, the commonest indian, who may have scarcely been outside of his own town in all his life, may start to go across the country. Astonishing incidents appear to create no more surprise in their minds than the ordinary affairs of every day. In January, 1898, we revisited Cholula. As we alighted from the street-car we noticed a boy, some fourteen years old, whose most striking characteristic was his smile. He wished to serve as guide, to show us the pyramid, the convents, the chapel of the natives. On assuring him that we knew far more about the lions of his town than he, he was in no wise abashed, but joined himself to us for the remainder of the day. He accompanied us to see the blessing of the animals in the great churchyard. He displayed an interesting knowledge of English, answering "yes" quite perfectly to every sort of question, and repeating the two words, which are well known the whole world over as American-English, on all conceivable occasions. When at evening he saw us safely on the street-car he left us with the same smile with which he had received us. On our next visit to Cholula much the same thing happened, but learning that we planned to stop at Cuauhtlantzinco on our way to Puebla, he stole a ride upon the car, for the sake of accompanying us. He was a rather handy boy, good-natured and anxious to please, so that, later in our journey, we hired him for several days and let him do what he could to help us.

Much later, when at home planning the details of our next extensive journey, the thought struck us that it might be well to make the boy with the smile a member of our party. It seemed as if, in going into districts rarely visited by strangers, it would be well to have the party as largely Mexican as possible. If, however, the boy were to accompany us, it was necessary that he should first learn something of our work and needs, and perhaps of English. Accordingly, I decided to go to Cholula and bring the boy up to the States.

The resolution was so hastily taken that there was no time to send word to the boy himself, Going straight to Cholula, I had some difficulty in finding his abode. I knew that the boy had no father, that his widowed mother had but one other child, a girl younger than the boy himself. I had once seen the mother and the little sister; I also knew the street on which they lived. Arriving at the street, however, no one apparently had ever heard of the boy. One and another through the whole length of the street was questioned, but none knew his name or recognized his description. Excepting that I knew that trait of Mexican character which assists acquaintances to seclusion, when they are sought by strangers, I should have despaired. As it was, I kept on asking, and finally, from a child who could hardly speak on account of youth, I discovered the house which I sought. It was a little hut set back behind a yard of growing corn. I had inquired at the houses on either side and at the house across the road, as also of a man working in the corn in the yard itself. But everyone had been profoundly ignorant of the boy's existence. Walking up to the house, I found the door open, and the mother and the little girl within. The moment the woman saw me, she said, "*Que milagro, Señor!*" (What a miracle, sir!) and rising, gave me a warm embrace. The little girl did the same. "And where is Manuel?" I inquired. "Ah, sir, he has gone to Puebla on an errand for a gentleman; but he will be back on the street-car at half-past ten. Pray wait, sir, till he comes."

The house consisted, like most of its class, of a single room. The walls were built of sun-dried bricks of adobe. Entrance was by a single door. There were no windows. The floor was clay. The flat roof was scarcely six feet above the floor. The furniture, though ample, was scanty. A little earthen brazier for heating and cooking, a stone *metate*, a rubbing-stone for grinding corn-meal, a table heaped with bundles and boxes containing the family clothing, and a chair were all. There were no beds, not even the mats which so frequently, among the poor of Mexico, take their place. Several pictures of saints and of the virgin were pinned against the wall, and there were signs of tapers which had been burned before them. A bird or two in wooden cages, a rooster and a little dog lived in the house with the family.

After answering various questions from the good woman and the little girl, I finally stated that I proposed to take Manuel with me to my country. He would stay with me there for six months, after which he would come back and accompany me for three months longer on a journey into southern Mexico. "If I have your consent," I said, "we leave to-day." Immediately the woman answered, "Sir, it is for you to say." Just then, however, the little girl, Dolores, began to cry. "Tut, tut, Dolores," said I, "I am sure you want Manuel to go away and visit a strange country and have a fine time; and think of the pictures that he can bring you to show what he has seen. And more than that, it is already half-past ten, and you shall go down to

The Cross; San Nicolas Panotla

The Boy with the Smile

the street-car to meet him, and tell him that he must come straight home, for fear that he will loiter on the way; but do not tell him I am here, nor say anything about his going away, for we wish to surprise him." Drying her eyes, and smiling almost as the boy himself, Dolores started to run to the street-car line, and presently fetched Manuel home in triumph. As he entered and saw me, he said, "*Que milagro, Señor*" and kissed my hand. Having asked, as Mexican politeness requires, a variety of questions about his welfare, I finally said, "Well, Manuel, how would you like to go to Puebla with me for the day?" "Sir, it is for you to say." "Very good," said I. "And if I should conclude that it was best to take you to Mexico for a few days, what would you say to that?" "I am entirely in your hands, sir," he replied, "to do your orders." "Well," said I, "suppose I took you to my own country and kept you there for six months?" and the boy replied, "Sir, you are my owner; it is for you to command." "Very well," said I, "get ready, and we will go on the street-car, at twelve o'clock, to Puebla."

Telling his mother that she should put together the few articles of which there might be need, we started for the noonday car. As we left, I suggested that she and the little girl come to the city, during the afternoon or evening, to bid the boy good-bye, as we should leave on an early train the following morning. They came at nightfall. She had his small possessions tied up in a carrying cloth, and her mind was stored with bits of excellent advice and admonition as to his conduct and behaviour in his new surroundings. After Dolores and her brother had given each other a farewell embrace, the mother said a few words to the boy, who knelt upon the floor of the room and crossed his hands upon his breast. The mother then gave him her parting blessing, and sent him forth into the outside world.

CHAPTER XI

IN THE MIXTECA ALTA

(1898)

OF all railroad cities in the Republic, Oaxaca is the most completely indian. It is the capital of a state the population of which is nine-tenths of native blood. Fifteen native languages are spoken in the state to-day. While some of these are related to each other, they are distinct languages, not dialects, even those which are related being as unlike as the French, Italian, and Spanish. The indians commonly seen on the city streets are Zapotecs or Mixtecs, but at times Mixes come from their distant mountain homes with burdens on their backs, or parties of Tehuantepecanas attract attention, by their fine forms and striking dress, as they walk through the streets. The market is crowded, even late in the day; ox-carts from the indian towns for miles around are constantly seen in the streets. Most of the sellers in the market are indians; they bring fruits and vegetables, dried fish from the Pacific, *jicaras* and strainers of gourds, beautifully painted and polished gourds from Ocotopec, honey, sugar — both the crude brown and the refined yellow cakes — and pottery. The indian pottery here sold is famous. Three kinds of wares are well known — a dull plain red, an unglazed but highly polished black, and a brilliant glazed green. The black ware is made into useful vessels, and also into a variety of toys, chiefly whistles and bells. Pottery would seem to be one of the least suitable materials for bells. Here, however, bells of pottery in many shapes are found — little bells, with handles like the upper part of a human figure; larger bells, with curious flat handles set transversely; others, still larger, like cow-bells in size and tone, and curious cross-shaped bells, really a group of four united. Among the whistles some are made into the shape of animals and birds and curious human figures; among the latter, some closely resemble ancient whistles from the prehistoric graves. This black ware is made at Coyotepec, and when the objects are first taken from the kiln they are almost white; before they are cold, they are exposed to dense smoke, and thus assume their black color. The brilliantly glazed green ware is the most attractive. Vessels made from it are thin, and, in the parts which are unglazed, resemble common flower-pot ware. The larger portion of their surfaces, however, is covered with a rich, thick, emerald-green glaze. Cups, bowls, saucers, plates, sugar-bowls, tea-pots, flasks, and censers are among the forms commonly made in this ware. The shapes are often graceful and the prices low. Most beautiful, however, and relatively expensive, are the miniature vessels made in this ware — scarcely an inch in height, but formed with the greatest care, and in such variety of dainty forms that one may seek some time to duplicate a piece which he has found; these little pieces are completely covered with the rich green glaze both outside and inside.

Our plan of journey for the year was first to make an expedition from Oaxaca to the north-west, into the Mixteca Alta; returning to Oaxaca, to strike eastward by way of Mitla, and the land of the Mixes, to Tehuantepec, from which place we should make a brief trip to the Juaves; returning to Tehuantepec, we should take the high road, by way of San Carlos, back to Oaxaca. Our first duty in the city of Oaxaca was to procure letters and orders from the governor. No governor in Mexico more completely realizes his importance and dignity than Governor Gonzales of Oaxaca. It is ever difficult to secure an audience with him; appointment after appointment is made, only to be broken when the inquiring visitor presents himself, and has been kept waiting an undue length of time. We had been through the experience before, and therefore were not surprised that it required four visits, each of them appointed by the governor himself, before we really had our interview. Governor Gonzales, is, however, an excellent officer. While we were waiting for our letters, after having explained to him our errand and plan of procedure, we had the opportunity to see a somewhat unusual and interesting sight. Like all public buildings and better-grade houses in Mexican cities, the governor's palace is built about *patios*, or inner courts. A wide balcony surrounds the court at the level of the second story and upon it the rooms of that story open. Having given orders that our letters should be prepared, the governor excused himself for a few moments, as he said that certain of his local authorities were ordered to meet him. We were seated where we could watch the reception. As we had entered the palace we had been impressed by the great number of indians, carrying official staves, who were waiting near the door. We now found that they were official delegates from the different towns, and that they had been sent from their homes to give the governor New Year's greetings. Having carefully arrayed himself for the meeting, the governor took his position in the wide balcony already referred to, with two officials of the palace stationed near, one on either side. The indians represented perhaps twenty-five different towns, the delegation from each town varying from three or four to fifteen or twenty persons. All were dressed in their cleanest garments, and all carried their long staves of office, most of which had ribbons of bright colors streaming from them.

The secretary of the governor arranged these delegations in their order, and they were presented one by one to the chief executive. As each delegation was presented, its members scraped and bowed, and the *presidente* and *secretario* kissed the governor's hand. A word or two of greeting having been exchanged, the spokesman from the village made a speech, sometimes read from a written copy, after which he presented a bouquet of flowers, real or artificial. The governor received the bouquet with a bow, placed the flowers on a little table near by, or, if the gift were a large bouquet of real flowers, handed it to one of the attendants standing near, and then made a polite speech of response, emphasizing it with vigorous gestures and plainly expressive of much interest and earnestness. The delegation then took its leave, always bowing reverently, and each man kissing the governor's hand as he passed out. As he received this mark of respect, the governor would make a playful remark, or pat the persons on the head, or otherwise treat them as a father might his little children. Instantly the flowers were cleared away, the next delegation ushered in, and the same ceremony gone through with.

Finally, all was ready for our leaving. The party consisted of five persons — myself, as leader, Mr. Lang, my American photographer, Don Anselmo, my Mexican plaster-worker, Manuel, and the *mozo*. All but the *mozo* were mounted on horses, more or less good or bad. The *mozo*, Mariano, a Mixtec indian, went on foot, carrying the photographic outfit on his back, and our measuring-rod in his hand. It was well on in the afternoon before we started, and hardly were we outside the town, before Mr. Lang's horse showed signs of sickness. His suffering was plain, and every person we met volunteered the information that unless something was done promptly, we should have a dead horse on our hands. Going to a little shop on the roadside, where strong drinks were sold, we stopped, and after preparing a remedy with the help of a passing indian, threw the horse down, wedged his mouth open, and gave him what seemed to be an unsavory draught. More than an hour was lost out of our already short afternoon by this veterinary practice, and long before we reached Etla, where we were compelled to pass the night, it was dark.

Leaving Etla in the morning, looking down as we passed out from the city upon a wonderful group of mounds, we passed rather slowly through the town of Huitzo. Don Anselmo and I loitered, as we found the whole country to be rich in ancient relics, examples of which were to be fcund in almost every house. As the afternoon passed, we found that we were likely to be completely left by our companions, and were forced to hasten on. The latter part of the daylight ride was up a continuous, and at times steep, ascent. As the sun neared setting, we reached the summit and found ourselves close by the station of Las Sedas, the highest point upon the Mexican Southern Railway. We had there expected to overtake the others of our party, but found that they had hurried on. It was a serious question whether we should try to overtake them. It had been wisdom to have stayed the night where we were. In this uncertainty, we met an indian boy driving mules toward Oaxaca, who volunteered the information that he had met our companions, who were just ahead, and that we would soon overtake them. This decided us, and we started down the trail. A heavy wind was blowing, and the night air was cold and penetrating. In a few minutes we met a half-breed Mexican, who, accosting us at once, urged us to go no further. His manner was somewhat sinister and disagreeable. He warned us that, if we attempted to make the descent in the darkness, we would at least lame our animals. He asserted that our comrades were fully three leagues ahead when he had met them, and that we would never overtake them. He also hinted darkly as to other dangers of the road, if we should succeed in making the descent without breaking the legs of our horses. Refusing his invitation to stop with him for the night, we pressed onward, and as we did so, he called out derisively after us.

The descent would not have been an easy one, even in the daytime, and in the gathering darkness there was really an element of danger in the journey. We left the following of the trail almost entirely to our animals. We were finally down the worst of the descent before night had actually set in. From here on, although the road varied but little from a level trail, we were obliged to go slowly, and it was with a feeling of true relief that, after floundering for a while in a brook in which our road seemed to lose itself, we heard ourselves called by name, from an indian hut situated a little way up the bank. As usual, the house consisted of a single room, of no great size, and was lightly built of cane. Two men, three women, a boy, and three little girls were the occupants. Our companions were already resting; their horses were unsaddled and were eating contentedly, and we were told that supper was being prepared for us. Entering the house, we found the women busy making *tortillas*, and fresh goat's meat, hanging from the rafters, gave promise of a substantial meal. When all was ready, we sat down to the finest of corncakes, beans, eggs, and tender kidmeat. We spread our blankets under a little shelter which stood in front of one side of the house. None of us slept well. It was very cold; dogs barked all night long; now and then a sudden outbreak of their barking, and curious signals and whistles, which were repeated in various parts of the mountain, gave us some uneasiness. At three o'clock in the morning, just as we were napping, Don Anselmo startled us by the statement that our mule was dead. In a moment, all was excitement. Mariano examined the animal and reiterated the statement. As for us, we were in the mood to care but little whether the mule was living or dead. Half frozen and very weary, our frame of mind was not a cheerful one. Just before day-break we could stand the cold no longer, and gathering some dry wood, we started a fire and crowded around it. The report about the mule proved to be false, and when morning came, there was no sign that anything was the matter with him.

It was nine o'clock before we started on our journey in the morning. We had three long hours of clambering up and down heavy slopes, and, much of the way, through a stream the bed of which was filled with slippery boulders and pebbles, over which the horses slipped and stumbled frightfully. Our horses slid down small cascades, but, when we came to larger ones, we had to mount the banks by ugly bits of road, descending below the falls. After much labor and weariness, we reached El Parian at noon. Having rested through the hotter portion of the day, we took the road again at two. We followed up the brook-bed to the point where another stream entered it, at an acute angle. Up this stream we turned, and after following it a little, struck suddenly up a steep hill, and then climbed on and on over a good road, cut in the limestone rock, up and up, until we reached the very summit. The vegetation here was a curious assemblage,— palms, cedars, oaks, and a mimosa-like tree, formed the chief types. The limestone rock upon the summit was curiously eroded, as if by rain rills. The masses presented all the appearance and detail of erosion shown by the great mountain mass of the country itself; looking at one of these little models, only a few feet across, and then gazing out upon the great tangle of mountain peaks around us, one could almost imagine that the one was the intentional reproduction of the other, in miniature. For a long time we followed the almost level summit; then a little climb and a slight descent brought us to Huaclilla. At the *meson* we found real rooms and true beds, and decided to stay for the night. The supper was less attractive. A brief walk about the village brought to light two cases of small-pox, and, on returning to the *meson*, we were charmed to find a third one in the building itself. Still, we slept well, and were up betimes next morning. The country through which we were passing was Mariano's *pais* (native land). Assuming that his knowledge was adequate, we left our *meson* early, with the intention of breakfasting at San Pedrito, where we were assured that everything was lovely; we were also told that it was but a short distance. The road thither was through a high open country, planted to wheat and oats and with some *maguey*. The road was discouragingly long, but after at least three hours of constant riding, we reached precious San Pedrito, chiefly notable for the amount of *pulque* drunk there. It was with the greatest difficulty that we succeeded in getting anything to eat; the breakfast was certainly worse than the supper of the preceding night. With the prevalence of *maguey* as a cultivated plant, the appearance of the houses and other buildings changed, as all of them were thatched with the broad, long, sharp-pointed leaves of the famous plant. Everyone in the district carries *tinajas*, or little sacks woven from splints of palm. Here, for the first time, we noticed that many of these had decorated patterns worked in black splints on the lighter ground. The blackness of these splints is given by exposure to the smoke of burning pine. Carrying-straps, also made of palm, are used for adjusting these *tinajas* to the back.

From San Pedrito the road is over a soft rock, which produces, when worn, a white glaring trail. The country through which we passed was fertile. Everywhere were fields of grain, wheat, oats, and, as we were descending into the lower land, corn. The little watch-houses for guarding the newly-sown fields are a striking feature of the landscape. In the higher districts they were small, conical or dome-shaped structures, made of the leaves of the *maguey*, and hardly large enough for a man to lie down in. Lower down, these were replaced by little rectangular huts, only a few feet across, with thatched roofs, the whole construction being raised on poles ten or twelve feet above the ground. It was scarcely more than noonday when we reached Nochixtlan, where the *jefe* of the district lives. Telling him that we desired to visit Yodocono and Tilantongo, he wrote orders for us, and charged some indians of Tidaa to show us the road, so far as they were going. The country through which we passed was a continuation of that preceding Nochixtlan. The road was nearly level, with but slight ups and downs, until a little before we reached our destination, when we had an abrupt up-turn to Yodocono, a pretty town on the border of a little lake, which has but recently appeared, and which covers an area which a few years ago was occupied by cultivated fields. Our letter from the *jefe* introduced us to Don Macario Espinola, a *mestizo*, owner of the chief store in the village, who showed us gracious hospitality. We were guests of honor. The parlor was surrendered to our use; the chairs were placed in such a way that, when supplied with mattress, sheets, and blankets, they made capital beds. Our meals were good. Don Macario, on hearing the purpose of our visit, placed himself entirely at our disposition. Unfortunately, he gained the idea that the people whom we wanted for measurement and photography were old folk, and the most astonishing collection of aged men and women was summoned from every part of the village and surrounding

Yodocono

neighborhood, and all had to be measured, although the measurements were afterwards discarded.

Leaving Yodocono at ten the following morning, we rode to Tilantongo. Though assured that the road was over a district as level as a floor, we found a good deal of up-hill riding. Tilantongo itself, with 2,266 inhabitants, is located upon the further slope of a hill, and but few houses were in sight until we were actually in the town. The public buildings surrounded a small open space, in the centre of which is a stone sun-dial. One side of this little *plaza* is occupied by the schoolhouse; the town-house and jail occupy the rear. The town is built upon a horse-shoe-shaped, sloping ridge, and the church is at the edge of the town, at one of the very ends of the horseshoe. Riding to the town-house, we presented our documents to the *presidente*, and ordered dinner for ourselves and food for the horses. We had letters to the priest, but he was not in town. The schoolhouse was placed at our disposal, and we moved two long benches close to each other, side by side; rush mats were brought, and these we laid upon the benches, and upon the teacher's table, for beds. Mr. Lang and Don Anselmo took the table, Manuel and I the benches, and Mariano had the floor. The cold was so intense that none of us slept much. We were astonished, in the middle of the night, and at intervals in the early morning, say at two or four o'clock, to hear snatches of songs. At first, we imagined it might be some religious festival, but on inquiring, we found that it was nothing but bands of drunken indians making night hideous.

We waited some time in the morning before beginning work, hoping that the *cura* might come and assist us with his influence. Finally, wearying of delay, we explained to the *presidente* the work we planned to do. We told him we must have subjects for measurement, photographing and modeling. He showed no great enthusiasm in the matter. One and another came to be measured, if they chose, but a number entirely refused. It was plain that something must be done. Quitting my work, I sent orders for the *presidente* to appear, and, after an intolerable delay, he presented himself. I told him that we were losing time; that subjects were not presenting themselves; that some of those who did present themselves refused to be measured; that I wished a *mozo* at once to carry a report from me to the *jefe* that my wishes were not regarded by the authorities, and that his orders had no influence; that the *mozo* must be ready at once, as there was no time to lose, and we should shortly leave his town without accomplishing our work. The effect was instantaneous. The official air of arrogance disappeared; he replied quiet humbly that subjects should be at once supplied, as rapidly as they could be brought in. I replied, "Here are two persons now who have refused; why wait while others shall be brought?" The fiat went forth, the two obdurate and not good-humored victims were marched up. As I measured them, they whispered to me that the *presidente* himself had not been measured, and begged that he be ordered to undergo the operation. The request was reasonable, and when they were through, they waited to see what would happen. Great was their delight when, turning to the chief man of the town, I said, "It is best for you to be measured next. It will set a good example to the rest," and without a word, although I knew that he had stated that he would not be measured, he stepped under the rod. From then on there was no lack of material. Our subjects were measured, photographed and modeled as rapidly as we could do the work. At noon the priest had come. As he passed where we were working, he gave us an extremely distant greeting and rode on up to the *curato*. From his

Mixtec Houses; Tilantongo

castle he sent immediate complaint because our horses had been put into his stable without his permission. I went to the good man's house and found him hearing confessions. Leaving with him the letters from the archbishop and the *jefe*, I returned to my work, leaving word that the horses would have to stay where they were, as there was no other suitable place for their keeping. After a hard day's work, the night started very cold, and we hurried to bed early. All were sleeping, but myself, when a rap came at the door. It was a message from the *cura*, begging us to come to the *curato*, where we would be more comfortable. Sending back a word of thanks, I stated that we would be there for the following night.

The *cura* had been away from home for several days. The result was that, on his return, his parishioners turned out in force to greet him, and hardly was he housed, when a procession bearing gifts marched to the *curato*. In front went one bearing flowers. Those who followed carried some kind of food,—great pieces of meat, fowls, eggs, corn, chilis, and other supplies. The following morning we were awakened by a great explosion of fire-crackers and rockets, and by pealing bells, announcing the early mass. After his religious duties were performed, the *padre* came down to the *plaza* to watch our work and use his influence in our behalf. When it was dinner-time, he invited us to go with him to that meal. We had thought that the donation party we had witnessed was a generous one; after that dinner, we had no doubt of the matter. Hardly had we disposed of the many good things on the table when the *padre* took us to a large room, the parish schoolhouse, and showed us the arrangements he had made for our comfort. Four beds, descending in grade of comfort from the one for myself to the one for Manuel, were shown us. Never was a party happier to move from one set of quarters to another.

Called away the next morning by his religious duties, the priest left us in charge of house and household. The work went merrily on in the *plaza*. We quickly found, however, that the town was getting into a condition of intoxication, and long before noon every person in the place was drunk. At noon we were waited upon by a committee, representing the town, who informed us that they appreciated the lofty honor which was conferred on the place by our presence, and stated that, realizing that we had brought with us letters from the President of the Republic and from the Archbishop of the diocese, they desired not to be lacking in the respect due to such distinguished visitors. Accordingly, they said, they had arranged for the brass band to discourse sweet music for us, while we ate our dinner. No sooner was the statement made, than preparations were begun. The band stood around us in a semicircle, chiefly notable for its unsteadiness on its legs, and regaled us with a series of most doleful pieces. When word came that dinner was ready at the *curato*, the band accompanied us to our stopping-place. The bandmaster announced his intention of personally serving us at the table. At the same time orders were given that the musicians, standing without, should continue to play pieces throughout the repast.

The last day of our stay at Tilantongo, the *padre* stated that it must be interesting to see the way in which a parish priest, returning from a visit to a neighboring town, is received by his parish. Accordingly, he planned that a picture should be taken of himself on horseback, with all the people gathered around welcoming him. Telling us that he would be ready when we should have made our own preparations for this photographic effort, he waited for our summons. We quickly found, however, that the proposition, although hailed at first with joy, did not create great enthusiasm. We recommended to the people that they

Mixtec Woman's Costume; Tilantongo

Mixtec Woman Carrying Water; Tilantongo

should get ready; told the musicians that the band should be prepared, and that soon we should send for the *padre* to be welcomed. When we finally succeeded in getting the matter under way, and were seriously thinking of summoning the reverend gentleman, it was reported that an old woman had been found dead in her lonely hut that morning, and arrangements were at once started for her funeral. In vain we suggested that they should wait until the picture had been made. Musicians and parishioners alike disappeared, going down to the house where the dead body lay. The afternoon was passing. It would soon be quite too dark for a picture. Meantime, the *cura*, having become anxious in the matter, hastened from his house on foot, to ask why he had not been sent for. On our explaining that a funeral was in progress, he was greatly outraged. We pointed out the house in front of which the funeral procession was now forming. He stood watching, as the line of mourners approached. The person who had died was an aged woman named Hilaria. The body was borne upon a stretcher, as coffins are not much used among these people. The procession came winding up the high-road, where we stood. The band in front was playing mournfully; next came the bearers, two of whom, at least, were sadly drunk. The corpse was clad in the daily garments of the woman, and the body sagged down through gaps in the stretcher; a motley crowd of mourners, chiefly women, some with babies in their arms, followed. One man, walking with the band in front, carried a book in his hand and seemed to read the service, as they slowly passed along. When the procession had come near us and was about to pass, the *padre* stopped it; expressing his dissatisfaction at the failure to arrange for the photograph which he had ordered, he told the bearers to take the corpse out behind the house and leave it there.

They did so, returned, and were arranged in a group with the *padre* in their midst, and photographed, after which the body was picked up again, the procession was reformed, and proceeded as if nothing had happened.

The following morning at six o'clock we were again upon the road. We first descended into the valley, passing the miserable hut from whence the dead woman had been borne. In all the yards we noticed peach-trees loaded with their pink blossoms. From the deep and narrow valley, we began to climb steadily upward. We passed along the side of a gorge, the bed of which had all the appearance of a giant stairway. Higher and higher we mounted, leaving San Juan Diusi on our right. Great masses of gray clouds hung upon the summits of the highest mountain, their lower line coming very nearly to our level. The wind beginning to blow, the gray mass soon was whirled and spread down like a great veil around us. We were indeed glad when we began to descend and have a little shelter behind us, against the wind, and dry skies instead of damp clouds above us. Making a sudden descent, we found ourselves in a cleared district, where the only trees left on the high summits were palms, which bore little round dates with round seeds; these were quite sweet and good. Small ranches were scattered, here and there, along the road. After another descent and ascent, we found ourselves in an extensive forest of great gnarled oaks, thickly covered with tufts of air-plants and with orchids. Many of the latter were in full bloom, forming masses of brilliant color. In making the descent from here, we found the slope composed of slippery limestone, with sharp, rain-channeled surfaces, where our horses with great difficulty kept their footing. Soon after we were down, we reached San Bartolo.

This purely Mixtec town was a delightful spot. It is large, and strung along two or three long straight streets.

The People Receiving their Padre; Tilantongo

The houses were in yards completely filled with fruit trees — *chirimoyas*, *limas*, *granadas de China*, *ahuacates* and oranges. Garden-beds of spinach, lettuce, and onions were frequent. The houses were of poles set upright, with thick thatchings of palms. Bee-hives in quantity were seen at almost every house. At Tilantongo we had seen but few women in native dress. Here almost every woman was clad in native garments, many of which were beautifully decorated. The men wore brilliant sashes, woven in the town. When we reached the town-house we found the doorway decorated with flowers,— stars and rosettes made of palm. We were well received, and a capital dinner was soon served, after which we were escorted around the town by the authorities, who arranged for photographing everything that seemed to us of interest. But, at three o'clock, we left this pretty spot. Again, we climbed much of the way over limestone roads. Santo Domingo, past which we journeyed, is a mean little town, with houses much like those of Tilantongo, but of a gray color instead of reddish-brown. From here we plunged downward, and when we ascended again, followed along the side of a rock-walled cañon with pretty cascades and magnificent masses of fallen rock. The last part of our journey was made by moonlight, along a brook-side over a road which seemed quite endless. With some trouble, we found the dilapidated old church and the municipal house; we took possession of the school, and after a miserable supper, thoroughly tired, lay down to rest upon the benches.

The town — Magdalena de los Comales — is so named from the *comales*, or earthenware griddles, made there. Besides this characteristic product, the town makes a good deal of unglazed but polished red pottery. The forms are chiefly candlesticks, censers and toys. Much weaving of palm is here done, and the hats of the place are rather famous. Famous, too, are the *mantas*, or women's dresses, of black wool, made in long rectangular pieces. The common grade sells for $6.00, and in using it, it is, like indian dresses generally, simply wrapped about the figure and held in place by a sash or belt.

Nowhere in our journey in southern Mexico had we met with the kind of scenery which we encountered between Magdalena and Tlaxiaco; its whole character was like that of New Mexico. Directly behind the town was a fine cart-road, worn in red sand pumice; before the town rose a magnificent cliff, which had been a landmark in our journey of the day before. The road running up the mountain, over gray and red pumice strata, was deeply worn, just like the road back of Cochiti, New Mexico. Here, too, were the same noble pines for forest. It was a full hour's climb to the summit, where we found a pretty brook tumbling over ledge after ledge into deep round basins of purest water. A long and rather gentle slope downward led to a valley filled with neat farm-houses and cleared patches. Our last ascent brought us to a mass of rounded hills, composed of brilliant clays — yellow, brown, pink, red and white. From among these hillocks Tlaxiaco, a magnificent picture, burst into view. It is compactly built; the flat-topped houses are white or blue-tinted; trees are sprinkled through the town; the old convent, with the two towers of its church, dominates the whole place; a pretty stream flows along its border; and a magnificent range of encircling mountains hems it in on all sides. The descent was rapid, and we reached Tlaxiaco with the morning but half gone.

The *jefes* of the districts of Mexico are frequently men of ability and force. Rarely, however, have we encountered one so prompt and energetic as Javier Cordova, then *jefe* of the district of Tlaxiaco. When he took possession of

Mixtec Houses with Beehives; San Bartolo

this district, not long before, deeds of robbery along the high-road were common. In many portions of the district, acts of violence were quite the rule. Perhaps the largest agricultural district in the Republic, it possessed few of the conveniences of modern life. Under Cordova's administration, vast improvements have been made. The roads are secure, deeds of violence are rare, the advantages of the district are being rapidly developed, telephone and telegraph have been introduced, and a railroad is talked of. Although we had no letter from the governor addressed to Señor Cordova, when we showed him the communications for other *jefes*, we were received with the greatest courtesy and everything was done to facilitate our work. We told him that we planned to visit the Triquis at Chicahuastla. He at once wrote letters to the town authorities and to Don Guillermo Murcio, living at that village. The plaster for our bust-making had not yet been received, but Señor Cordova promised, in case it came, to forward it after us promptly, and, in case it did not come, to send twenty miles into the mountains for the raw plaster, which he would have prepared and sent on to Chicahuastla. It was late in the afternoon, before we started for Cuquila, where we planned to pass the night. It was a mistake to make so late a start. For a time, the road was fairly level, but at last we went up a brisk ascent, reaching the summit near sunset. The road down would have been a bad one, even in the daytime. As it was, if we had not had a good moon, we could hardly have made the descent. From the depth of the cañon we ascended to Cuquila, thoroughly tired, somewhat before seven. It was with the greatest difficulty that we could find anyone of whom to ask our way to the townhouse. Our voices were sufficient to plunge any house into instant darkness and silence. After a long search, we found a man who agreed to seek the *presidente*. He and the rest of the town officials finally met us on the road, and, after reading our order, took us to the town-house. It was with difficulty that we got fodder for our horses. It was only after persistent and dire threats, that we secured food for ourselves, and firewood to make the room, in which we were to sleep, endurable. It was long past eleven before we were through our troubles and lay down on mats to sleep.

Though we had warned the town officials that we should leave at seven, and must have breakfast before we left, when we arose, we found no steps whatever taken for our accommodation. Yet the town officials had been up long enough to be thoroughly affected by their early morning drinks. Feeling that patience had ceased to be a virtue, we summoned the authorities, and told the *presidente* that he had paid no attention whatever to his *jefe's* order; that we had had far too much difficulty in securing the bad accommodations we had been furnished; that their promise to prepare a suitable breakfast had been completely disregarded. We told them that our duty was to send immediate complaint to Tlaxiaco; that we would, however, give them one more chance. We should not stop for breakfast, but would proceed upon our journey hungry; if, however, we sent him further orders regarding our return journey, we should expect them obeyed to the very letter. With this we mounted.

In vain the *presidente* and officials begged us to wait, promising that everything should be prepared. Time was too precious, and away we rode.

Soon after leaving Cuquila we struck a fifty-minute mountain, the summit of which we made at nine o'clock exactly. Here we sat in the shade and lunched on bread and pineapples, bought the day before in Tlaxiaco. From the summit, there was a slow and gentle descent around that ridge, and then a slow incline along an endless ravine, until at last we came out upon a crest, from which we looked down upon one of the grandest mountain scenes of the world. A valley of impressive size, surrounded by magnificent mountain masses, lay below us, and just to the right, at our feet, was Chicahuastla. Few people in Mexico are so little known as the Triquis. Orozco y Berra, usually a good authority, locates them near Tehuantepec, in the low country. The towns which he calls Triqui are Chontal; the five true Triqui towns are in the high Mixteca. The largest is the town which we were now approaching. The Triquis are people of small stature, dark-brown color, black eyes, aquiline, but low and rather broad nose; they are among the most conservative, suspicious and superstitious of Mexican indians. Most of them dress in native clothing, and all speak the Triqui and not the Spanish language. As a people they are sadly degraded, through being exceptionally addicted to drink.

Don Guillermo Murcio is a character. He and his family are almost the only *mestizos* in the place. He is a hale and hearty blacksmith, and has lived for fifteen years in this purely indian town, where he has gained almost unbounded influence among the simple natives. His word is law, and the town-government trembles before his gaze. He is impetuous in manner, quick-tempered, and on the slightest suggestion of disregard of his commands, freely threatens jail or other punishment. He received us cordially, and we lived at his house, where we were treated to the best that was available.

We have already referred to the beautiful location of Chicahuastla. Its appearance is most picturesque. Unlike the indian towns in the Mixteca which we had so far visited, it has many houses of circular form with conical roof. It is possible that this style of construction is the result of African influence. At Chicahuastla we were on the very summit of the great water-shed, and from it, when the air is clear, one may look down, over a sea of lesser summits and mountain ranges, to the waters of the Pacific. Along the Pacific coast, in the state of Guerrero, are whole towns of Africans, descendants of slaves, who build their houses after the circular pattern, so common throughout the dark continent. We did not find in the Triquis any admixture of African blood, but it is possible the mode of house-building may have been influenced by negro example.

Our first glimpse of the town suggested a veritable paradise. At eleven the sky was clear, the sun almost tropical, the whole country smiled under its warm beams; but at two there came a change. Fogs, so dense as to shut out the view of what was across the road, drifted down from the summit on which we had seen cloud masses forming. Deeper and deeper, wetter and wetter, colder and colder grew the mist. All, wrapped in their thickest blankets, were shivering, crouched upon the ground, trying in vain to keep themselves warm. At first we thought this might be a rare occasion, but were assured that it is an every-day occurrence, and from our own experience of four or five days, we can easily believe the statement to be true. How any people can live in such a spot, suffering keenly twenty hours in the day, simply for the four hours of clear sunshine and warmth is inexplicable; and the nights were torments! Don Guillermo's house is well built of logs and plaster, but no house could keep out that bitter cold night air which chilled us, as we lay in bed, until we could hardly move.

We have already stated that the people of Chicahuastla are conservative and superstitious. Our operations of measuring, photographing and bust-making filled the town with alarm and concern. It was hard enough to get our male subjects; the women were yet more difficult. At first we failed to secure any, but after we had several times

Don Guillermo and his Family; Chicahuastla

Group of Triquis; Chicahuastla

told the town officials that twenty-five women must be forthcoming for measurement, and Don Guillermo had stormed and threatened, the town-government began to plan a mode of carrying out our wishes. Close by Don Guillermo's house was the miserable little village *plaza*, where the women of the town assembled with corn-cakes and other articles for trade. There, they met the travelling peddlers coming from Tlaxiaco, from Cuquila and the coast, and drove their bargains, mostly a matter of trade, not purchase, with them. Waiting at the place where we were working, until one or two women were to be seen in the *plaza*, the town officials separated, going in two directions. In a few minutes an anxious watcher, from our point of view, might have seen a gradually contracting circle of men surrounding the *plaza*. Usually at the same time that this circle was evident to the watcher, it became also evident to the women. With cries of terror, the poor creatures would start off as fast as their legs would carry them, over the mountain trails, with the whole town government, sixteen strong, in pursuit, with yells and screams. It was like nothing but the chase of deer by hounds. Usually, the women, given strength by terror, escaped; but once out of three times, perhaps, the officials returned in triumph with their prisoner in their midst, who was at once measured and then, if need be, photographed. In course of time these hunts supplied the twenty-five victims desired.

It might not be uninteresting to describe the events of a single afternoon in a Triqui town. On one occasion, having eaten dinner, we had scarcely begun our work when we heard a great uproar and din upon the road toward Santo Domingo. Looking in that direction, we saw a crowd of men and boys struggling toward us. As they came nearer, we saw that six or eight of the party were carrying some awkward and inconvenient burden. It was a man, sprawling face downward; two or more held his arms, an equal number his legs; about his waist a belt, knotted behind, was tied, and then through the knot was thrust a strong pole, which was being carried by two men, one on either side. Struggling against those who carried him, raising his face and snarling and gnashing at the crowd, the prisoner presented a fearful spectacle. It seemed that, being drunk, he had quarreled with his friend, whom he had nearly murdered with his *machete*. About the middle of the afternoon we heard a loud crying in the other direction, toward the church and jail, and, on looking, saw coming toward us a man, whose head was broken open and from it was streaming blood, his head and face were covered, and his white shirt, to the waist and even below, was soaked with the red fluid. He was wringing his hands and crying in a piteous manner. When he came to where we stood, he told his tale of woe. He was the majordomo in charge of the church property. He had expected that the priest would make his visit to the pueblo on that day, and had so announced it to the people; the pious parishioners looked forward, with interest, to the coming of the *padre*. When the day passed, however, and the priest failed to appear, one of the more religious felt so outraged that he had broken open the head of the majordomo with a club, on account of his disappointment. We told the poor fellow to go home and let his wife clean him up and change his clothing, promising that, if he died, his assailant should be punished. That evening there was a little moonlight at Chicuhuastla, the only time during our stay. As we sat eating supper, we heard an outcry in the direction of the church and jail. Asking Don Guillermo what might be the cause, he replied that there was probably some trouble at the jail. We insisted on going to see what might be

View at Chicahuastla

happening. Don Guillermo, the plaster-worker, Mariano, Manuel and I, seizing whatever weapons were convenient at hand, started for the jail. We found an excited crowd gathered around the doorway. On a log before the door there sat a creature crazy-drunk. I have never seen a case more horrible. He screamed, yelled, gnashed his teeth, struck and snapped at everyone around. The whole village stood in terror. I addressed the policemen, who seemed quite helpless. "Why not thrust him into the jail? Quick! Seize him! In with him!" Encouraged by our words, they seized him, the door was quickly opened, and he was cast into the little room, which already contained more than thirty persons, the harvest of a single afternoon. When the door was locked, we saw for the first time why the policemen had been so timid. One of them came limping up to us, crying, and showed his leg. From its fleshy part a good mouthful of flesh had been cleanly bitten by the madman. The wound was bleeding profusely, and the poor fellow wrung his hands and cried with pain.

We had finished our measurements and photographs, but there had been no sign as yet of the plaster; concluding that Señor Cordova had forgotten his promise, we were prepared to leave town early the next morning. After dark two men came from Tlaxiaco, one of whom brought sufficient plaster for making two good busts. This plaster had been brought, in a crude state, twenty miles from the mountains to Tlaxiaco; had been calcined and ground there, by prisoners in the jail, and then sent fifteen miles to us over the mountains. We were interested in the men who brought it. One of them was a prisoner from the Tlaxiaco jail. He had been sentenced to ten days for drinking, and it was he who carried the plaster. The other proudly informed us that he was a policeman, and had come to make sure that the prisoner returned. Thoroughly delighted at their coming, we broke our custom and gave the men a trifle. Alas, the day! That very night both men, policeman and prisoner, were thrust into the local jail, helplessly drunk.

One evening, during our stay at Chicahuastla, Don Guillermo begged me to go into the kitchen to examine a baby, upon whom he was thinking of performing a surgical operation. The creature was a boy some three months old, pure indian. We had heard him crying at night ever since we had come, but had not seen him. A tumor, or some growth, was on his neck, below the chin. Don Guillermo handed me the razor, in order that I might remove the swelling, but I refused the task. The story of the child is sad. It is the son of a young indian boy and girl, not married. That would not be a serious matter among the Triquis. For some reason, however, the mother did not like the child, and scarcely was it born, when she went with it into the forest; there in a lonely place she choked it, as she thought, to death, and buried it in the ground. The town authorities, suspecting something of her purpose, had followed her and were watching at the moment. No sooner had she left the spot than they dug up the child, found it still alive, and brought it to Don Guillermo, who had kept it at the town's charge.

The last night of our stay at Chicahuastla, just after supper, a cavalcade came to the door. It was the *jefe* of the next district — Juxtlahuaca — with a guard of six mounted men. Apparently a pleasant fellow, he was at the moment excited over a recent disturbance in his district. In an attempt which he had made to adjust a certain difficulty, he and his guard had been fired on and stones thrown from the height above them, by the people of the pueblo. One of his companions died from the effect of the attack. The officer plainly feared an outbreak or up-

At Work; Measuring

At Work; Bust Making

rising, and was nervous and uneasy, though Don Guillermo assured him that in his house there was absolutely no danger. Finally, we quieted down and all went to bed, we with the intention of an early start the next morning.

After an uneasy night, I awoke about five o'clock. Just as I was thinking of calling my companions, I felt a faint trembling, which rapidly increased to a heavy shaking, of the house in which we slept. There was a moment's pause, and then a second shaking, which began stronger than the other, but which lasted about the same time. It was the most serious earthquake shock we ever experienced in Mexico. Had the house been made of brick and plaster, considerable damage might have been done. Everyone was wide awake in an instant. The whole town was in excitement. The church-bell was rung and the people flocked out into the street. The shock passed at exactly 5:20, and, in other towns, notably in Oaxaca, it did considerable damage.

Two days before, we had sent word to the authorities at Cuquila, that we should breakfast with them on our way back to Tlaxiaco, and ordered them to be ready for our coming. This was the opportunity which had been promised them for redeeming themselves and avoiding complaint to their *jefe.* Arriving at the town at 9:40, we were met at the roadside by some of the officials, who led us at once to the town-house. Here the whole town government was gathered to greet us; politely each one, stepping forward, removed his hat and kissed my hand; they then invited us to sit down at the table and breakfast,— whereupon eggs, chicken, *tortillas* and *frijoles* — the best the town could supply — were set before us. The whole government sat by, looking on as we ate.

Immediately after breakfast, in accordance with our order previously sent, we were taken to see a potter at work.

Cuquila is famous for two lines of manufacture, pottery and woolen garments. The pottery here made is skillfully shaped into wonderfully large vessels of different forms. The product goes throughout this whole district, and even down to the Pacific coast, a hundred miles distant. Along the roads it is a common thing to meet parties of three or four men carrying great loads of water-jars, large bowls, etc., for sale or trade. While we were inspecting the potter's work, a slight shock of earthquake, almost too gentle to be noticed, passed through the place.

At Cuquila, we found that we should not meet Señor Cordova at Tlaxiaco. He had passed through the town the night before, on his way to Juxtlahuaca, with a band of soldiers to assist his neighboring *jefe* in maintaining order.

Leaving our Cuquila reprobates in friendly and gentle mood, we started for Tlaxiaco, where we arrived at half-past two. Something after four o'clock, we heard a violent ringing of the church-bell and saw the people flocking out onto the streets; looking up at the church-tower, although we did not feel the shock, we saw that the whole church was being violently shaken, and that the ringing bells, which we had heard, were not moved by human hands. This third shock of the day was more strongly felt in other districts, than with us. In the City of Mexico, three hundred miles away, it was the most severe of the day.

The whole town was in commotion; people threw themselves upon their knees in the streets and prayed to the Virgin for protection. Later in the day, we saw a priest and a saint's figure passing through the streets, and as they passed the people paid reverence. Surely the little procession, illegal though it was, must have been successful, for there were no further shocks. We found here a most interesting superstition, which we had not met before, but which we heard several times later, in other districts. We were

View at Chicahuastla

assured that the earthquake was but one of many signs that the world was coming to an end. We discovered that thousands of the people expected the ending of the world in 1900, and when we asked why, were reminded that this was the last year of the century. This is certainly a survival of ancient superstition. The old Mexicans did not count their years by hundreds or centuries, as we do, but by cycles of 52 years each. It was believed that the world would come to an end at the close of a cycle, and important ceremonies were conducted to avert such a catastrophe. It is clear that the old idea, of the destruction of the world at the close of a cycle, has been transferred to the new mode of reckoning time.

From Tlaxiaco to Teposcolula, there was a cart-road, though it was possible that no *carreta* ever passed over it. It presented little good scenery. We passed the pueblos of San Martin Jilmeca, San Felipe, and San Miguel. Just before reaching the first of these towns, the road passes over a coarse rock mass, which weathers into spheroidal shells. At Jilmeca and some other points along the day's route the rock over which we passed was a white tufaceous material loaded with streaks of black flint. Sometimes this black flint passes into chert and chalcedony of blue and purple tints. Here and there, along the mountain sides, we caught glimpses of rock exposures, which looked snow-white in the distance. Between Jilmeca and San Felipe there was a pretty brook, with fine cypresses along the banks, and a suspension bridge of great logs. Having passed through San Felipe and San Miguel, a pleasant road, through a gorge, brought us to the valley in which Teposcolula lies. The great convent church, historically interesting, is striking in size and architecture. The priest, an excellent man, is a pure-blooded Mixtec indian, talking the language as his mother tongue. With great pride he showed us about the building, which was once a grand Dominican monastery. The old carved wooden cupboard for gold and silver articles, used in the church service, is fine work. The gold and silver articles for which it was built have long since disappeared. In the *patio* are many old paintings, most of which are badly damaged, and some of which have been repaired with pieces cut from other pictures, not at all like the missing piece. Among these pictures is a series of scenes from the life of Santo Domingo. Of the figures in the church, two are fairly good; one, which is famous, represents Our Lady of the Rosary. In a little chapel are buried the remains of the old friars; here also is a beautiful old carved confessional. In front of the old church is a great court surrounded by a stone wall, which is surmounted here and there with little, pointed, square pillars. To the right of the church is a mass of masonry, in reddish-brown freestone, consisting of a series of arches, now more or less in ruins. When the convent was at the height of its splendor, the crowd of worshippers was too large for the church itself, and these beautiful arches were erected to receive the overflow. In the church itself, the plaster in the domes of the towers and the coloring on the walls and domes had chipped and fallen, on account of the earthquake, the day before. In the ruins of the upper rooms of the convent proper, stone and mortar, dislodged from the decaying walls by the same shocks, lay in little heaps on the floor.

The *cura* had ten churches in his charge. He says there are 2,000 people in Teposcolula, few of whom are indians. In his ten churches, he has 12,000 parishioners. He seemed a devout man, and emphasized the importance of his preaching to his congregation in their native tongue and his. So convinced is he that the native idiom of the people is the shortest road to their heart and understanding, that he has prepared a catechism and Christian doctrine

Triqui Children; Chicahuastla

Mixtec Potter; Cuquila

in the modern Mixtec, which has been printed. The town itself is desolate; the *plaza* is much too large, and dwarfs the buildings which surround it, and signs of desolation and decay mark everything. With the fondness which Mexicans show for high-sounding and pious inscriptions, the municipality has painted, upon the side of the town-house, in full sight for a long distance, the words, "Nations to be great and free must be educated." From here to Nochixtlan there was nothing of special interest. For some four leagues the road was through a gorge; from this valley we mounted to the height, just before reaching the town of Tiltepec, from which we caught an extensive view down over the great valley in which Nochixtlan and this town lie. From Tiltepec we had a rather tiresome, hot, and painful ride, passing San Juan Tillo and Santiago Tillo. By half past one we were again in the city of Nochixtlan.

CHAPTER XII

THE MIXES REVISITED

(1899)

AFTER resting at Oaxaca, from our trip into the high Mixteca, we made preparations for our new journey, leaving at three o'clock in the afternoon for the land of the Zapotecs and Mixes. Our late start compelled stopping at Tule for the night. In the morning we went on to Tlacolula, where we nooned, in order to see the *jefe* in regard to our work. He is a competent man, showed great interest in our plan, and gave valuable advice, in addition to the orders to his officials. He warned us that we might meet some difficulty at Milta, where we were planning to make our study of the Zapotecs, on account of the *fiesta* then in progress. He told us to notify him at once in case matters did not go well there.

The *fiesta* at Milta should have been a three days' affair. This year, however, it began on Sunday with the result that it filled four days. Reaching there in the afternoon of Monday, we found the whole town in great excitement and dissipation. The *plaza* had been enclosed with a fencing of poles, and *toros* were the amusement of the afternoon. The country sports with bulls are different from the regular bull-fights of the cities. Any one takes part who pleases, and while there is little of trained skill, there is often much of fun, frolic, and daring. The bull is led into the ring from outside by a lasso. It is then lassoed from behind and dragged up to a post or tree, to which it is firmly tied to prevent its moving. A rope is then tightly

In Tlacolula

Typical Zapotec House; Tlacolula

cinched about its middle and a man mounts upon the back of the beast, fixing his feet firmly in the rope below, between it and the animal, and winding his hands into it above. The ropes which hold the bull are then withdrawn so as to set it loose. Dozens of men and big boys, with jackets and *serapes*, then torment the beast, which, plunging and dashing at them, scatters them in every direction. Sometimes the angry animal attempts to break through the fence, causing excitement and consternation among the crowds who have been hanging to it and looking over. When, as sometimes happens, he does break through, there is great scattering before him, and closing in behind him, until he is again captured. The man riding on the bull's back clings as long as he can, in spite of the plunging and other frantic efforts of the animal to unseat him; comparatively few stay long in their uncomfortable position, and when they are thrown, much agility is required to escape from the furious animal.

As we rode into town these sports were in full blast; everyone, save the bull-fighters, was drunk. Now and then a tube of iron filled with powder was exploded. A band in front of the municipal house was supplying music. A little group of men with *pitos* and *tambours* strolled from place to place, playing. Much selling was in progress in the booths, the chief articles offered being intoxicating drinks. A cluster of drunken vocalists, sitting flat upon the ground, but almost unable to hold themselves upright, were singing horribly to untuned guitars. In front of the town-house a bench had been dragged out by the authorities for the benefit of the *cura*, who, seated thereon, was watching the sports with maudlin gravity. The *presidente* and other officials were standing by the *padre*, and all were drinking at frequent intervals. Thinking the moment opportune, I approached the party and handed them my documents; but both *presidente* and priest were far too drunk to realize my needs. Surveying the drunken town, I felt that it was necessary to act promptly and firmly if we were to accomplish anything before the *fiesta* ended. The only member of the government who was not extremely drunk that afternoon was the *sindico.* Calling him to me, I addressed him, scorning both priest and *presidente.* I refused to drink with them, saying that they were already too drunk to know their duties, and that both should be ashamed of their condition. At this time the *cura* asked me if I were a clergyman. On my replying no, he remarked that I looked like one. I told him yes, that I was frequently mistaken for one; that a priest in the Mixteca had even thought that I was a bishop. He then drunkenly inquired whether I were married, and on my replying no, made the astonishing observation that then, it was certain that I could not be a priest,— that every priest had one wife, bishops two, and archbishops three. This drunken priest had just been making certain observations to the *presidente* calculated to interfere with my work, and I felt that I now had my opportunity. So, turning upon him, I gravely reproved him for his remark. I told him that, in his language and his drunkenness, he was setting a bad example to his parish; that he should go at once to the *curato*, and not venture forth during the time that we remained in the town. Half-sobered by my order, he arose without a word, went to his house, and did not again appear for four days. Having gotten him out of the way, I turned to the drunken officials and told them that, early the next morning, I should begin my work, and that they must make the needful preparations; that I wished to measure, photograph, and make busts of the population. I told them that at present they were too drunk to aid me, but that the following morning things must be different; that enough at least to attend to my orders must be sober. After supper, attracted by the noise and hubbub, we set out to see the *plaza*. Torches were flaring in every direction, and considerable business was being done at all the booths. Crowds of drunken people were squatting on the ground in all directions; at the town-house the band of music was playing the *jarabe*, and 40 or 50 persons were dancing this lively dance. Old and young, men and women, boys and girls, all were taking part; no one paid attention to any other person, but each seemed to be trying to prove himself the most agile of the party. All were drunk, some astonishingly so. Occasionally a dancer would bump against such an one, who would fall head over heels. Immediately picking himself up, he would go at it again, with even greater vigor; sometimes one fell, of himself, in a helpless heap, and lay where he fell, until kicked out of the way or until the music stopped. All around was pandemonium; yelling, singing, cursing, fighting were in progress; the jail was crowded, but every now and then a new case was dragged up; for an instant the door was opened, and against the crowd, pushing from within, the new prisoner would be crowded into the cell. At one time in the evening a cry arose that a murder was being committed in the jail. The door was opened, the policemen crowded in, and the two men who had clinched and were battling were torn apart. One was dragged outside and thrown into the woman's jail, and for a time the air was blue with the most insulting cries. Convinced that no work could be done in the afternoons, we labored with the greatest possible diligence each morning. The first morning, going to the town-house, we ordered subjects to be brought. The *presidente* was drunk; the *sindico* also; still, some of the town officials were found in a condition able to do our bidding. Having measured a few of the officials, we proposed to take such prisoners as still remained in the jail, from the batch of the preceding day. There were eighteen of these, and with them we made a good beginning. Among the prisoners we found our first subject for modelling. Oiling him, we began to make the moulds. The back-piece had been applied; the second piece, covering the lower part of the face and upper chest, was hardening, and we were busily engaged in putting on the final application over the upper part of the face. At this moment the *presidente* staggered into the jail. When his eyes fell upon our subject, he stopped aghast; for a moment he was unable to speak; then he groaned out the words, "O horrible spectacle! To think of seeing a son of this town in such a position!" As I was beginning to laugh and ridicule him, the old mother of the young man came bursting into the jail, weeping and trembling, to see what fate had overtaken her son. Wringing her hands, the tears rolled down her face, and her voice was choked with sobs, as she asked pitifully whether he must die; she told me that he was her only support, and that, without him, she was absolutely alone. Taking the old woman outside, while the mask should be completed, I chatted with her, and as soon as the pieces of the mould were removed, delivered her precious son, unharmed, into her hands.

Just as we were ready for a new subject, a young fellow, better dressed than most, passed by. We called him to come in and be measured, but with a somewhat insolent manner, he walked by, paying no attention to our words. Sending the policemen for him, they soon returned with the report, "*No quiere*" (He does not care to come). To allow a first refusal was not to be thought of, so we ordered his return. Again the policemen came back with no result. Thereupon I declared that no more work should be done until he came; that time would be lost thereby, and the

Organo Cactus; Tlacolula

Where Tree Ferns Grow

jefe's order would be disregarded, but that it was not our fault. Upon this the *presidente* informed us that the order was not explicit; it did not state that people must be measured; he would consult the civil code to see whether anyone but criminals must be measured. "Very good," said I, "do as you like; but unless that young man is brought in we shall send complaint to the *jefe*; send for a messenger at once to carry my report." At this stage, the policemen returned, telling me that the young man wanted did not belong to this town; that he could not be found, and probably had gone home. We told them that we did not believe them, but that we would proceed with our work; however, I said, that, if he really were a stranger but appeared again, I should order his immediate arrest and jailing. To this they all agreed; and we continued work until the town was again too drunk for anything to be done.

About the middle of the afternoon, when the bull-fighting was at its height, the young man wanted appeared in the ring as the chief fighter and attraction of the day. Stepping at once to the policemen I told them that he must be brought immediately to the town-house, — that the bull-fight must cease while our matters were arranged. With much grumbling and complaint they obeyed. The young man dismounted from his bull and was brought by the policeman before us. Here we asked the *sindico* the name and residence of the young man; and, as we supposed, he belonged in Mitla. Asking him why he had not come to be measured when he was told to do so, he replied that we had already measured him. Telling him that lying would not save him, I commanded him to appear the following morning for measurement,— that otherwise he would be sent a prisoner to Oaxaca. In the morning he did not appear until officials were sent to bring him. After he had gone through the ordeal of measurement he swore eternal friendship to me, and at no time afterward was I able to pass him, on the street or in the square, without his begging me to drink *tepache* with him.

Mitla is famous for its weaving; fine *mantas* of wool are made there in two chief styles — one a long strip of black or blue-black cloth, the other a rich red, sometimes banded or striped with black. These Mitla *mantas* are widely sold to Zapotecs, in all the district around, and form the characteristic women's dress. The Zapotecs of this district wear something on their feet that more nearly resembles true shoes than the footgear of any other indians in southern Mexico. The sandal of the man has a projecting heel-flap which is bound around the ankles by means of thongs, and forms a good protection to the hind part of the foot. The women have not only such a flap, even higher than that used by the men, but also a broad strip of leather over the forward part of the foot, leaving the toes peeping out in front; between the heel flap and the toe covering, the foot is quite as well enclosed, excepting for the toes, as in a white man's shoe.

It was quite impossible, with the amount of work we had to do, and the difficulties under which we labored, to give the least attention to the ruins. We arranged, however, to make a photograph of the town authorities standing in the great court of one of the fine old buildings — a court the walls of which are covered with beautiful mosaic decorations, betraying taste and skill. The motley crew of half-drunk officials, miserably dressed, degraded, poor, in this scene of past magnificence, called up thoughts of the contrast between the government of old Mitla and the present, — of past magnificence and modern squalor.

Having accomplished all we wished at Mitla, we again struck eastward toward the land of the Mixes. Late in starting, we made no attempt to go further than San Loren-

The Contrast; Past and Present — Mitla

zo that afternoon. The old road was familiar, and from there on, through the following day, everything came back to memory. Even individual trees, projecting rock masses, and little streams, were precisely as we remembered them from our journey of three years earlier. We reached Ayutla in the evening a little before sunset. Riding directly to the municipal house we summoned the town government. We had not provided ourselves with orders from the *jefe* of the district, as Villa Alta, the *jefatura*, lay far out of our course. We planned to use our general letter from the governor. When the officials assembled we presented our order and explained it; we told them what we needed for the night, and arrangements were at once made for supplying us; we then told the *presidente* of the work we had before us, and informed him that, because his town was small, we should ask for only thirty-five men for measurement, and that these must be ready, early in the morning, with no trouble to us.

The *presidente* demurred; he doubted whether the people would come to be measured; we told him that they would not come, of course, unless he sent for them. When morning came, although everything had been done for our comfort, there was no sign of subjects. That no time might be lost, we took the *presidente* and three or four other officials, who were waiting around the house; then, with firmness, we ordered that he should bring other subjects. The officials were gone for upwards of an hour, and when they returned, had some ten or twelve men with them. "Ah," said I, "you have brought these, then, for measurement?" "On the contrary, sir," said the *presidente*, "this is a committee of the principal men of the town who have come to tell you that the people do not wish to be measured." "Ah," said I, "so you are a committee, are you, come to tell me that you do not wish to be measured?" "Yes." Waiting a moment, I turned to the officials and asked, "And which one particularly does not wish to be measured of this committee?" Immediately, a most conservative-looking individual was pointed out. Addressing him, I said, "And so you do not wish to be measured?" "No sir," said he, "I will not be measured." "Very good," said I. "What is your name?" He told us. I marked it down upon my blank, and wrote out the description of his person. Then, seizing my measuring rod, I said to him quite sharply, "Well, well! Take off your hat and sandals. We must lose no time!" And before he really realized what we were doing, I had taken his measurements. Having finished with him, I turned again to the *presidente*. "And what other member of the committee particularly objects to being measured?" As I spoke, another man was indicated. Turning to him, I said, "Let us lose no time. Take off your hat and sandals while I measure you." In an instant the thing was done. The operation was carried through. Before I had finished with the second case, the others began to smile and snicker, and when I was ready for my third subject I simply asked, "Who next?" and they came one after another without complaint. Having measured all the members of the committee, I soberly addressed them. "Now, if there is any harm in this that I have done, you are all as badly off as can be. If I were you, I would try to get as many other people in the same position as I could; go out and bring in others." Before noon the work was done, and we were ready to go on to Juquila.

We rested, however, the balance of the day, and spent a second night at Ayutla. The day had been given to drinking, throughout the town. It will be remembered that the village proper lies on a terrace, upon a slope above the town-house. As we sat before the house, in the afternoon and evening, we heard from time to time yells and cries above. Some policemen, who were standing up there to keep order, would then appear upon the edge of the slope, and, waving their hands, would loudly cry for help; then the policemen from the town-house would run to their assistance, and in a little time the party would return, dragging one or more victims to the jail. This operation continued from early in the afternoon until late at night; fully fifteen or twenty persons were brought down from the village to the jail during that time.

We had hoped to find the valley of clouds, and the great cloud cataract, on the road to Juquila, but were doomed to disappointment. When we stood upon the summit, looking down into what before had been the sea of mist, the whole place was clear, and everything, to the very bottom of the valley, was visible. The further journey seemed more tedious than before, and the latter part of the road seemed truly endless. There was not a breath of air; the sun poured its hot rays down mercilessly. Long before we reached Juquila I felt, for the first time in Mexico, that I was suffering from fever. After seven and a half hours on the road, we reached the town at 1:30 in the afternoon, and went at once to the town-house, where we were well received, and arrangements were made for our comfort. When they saw that I was suffering, they brought out hammocks, of which I made no use. Making myself a bed of blankets upon the floor, I lay down in my misery and covered myself from the world, a blanket over my head. After some hours, I felt that we were losing time, and that we must, at least, make arrangements for the work of the following day. It was now dusk. I sent for the officials, and when they appeared, told them that, notwithstanding my suffering, I could not lose time, and that early in the morning they must bring persons for measurement. There was a good deal of discussion over the matter. The officials were dissatisfied that my order was not signed by the *jefe* of their district and dated from San Carlos. They suggested that we send a messenger to San Carlos to inquire whether the order was all right. I replied that four days would be consumed in going and coming; that time was precious, and that it was impossible for us to wait. Seeing that they were likely to refuse to do what I wished, I made a little speech, in which I told them they had better do what I asked, and that promptly. No one so far had recognized me as having been there before. I told them that they had never had better friend that I; that this was not the first time I had visited Juquila; that when I came before I had had difficulty; that my companion, presenting an order from the governor, had been badly received by their *presidente*, who tried to do him violence; that if I had reported this incident, they knew well what would have happened; that, however, being their good friend, I had never reported it. Having jogged their memory regarding the past, I suggested to them that a report of the previous occurrence, with their present disregard of orders, might be serious. I told them that they knew what I desired; that they might at once inform me whether it would be done or not; if they decided in the negative, the *secretario* and my *mozo* must start at once on foot to Oaxaca, carrying my complaint to the governor; that, as for me, having started them upon their journey, I should leave early the following morning going to some town where the people knew what obedience to the law meant. They at once promised that no time should be lost, and that, the following morning, I should have the subjects for whom I asked, viz., thirty-five men and twenty-five women. Nor was it simply promises; having told them that I would begin early in the morning whether I were well or ill, and that I wanted no delay, we found our thirty-five men waiting, at seven o'clock.

The Land of the Mixes

At Juquila the system of public crying from the *plaza* is fully developed. The town lies in a valley, and most of the houses are on slopes surrounding the little plain or terrace upon which the *plaza* is situated on which the government house is built. When aid was needed by the town authorities, whether *zacate* for our horses, food for ourselves, objects for inspection, or what not, one of the officers, whose business it seemed to be, stepped out upon the *plaza*, and, raising his voice would cry out what was needed by the authorities. Whoever had the things desired, coming out before their houses, would cry back the amount, description and variety of the articles they could supply. This we found to be the constant practice.

Nothwithstanding the clearness of the preceding day, our day of working was cold, damp, and foggy. The sea of cloud and cataract of mists must have been in full operation. Where we were, a heavy wind was blowing and, before night, rain falling. We had not thought of the possibility of heavy storms or damaged roads at this time of the year, but, before night came, the people of the village expressed surprisc that we should talk of leaving the next morning. They assured us that at Quezaltepec and Ixcuintepec it was surely raining heavily, and that the roads would be wet, slippery and impassable. Long before we went to bed, a gale was blowing and we felt doubts regarding further progress. In the morning it was still wet and chilly; all told of terrible roads and risks in proceeding; we delayed. Finally, we decided to press on at least to Ocotopec. We had tried to send the *mozos* forward with our baggage, but it was plain they would not move until we did. Finally, somewhat after nine, we started. It was still heavy and chilly; we found the road much better than we feared; at some points it was slippery, but not for long distances. Until we were on the final descent to Ocotopec we were sheltered from the cold wind. To be sure, here and there, where the road passed little funnel openings along the crest, we felt fully the cold wind loaded with mist.

We noticed, what on the other trip escaped my attention, the profound difference in vegetation between the two sides of the hill upon the crest of which we were travelling. The one slope, cold and damp, was densely forested with trees, loaded with air-plants and orchids. The other slope, warmer and drier, was far less heavily grown, and in large part, with pines. Among the plants noticed by the roadside was a species of pinguicula which was very common on damp clay-cuttings. Its leaves form a close, flat rosette upon the ground, from which a slender stalk rises, with a a single crimson flower. When we reached the final descent to the town, we caught the full force of the cold, mist-laden wind, which struck our faces and made us shiver. Yet it was on this very slope, so frequently cold and wet, that the oaks, covered with air-plants and blooming orchids, were at their finest. Ferns in astonishing variety, from the most delicate, through giant herbaceous forms, to magnificent tree-ferns; lycopods of several species, and selaginellas, in tufts, covered the slopes; and great banks of begonias, in fine bloom, showed themselves. Before we reached the village we were forced to dismount, on account of the slippery condition of the road, and entered town on foot.

In our other journey Ocotopec made no impression on us. It is really one of the most picturesque and interesting of the Mixe towns. It is built upon a slope, which is cut and built into a series of little terraced gardens; clusters or groups of houses stand on the terraces. The houses are rectangular, built of adobe brick and heavy thatch, with a thick comb of thatch riding the ridge. Unlike most Mixe churches, the church at Ocotopec is entire, and in good condition. It is built of stone. The town is purely indian, and the type is the best we had seen. Had there been light for photographing, we should have stopped there and done our work, instead of passing on to Ixcuintepec. As it was, we spent the night, and were well treated. Leaving early in the morning, we hurried to Quezaltepec for dinner, the road being better than we had anticipated. The town is prettily distributed upon a curved crest; the houses are neat, built of adobe or of poles daubed with mud. Much fruit is grown here, and coffee is an important crop. In almost every yard mats were spread out, on which coffee was drying, or being sorted by people squatting on the ground. Considerable cotton is woven at this point.

Leaving at 3:40, the evening ride through the forest was magnificent. The flora was such as we have before described. As we rode through the higher forests, we constantly heard birds, notable among which were the *clarins*, with their fine clear notes. It was dark before we reached Camotlan. Nowhere had we been better treated. We were shown at once into a clean room, and were soon surrounded by bustle and preparation for our comfort. There are but 143 inhabitants, of whom six — four men and two women — have goitres. We had been previously informed that the whole town was goitrous. There were three deaf-mutes, but no idiots, in the town. Inquiring for books printed in the Mixe tongue, we were informed that the choir-master had one. On expressing my desire to see it, they sent to bring him. We were astonished at his appearance. The messengers who brought him carried him in their arms, and set him down upon the floor, when we saw that he had been born without legs, and with sadly deformed arms and hands. Yet, when once placed upon the floor, he moved about easily, and had a cheery face and sunny temper. He was delighted to show us his book and took the greatest pride in reading from it. It is truly remarkable that he can do this. The book was written in the dialect of Juquila of more than 170 years ago. The dialect of Juquila was no doubt then different from that of Camotlan, and during the 170 years there have been great changes, even in that town itself. As I watched the man read from his book, I noticed that he pronounced parts of words differently from the way in which they were spelled; how he had worked out for himself, unaided, the proper meaning and purport of the words was a mystery. I had intended to purchase the book, but found him so attached to it that I gave up the plan. Had he been a normal man, I should have insisted; but then, if he had been a normal man, he would not have had the book nor known how to read it.

From Camotlan we rode steadily for five hours to reach Ixcuintepec. There were considerable stretches of slippery road to be passed. The two gorge rides, the bridges of vines, and the houses along the way, were beautiful as ever, but the magnificent mountain forests were left entirely behind us. The old church at Ixcuintepec is visible on the high crest for a considerable distance. As we made the final climb, the boys noticed in the trees structures one and a half feet or two feet in diameter, and somewhat dome-shaped. I should have taken them for wasps' nests, but the party insisted that they saw parrots come out of them, and that no doubt young parrots were in the nests. Immediately there was great excitement, for Manuel had all along wanted to capture a parrot to take home with him. The party stopped, and stones were thrown to drive out the birds, but with no result. Finally Mariano climbed the tree, creeping out along the branches almost to the nest; just at that moment an unusually well-aimed stone struck the nest, but instead of parrots, out streamed a great cloud of wasps, which flew straight towards the *mozo*,

View in Quezaltepec

who lost no time in getting down from his precarious position.

We found Ixcuintepec almost deserted; hardly any of the town officials were there. Almost everyone was off, working in the coffee *fincas*. We quickly saw that we had made a great mistake in waiting for our remaining subjects until this town. Not only were men conspicuous by their absence, but the women were extremely hostile. They objected to our photographing their houses or themselves. They drove the messenger whom I had sent to measure a house, for the purpose of making a miniature reproduction, off the premises with clubs. The *mozos*, who had accompanied us thus far, had no intention of going farther, and the problem of getting carriers — which had troubled us ever since we had left Mitla — assumed serious proportions. It was with great difficulty and much bluster that we secured the food we needed and the *mozos*. When the *mozos* came, three out of the four whom it was necessary for us to employ, were mere boys, the heartiest and best of whom was scarcely ten years old. In vain we declared that it was impossible for such little fellows to carry the burdens that needed transportation. It was plain that they were our only resource. Starting the three boys upon a short cut to San Miguel, the oldest *mozo* and ourselves went by another road to Coatlan. It was fortunate for us that the school-teacher at this town was interested in our work. We took possession of the school-house, showed our orders to the officials, and, after much difficulty, obtained our wishes. The town was almost as deserted as had been Ixcuintepec, but after infinite difficulty, we succeeded in getting sufficient subjects to complete our work.

We had thought ourselves unfortunate at Ixcuintepec and Coatlan; the worst lay before us. We found San Miguel deserted. Our three *mozos* who had been paid, and ordered to go simply to that village, and there to leave our things, had left before we arrived. The man who had come with us, we had dismissed before we realized conditions. The coffee had been gathered for the season; the chief man of the place was in the mountains; there was no town government; neither prayers, threats, nor bribes produced food for ourselves and our horses; two or three men around the place would not be hired as *mozos*. We finally were forced to leave our busts, plaster, photographic outfit and plates on a bench under an open shed, and go on alone to Santiago Guevea. It was a bitter disappointment, because our previous experience at San Miguel had been so pleasant and interesting.

When we left Coatlan that morning, it had been through clouds and drizzling rain. When we passed through San Miguel, conditions were but little better. From there, we went through a gorge road, everywhere passing little plantations of coffee, bananas, and tobacco. Finally, we began our last mountain or forest climb. The wind with the rain became colder and more penetrating. At the summit, we found a typical norther raging, and at points our animals and ourselves were almost blown from the crest. In good weather the road is long, but through this it was dreadful. Few towns compare in beauty of location, and appearance from a distance, with Santiago Guevea. It was nearly five when we drew up in front of the crowded town-house. It will be remembered that this town is Zapotec, Coatlan being the last Mixe town. The school-teacher interested himself in our welfare, securing for us a real sleeping-room with cots, putting our horses into the corridor of the schoolhouse, and arranging for our meals. Chocolate and bread were at once furnished, and at eight o'clock a good supper was sent to our room. In the *plaza* outside, the wind was blowing a hurricane and the cold cut like a knife; but the house in which we slept was tight and warm. In the morning, we found the wild weather still continuing. It had been out of the question to send *mozos* to San Miguel the night before, and it seemed wicked to start them out in such a storm of wind, fog, rain and cold. Still, our time was precious, and we ordered men sent to the place where our stuff had been left, to fetch it; meanwhile, we decided to wait until they should appear. Our animals had had nothing to eat the previous day, except a little corn we had brought with us from Coatlan. We therefore ordered *zacate* brought for them. The night before, I had inquired regarding the acquaintances we had made at San Miguel in our previous trip. I learned that the man had died less than a month before, but that the widow, the four boys and the little girl, having finished their work at the coffee *finca* at San Miguel, were in town. Accordingly we called at the house. The woman immediately recognized me, and asked after Don Ernesto. The boys were sleeping, bedded on piles of coffee, but were routed from their slumber to greet us. At first, none of them remembered me, but the little girl did, and soon Castolo also. Their house was comfortable, and piles of corn, coffee, and bananas were stacked up in the place. They invited us to stop with them, but we were already well housed by the authorities. As we left, the woman went to the corner, and, from a pile of similar objects, took two things neatly wrapped in corn-husks. On opening them, we found that they were eggs, which are frequently wrapped in this way for storage, in all the indian towns. Although we had ordered food for the horses, at seven o'clock it had not appeared. We called at the town-house several times, but still no *zacate*. Our dinner came, and the afternoon passed, but still no fodder for the horses was produced, and the poor animals had eaten nothing, practically, for two whole days, although subjected to hard work and the pelting storm. We anxiously watched for the coming of the *mozos* with our equipment. The storm, though still raging, was abating, and we could see well down the road. When, at half past three in the afternoon, there was no sign of either men or fodder, we called the town authorities to account. We told them that we would wait no longer in a town where our animals could only starve; that they must forward our boxes, plaster and busts promptly to Tehauntepec; that we should hold them responsible for loss or delay, and that all should be delivered at the office of the *jefe*. Paying no attention to their entreaties that we should wait a little longer for the fodder, which they promised, as they had so many times before, would come soon, we saddled our animals, and at 4:20 left the town. Just as we started, little Castolo appeared with two bunches of *zacate* sent by his mother, as a present to Don Federico.

Certainly, there must be a new and better road from Guevea to Santa Maria than the one we traversed in our other journey, and which again, following from memory, we used. It was a fearful trail, neglected and ruined, over slippery rock and rough, sharp-splintered stone. Still we pressed on rapidly, making even better time than we had been assured at the town that we might expect to make. Never were we more happy than in reaching Santa Maria, lovely in the moonlight, with its great church, fine municipal-house, cocoa-nut trees and thatched huts. Here was no sign either of the norther or the rain. The next day's journey was over the hot dusty road with glimpses now and then of the distant Pacific and Tlacotopec for destination. The following morning we pressed on toward Tehuantepec, through the dust and heat, reaching the city at noonday. To our great surprise, we found the *mozos*, with the plaster, the busts, and the boxes of plates, waiting for us since four o'clock in the morning.

CHAPTER XIII

ABOUT TEHUANTEPEC

(1899)

SINCE our former visit to Tehuantepec, that hot and dusty city had suffered terrible misfortune. Through a period of several months it was subject to frequent shocks of earthquakes; for a time these were of daily occurrence, and on one occasion there were seventeen in a single day. The town still showed the destruction produced by these earthquake shocks, although for some months past there had been none. Houses, stores, churches, all presented great cracks and bare spots from which plaster had fallen. Many of the people had left the city permanently; those who remained were completely discouraged and unwilling to spend trouble and money in the repair of their houses. Tehuantepec is, of course, a city of considerable size; situated on a railroad, it has lost its importance since that thoroughfare was constructed. It was, formerly, the natural point through which all the produce of the surrounding country passed; the railroad has given similar opportunity to other places, to the loss of Tehuantepec. Between earthquakes, the damage resulting from the railroad, and the location of the military forces at Juchitan, not far distant, the town is declining. It is still, however, the *cabecera*, and the *jefe* is a man of some force and vigor. Shortly after our arrival, I visited his office, delivered the governor's letter, and stated our purpose in visiting his city. He seemed interested, and at once stated that there would be no difficulty in carrying out my plans; that I would find plenty of women for measurement in Tehuantepec itself; that the 100 men had better be secured at San Blas, which, although independent in government, adjoins Tehuantepec. I suggested that it would be well to measure the women in the court-yard of his palace; he, however, replied, "By no means; it will be much better to go directly to the market, where the women are gathered in great numbers; a *regidor* will accompany you to arrange the matter with your subjects."

Although convinced that his plan was bad, we arranged to begin work the following morning; with instruments and *regidor* we presented ourselves in the market, picking out a suitable spot and preparing for work. Then I told the *regidor* to bring a subject. The market-place was crowded, probably two or three hundred women being there gathered. Approaching the nearest of them, the *regidor* politely asked her to step up and be measured. We were not, however, dealing with Triquis. The women of Tehuantepec are certainly the heads of their houses; the men occupy but an inferior position. Possibly, they are really larger than their husbands, but, whether that be true or not, they give that impression to the spectator. The lady indicated lost no time in assuring the *regidor* that she had no intention of being measured, and he returned crest-fallen to report results. He met with no sympathy. I told him he had been sent to bring the women, that my business was simply to measure them; that if he would do his duty, I would do mine. He made two other efforts, equally futile, and finally returning, said he thought an order would be necessary. I told him, if he had not already an order I did not know what an order was; that the *jefe* had distinctly told me what he was to do; that he was not doing it. He then said he had better go to the palace a moment; would I kindly wait. I waited. He soon reappeared, and started in bravely with a new subject, but was again repulsed. Returning, he said that we had better go up to the palace and interview the *jefe* again. I replied that I had no time to spare; that we had already lost two hours at the palace, waiting for the *jefe* to appear, and that I did not propose to lose more time; that he knew what I expected, and must either do it, or I would return to my hotel. He helplessly remarked that we had better see the *jefe*, whereupon I picked up my instruments and departed to the hotel. Leaving my instruments at the hotel, I decided, while matters were adjusting themselves — for I had no thought of bothering myself further — to call upon the bishop. Sallying from the hotel, I met upon the street the *regidor* and two other town officials, who were awaiting me. "Sir," said he, "will you not measure the women?" "No," said I, "I am going to call upon the bishop. I have no time to waste. We went once to measure the women, but you had no power; your *jefe* plainly is a man without authority." "No, sir," cried he, "the *jefe* has issued a strict order that the women must be measured." "No matter," I replied, "I have no time to waste. I shall make my call." With this I entered the bishop's palace, and had an interesting visit with that prelate. When leaving the palace, I found the *regidor* and four town officials, awaiting my appearance. He at once demanded whether it was not my intention to measure the women. He said that he had been to see the *jefe*, and that the *jefe* said my wishes must be obeyed. I asked him where it was proposed to measure the women, and he replied that it should be wherever I pleased. "Very good," said I. "We will measure them in the court-yard of the *jefe's* palace; have subjects brought there at once, and send a man to my hotel for my instruments."

To the palace we went, and thither shortly four policemen brought a woman from the market. With bad grace, she submitted to be measured, after which the four policemen went again to the market, and soon after reappeared with a second subject. So the work went on, with four policemen to each woman, until our full number was finally secured and the work completed.

Three years ago, on my return from Guatemala, I met in this city an English doctor named Castle, who has lived here for many years — a man of scientific tastes and interests, who has employed his leisure in studying the botany, zoology, and indians of the district. He is well-informed, and one of the few persons acquainted with the Juaves. I counted on his help in approaching that curious and little-known tribe. The doctor's house is full of pets; eight different kinds of parrots, a red and yellow macaw, a brilliant-billed, dark-plumaged toucan, an angora goat, a raccoon, dogs and cats, are a part of the happy family that prowls at large in his house. A little creature, an indian, no more than eight years old, has adopted the doctor for her father. She had come to him as a patient for a trouble by no means uncommon here — night-blindness; in caring for her, he gained the little creature's heart, and she will hardly hear of leaving him to return home. The doctor accompanied us on our first visit to San Blas, and told us many things, not only of the Juaves, but of the Zapotecs and other indians of the region.

From the hotel, in the heart of Tehuantepec, to the town-house of San Blas, is a walk of only twenty minutes. Here for three days we did our work, returning to our hotel for meals and lodging. The work went easily, the men presenting little or no objection to our operations; measurements, busts, portraits — all were taken. On the whole, the Tehuantepecanos do not present a simple, pure indian type. The women seemed to be purer than the men. The *secretario* at San Blas has been to school. He is one of the few indians of the district who has taken an interest in the study of his native tongue. He has already published a grammar of the Zapotec, as spoken in his village. He has also printed a little tract for lovers, in which high-sounding phrases are translated from the Spanish into Zapotec. He has also prepared, and holds in manuscript, a dictionary of the dialect containing some 4,000 words.

The visit to the Juaves we considered one of the most important and interesting of our journey. These people are conservative, and among the least known of the native populations of Mexico. There are but four towns, with a total population of probably less than three thousand persons. These towns are situated at a few leagues' distance from Tehuantepec, near the Pacific, upon narrow tongues of land, washed by salt lagoons. The nearest, largest, and according to Dr. Castle, the most conservative of the four towns, is San Mateo del Mar. We had hoped that Dr. Castle might accompany us on our journey. This, however, was impossible, but he suggested that he would go with us part of the way. To avoid the great heat, we travelled by night, as there was moonlight. Hiring a *carretero* at San Blas, we loaded our materials and instruments into the cart, and started it upon its way. At about four o'clock in the afternoon, we rode from Tehuantepec, taking a roundabout road in order to see the hill which gives name to the town. It was Sunday, and many women and girls had been visiting the cemetery, carrying bowls filled with flowers to put upon the graves of friends. We saw numbers of young fellows sitting by the roadside, and learned that they were the lovers of the young women, awaiting their return from the cemetery.

The name Tehuantepec means the mountain of man-eaters. These man-eaters were not men, but tigers, or ocelots. The story runs that long ago this mountain was infested with wild beasts who destroyed the people of the neighboring villages. Fearing extermination, the people of the town decided to consult the Juaves, who were famous for their *naguales*, or witches. The oldest and most skilled *nagual* of the tribe was employed. Having performed his incantations, he told them they might expect immediate deliverance; that he had conjured a deliverer from the sea. Soon there came forth from the water a gigantic turtle, who made his way slowly inland, until he reached the bottom of the hill, which was the home of the tigers. The dangerous animals were just descending from the mountain in a double line, but the moment they caught sight of the mammoth sea-monster, their bodies froze with terror and they were turned to stone. Terrified at the power of the creature he had conjured, the old *nagual* quickly made use of his most powerful incantation, with the result that the turtle also was transformed into stone. The proof of the truth of the story we saw in the lines of stone tigers on the mountain side and the stone turtle at the foot of the hill, as we rode by.

The doctor suggested that it would be well to take a guide with us from San Blas as far as Huilotepec, as there were many side-roads before we reached that town, and that, from there, we would need no help. We followed his suggestion. The road was almost level. It passed through a district covered with a dense growth of brush and thorny trees, except where the land had been plowed for planting corn. In the early evening we saw many birds. Flocks of parrots rose from the trees as we passed by; at one point Manuel shot a little eagle, which fell wounded to the ground. Our guide concluded to carry it on alive. All went well for some time, but at last, with no warning, the bird made a vicious dash, and with its claws tore through the trousers of the guide, making a great gash in his leg. The man promptly decided it was better, on the whole, to carry it further dead than living.

The doctor turned back at sunsest. We reached Huilotepec something before eight, and found it a large pueblo with houses built of bamboo or cane. Here we had a good supper, and dismissing our guide started out, by brilliant moonlight, for the last part of our journey. Shortly beyond the town, the road turned, for a moment, into the river, and after passing for a few rods in the river-bed, struck up again onto the bank. At this place we made a fatal blunder. When the road went down into the river, supposing that we were about to ford, we kept straight across the stream. Finding a road upon the other side we had no suspicion but what we were going well and travelled onward. For a long time we found trails of varying degree of badness. Sometimes the branches formed a complete tangle which, even in the daytime, would have required careful watching. As it was, the faces of the party were well scratched with thorns. Sometimes, we seemed to be on a good road; at others, we had hardly found a trail. At one place we passed a ranch — Corral de San Diego. A host of barking dogs announced our coming, and we cried out to the old man living there to tell us the road. His directions were not clear, but in attempting to follow them, we retraced our trail, and then struck into another road. Keeping to it until we really could not follow it further for the tangle, we retraced our steps until we came to a cart-road crossing that on which we were. We started first to the right upon this; then, concluding we were wrong, turned about and went the other way. We soon found ourselves off the road again, and travelling blindly through the brush. Coming to a round patch of clear sand, to which the trail on which we were seemed to have led us, we could find no way out. Convinced that we were hopelessly lost, we camped out upon the sand for the night. Fortunately we had a little corn with us which we gave to the horses, after which we tied them to the trees. As we lay upon the sand in the bright moonlight, we could hear the dashing of the sea waves not far away. The heat was intolerable and the mosquitoes venomous. We secured no rest, and, at the first signs of day, were ready for our start. The two boys went out to hunt a rabbit, but returned with most discouraging reports. While they were absent, Don Anselmo and myself were left in camp. Suddenly he cried out that our horses were running away; such was really the case. The last one was just disappearing in the brush and Anselmo started after them, leaving me to keep the camp. When the other two returned, they, too, started in pursuit. After a hard chase, the animals were captured and brought back. By seven we had mounted and were on our way. We retraced our trail of the night before, going back to the cart-road. A little before eight we came upon a ranch, the Ranchito del Boca del Rio. Here we asked our way, and found that we were still as far from San Mateo, as when we left Huilotepec the night before. Eating a light breakfast, we secured a guide who took us, by the shortest way across the river, back to the main trail for San Mateo, where he left us. The road was long and hot and sandy. Our horses could hardly keep up a decent walk. It seemed that we would never reach the town. More than an hour before we arrived at the town, we encountered little ranches belonging to it. Everywhere we saw flocks of sheep, cows and horses. Curiously, the Juaves have always had herds, since our first records of them, but they eat no meat. The country was more tropical than any through which we had passed. Clumps of palmtrees were to be seen here and there. Pools of standing water, where horses and cattle stood cooling themselves, were frequent. The people whom

Juave Indians; San Mateo del Mar

Juave Fisherman; San Mateo del Mar

we met wore little clothing. Men frequently had nothing but the breech-clout and hat. Women wore a skirt, but no upper garment. Children up to ten and twelve years of age ran naked. Reaching San Mateo at twelve o'clock, we found the village excited at our non-appearance. Our *carretero* had arrived long before with our luggage. He had told the *presidente* of our intended coming, and men from the town had been sent through the by-roads to seek for us. The town lies on a level stretch of sand, and the houses are built of canes and thatched with palm. Most of the trees in the village are palms; some, cocoa palms. The *plaza* is a large open space. On one side of it is the church, of stone and brick; on another side is the town-building made of brick, covered with plaster, and consisting of three portions,— the *presidencia*, *curato*, and jail. A brick-paved corridor, roofed above, runs before the whole building. We were given the jail and *presidencia* with the corridor. Here hammocks and a bed of palm stalks were prepared for us, and orders issued that eggs and *tortillas* should be brought us. The Juaves ráise no crops. They are fishermen, and their food and living come from the sea. Their dried fish and shrimps, and the salt, which they make from the brine-soaked bottoms of dried lagoons, go far and wide through the country, and for these they get in trade the corn, coffee, chocolate, and raw cotton which they need. We have already spoken of their cattle, which is a source of income, though, as stated before, the Juaves rarely eat meat food.

The Juaves present a well-defined physical type. They are of medium stature or tall. Their noses are the largest and most prominent in indian Mexico, and are boldly aquiline. The men are rarely idle; even as they walk, they carry with them their netting, or spindle with which they spin cord for making nets. It seems to be law, and is certainly custom, that persons coming to the *plaza* are expected to be more fully dressed than when travelling on the road or when in their homes. Usually white cotton drawers and shirt are worn in the *plaza*; outside, practically nothing but the breech-clout.

There is an interesting commerce carried on in Juave towns by Zapotec traders from Juchitan. As might be expected, this is entirely in the hands of women. Some women make two journeys weekly between the two towns. They come in ox-carts, with loads of corn, fodder, coffee, chocolate, cotton and the like. These they trade or sell. When they return to Juchitan, they carry with them a lot of salted and dried fish, shrimps, salt and eggs. Upon these expeditions the whole family accompanies the woman; the traveling is done almost entirely by night. These Zapotec women are shrewd at bargaining. They must be doing a paying business. It was interesting to see the primitive devices for weighing. The scales consisted of two tin pans of equal size and weight hung from a balance beam. The only weight was a stone weighing a pound. In case a Juave woman wished to buy a quarter-of-a-pound of cotton, the procedure was as follows: The weight was put into one pan of the scales and a pound of cotton weighed out into the other; the weight was then removed and the cotton divided, so as to balance in the two pans; one of the pans was then emptied, and the remaining cotton again divided, with the result that a quarter-of-a-pound of cotton had been weighed.

One curious feature, which we had not seen elsewhere, but which Dr. Castle had warned us we should find, was the nightly guard set upon us. As we lay upon our beds at night, looking out upon the white sand in front of us, we could see, by the moonlight, at some little distance, a circle of eight or ten men who spent the night sleeping within call. Another striking feature was the music which we heard in the late evening and early morning. In the early morning, five o'clock or earlier, and at sunset, there was service in the church. Later on, at eight, there was again singing in the churchyard, lasting until quite a late hour. One evening, on investigating, we found eight or ten men kneeling on the sand before the church door, singing in the moonlight. They were practicing for the procession and special service of the second Friday of Lent.

The water-life of the Juaves is at once picturesque and curiously tame. The men spend much of their time on or in the water. They make great dugout canoes from large tree trunks. There are usually no paddles, but poles are used to propel the craft sluggishly over the waters of the lagoon. Few of the men can swim. The fish are chiefly caught with nets, and both seines and throw nets are used. The lagoons are said to abound in alligators, and the men, when fishing, generally carry with them spears with long iron points which are said to be used for protection against attacks of these reptiles. Great respect is shown the alligator, and curious superstitions prevail regarding it.

Between San Mateo and the nearest of the great lagoons, the country ceases to be level and is covered with sand dunes. On these dunes there are great numbers of hares of a species peculiar to the locality. They make excellent eating, and Manuel kept our larder supplied with fresh meat, which was welcome, and which we could not otherwise have had among these non-meat-eating folk. An old Zapotec woman, seventy years of age, with snowy hair and gentle face, was deputed by the town authorities to do our cooking. Her relatives live in Juchitan, and why she had chosen to live among these people I do not know. She took a motherly interest in all our party. Nothing was too good for us. She spent her whole time in hunting supplies and cooking and serving food. Not only did she insist on all our purchases being supplied at cheapest rates, but her own charge for help and service was ridiculously small. From early morning until late at night the poor old soul was busy in our behalf. On our leaving, she took my hands between her own, and kissing them, begged that we would send her a picture as a remembrance.

The road to Tehuantepec at night was one of no adventure. We were impressed with the great number of families travelling in ox-carts over these roads in the cool night air. It was a custom and habit of which we had before no realization. It lacked but ten minutes of one o'clock when finally we rode up to the hotel in Tehuantepec. From the hostler we learned that every room was full,— five persons in some cases sleeping in a single room. So we were compelled to lie down upon the porch outside until the morning.

CHAPTER XIV

ON THE MAIN HIGH-ROAD

(1899)

AFTER a day or two of rest, we started from Tehuantepec upon our return to Oaxaca. For the first time, we were to follow the usually travelled high-road. Our hearts failed us, as we thought of thus neglecting the lovely land of the Mixes, but it was on our program to see the Chontals. Starting at seven, we lost a little time in having a photograph of our party taken as we left the city, so that it was really 8:15 before we were on our way. Our plaster had been sent by *carreta* to Xalapa. We had a hot, hot, hot ride over a heavy, difficult sand road. At least half a dozen times we forded the Tehuantepec river, and everywhere at places which would have justified the name, Xalapa, "the sandy water." Finally, arriving at Xalapa at four o'clock, we found it a large town, of the usual hot, dusty Zapotec kind. The authorities bestirred themselves vigorously to locate us in comfortable quarters, with an old lady of regal apppearance and dignity. From the start, we feared that this royal appearance and dignity would be paid for, but the opportunity for comfort was not to be neglected. One of the houses of her royal domain was vacated for our use, and two good cots and a hammock were put at our disposal. The supper was abundant, and capital in quality, and there was plenty of food for the horses. Strolling down to the river after supper we found it broad but very shallow; it did not reach our knees at any point, when we waded across it; the bottom was, as we imagined it would be from the name, moving sand. After a bath in the much too shallow stream for swimming, we returned refreshed to our comfortable beds. As anticipated, we found the bill, when presented in the morning, truly regal; after some demur, our queenly hostess reduced it slightly, but, even so, we were reminded of the summer-resorts of our own country.

Tequixistlan, perhaps the largest of the Chontal towns, we found without an official head. While we were in Tehuantepec the *jefe* received notice of his father's death. This notice had been duly sent to all the villages and towns within the district, and, on a certain day, the *presidente* and other chief officers of the different pueblos gathered at Tehuantepec to express their sympathy by speeches and to present flowers to the official. It was for this errand that the *presidente* of Tequixistlan had gone to the *cabecera*. Had he been at home, perhaps we would have had no difficulty, but as it was we found the government disjointed and nerveless. Constant nagging and harrying were necessary in carrying out our wishes. The town itself was not bad. It stands upon a sort of terrace, at a little height above the neighboring river. The town-house is a long building, occupying the whole upper end of the large rectangular *plaza*; at the lower end is the fine church and *curato*. Along the sides were *tiendas*, school, etc., well built adobes and plastered over with tinted plaster. Behind the church beyond the river rises a handsome background of mountains. The long corridor in front of the municipal-house was fine and broad, with a high roof and brick pavement. Oleanders bloomed before this corridor. The view from it was fine, and the air cool there even in the middle of the day. We accordingly took possession of it, working and sleeping there. So far as personal comfort was concerned, we were well cared for. We had good meals, comfortable cots, plenty of food for the horses, but, as we have said, the work lagged, and it was only with the greatest difficulty that we could accomplish it.

There is little distinctive about the Chontals, as we saw them. The women dress much like the Zapotec women in the neighboring towns. The men present nothing notable in dress. Outside the *plaza*, the houses were built of light materials, and resembled the ordinary cane-walled, thatched huts of the Zapotecs. The people appeared to be badly mixed, and this not only with white, but also with negro blood. Nevertheless, as we worked upon subject after subject, a fairly defined type seemed to grow upon us. We could see that the Chontals are tall, with rather well-shaped faces, though somewhat high cheek-bones, with light complexions, and with wavy or curly hair. When the work was finished, we had great difficulty in securing carriers to bear our burdens to San Bartolo. Enormous prices were demanded, and at last, angry over the attempted extortion, we threatened to leave all our stuff behind us, and hold the town responsible, reporting them to the authorities when we should reach Oaxaca, demanding that damages should be collected. These threats had the desired effect. The *secretario*, who had been the only member of the town government displaying energy in our behalf, promised by all that was sacred that our goods should be delivered promptly at San Bartolo; that if they were not already there on our arrival, we might safely arrange for further transportation from that town, convinced that the goods would come before we left.

That we might not be too much delayed by this palaver regarding carriers, I had started the balance of the party ahead, and rode on alone after them. They had left at 10:15, and we all had a hot, dry, dusty, thirsty mountain ride until five o'clock in the afternoon, when we reached the ranch, Las Vacas. It consisted of a dozen houses. We rode to the last one in the place, which consisted of brush and leafy branches, and had an enclosed *corral* adjoining it, where we asked for lodging. The owner was a young Zapotec, who, with his wife, was strikingly neat and clean. A little girl of seven was the only other member of the family. The house had but a single room, but there was a *coro*, or cane platform, and loft. Having fed our horses and eaten our own supper, I mounted to the loft, despite the advice of all the members of the party, who predicted smoke, heat, mosquitoes, fleas and other trials. They stayed below. There is no question that they fared worse from all the sources mentioned than myself. The woman worked until midnight, making *tortillas* and cooking chicken for us to carry as luncheon on the road. We had started by four in the morning, and pushed along over a mountain road. The first portion of the road was well-watered, but afterward it became hot, dry, and stony. Having gained the pass looking down upon the valley, we could see, at its further side, lying on a terrace, the pueblo of San Bartolo, stretching out in a long line near the front of a mighty mountain, upon which plainly our way would pass. It was almost noon when we reached the municipal-house, and found that our carriers had already arrived, and left the luggage. Here things were really quite as bad as at Tequixistlan, but here fortunately we had no work to do. The town was Zapotec. One might suppose, from its being upon the main high-road, that they would be accustomed to see strangers. We have hardly found a population at once so stupid and timid. It was with great difficulty that we found food to eat. Here we had to pay for beds (made of sticks tied together), belonging to the municipality, a thing which we had never done at any other town in Mexico.

The people wear curious and characteristic garments.

View from our Corridor; San Bartolo

All the stuff used for clothing is woven in the town, and not only the women's *camisas*, but the men's *camisas* and trousers, are decorated with elaborate designs — birds, animals, and geometrical figures — worked in various colors. Even in purchasing examples of these clothes, we were compelled to make a vigorous display of our civil and religious orders. After some bickering, we arranged for carriers to San Carlos, which is the *cabecera* of the district. Starting by moonlight, at two o'clock in the morning, we struck out over the enormous mountain mass to which we have already referred. Roads in the Zapotec country do not go directly up the hillside, as in the land of the Mixes, but zigzag by gentle diagonals up the slopes. The road was largely composed of jagged rock; two hours and fifteen minutes were necessary for the ascent; the descent was bad enough, but a distinct improvement. At one place, however, we wandered from the main-travelled road, and found ourselves in an abandoned portion of the road, full of great holes which were filled with drifted fallen leaves, so that their presence was not betrayed until our horses fell into them. The latter part of this descent was slippery, being over hard stone, which was worn almost to a glassy smoothness by the passage of many hoofs. A little before reaching Manteca, as we looked down from the height, we saw an immense train of pack-mules coming. In the good old days, before there were railroads, such trains as this were frequent. From Manteca the road penetrated into contracting valleys, until finally it might, with propriety, be called a cañon road. At half past eight we reached San Carlos, a mean town with no *meson* or other regular stopping-place. We left the horses under the shady trees with the old farrier. While we rested and waited for breakfast, I called upon the *jefe politico*, who had received several communications from me, and had become interested in my work. Our luggage was all at his office, and he promptly made arrangements for its further transportation. At breakfast, we received the cheerful news that Mr. Lang's horse had the lockjaw and showed signs of dying. On inspection, this proved to be quite true; the poor animal was in great pain, and could eat nothing, though making every effort to do so. Our first thought was a shot in the head to put it out of misery, but the old farrier wished to try a *remedio*. He did his best, and it looked as if the animal might recover; it was plain, however, that he could not be used again that afternoon. Accordingly, an extra horse was rented for Mr. Lang's use. The remainder of the party was started on the road at 1:50, while I waited to give the *remedio* a chance to operate and the beast an opportunity to rest. At three I started, leading the sick horse. We had a fine ride in the cool of the evening, over a mountain road past the little ranch El Quemado, beyond which we found an immense ascent. When we reached the summit, it was fast darkening, and I pressed on as rapidly as the led horse would permit. Finally, I reached Escondido at seven. Several large parties of packers, with their trains of mules, had already settled for the night; campfires were burning. Here and there drinking had been going on, and there was noise of loud laughter, singing and dancing. Our party was already eating supper when I arrived, and my own meal had been ordered. Shelter was supplied us adjoining the house, where we spread our blankets and spent a comfortable night. We were late in starting, and were not upon the road until seven in the morning. We found the high-road most uninteresting. For long distances we descended, passing a ranch and emerging finally into a deep, hot gorge. By the time we reached Pichones we were tired, hot and thirsty. There, however, we could get no water, for man or beast, for love or money; suffering with

Our Party Leaving Tehuantepec

Zapotec Women and Girls; Tlacolula

thirst, the road seemed long to the river near Totolapa, where we refreshed ourselves with water, but a heavier road than ever had to be traversed. Much of the way we followed the stream-bed, fording repeatedly; the remainder was through deep sand and over rolling pebbles. Passing Juanico, on a high bank overlooking the river, at noonday, we were delighted to strike upon a rock road, high on the river bank. Keeping to this trail, passing from plantations of bananas lying at the river level below us and catching many pretty views of valley and of mountain, we at last reached Totolapa, completely worn out with the journey and the heat. Here we rested until the heat of the day should be past.

We had expected at this town to secure a muleteer, as the one we hired from San Carlos had agreed to come only to this town. Here, too, we had expected to rent a new horse for Mr. Lang. Our muleteer, however, was much taken with the party, and declared that he should hire himself to continue with us to Tlacolula. We quickly arranged with him, and at four o'clock prepared to leave. The sick horse was then at its worst; it had lain down, and for a time we believed it was really dead; it was out of the question for it to go further; so, calling one of the villagers, I told him that he might have the horse, and if there was any possibility of curing, it, he should do what might be necesssary.

From four to seven it was a tiresome climb, largely through stream-beds to Carvajal. It is a large *rancho*, but we stopped at the first house we came to, a miserable place, where, however, we got coffee, bread, beans and eggs, and some mats for beds, which we laid out upon the ground, under the open sky. Taking early coffee and *tortillas*, we were again mounted at four and on our way. It was the last ascent. The moon was shining brightly, and we could see that the road followed the edge of a fine gorge. When we once reached the summit, there was no further descent to make. We were on the high, flat, table-land of Oaxaca, and from here to the capital city of the state, the road is level, and passes through a rich agricultural district. Passing San Dionisio at seven, we pressed on as rapidly as possible to Tlacolula, where we arrived before noon, ready for the good meals and comfortable quarters which we well knew awaited us there.

Tlacolula is a large town, in the midst of a dusty valley. Its houses are large, rectangular constructions, well built of poles, with fine thatched roofs. They stand in yards, which are enclosed by fences of organ-pipe cactus. The people dress well, and at almost every house they own an ox-cart and a yoke of animals. While photographing there that afternoon, we suggested that we wanted a group of girls and women in native dress. "Very well; I will take you to the house, where you can get one." Arrived there, the policeman at once led out five women and four children, whom he placed in line. After the picture was taken, we expressed our satisfaction and surprise that so good a group had been so readily secured at a single house. "Oh, sir," he replied, "we struck a lucky time; there is a funeral going on there."

In the Hot Valley; Cuicatlan

CHAPTER XV

CUICATLAN

(1899)

BETWEEN Tehuacan and Oaxaca the railroad passes through a low, deep valley which is ever hot. Few people on the train pass through this valley without feeling its depressing influence. It would seem that travelers would hardly stop at stations within its limits, unless impelled by actual necessity. The most important of the towns in this valley is Cuicatlan. Little of it is to be seen from the railroad, but in reality it is a notably picturesque village.

It is the *cabecera* of a district in which dwell three most interesting tribes — the Cuicatecs, Chinantecs, and Mazatecs. We had time to visit only the nearest of the Cuicatec towns. Cuicatlan itself is situated near one side of a valley, through which runs a considerable stream. The distant bank rises in two magnificent mountain masses. The nearer bank, at the very base of which the town nestles on a series of little hills, rises into almost sheer precipices of purple conglomerate. These cliffs are hundreds of feet high, and are, apparently, due to a gigantic landslide. The mass which fell must have measured fully two miles in length, and still lies, broken and heaped up, at the base of the cliffs. The face of the cliffs, and the fallen masses of rock at its base, are cut into narrow gullies and gaps by water. The town consists of several clusters of houses, scaled along the slopes of little hillocks and settled into the spaces between them. Gigantic cactuses surround the town, and cocoa palms rise to great heights within it.

It is customary for travelers to emphasize the slowness of the Mexicans. Either we have been exceptionally fortunate, or the reputation is largely undeserved. We have been rarely delayed by sluggish action. Here, however, we found a *jefe* who would surely satisfy the most complaining. He was mild in manner, gentle in speech, fond of brilliant plans and schemes, all of which, however, were to be put in operation to-morrow and not to-day. It was with difficulty that we impressed upon him our necessity. We told him that we wanted animals to carry us to Papalo. In reply, he told us that Papalo was but a poor town, and he outlined a journey the traveling alone in which would occupy some eight or ten days. When we assured him that we had no time for such an enterprise, he said that it would be much better for the towns to come to us in Cuicatlan. He proposed sending to-morrow to those towns, and assured us that, at the end of a week's time, we would have all the subjects we needed. So, when we suggested that this, too, was loss of time, he had other brilliant plans, all quite as useless. With the utmost difficulty we finally succeeded in getting him to arrange for animals to go to Papalo. From the very start, the road was up-hill. Passing first through a section covered with a magnificent growth of tree cactuses of two species, in fine fruit and flower, we found the vegetation varied as we mounted, and at last came up among the pines. There was a great variety of landscape and geological formation. Purple-red conglomerate, with horizontal layers weathered into massive forms; granitic schistose rocks, over which we later passed, gave their peculiar scenic outlines. We climbed steadily for fully four hours, and then looked down, along a gently sloping hill trail, to our town, perched upon a slightly lower hill. Just at the edge of the town, we passed a gang of men and boys at work, making a level platform

Cactus; Cuicatlan

for the new *plaza* and town-house. We congratulated ourselves that we should have no difficulty, here, in finding subjects. The town claimed three thousand population. Many of them were certainly away upon their fields and ranches, scattered through the mountains, and working *fincas* for wealthy landowners. The town itself is picturesque in the extreme. Notable among its features is the ruined church, the roof of which has fallen in; the walls still stand, bare and broken, but the decorations, some richly carved and gilded, are still unmoved within the demolished edifice. The damage was recent, and represented a double catastrophe — lightning and earthquake.

We could not begin work until the *mozo* came with the instruments. Finally, at four o'clock in the afternoon, we began measuring with no great difficulty. Before night, fifteen subjects had passed through our hands and one bust had been made. Even when we arrived, at midday, it was too cold for us to stay with comfort in the town-house, though it was hot enough outside in the sunshine. When night came, it was bitter cold, and we went to bed early in hope of keeping warm, a hope without foundation. Early the next morning, we were ready for our work. Every one had disappeared, except those whom we had measured the night before. We requested the town authorities to bring in subjects. A few stragglers were dragged in and measured, and some pictures taken. Notwithstanding the poor way in which they had done their work, the policemen struck, declaring that they would not bring others until they had been paid. It was plain the town needed a lesson. We promptly paid the demand made upon us, and, then, calling the *presidente* and the *secretario*, we told them that we must have a receipt for the payment to show the *jefe*. We said that such a thing was unheard of; that, for town officials to demand pay, before they would agree to obey the order of their chief, was mutiny. At first they flatly refused to give the receipt, but after a little consultation were anxious to return the money, and threats were freely made to throw the whole police-force into jail. We said that this was not our desire; we were surprised at the demand, but, having met it, we insisted upon having our receipt. A meeting of the town authorities being held to consider the matter, our request was again refused, but attention was called to the fact that some subjects were waiting outside to be measured and photographed. I thereupon refused to measure or photograph any person until my demand had been met. I showed them, clearly, the position in which they had placed themselves; I stated that when they had done a wrong, and a stranger demanded an official statement of the case, their duty was simple and clear. By this time my own party was in arms; photographer, plaster-worker, Manuel, all were scared. They insisted that our throats would be cut that night. They called attention to the ugly manner and black looks of the town authorities. They declared that we had better flee, while yet there was opportunity; they insisted that they had not left comfortable homes to be murdered in cold blood; they begged that I would, at least, retreat from the position taken, and consent to measure the subjects who were waiting. I assured them that it was far more important to teach the town a lesson regarding their duty to their higher officials, than to measure a few indians. Finally, after hours of uncertainty, black looks, mutterings, and refusals, the town capitulated, and the receipt was in my possession. Having gained my point, I called the attention of the town officials to the bearings of the case. I emphasized their duty to the *jefe*. They knew, quite well, that it was out of place to demand money for obeying his order; I stated that I appreciated whatever work the policemen

View at Cuicatlan

might have done, and that, in due season, I might have recognized it by a gift, but that demands were quite another thing. I showed them how important it was, that, when trouble rose between them and a stranger, they should furnish any statement of the case he might, in justice, ask. Having stated the matter fully, I consented to receive back the money, and tore up the receipt much to their relief.

Still the work went slowly. No one was left in town but the officials and some women. The latter locked and barred their doors, at the approach of any of the town authorities, and neither threats to burn their houses above their heads nor bribes would bring them forth. It was only after three days of hard work that eighty men and twenty-five women were secured. By that time, it was plain that the other men were safely out of reach, and we concluded that naught remained but to return to Cuicatlan, to complete our work with representatives from other towns. This we did, although we found our *jefe* still gentle, mild, and slow.

Once in the hot valley, we concluded that we might as well see more of it. Leaving Cuicatlan at noon, a few minutes' ride brought us to the station at Tecomavaca, perhaps the hottest of the hot valley towns. Within it are ruins which have been strangely neglected by all tourists and investigators. Probably, the great heat has killed whatever little enthusiasm may have been kindled in those who have seen aught of these ruins. When we reached the station, in the hottest portion of the day, the valley seemed to glow; all looked hot and desolate. There were no *mozos* to help in carrying baggage, though the town was fully half a mile from the station, behind bare, hot, sandy hills. It is one of the poorest and meanest of the Mexican towns. A dreary *plaza* is surrounded by miserable adobe, or adobe-plastered, buildings. The only edifices that looked clean and neat were the school, jail, and town-house. We found shelter at a sort of a *meson*, where we could get no supper until nine, or possibly till ten. Rather than go inside the rooms, we took possession of the corridor, and there, with two cots, a table, and the floor, lay down to rest. But not to sleep! The town, small as it was, had twenty cases of *la grippe*. The woman of the house where we were stopping was one of these. Her husband, who came back from the mountains long after dark, appeared to have an affection and solicitude regarding her, which, under other circumstances, might have been quite touching, but which, then, was thoroughly exasperating. While he cooked his own supper, made chocolate for her, and heated hot water for her use, he kept passing back and forth, between the kitchen and the sick chamber, until later than two o'clock in the morning. The noise which he made, and these repeated movements, kept us all awake the whole night long. The night was hot and close, and new and unknown insects troubled us extremely. We were glad to be dressed and mounted, the following morning. Riding across the river, we made the ascent to the summit, on which were the ruins of Tecomavaca Viejo. The ascent was so abrupt that our horses were repeatedly compelled to stop for breath. The trail passed through cactuses, and spiny shrubs and trees, which tore our clothes more than all we had endured during weeks of travel. The ruins are unquestionably old. The hilly slope presents a succession of terraced platforms, one behind the other, at different heights. The rock walls between these are banked up and faced with rock, coated with plaster and mud; there are many pyramids and mounds; there are also curious subterranean, stone-faced, graves. Many curious disks of stone were found, a foot or eighteen inches in diameter, and three or four inches thick; these were all reddish grit, and had

Cactus Near Cuicatlan

View in a Tlaxcalan Barranca

plainly been piled one upon another to form pillars. Along the forward edge of some of the terraced platforms, we found the lower discs of some columns still in place. While the amount of work, represented in these cut terraces, banked rocks, and subterranean constructions, impressed us greatly, it was difficult to get a clear idea of the relationship of the parts.

When, however, we found ourselves at the station, waiting for the train, we looked back across the river to our three ruin-crowned hills. Then, for the first time, having visited the spot, we could clearly make out the relations. Three natural mountains or hills, the greater, central one flanked on both sides by lesser, had been utilized by the old builders; the natural rock masses had been cut and walled, until they practically formed masses of construction, rising terrace behind terrace, to the very summit. When the terraces were entire, with their temple-crowned pyramids, and with embankments and walls in full repair, these vast constructions must have been indeed impressive.

CHAPTER XVI

IN TLAXCALAN TOWNS

(1900)

A STREET-CAR line, running for most of the distance down hill, connects Santa Ana with Tlaxcala, the towns being separated by seven miles. When making this little journey to Tlaxcala in January, 1897, we noticed in the car with us, a stout, purely indian man, who seemed anxious to engage us in conversation. Knowing a few words of English, he was particularly anxious to practice them. He called our attention to the various villages, streams, and mountains in the country through which we were passing, and took delight in analyzing the native names and explaining their meanings. When we were returning in the afternoon, we met a gentleman who had been in the same car with us in the morning, and we inquired regarding our indian acquaintance. He told us that he was a full-blooded indian, whose native tongue was Aztec, and who lived in Santa Ana. Being the child of poor parents, the state had assisted in his education; he was now studying law in the city of Puebla. He was also a musician, and on this occasion had been upon his way to a public appointment, where he was to sing.

Later, in Puebla, we called upon this gentleman, whose name we found was Quechol, meaning a bird with a crooked neck, perhaps a flamingo. He was interested in our study, and said we ought some time to visit the indian towns of his people upon the slopes of Malintzi. In January, 1900, having been delayed in our plans, we decided to spend a few days in Tlaxcala, and secured his company. Our preparations were made at Santa Ana; at the home of his parents we were hospitably welcomed, and chocolate and bread were furnished, before we started on our journey. While this refreshment was preparing, we visited the old church, in front of which stood an aged cypress tree, hung with gray moss and blazing with red flowers. We also entered some of the houses, where, on domestic looms, the *serapes* for which the town is famous are manufactured. We visited also a private school for girls, established by a Señor Barela, who is noted as the first to introduce the industry of weaving wool into this community. While the memory of this gentleman is held in high esteem by this people, that of his wife is by no means savory. It seems that she was an avaricious, vain and selfish woman, with no sympathy for his schemes for the betterment of the people. Her feeling was well known, and she died heartily hated by all. When the time came for her burial, the grave was prepared, and her body placed within it. But the earth twice refused to receive the corpse. It was then carried to to the Sawapa, near by, and thrown into its waters. The stream overflowed its banks, and tossed the body upon the ground; again the effort was made to thus dispose of it, but again it was thrown upon the shore. It was then suggested that it be carried to "the Cuezcomate," an extinct geyser-crater, famous through all the country, and popularly believed to be the mouth of hell; when the body was thrown into this opening, it is said the devils were seen to swarm upward to receive it.

It was almost noon as our little party started on foot in the direction of Malintzi. Our indian friend, his brother, a white friend, our photographer, our Mexican boy and ourself, made up the party, and we were followed by three *mozos* on foot carrying supplies of food. We struck out over a sandy plain, where the foot sunk deep into dry sand, until we finally reached a well-built wall of stone, considered in the district a notable piece of engineering. It was constructed to turn the course of a little stream which, in times of flood, has frequently done damage to the town. From here, our trail led us on through the sandy pine-scrub, broken now and then by narrow gullies, called *barrancas*, with almost vertical sides. In every case, we were obliged to descend into these gullies and climb out upon the other side. After one and a half hours of walking we reached the village of San Pedro, where we stopped for dinner. The two Americans accompanying us lay down upon the ground, completely tired out, and were fast asleep within five minutes. Manuel assisted the local cook in preparing dinner, while we talked with visitors until the meal was ready. The houses of San Pedro are well constructed of stone, set in adobe, and have well-thatched roofs. The granaries, or *cuezcomates*, are of unusual size and well built. They range from six or eight feet in height to twelve or more, and are shaped like great urns, open at the top, which is protected by a thatch, generally two-pitched. The *temascals* were also unusually well built of stone, and frequently were neatly covered with white plaster. Soon after leaving San Pedro, in the afternoon, we came upon two indian boys digging in the ground. Inquiring what they were doing, we learned that they were hunting honey-ants, and in a moment our whole party was engaged in the same operation. These ants were found some inches below the surface, either singly, or in roundish holes containing half a dozen or more; the abdomen was swelled until it was as round as a pea and as large as a fair-sized currant, and was filled with honey. To get the sweet liquid, one takes the insect by the head or forward body and pressing the honey bag sucks out the contents. It is sweet and rich, with a little twang, as if fermented, and people in the district call it honey-wine. Three quarters of an hour brought us to San Francisco, though we had to go down and up two large *barrancas* before we reached the town. It was almost sunset when we arrived. Sitting down before the town-house, we sent for the *agente*. Soon after our arrival the church-bell rang furiously, and the din and clangor was kept up a long time. While waiting for the official, supper was prepared, though we had had some difficulty in arranging for it, and were in doubt as to where we were to spend the night. Before supper was ready, a motley crowd poured into the room in which we sat. One large fellow carried a great sword strapped at his side, another bore a short sword, another a knife, another a large and ancient gun. Probably there were other weapons not in sight. This group of indians was the *agente* and his *guardia*. We were objects of suspicion, and much argument, and an abundant supply of *huitzatl* — strong drink — were necessary, before we secured permission to spend the night at the house where we were to have supper. No sooner had this company withdrawn and supper been eaten, than we prepared for bed. One wooden bed, with a mat of rushes, served for Señor Quechol and myself. A second mat, laid on the floor, formed the bed for our four companions. In the morning, we took a walk to Akxotla, where we wished to see an ancient painting. Here we encountered greater suspicion than before, and, after wasting the greater part of the day, accomplished nothing. It is true an indian made a *camalpa* for us. This is a stringed musical instrument; though the name is Aztec, it is unlikely that it was known before the coming of the Spaniards. Quechol says the word means mouth-harp, coming from the Aztec *cam*, mouth, and the Spanish *harpa*, harp. We returned to San Francisco for our dinner, and at four o'clock again started on our journey.

It was after five before we reached San Bartolome. As we drew near the village, we saw a magnificent double rainbow, brilliantly displayed upon the eastern sky against a cloud of almost inky blackness. Looking westward, as we entered the village, we saw the sun setting in a sea of gold, between Popocatapetl and Ixtaccihuatl. Watching this magnificent sunset, we sat down before the old church, and almost instantly a crowd gathered to see what the strangers might want. Don Romualdo, in wandering through the village, found a *temascal* in use, and húrrying to us, led us to see the method of its use. It is a dome-shaped structure, with an entrance so low that one must crawl upon his hands and knees in entering; it is a sweat-bath, used for cleanliness and health. A quick fire, built inside, heats it thoroughly, after which water is thrown upon the hot stones to produce steam. Four persons, of both sexes, were in the one in question, taking a sweat-bath. When we returned to our companions, sitting before the church, an indian of the village, accosting Don Romualdo, claimed to know him; he also claimed my acquaintance, and reminded me that he had been one of the subjects I had measured two years before in Tlaxcala. A score or more of natives had gathered, in the moonlight, around our party. Having heard some indians singing, we tried to get these to sing some native songs. Only after Louis and Frank had sung some English songs, which were well received, were we able to hear Aztec songs in exchange. After a long delay, we were taken to the school-house for supper and the night, and spent the balance of the evening in taking down a native song, *The Tlaxcalteca*, and witnessing a dance which accompanied it. A bed was made up for the party by putting various benches and tables together.

Most of the following day was spent in visiting in the

Tlaxcalan House with Temascal

The Mapaho in Use; San Juan Zautla

village, purchasing idols and in making notes on life and customs; at four o'clock in the afternoon, we set out for Ixcotla. Near sunset we reached the house of Quechol's uncle, old Isidro. Almost eighty years of age, he was straight and lithe as a man of thirty. His house and all the lesser buildings of his place were excellent and in fine condition. A flight of steps led to the flat roof, from which we watched the sunset. In the yard, were half a dozen hives for bees, made from the stocks of the *maguey*. The old man was rich, and owned other houses, but he lives alone, his wife being dead and his daughters married. He is a master of the Aztec, and uses it in its most poetical and figurative style. He does not speak like common men, but his conversation abounds in metaphor and flowers of speech. When once one spoke to him of his lonely and solitary life, he said, "Alone and solitary! No, we are three! There are here myself, my good angel, and my bad angel. I am never alone." Isidro knows all the boundaries of the fields, and can trace all the titles, and is frequently appealed to in land disputes, and even in law cases, is summoned to give testimony. He received us heartily, offered cigarettes and ordered supper. To refresh us, he broke fresh leaves from the orange-tree and steeped them in hot water, sweetening with sugar. After supper, good beds were made upon the floor, with plenty of mats and blankets.

We had hardly risen in the morning, when the village was thrown into great excitement by the appearance of a band of soldiers. They had come to arrest a young man supposed to be a leader in the local opposition to Governor Cahuantzi. This opposition was just at fever heat; the election was approaching, and a fierce effort was being made to oust the governor. Forty-four towns were in open rebellion, among them, all of those which we had visited.

There had been new laws passed regarding land and taxes; these had been resisted. The governor had threatened to send engineers to make new surveys, and to bring land-titles into question. The suspicion and distrust which we had met were doubtless, in large part, due to these measures, and the fear that we were government spies. So great was the discontent, and so openly expressed, that it was said that on the Saturday preceding, in the Plaza of Tlaxcala itself, there was a riot, with cries of derision and contempt, and firing of guns upon the palace. We were told that the nearest *haciendero*, who was friendly to the governor, was marked for assassination and would be killed within the next few days.

Leaving at ten next morning, we skirted Santa Ana, and, having passed through San Pablo, came out upon the banks of the Sawapa. This pretty stream has reputed remedial power, and in May hundreds of people bathe in its waters, to protect themselves against smallpox. As we crossed the great stone bridge, we met a drunken indian who attached himself to our party. Between him and the Mexican members of our party, there arose hostility and an exchange of angry words. To us, personally, he was maudlinly affectionate and respectful. Finally, shaking him off, after climbing a considerable height, we stopped at Belen for a noonday rest and lunch. Dinner having been ordered, we seated ourselves in the shade, when our drunken friend again appeared upon the scene, and in great excitement, begged me to move, as it was certain death for a heated and perspiring person to sit in the shadow of a Peru tree. So persistent was he, that Quehcol and Manuel lost all patience, and ordered the local officials to arrest him.

About the middle of the afternoon we were again upon the road; having passed the bare, fortress-like church of

San Mateo, and descended a long hill, toward evening we crossed a fine bridge over a gorge of black basaltic rock, and shortly reached Santa Maria Atlihuitzia, where we planned to spend the night. Here is a fine old church, with a façade absolutely covered with elaborate carving; a square tower rises at one corner. The great altar is a magnificent piece of carving and gold work; the windows are set with thin slabs of onyx. Within, near the church-door, are two paintings representing the scene of mayrtrdom for which the town is famous. These pictures are ancient, and represent some interesting details of indian life at the time of the Conquest. The head-dress and mantle of feathers worn by the old chieftain, the dress and hair-dressing of his wife, war weapons and buildings are all shown. Here, in 1527, the boy Cristoval, child of the great chief Acxotecatl and his wife Apalxitzin, was killed by his father because he would not renounce Christianity. The little lad was only thirteen years of age, and had been trained by Spanish priests. He was the proto-martyr of the new world, and the story of his martyrdom and the early church in Tlaxcala, have been charmingly narrated by Mendieta. Close by the church stand the ruined walls of the monastery, impressive for their massive construction and the enormous space which was enclosed. It was dark before we finished the examination of these quaint and interesting old buildings, and we were glad enough to go to the house of the *secretario*, where we found good beds and elaborate furniture. In the room where we were to sleep there was a *nacimiento*, made in connection with the Christmas season. The table was covered with little landscapes, scattered over which were figures of many kinds, including a group of San Jose, Maria, and the infant Christ.

Santa Maria is purely *mestizo*. In the morning, finding breakfast somewhat slow, we started for a walk, and passing by the old church, came shortly to the spot where the boy martyr was killed. From here we descended, over a long slope of gray tufa, to a pretty stream flowing through black basalt. The rock is hard and shiny with cells or air-bubbles scattered through its mass. Close by the water's edge we were shown some curious impressions, on the nearly level surface of the rock, which were said to be the imprints of the knees of the Holy Virgin as she knelt here to wash clothes in the brook; there are also grooves made by the Virgin's fingers as she scrubbed the clothing on the rock; by the side of these impressions are two hollows, marking the spot where the Holy Child sat with its mother as she worked. On the rock behind is the impression of a mule's foot. Formerly there were two of these impressions, but in 1888 a tornado broke away the mass of rock, on which was the other impression. Just below this place the stream leaps in a pretty cascade which, with its white foam, contrasts strikingly with the black rock. The trail followed by Cortez on his way from Vera Cruz to Tlaxcala was pointed out to us and we were told that Atlihuitzia in those days was an important city, numbering five thousand *solteros* (unmarried men). On the way back to the village, we visited the *arbol huerfano* — orphan tree — a cypress, so called because it is the only tree of its kind in this district. Quechol says that a long line of such trees, at a distance of several leagues apart, was planted by the Spaniards, and he and the villagers mentioned a number of them in different places. Passing once more by the spot of martyrdom, a white *capulin* was pointed out, as being the very tree represented in the picture of the killing.

It was now almost ten o'clock and we found breakfast waiting. At Quechol's request, it was a purely Mexican meal, consisting of Aztec dishes. We had *tamales*, *atole*, and, for the first time, *champurado*. The latter is *atole*

— corn gruel — mixed with chocolate, and is really an excellent dish. After breakfast, we left our friends of Atlihuitzia and hastened back over the same road past San Mateo, Belen, San Pablo, and Santa Ana. The way was long and the sun was hot, but the road was beguiled with many stories regarding the places that we passed, for the whole state of Tlaxcala abounds in legend.

CHAPTER XVII

IN THE CHINANTLA

(1900)

ONCE more we found ourselves in picturesque Cuicatlan. Walking up the familiar street, we again found lodging with Doña Serafina. Having settled, and taken a look out over the beautiful landscape visible through our windows, we interviewed the *jefe politico*, whom we we found the same nerveless, well-meaning individual as ever. After grumbling, and insisting that it was impossible to fit us out on such short notice, he finally promised that all should be ready the next morning. It was a sorry outfit that we found; one medium-sized mule for myself, and four small *burros* for the other members of the party. A boy from the jail was sent with us as *mozo* to carry our instruments. It was still early when we started through the hot, sandy, flat land, covered with gigantic cactus trees, which swarmed with little birds of many beautiful kinds. We soon began to climb the great, red rock cliffs, up, and up, and up, endlessly. We had forgotten how long the road was; but it was longer than ever on account of the beasts we rode. Long before we reached Papalo, Manuel and Louis were on foot, rather than longer submit to the torture of riding their little *burros*. As we neared the town, we were surprised to find a cloud effect almost as fine as that near Juquila in the Mixe country. Had it had clearly defined banks on both sides, its resemblance to a cataract would have been complete. As it was, there was no boundary back of the side towards us, and the clouds plunged over and downward as well as in the direction of the flow of the main mass. No one in the town recognized us. Supper and a night's lodging were readily supplied, but when we wished to secure new animals for the onward journey, there was difficulty. They were promised, indeed, for seven o'clock, but it was long after eight before we saw any signs of their appearance. Remonstrating, we were told that there was other business to attend to, and that the town officials could not devote themselves to us. With great difficulty, by 10 o'clock all preparations were made, and we started on the journey. The animals were not bad, but we had been told that there were eight leagues of hard road between us and Tepanapa, and six more from there to San Juan Zautla, our destination; we were told that we should spend the night at Tepanapa, reaching Zautla the second day. As we left the town we overtook a funeral procession on its way to the little hill-crest cemetery which we passed soon after. At first the road was good, gradually ascending. It led us up a rising pine-covered crest, with a little hollow of deciduous trees in the midst. We were again getting into a region where the great hills presented two differing slopes, one dry, pine-clad; the other moist and covered with the dense tropical forest. We soon found ourselves upon the damp slope in a forest, almost the counterpart of those with which we were familiar in the land of the Mixes. Great oaks were loaded with bromelias and dotted with orchids; ferns of many beautiful kinds grew along the roadside. Unlike the forest of the the Mixes, the trees here were hung with masses of golden-yellow moss, presenting a curious and mysterious aspect. From here, the trail descended rapidly over surfaces of slippery stone and patches of mud; the air was heavier and heavier with moisture. Ferns abounded, and presently great tree ferns were to be seen, here and there, in all directions. Shortly, our road was through a true gorge, where the footing for the horses was precarious. Great masses of lycopods of several species covered the rocks and little round tufts of a dark green plant with feathery foliage dotted the decaying tree trunks. The descent seemed endless, and for more than two hours we descended deeper and deeper into the dampness and darkness. It was six o'clock when we came out upon a slope where the trail was easier and almost level, and it was after dark before we reached the first hut of the miserable *ranchito* of Tepanapa. Checking our horses, we called, but received no answer. Sending our *mozo* to the house, we asked for food and shelter, but were refused everything, as they said that they were in bed. A little lad, however, agreed to show us to the next hut, and we followed him as well as we could in the darkness and over the slippery road, some rods further. We found there two empty huts within an enclosure, and, taking possession of one, brought in our things out of the mist, and soon had a fire built and a candle lighted. In vain we urged our *mozo* to hunt for food. He said that all the houses were empty, and, if perchance one were occupied, no one would turn out so late to supply us. All were extremely hungry, as we had eaten nothing since morning except a *tortilla* or two with some eggs as we rode along. Manuel, Louis and Frank slept in the loft, Ramon and I upon the floor below. The two *mozos* with the saddles slept in the other hut. The night was cold and the damp air penetrating. We arose early to go upon our way, but unfortunately yielded to the request of Louis and Ramon, permitting them to go in search of food. Two full hours passed before they returned with a few *tortillas* and two eggs; so that it was half-past-eight when finally we started.

The road was slippery and muddy, descending constantly; a large portion of the way was through woods: at the

San Juan Zautla

bottom of the slope we found ourselves by a fine brook, which we forded. Then began an ascent as precipitous, slippery and unpleasant. The trail followed the bank of the stream. Passing through a dense jungle of vegetation, where the air was hot and wet, the flora was characteristic. Trees with large, coarse, broad pods enclosing two or three great seeds, trees with acorn-shaped red fruits, quantities of sensitive plants covered with pink flowers, occasional orchids bearing flowers of brilliant flame color, and vines with lovely blue pea-flowers made up the bulk of the tangled growth through which we passed. At two places we crossed pretty streams, with cascades and narrow gorges, opening on to the gorge along the sides of which we were travelling; where these streams crossed our trail there were great masses of caladiums with their leaves of green velvet. We passed two little coffee plantations, the first of which was sadly neglected and overgrown with weeds, the second neatly kept. From this we rose again, and having gained the summit, looked down upon the village of San Juan Zautla.

Riding to the town-house, we met the *presidente* and *secretario*, the latter an intelligent fellow, who told us that the town was dwindling, numbering at present but 80 *contribuentes*. He ordered a capital dinner for us of chicken, fried bananas, eggs, *frijoles*, *tortillas* and coffee. Though the *secretario* was intelligent, the *presidente* was otherwise. He was good-natured, but a fool. With pride he frequently remarked, "*yo soy presidente*" (I am president). Then he whispered and mumbled, kissed my hand, assumed an air of great intelligence, and walked off with a peculiar tottering movement. These performances took place not once or twice, but every time the official made his appearance. Having fed us, the *secretario* disappeared, and did no more for us. While waiting for him, our attention was attracted by a curious drumming noise. It was due to women who were beating cotton. At the first house we visited we found three women all busily occupied. An old woman sitting in the doorway was spinning thread; a second, somewhat younger woman with a baby in a blanket on her back, sitting on the ground, was weaving cloth; a third woman sat, with a great cushion of moss in a bag of matting on the ground before her, over which was spread a deer-skin on which was laid raw cotton, which she briskly beat with beaters made of five or six divergent sticks fastened together at one end. Such beating sticks are called *mapaho*; one is held in each hand, and the beating is briskly done, alternately with one and the other; the beating is intended to spread the raw cotton into a thin and even sheet before it is spun into thread. Returning to the town-house, we began our work, but were soon interrupted. The town is situated on a slope over which the houses are scattered. From the porch of the municipal house where we sat, we could see several huts upon the slope above. Groups of women and children gathered on the little terraces before the houses to look down upon us at our work. The *presidente* and other officials had gone to bring us subjects, when we heard an outcry upon one of these terraces. A man cried out to the officials; struggled, apparently with a woman, then fell. The police rushed up the path. A moment later a surging crowd of a dozen persons were struggling together with cries and shouts. In spite of the commands of the *segundo secretario*, we started for the scene of the disturbance, but long before we reached the spot, met a big *topil* with his head cut open and blood streaming down his face, soaking his garments. His arm was thrown around another man's neck, whose wrist he held, dragging him thus a prisoner toward the jail. Two others followed, holding a bad-looking little man between them. The two had fought, and when the *topil* tried to take them, the little man, seizing a rock, split open his head. The two persons were thrust into the jail and a guard set. Great effort was made to find the stone with which the blow was dealt, in order that it might be used as evidence. The *secretario* told the *topil* not to staunch nor wash the wound. With natural curiosity, the *presidente* and other men were clustered around the jail, looking in at the prisoners, when the *segundo secretario* ordered them from the door.

This man is a strange one. He is a Cuicatec, who married a Chinatec wife. He is little, but important. He ever carries a queer old sword. When he first appeared before us, he impressively said, "*No tengas cuidado*" (Have no care.) He told us that our comfort and our orders should be cared for, even though we were in a pueblo of mere brutes, unreasoning beings; he should charge himself and the officials with our needs. There were scarce three hours of daylight in the afternoon, and night set in chilly and damp. Meantime, the *secretario*, the *segundo*, the *presidente* and the *topils*, all had disappeared. In vain we urged that arrangements should be made for fuel, for beds, and for a *mozo*, whom we had ordered should be supplied to accompany the man from Papalo back to that town with the horses. It was now dark and late, with no sign of attention to our wishes. Through the darkness, we picked our way over a muddy road, slippery and soaked with water, to the *secretario's* house, where we forcibly made known our wishes, and said that attention must be paid to them. Before we got back to the town-house our shoes were soaked with water and heavy with mud, while our clothing was soaked through with moisture from the air filled with mist and drizzling rain; and this in the midst of the dry season!

During the afternoon, we had seen a curious-looking

indian, dressed in a red flannel shirt, white drawers and a cap, but with the regular red Chinantec neck-cloth. He was a Mixtec from San Francisco Huitzo, who is in charge of the well-kept little coffee *finca* which we passed upon the road. He showed us a bottle of coffee essence of his manufacture. It was a heavy, oily, clear liquid which I understood he had distilled from a weaker and darker coffee extract. It was exceedingly strong, and was supposed to be used for making coffee, a small quantity of the essence being put into a cup with hot water and sugar. He desired us to test this, but a look at it was quite sufficient. He was a handy fellow, and did much to hasten the fulfillment of our orders. Under his direction, sleeping mats were brought, and he, himself, served our supper, when finally it was ready. We were so tired that directly after supper we laid down upon the mats spread on the damp earthen floor. We had hoped to start our man from Papalo back with our horses early; the officials had promised that the *mozo* to accompany him should be ready; but, of course, neither breakfast nor *mozo* was to be seen. So we again started for the *secretario's* house. The *secretario* himself was lying drunk in bed, and the *segundo* was almost as bad. In vigorous words I made known my dissatisfaction. The *segundo*, with his sword in one hand and *tortillas* in the other, almost too drunk to walk, led us to the town-house and summoned the people before him. He thundered forth his orders: "You dogs, children of a degraded race! Wretched brutes! What do you mean? Why are you not bringing in breakfast for these gentlemen? Eggs, *tortillas*, *frijoles*, chicken? Why are you not supplying them? Obey his order. Fulfill your duty. You hear? If you do not fulfill your duty, you shall be punished. Hear and obey at once." Under this impulse the men started and breakfast was soon disposed of.

Work being slack, the boys went bird-hunting. Manuel fetched in a *rara avis*, a little old man of 95 years, who had an extra thumb on his right hand. Notwithstanding the small population of the town, there were three cases of extra digits. In addition to this old man with his extra thumb, two persons in the town each had an extra toe upon one foot. We have already stated that the *presidente* of the village was a fool. He had plenty of companions. One of the men, who made himself quite useful to us was an imbecile; he crossed himself, kissed our hands, nodded his head, and told us the most surprising things in regard to the subjects whom he brought before us. In connection with each case he cried and carried on at a great rate, and finally insisted that he was going to bring me a raw egg as an offering of friendship, which he did. One of his subjects was his cousin, who was both idiotic and a deaf-mute. My impression was that there were several cases of deaf-mutism in the village. One man, whenever any of our party spoke to him, or in any way turned our attention to him, piously and vigorously crossed himself, grimaced and gesticulated as if in a fit. One man, who seemed cxceptionally intelligent, after he had seen us make a plaster bust of one of his townfellows, stated with great delight, that it was an idol, representing Jesus Christ, and that we were going to use it in the church. Unlike any other indian town we have visited, there is not even the pretence of an open school in this place. Nowhere else have women and children showed so great a fear of us and our work. From the moment that I showed an interest in the *mapaho*, the beating of cotton ceased, and the village was quiet. At no time during our stay did women or children come to the town-house. Shortly after sending back our horses to Papalo, we found that there were no animals for riding in San Juan Zautla. Fortunately, our next point, San Pedro, was but two leagues distant, and rather than wait until animals could be brought from Cuicatlan, we decided to walk. The night before we were to leave, we made arrangements for our carriers. The *secretario* had set the price at two *reales* a man; four were ordered, and an early hour set for the departure. When the time came, our men were in open rebellion. They refused to go upon the journey. We told the town officials that, if these men failed us, they themselves must do the work. The men were really scared, and stated that the people of San Pedro had threatened to kill us all, if we came to their town. In vain we argued — they were sure that the whole party were going to their doom. For such a paltry sum no man would risk his life. At last, however, the officials decreed obedience, and our party started. At first we led the company and the carriers came behind. The road led straight down the mountain-side to a brook, and then up the opposite side to the summit, just beyond which lay our goal. As we started, he who had recognized the bust of Jesus insisted upon accompanying us a way for friendship, and on the journey made various wise remarks regarding the busts. Hardly had we started when our men again rebelled; they would not make the journey for the price agreed upon, the risk was too great; they must be paid more, if they went at all. I felt that patience had ceased to be a virtue. Telling them that we would no longer go ahead, we ordered them to take up their burdens and precede us, at the same time threatening to shoot them, if they stopped without permission. After marching along in this new order for a time, they indicated a desire to parley. They would carry their burdens to the foot of the hill, where they would leave them by the brook-side. We could then go on to the village of San Pedro and send back carriers to bring them. To this proposition we gave no encouragement. The descent was abrupt. At the bottom was a fine brook, with a hanging bridge of vines swinging from tree to tree across it. Here we stopped to drink the fresh cool water, cut some sugar-canes, catch butterflies, and take views. One of the trees from which the vines hung was a perfect mass of ferns, orchids and bromelias of many kinds. On the great slope back of us, toward the gap through which the brook had broken, were great cliffs of massive rock; otherwise the whole mountain slope was a sheet of richest green. The ascent was long and difficult, and the party went slowly, with many rests. It was amusing, how, even at this distance, as we mounted the slope, we could hear the constant beating of the *mapaho* in the village behind us, as if in rejoicing at our departure. As we neared the summit, our carriers again made signals of a desire to converse. They would fulfill their whole duty, and would carry their burdens to the town-house in San Pedro, but would we have the kindness, from here on, to take the lead? Oh, yes, we answered, we would take the lead, and they should see that nothing would happen. No one would harm us; we were not about to die.

To make a favorable impression, we asked for a drink of water at the first house we came to, and passed a greeting with the few men, women and children whom we met on our way into town. The greater part of the population was at church, where we found a service in progress, and we were obliged to wait until it was over before we saw the town officials. I told the *secretario* to summon the town government to the municipal-house, which was a small affair, no more than 15 or 18 by 20 feet, with walls of lashed poles and a palm roof. A narrow bench ran around the four sides, and two tables, one long and one short one, set at right angles, occupied the greater portion of the open space. A long wide bench was placed alongside of the larger. At one end there was a *santo*, in a little shrine decorated with flowers and leaves. A little fire was built upon the floor, over which wax was melting, in which candles were being dipped.

The *secretario* chanced to be a man whom I had met at Cuicatlan the year before. He recalled our work, and taking us to his own house, we soon had an excellent dinner. He seemed to be well-to-do, and had two houses built of slabs lashed vertically together. Nets full of *jicaras*, great stacks of corn neatly laid out, good tableware in quantity, and a kerosene-lamp, all were evidences of his wealth. We ate at a good table, in the house, where the corn was stored. The most astonishing thing, however, in the house was an old-fashioned piano, long beyond use. How it was ever brought over the mountains to this village is a wonder. When we asked him, what we were to pay for the dinner, he replied, nothing; that we would begin to pay later. The impression made upon us by San Pedro was more agreeable than that produced by Zautla. The town government is large and vigorous, comprising a dozen well-built young fellows. On account of the church festival, plenty of subjects had been brought together. We did not understand what the *secretario* expected, and therefore took up our quarters at the town-house. We paid dearly for our misunderstanding. We waited long for supper, but none came. The *presidente* and the older men were at church. The *secretario* was nowhere to be found. While we were waiting, the young fellows who were making candles, and a crowd of boys, crouched about the fire and watched the work. Presently they lay down a couple of *serapes* on the floor, and the whole group, eighteen or twenty in number, dropped down upon them, a perfect mass of humanity, packed close together in the most curiously twisted attitudes, and were fast asleep in no time. They had no covering, but seemed to keep each

Chinantec Girl Spinning; San Juan Zautla

Chinantec Weaving; San Juan Zautla

other warm. After they were fast asleep, some of the other men appeared, and we urged the bringing in of supper. A handful of *tortillas* and two fried eggs were not a hearty meal for six hungry persons, nor were our sleeping accommodations satisfactory. With difficulty we got some mats, and I lay down upon the smaller table, Frank on the larger, Louis and Manuel rolled up on the ground below the latter, and Ramon and the *mozo* on the long bench. Half a dozen of the older men remained sitting about the fire. It can be understood that the room was fairly full. The men made no pretense of sleeping until past ten o'clock, and two or three times during the night they broke out into loud conversation.

Just outside the town-house, under a thatched shelter, a group of old women were cooking *atole* in great *ollas* until a late hour. This gruel they ladled out to those men and boys who had been working, and doled out to them drinks from black bottles. The men and boys, with their red head-cloths or neck-cloths, went forth from time to time in groups upon some public errand. Towards evening, eight or ten little fellows came from the forest with bundles of firewood upon their heads and great *machetes* hanging at their sides. In the morning, the same group of youngsters came in loaded with bunches of green leaves and holly to be used in decorating the church. At eight o'clock there was a procession in the churchyard; the saint, dressed in flowing garments, was carried about, accompanied by banners and a band of music. During the festival, everyone drank; even the little boys of eight or nine years, who brought in their loads of wood, received their spirits, which they drank like old topers. There was no evidence of bad temper as a result of this drinking, but an increasing stupidity. When, in the morning, we found our breakfast to consist of nothing but coffee, we realized our mistake of the night before, and promptly betook ourselves to the house of the *secretario*, where we spent the following day. The demands of the church during the day were so heavy that we did little work. The day itself was dark and dismal. In the late morning the boys brought in great loads of poinsettia, from which they fashioned brilliant rosettes and garlands for the church. At night, a wooden platform was brought in for a bed, upon which Louis, Manuel and I slept, while the others made a bed of broad boards upon the floor. Being behind with his developing, Louis set to work as soon as the lights were out, and kept at it until half-past-one. Scarcely had he come to bed and promptly fallen asleep, when there was a pounding at the door, which was almost immediately after broken in. Rising, I called out to see what was wanted, and four or five indians, all very drunk, came staggering in. The oldest of the party carried a great *machete*, and one of them closely hugged a bottle full of spirits. After begging pardon for disturbing us, they built a smoky fire, near the drying negatives. Fearing that their drunken movements and the smoke would work disaster, I made them change their place of rest and fire, moving them to the other end of the room. There they built another fire, and, before morning, they had consumed three bottles of spirits. What with the firelight and smoke, the noisy laughter, the loud talking and constant movement, it was impossible for me to sleep. Only for a single hour, when they fell back upon the floor in drunken slumber, and their fire burned down, did I get a bit of rest. It seems that they were an official guard put to watch the town store of grain which was kept in the building, and which was subject to the depredations of animals. During the following day we completed our work upon Chinantecs. The type is one of the best marked. In the child, the nose is wide, flat at the tip, with a straight or even concave bridge; the eyes are widely separated and often oblique; the mouth is large, the lips thick and the upper lip projects notably beyond the lower; the face is wide, and flat at the cheek-bones. With age, this type changes, the nose becomes aquiline, and of moderate breadth, the upper lip becomes less prominent, the skin lightens.

For two days more, days of darkness, rain and cold that penetrated to the marrow, we remained prisoners in the village, waiting for the horses for which we had sent the day of our arrival. It was impossible to make photographs, nor was it feasible to look around the town, or into the adjoining country. The *secretario*, indeed, showed us the way in which spirits are distilled from the sap of sugar-cane, and we had ample opportunity to examine the dress of the people and the mode of weaving. All the women dress in garments of home-woven cotton, and the red head-cloths, so characteristic a feature of the dress of men and boys, are woven here from thread already dyed, bought in other places. The little figures of animals or birds or geometrical designs worked in them in green or yellow worsted are woven in, at the time of making the cloths, with bright bits of wool.

At last our animals appeared. They had been sent from Papalo, and we made arrangements, as we supposed, for using them through to Cuicatlan. The animals arrived at 9:30 in the morning and the *mozo* with them reported that the roads were bad from the constant rains of the past several days. We decided to leave that afternoon, stopping at Zautla for the night, and then, making an early start, to push through in a single day. The *presidente*, *alcalde*, and other town officials accompanied us to the border of the village, where they bade us adieu, begging for a *real* for drink. As we left, the sky was clear and the mists were rising from the valleys. For the first time we gained some idea of the beauty of the country all around us. The houses of the town are well built, with walls of poles or narrow slabs neatly corded together in a vertical position. The roofs are thatched with palm; they pitch sharply from a central ridge and the ends pitch also from the ridge in independent slopes. The top is crested with a comb of thatch, neatly applied. Off to the right from the village lay a magnificent valley, with massive rock walls clad with green forest. The low masses of clouds and great banks of mist but emphasized the impression made by those parts of the scene that were visible. Soon we had passed the ridge and looked down again into the Zautla valley. The road was not as bad as we had anticipated. As we made our upward climb, we found that the flame-colored orchids, few when we last passed that way, were out in quantity. They are a terrestrial species, and the colors are a beautiful combination of flame-red with chrome-yellow. The other day only the outer and lower flowers of the racemes were blown, but on this occasion the whole cluster was in bloom. We noticed strikingly, what had before suggested itself to us, that through this district flowers of certain colors mass themselves together. Thus, on this slope, the hundreds of bunches of flame-colored orchids were rivalled by clusters of a tubular flower perhaps an inch in length, of almost the same hues. Along the glen-road near Tepanapa all sorts of flowers seemed to be pink or flesh-colored, while along the jungle-bank, near the coffee plantation, everything was blue or purple. When we reached Zautla, neither the *presidente*, the *secretario* nor the *segundo* was in town. The big *topil*, whose head was healing, did the honors of the place. We had intended to make an early start, but it was half past six before we mounted and were on our way. Going back over the old road, we soon reached the little coffee *finca* in charge of our Mixtec friend, and here we left the familiar trail, for what our guide insisted was a better one. We struck up and up and up the slope to avoid little ravines which he assured us were very bad. At last, when it was certain that he had completely lost his way, we started down into the forest. For a time we followed a bad and disused trail, but soon even this disappeared, and we tore our way through the tropical vegetation as best we could. Often the men had to cut the way with their *machetes*; sometimes we slid for yards over the wet mud; frequently our heads were caught by hanging vines, and faces and hands were scratched with brambles. When at last we came out upon a cleared space, we found ourselves at the Chinantec village of Santa Maria. Perhaps there were four houses in the village. Our appearance caused great excitement. Our pack-animals bade fair to destroy the maize and other plantings in the field. In the trail were oxen, which had to be gotten out of our way for fear of being driven to frenzy by our mere passing. They assured us that we were on the road to Tepanapa, so we completed the descent to the brooklet and started up a trail which at any time would have been steep, stony, slippery, all at once. We were compelled, finally, to dismount and lead our animals; Frank, before he did so, tumbled his horse three times down the bank. At one place two of the horses fell together in a struggling mass, and for a moment things looked serious. All the animals but my own fell, at least once, before we reached the summit. From there, it was an easy ride over a level district until we were in sight of Tepanapa, which, by sunlight, presented a most attractive appearance. The houses are spread over a gentle slope, to the very edge of a little *barranca*. Each had a little enclosure, with a group of banana plants. Butterflies of brilliant hues lazily flew about, and a few birds uttered their characteristic cries. We could not, however, delay.

Before us lay a tremendous ascent; the first part, which we had passed after dusk, we found rougher than we realized; rock masses here were covered with a thick cushion of brilliant crimson moss, a kind of sphagnum. The gully trail had not been improved by the recent rains, and it taxed our animals severely to reach the summit. Arrived in the district of the trees loaded with beards of golden-yellow moss, we caught a magnificent view back over the valley. With one sweep of the eyes, we could almost follow our whole round of wandering. The ridges on which lay San Juan Zautla and San Pedro Soochiapan both were in sight, as were the valleys in which Santa Maria and Tepanapa lay. But the only actual feature which we could see and recognize was the little coffee *finca* this side of Zautla. The combination of green mountains, blue ridges and bare rock cliffs was grand. Here our road forked, and at this point we had a moment's excitement. We met an old indian man with a baby tied upon his back, and his old wife, carrying a burden, followed after. Before them a black bull was calmly walking. The moment the old man saw us, he waved his arms and cried out, in great excitement, "*Toro, muy bravo!*" (Bull, very fierce!) and hastened forward to catch the lasso wound round the horns of the beast to lead him out of our way. Just then the bull took matters into his own control, and, with a snort and plunge, started wildly away, dragging the old fellow at a wild run down the trail, finally whirling him and the baby into a heap by the road-side, while he himself took up the mountain-side. It was after dark before we reached Papalo.

After much grumbling, supper was prepared and a solemn promise given that we should leave at seven in the morning. When we were ready, no animals were to be seen. The *presidente* asserted that the price which we had paid was only to that point, and that if we wanted animals for Cuicatlan we must make a new arrangement. This was sheer blackmail, because there had been no misunderstanding in the matter, and a liberal price had been paid. After wrangling for an hour, we shook the dust of Papalo literally from our feet, and started to walk to Cuicatlan, telling the town authorities that our burdens must be taken by *mozos* to the *cabecera* before three o'clock, and that we should pay nothing for the service. Probably we should not have been so ready to take this heroic action if we had not remembered that the road was down hill all the way, and good walking. Still, fifteen miles is fifteen miles, and the sun was hot, and though we left at 8:30, it was two o'clock before we entered Cuicatlan. We had no adventures by the way, except the killing of a coral snake which lay in the middle of the road. At three the *mozos* with their burdens arrived, and felt it very hard that we kept our promise of paying nothing for their service.

CHAPTER XVIII

TO COIXTLAHUACA

(1900)

FOR a day we rested at Cuicatlan to make arrangements for a trip to the land of the Chochos. We complained bitterly to the *jefe politico* regarding the miserable animals which had been supplied us for our last journey, and demanded something better.

Frank had had enough of practical anthropology, and left us, so there were but four to be provided. At eight o'clock the following morning, four decent horses and two pack animals were waiting at our door. A mounted *arriero* was in charge, to accompany us. Although he had been inefficient on the preceding journey, the same jail-bird was sent with us, as *mozo*, whom we had had before. At 8:30 our party of six persons started; passing the river, which we forded, an excellent road took us, for a league, over the sandy plain, which was fairly grown with trees, supplying a little shade. The great *pitahayas* were in bloom, and their white flowers looked well against the ugly, stiff green branches. The roadside was bordered with *acacias* which, in full bloom, presented masses of golden balls and perfumed the air with their delicate odor. Passing a considerable sugar *hacienda*, the trail struck into the mountains, and for three hours we made a steady ascent. The road itself was excellent but the sun beat down with fearful force, and the heat was reflected from the bare road and the rock cliffs along which we travelled. At one place the vegetation consisted of a curious mixture of gigantic cactuses, rising as single stalks as high as telegraph poles but larger in diameter, and palms. Arriving at the crest, we saw a long plain stretching before us, presenting a mingled growth of palms and pines. At the very border of the ridge stood a hut of poles, where we stopped to drink *tepache* and to eat broiled chicken which we had brought with us. We found the old woman, an indian — neither Cuicatec, Chinantec, Mixtec, nor Zapotec, as we might expect — but a full Aztec from Cordoba. She was bright and shrewd, and, as we chatted with her, we noticed a little chicken a few days old awkwardly running about with curiously deformed feet. Upon my noticing it, the old lady remarked that the moon made it so. I inquired what she meant. She said, "Yes, we know it is the moon which shapes the bodies of all young animals." We followed the road a long distance over the hot plain, passing San Pedro Jocotepec to our left, and shortly after, struck up the mountain side and had another long and steady climb, until, at last, we reached the crest of all the district. Here and there, we encountered bits of limestone, which always, in this southern country, makes the worst roads for travel. The rain erodes it into the oddest of forms, leaving projecting ridges almost as sharp as knife-edges, with irregular hollows pitting the surface, so that it forms a most insecure and unpleasant foot-hold for the animals. Not only so, but the surface, rough as it is, is frequently as polished as glass, and, whether wet or dry, is slippery to the tread. Walking over these jagged surfaces of limestone is destructive to any shoes. A single afternoon of this will do more wear than a month of ordinary use. Troublesome as these limestones are, as roads, they are ever interesting, because the masses by the roadside present the most astonishing and beautiful forms of waterwear; upon a mass eight or ten feet across, there will be worn a system of ridges and intervening channels, which, in miniature, seems to reproduce the orographic features of the whole country.

While we were passing over one of these limestone stretches, a little before reaching the summit, we found a spot of unusual difficulty. The two pack animals were together, one tied to the tail of the other; the second had several times acted badly, but in passing over this bit of road, he jumped and plunged, so that his pack loosened and slid to one side. Plunging, kicking, and falling, he dragged down the unfortunate beast to whose tail he was tied; the old rope tugged and creaked, and, for a moment, we expected to see the very tail of the forward animal pulled out, and both packs destroyed by the struggling beasts. Fortunately, at this moment, the rope itself broke. The forward animal was loosened and quickly quieted; but the other one kicked and struggled, with our load of plates and developing trays under him. Quickly cutting the ropes that held the burden, we tried to release the animal, but it lay exhausted, and, for a moment, we thought it dead. Really, however, it was not hurt at all, and the loads themselves appeared undamaged. The burdens having been repacked, we again started on the journey. At several places on this road, we had noticed cairns, or heaps of pebbles. On inquiring from Don Manuel — the funny little man, who had the animals in charge — we learned that every Chocho indian passing the place adds a pebble to the heap, to secure good luck and insure his safe return home. At the summit, we found one of these piles of stone surmounted by a cross, and learned that when the Chochos reach this spot, they always stop, repeat a prayer, and dance for good health and fortune before the cross. It was now almost dark. Soon we saw the downward slope, at the foot of which Huautla lay. We hastened down the slope, passing through a grove of oak trees, heavily loaded

Chinantec Women with Babies; San Juan Zautla

Cairn, on Road to Coixtlahuaca

with bromelias; at the foot of the slope, we crossed a stream of clearest water, bordered with handsome cypress trees, and passing several houses, came to the one where we planned to stop for the night. It was now dark. There was no opportunity for sleeping in the hut, and so we prepared to lie down outside. The people in the house prepared *tortillas* and beans, and, after eating, we rolled up in our blankets and lay down on some dried corn-husks on the ground. It was a night of suffering; the cold was so great that our blankets furnished no protection, and the place swarmed with fleas innumerable. At last, at four o'clock, two hours before sunrise, we started on our journey in the hope of getting warm. The air was damp and heavy, and, until the sun rose, we had a desolate journey. We were again upon a limestone district, with interesting features of scenery, and with few difficulties in the road. We passed many oblong hills of limestone, the horizontal layers of which upon the slopes present tiers of steps, one behind the other. These hills were astonishingly overgrown with trees, and formed masses of the darkest green. There was a great deal of subterranean water, and sink-holes produced by caving over such streams were frequent. The soil generally was a residual red or brownish clay. Flocks of gray pigeons were startled from their roosts by our passing; and little doves were plentiful; great hawks and small eagles were seen in pairs, hovering high in the air. We passed several little ranches, to one of which the name of El Zapato is given from a foot-print which is said to be painted on the rocks at that point. Finally, we saw before us the hill behind which, Don Manuel assured us, lay Coxitlahuaca. To mount and drop down behind it seemed a simple thing, but we had to traverse the whole length of the rather irregular ridge, which seemed interminable. The road which led up to it was called the Rio Blanca — white river — an appropriate name, as it was broad and deeply worn into the soft rock of which the ridge consisted. When we reached the crest, we found the ridge extending as a flat plain of light, buff-colored tufa, with many trails worn deeply into it, and giving out, under the bright sunshine, a frightful reflection of light and heat. Long before we reached the end of this dreary stretch, we saw Coixtlahuaca and its adjoining indian villages, Nativitas and San Cristobal. As we drew nearer, the view was striking. The town is broad, but of little depth; its streets are laid out with regularity; its great church, with masses of ruin on either side, is conspicuous; the *plaza* is large for the size of the town. To one side of it are the *portales* and the town-house and *jefatura.* To the right of the town and behind it is a large, walled cemetery with many gravestones. Back of all, rise hills of tufa, such as we had just traversed. The houses, similar to those at Huautla, and in the country between there and here, appear to be constructed with a view to cold. At least, two houses usually occur in one inclosure; the one, more important, corresponds to the god-house of the Aztecs and the other to the cook-house. The former is better built, and has low, carefully constructed walls, and a high abruptly four-pitched, heavily thatched roof. Going to the *jefatura*, the young clerk there was much impressed by the documents we presented, and asked us if we would accompany him to the *jefe's* house, as thus no time would be lost. Upon arriving at the house of the *jefe*, we found that a wedding was about to be celebrated in the church. The *jefe* received us with magnificent promises; we should room at the palace, arrangements should be made for boarding at a private house, beds and other proper furniture should be brought immediately, and the following day we should journey on horseback through all the indian towns of the vicinity. This was all very fine, but we told him that meantime we were hungry — we had eaten nothing since the night before and then had fared badly — and that we must unload our animals, which we had left with the rest of our company, standing in front of the palace. The unloading was done at once and we were given the school-house for our quarters, at the rear of the *patio* of the palace. At this moment, however, everything else was neglected for the wedding. This we all attended, and it was, indeed, an occasion. The bride in white, with veil and orange-blossoms, was accompanied by her mother, god-mother, and other female friends. She was really a pretty and wholesome indian girl, and the groom was a decent young *mestizo*, with gray wool sombrero, and linen jacket, cloth trousers, etc. He and his god-father were bustling about attending to all sorts of preliminaries. In the solemn procession which took place to the church, the company of ladies preceded; the *jefe* and myself led the line of male friends, and, when we filed into the church, the building was fairly filled. The special friends, including our party, moved in procession to the high altar, where the ceremony was performed. The bridal company knelt with candles in their hands. Other candles, some of enormous size, were burning in various parts of the church. The priest, with much ceremony, gave the sacrament of the communion to the couple, and then fastened two golden chains, crossing, about both their necks. A scarf of satin was placed upon them so as to cover both, passing over the head of the woman, and the shoulders of the man. From the church, our procession, dwindled to the particular friends and guests of honor, walked through the village to the justice-court, where the civil ceremony was performed. The matter having been accomplished with full respect to the requirements of the law, we thought again of dinner. The *jefe* told us that to-morrow we should go to our boarding-place, but that to-day we were to dine together in state. Time passed, hour after hour lagged by, until the *mozo* and *arriero* struck for money, with which to buy themselves something to eat. Meantime, we waited. Finally, at three o'clock in the afternoon, we were summoned, and the *jefe*, myself, and our companions, started down the hot, dusty, main street. On and on we walked, until, at last, the *jefe* himself impatiently demanded of our guide how far we had to go. At last, we heard the strains of music, and, shortly, found ourselves in a yard crowded with people, among whom two bands of music were present, one with stringed instruments and the other with brass. It was the house of the bride, and after a moment's waiting in the yard, we were ushered, by the *jefe's* clerk, into the building. It had been cleared of all its contents and a long table, set in the middle, ran lengthwise of the place. Benches were placed beside it. A line of vases, filled with bouquets, occupied the middle of the table and between these were bottles of wine, *catalan*, *mescal*, *pulque*, *tepache*, beer, etc. The ladies were already seated; we took the remaining seats. The company consisted of the bride and groom, their parents, godparents, families, and particular friends. And then, we had a dinner which amply compensated for the thirty-six hours through which we had been fasting — good bread, soup, stews, broiled meat, *mole*, *mole prieto*, chicken, beans, sweetmeats, coffee, with the beverages before mentioned. Dishes, when they came in, were politely passed across the table to the ladies opposite; no one ate till all were served, and when we were through, the place was cleared, and another room full of friends sat down to the bountiful repast. And then a third, and then a fourth, till everyone had feasted, even to the commonest, and the musicians, to whom abundance was carried after those invited in had eaten. Through

Coixtlahuaca

all this lengthy feasting the bands of music alternated with each other. When all had eaten, the women quickly cleared the house, the tables were moved, and all the chairs of the neighborhood were set stiffly around the walls, after which dancing began, continuing through the night.

After having eaten, we stepped outside to visit with the crowd. Among them, several drunken men showed special friendliness. One of these insisted upon showing us an idol, which, from his description, should have been a rather beautiful piece. It turned out to be a very crudely-made head, wrought in coarse, cellular lava. Considering the material, the work was really fine; nor was it a fragment broken from the body, as there had never been more than what we saw. From here, a yet more drunken *dulcero* insisted on our going to his *dulceria* and bake-shop, where he told us that he had a much finer piece. We found he really had an enormous head, made of coarse, but rather bright, red stone; it was another example of the same type of separate head, a type which must be characteristic of the district.

Nothwithstanding the fine promises, we found no beds or other furniture when we returned to our room. This was not, perhaps, surprising, in view of the excitement over the wedding, which might drive lesser matters out of the mind of the great official. With difficulty, we secured some mats from the chief of police, and made our beds with these upon the desks and benches of the school room. But, though we remained in Coixtlahuaca several days, no beds were forthcoming, though we referred to them often enough; nor did the private boarding-house materialize. We, however, found a little place in the village where we got plenty of good food cheaply. Nor did the ride on horseback through the neighboring villages, which had been so pleasantly suggested by the *jefe*, materialize. However, each day of our stay we were assured that all arrangements had been made for it to take place on the morrow.

We have already mentioned the *plaza* as large in proportion to the size of the town. On Sunday it was crowded, and while many things were bought and sold, the trade in *sombreros* surpassed all others. This is a specialty of all the district; throughout the Chocho towns, they make an excellent grade of palm-hats and everyone engages in the making. Both men and women braid palm, and in every yard there is excavated in the soft, tufaceous rock, a *cueva*, or cave, in which they work. Here the palm is left between times, and here two persons generally work together, each braiding at a hat, while a little cross, cut in the rock-wall, looks down upon the work, for good luck. These caves have a narrow opening upward and are scarcely large enough to admit the two persons who sit at their work. The object of the cave is to keep the work moist, as the plaiting cannot be well done, if the palm dries out.

The Monday we were there, the victory of February 5th was celebrated. The day began with music by the brass-band, from the roof of the *presidencia*. The band, a large one, consisted almost entirely of boys about fifteen years of age. Only the director and one among the players were men grown. At sunrise the national flag was raised, and at seven the church-bells were rung. Through the afternoon, games of ball and cock-fights furnished amusement. Among the crowd, at the house of the bride, we had met a little, stout man of about twenty-five or thirty years, who considered himself superior to the other people, and who variously attempted to make himself familiar. At several times during our measuring and bust-making, he had hung around, making smart remarks, but we had never invited him to submit to measure, as he did not seem to be a really full-blood indian. He had made a nuisance of himself, but, finally, one day, when he was standing in the crowd, which was looking on, he called my attention to a friend of his, remarking that here was a good subject. On calling this young man to be measured, we met with unexpected resistance. He was purely indian, short, well-dressed, and well-mannered, but he refused to be measured. We had had some little trouble with our subjects that afternoon, and therefore insisted that he should undergo the operation. He refused. Of course, the officials were on our side, and the police led him off to jail. When he saw that there was no escape, he consented to be measured, and they brought him back, under guard, until the operation was performed. So much feeling had been raised by the matter, that his foolish friend, to whose jocularity he owed the unpleasant experience, thought best himself to be measured. Accordingly measures were taken, although it was after dark, and a candle had to be used in reading. As our day's work was done, we returned to our room, making ready to go to supper. The crowd had departed. To our surprise, we found these foolish fellows at our door awaiting us. "Sir," they said, "we would speak with you a moment." Going aside with them, I asked their wishes. They then launched out, with weeping and groans and much wringing of hands, into a dreary tale. They were young teachers waiting for appointment; one of them had a little family; it would be a dreadful thing for them to be taken away and forced into the army. It was impossible to convince them that there was no harm in the matter. After long discussion and elaborate explanations, they cheered up somewhat, but insisted that I must go to the house of one of them, the one who had given trouble, to take *pulque.* We went, three abreast, each one of them taking one of my *brazitos queridos* — "beloved little arms;" as we went, they alternately indulged in admiring exclamations — "Ah,

Severo, what a *maestro!* how fine a gentleman! how amiable! Say Manuelito, was there ever such a one." At the house, which was neat and clean, I met the mother and two little ones, who would be left behind in case Severo were forced to go into the army. Then the *pulque* was brought in and sampled. As I was leaving to go to supper, they said, no, I must go to my room; they would accompany me. In vain I reminded them that my companions were waiting for me at the eating-place; I must be seen back to my very door, then I might go where I pleased; but with them I had gone forth, and until they saw me home again, they would be responsible for my person.

Coixtlahuaca itself is largely a *mestizo* town. But immediately in its neighborhood, and on its outskirts, are indian villages. All Chochos know Spanish, and but few talk their own language. There is little of interest in their life and nothing characteristic in their dress, which is that of *mestizos* in general. But the physical type is well defined. The stature is small; the face is short and broad; the nose is wide and flat, with a fat, flattened tip; the hair is somewhat inclined to curl, especially on top behind.

Despairing of the promised trip through the villages, we issued orders for our animals to be ready early one morning. Only after vigorous complaints and threats were they actually ready. The owner of the beast which I, myself, mounted went with us on foot, and a *mozo* was supplied for carrying instruments. In spite of fair promises that we would leave at three, it was 4:40 before we started, though we had risen at half-past-two. Our *arriero* was the best we ever had; far from sparing his good horse and grumbling at our speed, he was continually complaining at our slowness. "Why don't the boys want to go fast?" he would say. "Don't you want to get there at a good hour? Why do you go so slowly?" And then, striking the horse,

Chocho Houses; Coixtlahuaca

he trotted along at wonderful speed. We reached Huautla at half-past-eight, stopping an hour to feed our horses and to eat beans and *tortillas*. We then pushed on down the slope, and out over the long ridge, passing the hut of our Cordoban Aztec woman. It was the hottest hour of the day when we descended the broad road, over the hot rocks, and saw Cuicatlan in the distance. Thanks to our *arriero*, we drew up at Doña Serafina's when it was but 3:40 in the afternoon, having been upon the road eleven hours.

CHAPTER XIX

HUAUHTLA AND THE MAZATECS

(1900)

A SHORT ride upon the train, through the hot and dusty valley, brought us to the miserable station of San Antonio, from which, we had been assured, a coach ran daily to Teotitlan del Camino; arrived at the station, no stage was in sight, and we were told that it sometimes came and sometimes not. Accordingly, leaving my companions at the station in care of the baggage, I walked to the village, half a mile away, to see what arrangements could be made for transportation. It was hot, and it seemed difficult to arouse interest on the part of the town authorities. Neither conveyance nor animals were to be had. Accordingly, a foot messenger was sent to Teotitlan, which is a *cabecera*, asking that some arrangement be made for transporting us. As there was no hurry, and it would be some time before we could receive an answer, I sat under the thatched roof in front of the town-house, resting and enjoying the little breeze which had sprung up. Suddenly the belated coach, itself, came into sight, bound for the station. Starting to mount, the driver told me it was better for me to remain sitting comfortably in the shade, and that he would pick up my companions, of whom, I told him, there were three, and that I could join the company, as they passed. As arrangements had already been made regarding the transportation of the baggage by mules, the advice seemed good, and I remained where I was. A long time passed, and when, at last, the coach arrived, it contained but one passenger, a dignified *licenciado.* When I asked the driver where my companions were, he answered that they had refused to come because I had sent no written order to that effect. I suggested that we should turn back and get them, but to this proposition he gave refusal. Not only so, but the *licenciado* expressed vexation at the delay which he was suffering, and demanded that we should go on at once. Argument, persuasions, threats were all of no avail, and, as it was necessary that I should see the *jefe* at the earliest possible moment, I was forced to mount the coach and leave my unfortunate and obedient companions to their fate. For an hour and a half the coach lumbered slowly over a hot and dusty road, which passed between small, bare, gray or brown rock hills, rising to a higher level only a little before we reached Teotitlan itself.

Hastening to the *jefatura*, I discovered that the *jefe* had gone to Mexico, leaving the *presidente* of the town as his lieutenant. This man was neither willing, interested, nor efficient. He had little authority, even with his own policemen and townsmen. I requested that the first thing should be to send for my companions and bring them to town within the briefest time. Orders were sent by the policemen to the driver of the coach, that he should return at once to the station; to these orders, he sent the false reply that his coach had broken down, one wheel being completely ruined. After some wrangling and delay, the *presidente* sent a foot-messenger to San Antonio with orders to the authorities of that village to supply three animals for the travellers. The messenger left at five in the evening. Meantime, we arranged with difficulty for beasts for our further journey. Although we were assured that no animals from the town could accompany us further than the first *ranchito* in the mountains, named San Bernardino, they assured us that fresh animals could be obtained there for the remainder of the journey. Going to the regular hotel in the village, we found the prices higher than in Oaxaca or Puebla, and equal to those of a first-class hotel in Mexico itself. As the landlady seemed to have no disposition to do aught for us, we decided to look elsewhere. At a second so-called hotel we found a single bed. At this point, a bystander suggested that Don Pedro Barrios would probably supply us lodging; hastening to his house, I secured a capital room, opening by one door directly onto the main road, and by another, opposite, onto the large *patio* of his place. The room was large and clean, and four good cots were soon in place. Having ordered supper at a little eating-house, for four persons, to be ready at seven o'clock, I spent a little time in looking at relics found in the neighborhood. Pottery figures and heads are quite common and frequently painted brilliantly; small heads and ornaments of green-stone are not uncommon; curious clubs of stone for beating bark-paper aretalso found; objects of gold and silver have been found in ancient graves, near the foot of the mountains, on the outskirts of the village. These were of curious forms and excellent workmanship, and included large ornaments for the ears and pendants for the neck, made of thin sheets of gold; turtles and human skulls cast in a single piece; and most curious of all, odd pieces of filagree where the gold-wire was coiled into strange human heads. One of these was made half of gold and half of silver wire.

At seven, no sign of my companions had appeared. A policeman went to tell the keeper of the eating-house that we would eat at eight, and, putting my chair outside the open door, I sat in the cool air and watched the people passing in the moonlight. Eight o'clock came, and no companions. The supper hour was postponed to nine. Between nine and ten, Don Pedro and I talked over various

View of Huauhtla

matters, and at last, yielding to his solicitation, I went to supper, he promising to send my comrades in case they should arrive during my absence. I had just finished supper, at half-past ten, when my three hungry companions arrived, with big appetites for their own meals, and it was after eleven before the party was through its supper.

They, themselves, had by no means spent a dull afternoon. The station agent and his lady wife had indulged in a vigorous battle. Both were drunk, shot revolvers recklessly, bit one another, tore hair, and clubbed most vigorously. The man finally took $6,000 in money out of the company's safe and left the station, vowing that he would never be seen again. Though the authorities at San Antonio had received the order to supply animals at six o'clock, it was after nine before they had the beasts ready for the travellers.

After an excellent night's rest we started our pack-animals, and were ourselves ready for the journey at nine, when we found that no arrangements had been made for a foot *mozo* to carry our instruments. This again caused delay and trouble, but at last we were upon the road, and started out through the little village towards the mountains. My animal appeared a beast of vigor and spirit, and my hope ran high. The moment, however, that we struck the climb, matters changed. He then stopped every few yards, breathing as if it were his last gasp. This he kept up for the whole ascent, and there seemed doubt whether he would ever reach the summit. For a long distance, the road followed the side of a gorge in which a fine brook plunged and dashed. We passed and repassed picturesque groups of Mazatec indians with their burdens. The women wore *enaguas*, the lower part of which was brown, the upper white. Their *huipilis* are among the most striking we have seen, being made of native cotton, decorated with elaborate embroidered patterns of large size, in pink or red. The favorite design is the eagle. Men wore *cotones* of black or dark blue wool. We had been riding steadily for two hours before we reached San Bernardino, where the *mozos* and pack animals were changed, and where we rested for a few minutes. We then rode for a long time, gently ascending through forests of pine or oak. Here and there the air-plants on the oak trees were notable. Finally, we mounted to a road along a narrow ridge, like a knife's edge, and from here on had one of the most remarkable roads that I have ever travelled. Keeping continuously upon the crest, we had upon the one side the dry slope, with the pine forest, and on the other the damp slope, densely grown with low oaks, heavily clad with orchids and bromelias and weighted with great bunches of gray moss. The road passed up and down gentle and abrupt slopes separated by level spaces. When we first caught sight of Huauhtla it looked so near, and the road to be traversed was so plain, that we expected to reach the town before three o'clock; but the trail proved drearily long. True, the scenery was magnificent. The great mass of mountains; curious ridges extending out from their flanks; the multitude of horizontal, parallel long roads following these; the little towns, San Geronimo, San Lucas — all were attractive. From the great slope opposite Huauhtla, the view of the town was most impressive. Before us opened a narrow valley, the depth of which we only realized after we had traversed it. An hour and a half was necessary for making the descent and the up-climb. From the point whence we were looking, the church, town-house, and clustered houses of the village were above us. Below stretched a line of *nublina*, and beneath it the whole great mountain flank was checkered with the irregular brown and green fields belonging to the villagers. It was already five o'clock when we began the descent from

Mazatec Houses; Huauhtla

this fine view-point, and, on our way down the slope and up the opposite slope to the village, we met great numbers of drunken indians,—as it was Sunday,—usually a man and woman together. Two of the men we met had been fighting, and were covered with blood; the face of one of them was livid with the blows which he had received. Many of the parties were noisy and quarrelsome, and some of them showed a tendency to meddle with us, as we passed.

The greater portion of the journey had been over fine, dry roads; after we reached the knife-edge ridge, however, whenever there was a descent or ascent, we found the road of clay, moist and slippery; in the rainy season these bits would be bad enough. At this time of year they are due to the *nublina*, great masses of which we saw from the time we reached the crest-road, and, at times, we passed through great sheets of it which cut off all view and which soaked our clothing. Upon our last descent and ascent, we were almost discouraged, and the last half-hour of our journey was made by the light of the moon, struggling through *nublina*. Though it was dark, when we reached the village, we were impressed with the fineness of the municipal-house, the best constructed we have seen in an indian town. Its location, near the edge of the mountain slope, giving a magnificent outlook over the great valley, is very fine. The houses of the Mazatecs are picturesque. The walls are built of mud, or slabs or posts daubed with mud, while the roofs are thatched with palm. The ridge pole extends, at both ends, in projections which themselves are thatched, forming curious and striking horns. This same mode of thatch, picturesque in the extreme, is also used above the little granaries which are raised, on poles, several feet above the ground, in order to keep the contents from the attacks of animals. Huauhtla is a large town. The village and its immediate dependencies have a population of 7000. Until lately the town was jealous of visits from outside, and little inclined to hospitality towards travellers. If this were formerly true, it has ceased to be so. We were received most heartily; the large and enthusiastic town government, after learning our errand, expressed their willingness to aid us in every way. They at once cleared a fine large room in the town-house for our occupancy, prepared four beds of boards covered with *petates*, and brought from the priest's house, hard by, blankets, sheets, and pillows for my own use. Arrangements were also made for our eating with the priest, Padre Manzano, with whom we fared in truly regal fashion. In the days we stayed at Huauhtla, there were no delays in our work and everything went in orderly fashion. It is true, our subjects for busts were an awkward and trying lot. The first subject broke the back-piece of the mould to fragments, and, when the plaster was being applied to his face, he opened his mouth and talked, opened his eyes, and drew out his nose-tubes, with the result that eyes, nose and mouth were all filled with the soft mixture, and it was all that we could do to clean him without damage. As for trying to take his bust again, that was quite out of the question. The second subject was all right, until the last application had been made, when he turned in the partly hardened mould with truly disastrous results. The third one acted so awkwardly. that a piece of mould, which should have come off singly, was taken off in ten fragments.

The dress of the Mazatec women is elaborate and striking, both *enagua* and *huipil* being made from the cotton woven by themselves. At the base of the *enagua* is a broad and heavy band of wool, embroidered in geometrical patterns, the color being cochineal. Above these bands, there are embroideries in the same colored wool, animal and human figures, and geometrical designs. Un-

Mazatec Women; Huauhtla

Heavy Braids; Mazatec Women; Huauhtla

fortunately, cochineal, while brilliant, is by no means permanent, a single washing of the garment spreading the color through the white texture. The *huipilis* are ornamented frequently with red, purple and crimson ribbons, bought in stores in the town, which are sewed to the garment in such a fashion as to divide it into rectangular spaces. These, in turn, are occupied with the elaborate large patterns in pink representing the eagle and other designs already described. It is uncommon among Mexican indians to find a native use of silk. Here, however, silk-worms are reared and carry-cloths, kerchiefs and belts are woven from their product. These are worn by both men and women. The mode of wearing the hair among the Mazatec women is in two broad, flat braids hanging down the back. The women made no demur whatever to being measured, but everyone, who presented herself for the operation, came dressed in her best clothing, with her hair elaborately braided, and showed serious disappointment and dissatisfaction if not invited to be photographed.

The town has a most curious reputation, as devoted to commerce, and not to manual labor. In fact, it is considered disgraceful for a man of Huauhtla to indulge in work. The people of San Lucas, the nearest town, and a dependency, are, on the other hand, notably industrious, and it is they who carry burdens and do menial work for the lordly Huauhtla people. Mrs. de Butrie told us that she tried in vain to get a cook in the village. The woman was satisfied to cook and found no fault with the wages offered, but refused the job because it involved the carrying of water, and she feared lest she might be seen at such ignoble labor. Mr. de Butrie a while ago bought a set of shelves from a man who had them in his house. As they were dirty, he suggested that they must be cleaned before he would receive them. The seller said, very well, he would send for a man of San Lucas to clean them. It was only lately that they condescended to carry stuff to Teotitlan to sell. In the town-house they cherish two much-prized possessions, the *titulo* and *mapa* of the town. The former is the grant made by the Spanish government to this village, in the year 1763. It is an excellently preserved document in parchment and the old writing is but little faded. As for the *mapa*, it is a strip of native, coarse cotton cloth, seven feet by three feet nine inches in size, with a landscape map of the surrounding country painted upon it in red, yellow, black and brown. It is a quaint piece of painting, with mountains valleys, streams, caves, trees, houses, churches and villages represented on it with fair exactness. It was probably painted at the same time that the *titulo* was given to the village.

The morning after our arrival, we witnessed a quadruple indian wedding in the church at seven. The brides were magnificent in the brilliant *huipilis*, and the godmothers were almost as much so, with their fine embroideries. The ceremony was much like that at Coixtlahuaca, already described. The bride put a silver ring upon the groom's finger, and he did the same by her; the priest put money into the man's hands, he transferred this to the woman, and she to the priest; single chains were hung about the neck of each of the party, both men and women; the covering sheet or scarf was stretched over all four couples at once, covering the heads of the women and the shoulders of the men.

Near the town-house, along the main street, is a series of sheds or shacks used as shops, altogether numerically disproportionate to the population. Great was our surprise to find that one of these was kept by a Frenchman, who spoke excellent English, and who is married to an English lady. They were the only white people living in this great indian

Mazatec Carriers from San Lucas

Mazatec Laborers from San Lucas

town. Monsieur de Butrie has a coffee plantation in the valley a few miles away, at Chichotla, but he finds the climate bad for himself and lady. Accordingly, they had moved up onto the high land, and it is easy for him, when he must give attention to his *finca*, to go to it for the necessary time. They have some pretty children and are doing well. We called at their house, quite like the others of the town, and were hospitably received with chocolate and sweet English cakes. During our stay, this gentleman and his wife did their utmost for our comfort, and gave us many interesting bits of information regarding the people, their customs and their superstitions. We have elsewhere described in detail their witchcraft practices, their belief in transformation into tigers, and their ideas regarding the destiny and condition of persons after death.

Just across the way from the town-house, was a large house of the usual fashion, which we quickly learned was the rendezvous and practice-place of the town band. This consisted entirely of boys, none of them more than twenty years of age, and numbered upwards of thirty pieces. The leader was a man of forty, a capital trainer. The daily practice began at 4:30 in the morning, and was kept up until noon; then ensued an hour's rest. At one, they were again practicing, and no break occurred until long after dark. During the days that we were there, a single piece only was being practiced. It was our alarm clock in the morning, beat time for our work throughout the day, and lulled us to sleep when we retired for the night. Señor de Butrie insists that during the year and more than he has lived in the village, several boys have blown themselves, through consumption, into early graves. Our pleasant stay at Huauhtla came to an equally pleasant termination. Having stated the number of animals and human carriers necessary, and the hour at which we wished to start, we found every preparation made on awaking in the morning, and at 6:25, after an excellent breakfast with Padre Manzano, we sallied forth. Six human carriers bore our busts and baggage, and four capital horses carried us rapidly over the good road. It was a magnificent morning, but later in the day, as the sun rose, it became hot. We arrived at three in the afternoon with our carriers close behind. The following morning we forgave the crabbed *cochero* at Teotitlan sufficiently to take his stage coach for San Antonio, where we arrived in fifty minutes, having two hours to wait before the north-bound train took us towards Puebla.

The Band; Mazatec Boys at Huauhtla

CHAPTER XX

TEPEHUAS AND TOTONACS

(1900)

LEAVING Puebla on the early morning train, and taking the Pachuca branch at Ometusco, we changed cars at Tepa onto the narrow-guage Hidalgo road for Tulancingo, which took us by a winding course through a great *maguey* country. After two hours of riding, in the latter part of which we were within sight of a pretty lakelet, we reached Tulancingo. Broad avenues, bordered with handsome trees, connected the station with the town, in the *plaza* of which we shortly found ourselves. This *plaza* consists of a large square, planted with trees, with an open space before it, and is surrounded by various shops and the great church. It is pretentious, but desolate. In front of the treed space, were temporary booths erected for the carnival, in which *dulces*, *aguas frescas*, and *cascarones* were offered for sale. Hawkers on the streets were selling *cascarones*, some of which were quite elaborate. The simplest were egg-shells, dyed and stained in brilliant colors, and filled with bits of cut paper; these were broken upon the heads of persons as they passed, setting loose the bits of paper which became entangled in the hair and scattered over the clothing. Some had, pasted over the open ends, little conical caps of colored tissue-paper. Others consisted of a lyre-shaped frame, with an egg-shell in the center of the open part. Some had white birds, single or in pairs, hovering over the upper end. The carnival was on in full force, and we saw frequent bands of maskers.

They went in companies of a dozen or so, dressed like clowns, with their clothing spotted and striped with red. Their faces were concealed by cloth. They walked rapidly, almost ran, through the streets. They spoke to no one, and did nothing except to keep up a loud and constant trilling of the most ridiculous kind. Packs of youngsters chased behind and crowded upon them; they also pelted them with stones, and the head of one of the maskers was bleeding quite profusely, but he still kept up his headlong run and trilling. We had counted upon the assistance of the *jefe*, but found him too dignified to receive us outside of office hours, and therefore we arranged the matter of our transportation to Huachinango. The price was high, the coach inconvenient, and the *cochero* unaccommodating. In vain we tried to have all of our plaster taken in the load with us; only one-half could go, the balance must follow the succeeding day. Finally, at about ten in the morning, we lumbered heavily away, and were soon out of the town, passing through a brown, hilly district, at first devoted to *pulque* plantations, but further along becoming fine pasture-land. Neat fields, separated by bands of yellow, unplowed stubble, and true farm-houses of good size, were striking features. We passed through quantities of pine groves, and everywhere a cold wind blew strongly in our faces. At one place, we were obliged to dismount and walk, on account of the sharp descent, and found ourselves upon an ugly piece of limestone or sandstone rock, which soon, to our surprise, we found replaced by a solid mass of obsidian. The *cochero*, says that the place is known as *itzlis* — the obsidians, the knives. It was 2:30 when we reached Aguazotepec, where we called upon the *presidente*, and engaged a *mozo*, for a *peso*, to convey our instruments the balance of the journey, as we were completely tired out with carrying them upon our knees. We also arranged with that official to forward the balance of our stuff to Huachinango the following day. We also arranged to pay for horses from Aguazotepec to Huachinango. Having eaten an excellent dinner, when ready for resuming our journey, we discovered, with surprise, that the stage was still our conveyance to Venta Colorado, only a league from Huachinango. There we were to secure the animals for which we had paid, though we were warned that only three could be supplied. Manuel and Louis at once tossed coins to see which should ride first. Although we had paid the full cost of the coach, two other passengers were crowded in upon us, and the man, for whom we had paid the *peso* to carry our instruments, ran alongside the coach on foot, throwing stones at the mules, while we had again the pleasure of carrying the instruments and boxes on our knees. The country through which we rode was much as before. For some time we passed through a fine pine forest; then we made a deep descent into a valley, at the bottom of which flowed a large stream, which was bridged by a grand old structure of stone and cement. This descent, and the opposite ascent, we were obliged to make on foot, as the approaches were bad. We have been impressed strongly with the fact that everywhere in Mexico the worst bits of road are those which, in old Spanish days, were handsomely and well paved; and which, during the disturbed period of the early Republic, were neglected and allowed to go to decay. It is depressing to see so many evidences of past magnificence and present poverty. It was almost dusk when, after skirting the edge of a deep gorge, we reached a piece of bad road, where the coach with difficulty made its way, with frightful jolts and pitchings, till we drew up at Venta Colorado. Here the coach was finally abandoned. Our animals were packed and mounted, and after fussing and quarreling with our ugly *cochero* as to whether he or we should carry the bulk of our baggage, we started. The distance was not great. It was down hill, and we had to pick our way with great care over the rough road, filled with loosened and separated blocks of ancient paving.

This district, in one respect, reminded us of the Tarascan country. Every house along the road was a salesplace, where drinks, cigarettes, fruit and bread were offered, and each had the little boarded window, open when sales were solicited, and closed when business stopped. The houses, too, were log structures with shingled four-pitched roofs, and the houses in the town were well built, cement-walled, with low-sloped, far projecting tile roofs supported on trimmed beams. One might as well have been in Patzcuaro, Uruapan, or Chilchota. Again the *cochero*; we had told him that the stuff should go to the *jefatura*, and not to the hotel; he told us with great insolence that the *jefatura* was closed, and that it would be impossible to see the *jefe* and that the stuff would remain at the hotel; he followed us, when we went to the *jefe's* house, and great was his surprise when he found our order efficacious. We had a long talk with the *jefe*, who told us that few indians lived in the town, and that none of them were Totonacs; he assured us that, though there were no Totonacs in Huachinango, we could find them in abundance at Pahuatlan, to which he recommended us to go. The nearest indian town to Huachinango is Chiconcuauhtla, but it is Aztec. The next day was spent in town, waiting for our other baggage, and for the *jefe* to arrange our orders and lay out our journey. My day of fever was on, and I spent it mostly in bed. There were many indians in the market, most of whom were Aztecs, though a few were Otomis. The men wore dark brown or black *cotones*; the *enaguas* of the women were wool and were dark blue or black. Many carried on their shoulders carry-pouches, consisting of two rectangular frames of sticks, corded together along the lower side, and kept from opening too widely, above, by a net of cords at the ends. The indians of Chiconcuauhtla are easily recognized by their little flat, round caps. Late in the afternoon the bands of maskers, here called the *huehuetes*, were out. There were a dozen of them, dressed in absurd costumes; a bewhiskered Englishman in loud clothing, a gentleman, a clown, a lady, etc. These all went, by twos, on horseback; a clown and a devil and a boy with a prod, on foot, accompanied them. The duty of the latter, who remotely resembied death, was to prod the unhappy devil. They were accompanied by noisy crowds the several times they made the rounds of the town, keeping up the peculiar trilling, which we had noticed at Tulancingo. At dusk, these maskers dismounted and promenaded in couples about the *plaza*.

Nowhere, as in this region, have we had so much difficulty with regard to animals. The demands were so exorbitant that we insisted upon the *jefe* making the arrangements. He received us in anything but a pleasant mood, but acceded, and finally we secured four horses and four mules, for which we were to pay for two full days, and a foot *mozo* to whom we also were to pay two full days' wages. As the *jefe* himself had made this arrangement, we consented to it, but the man who was outfitting us then demanded pay for the *mozo* who went to bring back the horses and for the fodder of the animals. At this, even the *jefe* balked, declaring that he was not in favor of really robbing the gentlemen. Paying him the seventeen dollars and twenty-five cents, in order that there might be no further discussion, we started. Just as we left, the man who supplied the animals decided that our loads, which before had been so large, were really not too large for three mules, which number was actually sent with us, though we had paid for four. We were ready for starting at seven, but it was ten before we left. Meantime, clouds had gathered, and just as we started, rain began. There were first several separate showers, and then a steady downpour, which lasted almost till we reached Pahuatlan. All the blankets had been packed away, and we rode through the rain until our clothes were drenched through and through. For three hours this continued, and it was impossible to see anything of the country through which we passed. Finally, however, as we reached a great crest, and looked down into the valley beyond, the sky was clear and we could see something of the scene about us. The descent we were to make, and the slope in front, were covered with sugar-cane, broken here and there by great patches of pineapples. With each plantation of sugar-cane there was a little shelter of poles under which was a sap-trough or boiling-tank, while at the side of and behind the shelter was a rude mill, the power for which was furnished by a yoke of oxen. Boys fed the fresh cane between the crushing rollers, and the sap, as it ran out, was carried in little troughs to vats. Not at all these little shelters was sugar-making in progress, as we passed, but over both slopes many columns of smoke indicated places where the work was going on. The fire in the vat kept the sap boiling, and a man standing near with a great ladle, pierced with holes, kept dipping up and pouring out the hot sap. When we started up the great ascent we had no hint of Pahuatlan, and, when we reached the summit, could see nothing of it. But hardly had we begun the descent before we saw the large and handsome town below, but still with a long slope and a sharp ascent to be passed, before we could reach it. From the brookside, at the bottom of the valley, almost to the village itself, we passed through a dense growth of bananas, which seemed to have suffered some damage, as many were dry and yellow, and individual leaves were curiously tattered and jagged. Among them grew other plants, coffee, orange-trees, peaches, and cane. When we reached the town, my heart sank; a church with handsome dome and modern tower, a planted *plaza* with central fountain, buildings, of two stories with gaudy fronts and *portales*, surrounding three sides of the square, augured better for comfort while we were in the place, than for work on Totonacs. We rode up to the *municipio*, where we found the *presidente*, a rather stylish young fellow, who was interested in our work and helpful. The town controls fourteen thousand persons, and its name is derived from that of a large *ahuacate*, the Aztec name of which is *pahuatl*. The *presidente* assured us that there was no Totonac town, properly speaking, within the limits of the *municipio*. For all this district, Orozco y Berra makes many errors. Atla, which he lists as Totonac, is really Aztec. The *presidente*, upon a local map, showed us the interesting way in which natural barriers limit idioms. Two little streams, coming together at an acute angle, may divide three languages — one being spoken in the angle and one on either side. In Tlaxco, a small village in this *municipio*, four idioms are spoken — Aztec, Otomi, Totonac and Tepehua.

Two years before, just as my work was ending, we were in the great Otomi town of Huixquilucan, in the state of Mexico. While resting at midday, I noticed a neatly-dressed and clean young indian, plainly not Otomi, with whom I conversed. He was an Aztec, and much interested in the work we were doing. In our conversation, he told me that I would find much of interest in the state of Hidalgo, and particularly called my attention to the making of paper from bark, which he had observed in the town of San Gregorio, two years before. This particularly interested me, and I then made notes regarding the method of getting to San Gregorio. I was advised by him, in case of going to that place, to talk with Don Pablo Leyra, of Huehuetla, who was himself an indian and a man of consequence in the district — a sort of *cacique* among his people. Several years ago, I had first learned from Señor Eurosa, a Mexican Protestant clergyman, that in the little town of Tlacuilotepec, there still survive interesting pagan practices. In planning our present journey, I had arranged to visit San Gregorio and Tlacuilotepec for the purpose of investigating this manufacture of paper and these pagan customs. Inquiring of the *presidente* of Pahuatlan about his indians, I asked regarding paper-beating, and discovered that it was done at the nearest indian village of San Pablito, Otomi. We were told that bark of several species of trees was used — *jonote*, dragon, and mulberry; that the paper is usually made secretly and in-doors; that the passing traveller can hear the sound of light and rapid pounding as he passes through the village; that it is made in every house, and the proper season is when the sap runs, April to June; San Pablito is the only village in the *municipio* where it is made. It is used in *brujeria* (witchcraft); other paper can be bought much cheaper, but only this kind is serviceable. It is cut into *muñecos*; representing human beings and horses and other animals, and these are used to work injury to human beings and beasts, being buried in front of the house or in the *corral*. The judge, who was sitting by, told us that a prisoner brought before him for trial was found to carry such a paper figure, which was sewed through the body with thread and had its lips sewed also; he learned that this figure represented himself, and that the lips were sewed to prevent him from pronouncing judgment on the prisoner. They assured me that the nearest point for finding Totonacs or Tepehuas, in sufficient numbers for my purpose, was in the district of Tenango del Doria, where, at Huehuetla, we would find the largest Tepehua town, and that in Pantepec, which is in the district of Hauchinango, and near Huehuetla, we would find Totonacs. We had had such ill success in locating Totonacs so far, that, at our suggestion, they telephoned to the *jefe* at Tenango inquiring regarding the populations of Huehuetla and Pantepec, with the result that we decided to visit those towns.

At Tulancingo, we had been snubbed by the *jefe*, who would not treat with us outside of office hours. When the *presidente* of Pahuatlan took us to the house where arrangements had been made for our accommodation, we found a garrulous, simple-minded, individual who was set to clear our room and make our beds. To myself, as leader of the company, he was attentive and ceremonious in the highest degree, and on several occasions he took my companions to task for their ignorance regarding the proper deference to display toward me. He inquired whether we were acquainted with Señor Arroyo, *jefe politico* of Tulancingo, and then informed us, with pride that that gentleman was his "Señor Padre." "If so, Señors, you may well ask why you see me thus dressed in *calzoncillos*. For two reasons: first, I am not a legitimate son, no, Señors, my lady mother, who bore me was an Otomi indian, but I am the acknowledged illegitimate son of my honored Señor Padre. Second, I had the misfortune to be involved in trouble in the district of Del Doria, which forced me to flee from that district to escape the *jefe*. But, sir, my Señor Padre said to me, 'son, I am the *jefe politico* of Tulancingo and the governor of the State is Pedro L. Rodriguez; I am his intimate friend, and we shall succeed in ousting that *jefe* in Tenango del Doria who has ordered your arrest.'" He also told us of one time, when his Señor Padre and an inspector visited that unfortunate district as an investigating committee, and found the *jefe* guilty and put him in jail *incomunicado*. He also told us of the band of Pahuatlan, justly famous, which made so great an impression in one town it visited, that it determined to go to Tulancingo to serenade the *jefe* of that district, his honored Señor Padre. "And I was invited, sir, not that I am a musician or know one note from another, but because I am of the family of the gentleman who was to be honored, and as a mark of distinguished favor to both members of the family. The band played so beautifully, that it was not allowed to stop until half-past-eleven at night, when it retired in great triumph." All this was very interesting, the first time it was told us, but the natural son remained while we ate supper, and afterwards, following us to our sleeping-room, kept up the repetition until two were already in bed and asleep and the others wished to be, when, finally, we turned him out and locked the door upon him for the night. We have stated that we paid for four animals to bring our baggage hither, while but three were actually employed; the animals, both pack and passenger, started on their journey for Huachinango at half-past-four in the afternoon, though we had paid both beast and man two full days' wages.

Tlacuilotepec is a dependency of Pahuatlan. We started for our day's trip thither on a good lot of animals, at eight o'clock in the morning, with two foot *mozos* for carriers. The journey was delightful. For a little, we followed a trail down the left-hand bank of a fine ravine. Nearly at the foot we struck to the left, through a little cut, and were surprised to find ourselves upon the right-hand slope of another gulf of immense depth. A few minutes later, we reached the point where the two streams united. And from there on, for a long time, we followed the bottom of a great gorge. The rock walls were bold and often sheer, and the upper line of mountain horizon was graceful and

The Hope of Indian Mexico; Huauhtla

Totonac Mothers with Babies; Pantecep

varied. The cliffs were mostly limestone, and presented remarkable examples of folding and dislocation. The long roots of trees, following exposed rock surfaces downward for yards, and twisting and bending to find lodgment in the crevices, were curious. Great tufts of a plant with long, narrow, light-green leaves hung down along vertical rock faces. In little caverns, at the foot of cliffs, were damp spots filled with ferns and broad-leaved caladiums, and brilliant clusters of begonias in bloom. At several places, the water of springs or underground streams gushed forth, in natural rock-basins, or from under projecting ledges. At one spot, there was a dainty basin of limestone into which a pretty veil of spring water fell gracefully. We crossed and recrossed the stream many times. Everywhere we were within sound of the creaking sugar-mills, and in sight of the ladling of boiled sap; everywhere we met *arrieros* driving animals loaded with little loaves of native sugar; everywhere the forest was broken with little patches of sugar-cane, growing on the slopes. Here and there, we saw cables slung across the streams, for passing cargoes at high water. At one place was a fine display of basaltic columns, the position of which was horizontal, the flow having come up as a sheet injected from below, and not as a surface out-flow, where the jointage would have been vertical. Finally, leaving this beautiful ravine, we made a rapid ascent, passing a little village consisting almost wholly of a school, noisy with study, and a church, with a separate square tower. Shortly after reaching the summit, and dipping slightly, we found Tlacuilotepec. It is not a large town. At its center *mestizo*, it has charge of several indian villages. We had been referred for information concerning surviving paganism to a Señor Martinez. We were interested in finding that the *presidente* of the town was a brother of this gentleman, and that both were Protestants.

We were received with great cordiality, not only on account of our official introduction, but also because we brought an unofficial introduction from Protestant friends. Two charming beds were arranged in the little meeting-place in Señor Martinez's own house, and two others, almost as good, were secured for the others of the party, in the little *meson* of the village. As we chatted, we were refreshed with a delicious orange-wine, which is made here, and during our days spent with Don Quirino, we had meals fit for a king. The indians under his charge are Otomis, and in one little village, Santa Maria, Totonac. When we came to inquire regarding the pagan practice for which we were searching, we learned that it was peculiar to the Otomis, and formed their annual *costumbre* — custom. They believe that Montezuma is to come again. Meantime, from him come health, crops, and all good things. Their *costumbre* is a feast given in his honor, of which he is believed to partake. A *jacal* — hut — is prepared in a retired spot; a table is constructed full length of the house within, and upon this a feast is spread of which all partake.

Upon this table they place many *muñecos* of paper; formerly these were made of the bark paper, but they are now made of ordinary paper bought in the stores. There may be so many of these that they cover the table an inch or two thick. The feasters shove money, usually small pieces of silver, beneath these figures. They then kill turkeys and hens and chickens, and sprinkle the blood from the headless bodies over the *muñecos*. This they do that Montezuma may be propititated, and give them what they desire; the money and the *muñecos*, sprinkled with blood, are left upon the table after the feast, the former being stolen by passing *mestizos*.

The *presidente* stated that, at the *pueblito* of Santa Maria, where we should go upon the morrow to see some Totonacs, they had just celebrated their annual *costumbre*. He said that it might be somewhat similar, as they had sent him a headless turkey, as a gift. In the morning, we visited this village accompanied by the two brothers. A half hour's ride brought us to the spot, from which one gets one of the most lovely views in all this picturesque country. Standing on the end of a little spur upon which the village lies, one sees the handsome river below, which separates this *municipio* from that of Villa Juarez. To the left, rise magnificent mountains covered with brilliant green vegetation, broken here and there by bare rock faces, from the base of which gentle slopes, extending down to the river, are covered with little corn-fields. Cuauhtepec, a Totonac pueblo, where all are said to dress in white, lies upon this stream, and immediately back from it the cultivated fields of the village stretch up to the very crest. To the right, is seen the little ranch Tanchitla, with its fields, a strip of green forest separating these from the fields of the next village, Tlapajualla. The stream abounds in fish of various kinds, which form an important food supply. They are, however, rapidly being destroyed by the practice of exploding dynamite cartridges in the water, by which not only the adult fish, but the young, of all ages, are killed. Unless the practice soon ceases, and there are rigid laws against it, there will soon be no fish left in any of the streams of this whole region. This particular stream bears different names in different portions of its course — thus it is called Tanchitla, Pahuatlan, San Marcos, Caxones, Xico, etc.

Having noticed that here, as at Pahuatlan, the banana trees were badly injured, we learned that this havoc was the result of two recent hail-storms, which were felt over a wide area, and which were of almost unexampled severity. By the time we had enjoyed the outlook, and learned a little of the village, the messenger who had been sent to call the people together had performed his duty, and a picturesque group of our long-sought Totonacs were at hand. The women wear *quichiquemils* of native cotton cloth, the neck opening of which is over-hemmed with black wool. Lines of crosses, rosettes, birds, etc., are worked in various-colored wools upon them. Many of them have a broad line of color, in geometrical combinations, running vertically up the middle. The men wear *cotones* of black and white.

Twenty-five or thirty of the more important men of the village were now taken to the school-house, where the *presidente* inquired, for me, in regard to the *costumbre.* At first a little hesitancy was shown, but soon all were interested and talked freely. The *costumbre* comes at about the same time each year, though not upon a fixed date. Its purpose is to secure health, good weather and crops for the coming year, though it may be held on the occasion of pestilence. Everyone, even widows and old maids, brings something for the feast. The celebration is held in some large house, and lasts through two days; floral decorations are arranged in the four corners of the room, candles are lighted, and *copal* is burned. The first day, each person brings a handful of earth from his field, which is placed in a heap upon the floor. Fowls and animals are slaughtered for the occasion; their heads are cut off and their blood is sprinkled upon the earth. After feasting and drinking, a dance follows, the dancers wearing crowns and necklaces of yellow arnica flowers, and carry in their hands wands made of pine-splints wrapped with corn-husks, and with a flower of arnica tied to each end. The second day, corn on the ear and beans are brought instead of earth, and these are sprinkled with blood. On both days, blood-sprinkled material is carried home, and the seed and earth are later put into the field. In the feasting-room, two paper lanterns are hung from the ceiling; these are stuck over with gilt and colored paper disks and stars. They represent the sun and stars. Upon these lanterns a cross of blood is made, at the time when the earth and seed are sprinkled. After the dance ends on the second day, children shoot at the lanterns with small arrows and try to break them. Disappointed that no mention had been made of bark paper in connection with this ceremonial, we asked whether they ever used it. They answered promptly in the affirmative. For what? To wrap *ocotes*. With this, the man who told me hastened out and came back with a little parcel in his hand. This consisted of twelve little sticks of pine about three inches long; they were tied together with a band of thread or bark fibre, and were stained with blood; these were wrapped in a piece of green banana leaf, the upper face of the leaf being placed inside and the base of the leaf kept downward. When it had been thus carefully folded, it was carried to the field and buried in a hole, carefully dug, so that the top of the package was close to the surface of the ground, and the face of the leaf wrapping was directed toward the rising sun. To anyone who has studied American indian religions, these two *costumbres* suggest much of interest.

The young man who had been most interested in our proper understanding of the *costumbre* was anxious that we should see the village idols. These are kept concealed, apparently in a cave, though it is possible that they are buried in the ground. At all events, they exist, and in considerable number. A lively discussion ensued as to whether it would be proper to show them to us, and it was decided that nothing ought to be done until the old woman, who is at the head of the pagan practices of the village, should be present. It seems that in the *costumbre*, already described, there are four priests or leaders. One of these is the old woman just mentioned, and the other three are men. She was sent for, and while we waited, we were told that, if we desired to see the lanterns that were used in the last *costumbre*, they were still preserved in the *santocalli*. *Santocalli* is a mongrel word — from Spanish *santo*, saint, and the Aztec *calli*, house. It was a little structure of adobe and canes, close to the school-house, and fronting with it upon the little *plaza* of the village. It had a two-pitched thatched roof and a single door in the front. After some demur, it was opened, and we entered. It consisted of a single plain room with two benches made of beams along the wall. At the back was a terrible Christ and Virgin, and, to the right and behind, another Virgin. These Virgin figures were both small and unattractive, and both wore *quichiquemils*. In front of the Christ and larger Virgin was a simple altar built against the wall. In the floor, directly in front of it, were four small hollows. To the right of the altar, a flat stone was set into the floor. In front of the altar stood a small table on which were censers and candle-sticks. Underneath this table, the space between the four legs was occupied by a heap of ashes; in front and behind this were ill-defined basin hollows. To beams in front of these were hung the almost globular paper lanterns already mentioned. When we had seen these lanterns, and were about to leave, the old *bruja* appeared, with her female acolyte. She was furious over the desecration of strangers entering the *santocalli*, without her presence. She was a striking figure; very small, with a wrinkled, shrewd and serious, but not unkind, face; her white hair was almost concealed by her *rebozo*, which was folded square and laid upon her head with a portion flowing behind. The most striking thing was her great devotion, and complete unconcern regarding all around her. Entering, she hastened to the altar, knelt,— touched her forehead to the edge — and in a clear but not loud voice crooned an impassioned cry to Christ, to San Jose and to the Virgin.

Imperiously turning to her acolyte, she seized the censer filled with copal, and, having lighted it, incensed the figures. Turning to the *presidente*, she asked whether he were going to placate the saint for invasion by giving *aguardiente* and candles, both of which appeared, as if by magic, when she was given money. Pouring *aguardiente* from the bottle into a glass, she poured into the four basins in the ground before the altar, before the Virgin, before and behind the heaps of ashes under the table, and then placed it to the lips of the Virgin and Christ, lovingly requesting them to partake. She then compelled each of the three men priests to make the same libation. Taking the unlighted candles, she made passes with them, over and across the figures, first to one side and then to the other, brushing the wicks against them. This, too, had to be done by the three assistants, after which the old lady began to make vigorous personal use of the bottle of spirits, though she was not at all selfish, urging, not only her acolytes, but the *presidente*, his brother, and the chief guest, to partake. It was too late to suggest a visit to the idols, but the curious scene we had witnessed gave sufficient food for thought. Hurrying back to Tlacuilotepec, we ate a last excellent dinner, which had been long waiting, and at three left for Pahautlan. Our host, who had been unremitting in his attention, refused all money. At certain indian houses which we passed upon our homeward way, we saw curious pouches made of armadillo-shells, hanging upon posts or on the house walls. We learned that they were used at planting-time for holding seed-corn. When the shell is freshly removed from the animal, it is bent into the required shape, and then packed full with wet ashes, to make it retain its form in drying. Though it was half-past three when we left, the way was so cool and delightful that we made the journey in three hours.

During our day at Pahuatlan, with a guide furnished by the *presidente*, I made the journey on foot to Atla, an Aztec town, famous for the little cotton sacks with red wool patterns, which are almost universally carried by men throughout this district. White *cotones*, with narrow, dark stripes and a transverse band of red decoration at each end, and white *quichiquemils*, decorated with brilliant designs in red wool, are also made here. Our object was not so much to see the village and the garments, as to visit a famous witch's cave, situated in the noble pinnacle of rock, plainly visible from Pahuatlan. The whole party started out from Pahuatlan, but at the bottom of the great slope, I left my companions to swim, while the guide and I, crossing a pretty covered bridge, scarcely high enough for a man of my height wearing a *sombrero*, went on. It was a long climb to the village, but, when we reached there, my *mozo* with great glee called my attention to *brujeria* directly at the side of the church. In front of the building, to the right of the door as one enters, is a hole in the ground, into which a few large stones have been clumsily thrown or laid. Here chickens, flowers, eggs, etc., are buried, in order to secure good luck or to restore health. Carefully removing some of the stones, we saw ample evidences of such offerings, in bones, bits of egg-shells, and dried flowers. From here, the climb was easy to the crest overlooking the village, and to the curious tower-like mass projecting conspicuously from it. The cave is situated in this mass of rock and faces almost east; it is a shallow cavern, well-sheltered and dry, perhaps fifty feet wide along the cliff's front, though only the eastern third, which is the more completely worn out, is used for ceremonies; it is, perhaps, no more than eight or ten feet deep, and has greater height than depth. Within the cave itself we found a little table, a small chair, and two blocks for seats. On either side of the table, a pole was set obliquely

The Pagan Priestess and her Acolyte; Santa Maria

The Witch's Cave at Atla

against the wall. The upper end of the left-hand pole was tied with a strip of palm which was looped through a hole in the rock wall. At two or three other places, strips of palm had been slipped through natural holes in the wall, behind bars of stone, and then tied. To the left, were a censer and two candle-sticks, behind which, lying obliquely against the wall, were twenty-five or thirty dance-wands. These were sticks wrapped with corn-husks and tufted with clusters of flowers tied about the middle and at each end. The flowers used were mostly the yellow death-flower and purple everlastings. Two or three of them were made with the yellow death-flower — *cempoalxochil* — alone. A few were made of *xocopa* leaves. While only twenty-five or thirty were in position, hundreds of old ones lay on the bank to the left. Three small crosses of wood were placed near the wands; much white paper, clipped and cut into decorated designs, was lying about, as also wads of cotton, colored wools, long strings of yarn, and bits of half-beaten bark fibre. Near the front edge of the cave was a hole with large stones; here, with a little scratching, we found feathers and bits of bone of turkeys and hens, that had been sacrificed, as well as splints of pine tied together with bark string. Wooden spoons, probably used in the banquets of the witches, were stowed away in crevices of the rock. Chains of the yellow death-flower were looped up against the wall. It is said that the people of the town never enter here, but only *brujas*. Nor is it the exclusive property of the witches of Atla, of whom there are but two or three, but those of several pueblos make their rendezvous in this cave. In fact, from the crest, we could see two other little towns that are interested in this cave, though located in another valley.

Don Antonio, at whose house we stayed, told us that San Pablito is worse for *brujeria* than Atla. He says the people of that town make use of *muñecos* of wood, of various sizes. For these he makes many little shoes, for which he charges five or six *reales* a pair; at that time he had orders for three pairs, and showed us the little forms or lasts he employs, and the special leather; they are particular about this, using black for shoes for males and red for females. He says they also use little hats, *serapes*, *enaguas* and *quichiquemils*, for their *muñecos*. Some of these dolls they place on the altar in the church, and consider them as sacred, though they remove them when they expect the priest. Others they take to a lake in the district of Tenango, near San Pablo el Grande, and leave them there as offerings. They also throw money and other offerings into the lake.

We started at eight o'clock the following morning, bound for Tenango del Doria. For a little time, after leaving Pahuatlan, we mounted, soon finding ourselves at the top of a magnificent crest. From here the descent was rapid and profound; in front of it rose an equally abrupt slope to an even greater height; toward the left this presented a wonderful knife-edge crest, jagged and toothed astonishingly, and on this great slope, below the level where we were, we saw San Pablito, prettily located. As it was Sunday, most of the people were on their way to market, and we saw many Otomis, whose dark color and broad faces reminded us of those in the state of Mexico, though they did not present so marked a type. The *enaguas* of the women consisted of an upper white strip and a lower striped one, the colors in the latter being blue and white, or white with a broad band of purplish blue, in which were woven white designs. Their *quichiquemil* was usually rather plain; white with a broad band of red, magenta or purple, parallel to the edge. It might, however, be decorated with a number of very small geometrical, floral, and animal figures, worked in brown, purple and blue, which were never so crowded as to destroy the white background. At 9:30 we reached the school-house and called out the teacher, to whom we delivered a letter which the *presidente* of Pahuatlan had given us for him. He summoned the town authorities and we made known our wish to see some of the bark paper. At first there was some hesitancy, but, at last, an old woman produced two sheets which, she said, she made the day before. At our wish she then brought out the *tabla*, or board of wood on which the beating is done, and the stone for beating. The latter was smaller than the ancient beating-stone, and not grooved upon the beating surfaces; it had, however, the side notches for convenient holding in the hand. The board on which the beating is done is smooth, and is constantly cleaned and soaped. Two kinds of bark are used, *moral* and *xalama*, the former giving white, the latter a purplish paper. The bark is thoroughly washed with lye-water taken from soaked maize; it is then washed with fresh water and thoroughly boiled; it is split into thin strips which are carefully arranged upon the board. First the border is laid out the size of the sheet to be made; then, within this, strips are laid lengthwise, side by side. All of this is then beaten with the stone until the sheet of paper results. The paper when finished, presents two sides quite different from each other; one, smooth and finished, is the surface that was below in the beating, while the other, rougher, is the one that was beaten with the stone. The sheets are dried in the sun, carefully folded into convenient size, and done up in packages of a dozen, which are sold to the indians in all the country round about. We secured seventeen dozen sheets of this paper, and samples of the bark, and the board and stone used in the beating.

While arrangements were being made for showing us these details regarding paper-making, we visited the village church, which was very mean and bare; we were disappointed to find nothing suspicious in the way of *muñecos*. It was suggested that we should visit the *oratorio*, where we found more. Here they held their *costumbre* in June, or thereabouts. Saints were arranged in the back of the room on a raised altar; in front of this, running through the middle of the room, was a table on which stood censers and small candlesticks of rude pottery. Upon the wall, over the saints, were decorations of rushes. Here the whole village feast and dance. There were no *muñecos* present, but we found plenty of cut paper, most of which was probably decorative; the most curious was cut into groups of human figures, some of which had crowns and horns, or tufts of hair, upon the top of their heads. These were said to be decorations for Montezuma, in whose honor the feast was given. Leaving San Pablo at eleven, we rapidly made what remained of the great ascent. As we neared the jagged crest of rock, it appeared more irregularly gashed and pinnacled than ever. At the crest, leaving the old road, which passed directly through the fantastic mass of rocks, we reached San Nicolas, from which, on looking backward, we gained a magnificent view of the valley and a fine waterfall, which shone like a sheet of polished metal, far up the mountain side. From here our road descended gently, but winding, in and out, through a series of narrow valleys, lying between parallel ridges. As we passed the crest, we saw a level field of green corn, which looked as if we must reach it in a few minutes. But the curves of the road proved frightfully long. It was after two o'clock before we reached the green field, and, just below it, Tenango del Doria, and made our way to the *jefatura*.

When the *jefe* came, we found, to our surprise, that he was the Don Pablo Leyra of whom Xochihua had told us two years before. He is a pure indian, tall, smooth-faced, of gentlemanly manner, and with all the reserve character-

Indians Fishing in Stream

Paganism and Christianity

istic of his race. He has lived at Huehuetla since boyhood, forty-four years, till just now, and has but recently come to take the position of *jefe politico*. He has not yet moved his family from Huehuetla, and occupies a single room in his office-building. He secured us a pleasant room, with good beds for the older, and good mattresses for the younger, members of our party, in a house near-by upon the hill. The *jefatura* fills one side of the little *plaza*; around the other side are *tiendas*, with high-pitched single roofs, and private houses. The town suffers much from *nublina*, and is cold most of the time.

We asked Don Pablo about the lake, concerning which we had heard. He says it is not as much visited as formerly. While used by Otomis, and others of this district, it is most favored by the Huaxtecs, parties of whom go there from long distances. They visit it when there is drought, for fear that the siren, who lives in it, is annoyed at their neglecting to make gifts; when there is too copious rain, they visit it to beg her to desist from sending more, and, when crops have been destroyed, to placate her anger. Sometimes two or three hundred indians are in these companies. They bring *muñecos* of wood, cloth, clay, or even metal; such are shod, clad and hatted. They leave these upon the shore. They also bring seeds and strew them in the water, and some throw money in. They also make offerings of turkeys and hens. Sometimes these bands spend several days on the shore, dancing and eating.

We found that Don Pablo had arranged all our plans. We were to leave at nine, dine at twelve at San Bartolo, leave there at one, and reach Huehuetla between five and six. It was really only a quarter-past-nine when we did start, and the *jefe*, himself, saw us on our way. The journey was uneventful; the descents were gradual; we saw San Bartolo long before we reached it; and, between it and us, there lay a valley, like a narrow gash, down which we had to go, and up the other side of which we had to climb. We passed Santa Maria, an insignificant town, just before reaching the edge of this gully. From there we saw, in the mountain ahead, above and behind San Bartolo, a great cavern which we believe must belong to witches. Arriving at San Bartolo, we found the market in full progress, and had ample opportunity to see the characteristic dress of the women, with the little black, red and purple designs embroidered upon the white ground. We were impressively received at the town-house, for Don Pablo had telephoned them to be ready. Still, we waited a long time for the promised dinner, but at half-past-one climbed up a steep hill, in the rear of the town-house, to the home of the *presidente's* father, where a very elaborate meal had been prepared, with wine and luxuries. All payment was refused, and, after we had rested and refreshed ourselves, we left at half-past-two. The road was long; it followed the side of a great gorge, into which it descended abruptly; in this gorge we saw magnificent vegetation. The trees were heavily hung with long vines and ferns; parasitic fig trees, hugging victims whose life sap they were stealing, were abundant. The country was of limestone. On the whole, the road was good, but, here and there, were patches where we traveled over sharp and jagged out-croppings of rock, and near Huehuetla we were forced to make some stiff climbs up the cliff sides. Flocks of parrots were numerous, especially toward evening. The stream was a handsome one, with clear, deep water; we crossed and recrossed many times. The foot-paths rarely crossed, being cut sometimes, as a narrow trail, in the rock of the cliff. Noticeable were numerous silvery lines of water falling over the cliff, several of which must have been hundreds of feet in height; these little threads of water were impregnated with lime, and deposited material in a sheet upon the bank over which they flowed, so that trails of brown tufa marked their location; the lower ends of these deposits expanded into fan-like masses of tufa, over which the water trickled, dripped or fell. Where there was not sufficient water to produce a stream and fall, but enough to keep the tufa moist, the growth of ferns, and other delicate vegetation, was brilliant and striking. We passed a number of coffee and sugar ranches on the road. It was dark long before we reached Huehuetla, and had it not been for the moonlight struggling through the clouds, we should have had difficulty in traveling the last portion of the road. At 7:35 we arrived, and went at once to the large and handsome house of Don Pablo himself, where we were expected, and where an elaborate supper was being made ready. The largest room in the house was put at our disposal and good beds and cots, beautifully clean and carefully made, were ready. Formerly, Don Pablo was the *presidente* of the town. His successor was at the house to meet us, within five minutes after our arrival, and took supper with us. It is needless to say that in this town we met with no delays in our work. To our surprise, we found a fellow countryman, a civil engineer named Culin, from Philadelphia, who has done and is doing much work for the pueblos of this region.

Huehuetla is a large town, occupying a long valley hemmed in between mountains and bordering a stream. The streets are regular, and the view from the hills about, looking down upon the well-built houses and the intersecting streets, is very pretty. The houses have substantial walls of stone and mud, and many of them are white-plastered outside; all have a thick and heavy thatch. The *plaza* lies before the house where we stopped, and, to the right, the large church stands on a terrace somewhat above the town. A large school building, finer than many of the best in some large cities, was just being finished; its construction was due to Don Pablo's influence, and it was soon to be occupied. Meantime, the children were given instruction in the church, and at noon and evening, when their lessons were closed, they marched in double file, down the flight of steps in front of the church and across the *plaza*, where they separated and made their way home. During the time that we were working at this town, when the school children filed past, they always removed their hats in the most respectful manner. While there are many *mestizos* in the town, it may truly be called an indian town, the largest of those belonging to the Tepehuas. According to Orozco y Berra, Tepehua is not related to any other language in Mexico. We have not studied it sufficiently to be sure that he is right; it is, however, certain that the language has been much affected by the Totonac, if it is not related to it, and many words in the two languages are the same. The people of this tribe have a great reputation, more or less deserved, for cleanliness; probably it is comparative, contrasting with the neighboring Otomis, rather than positive. However that may be, both men and women are usually dressed in clean white clothing. The *enaguas* of the women are plain white; their belts have a foundation of white cotton, but raised designs of black wool are so thickly worked upon them that the white is quite inconspicuous.

The *camisas* and *quichiquemils* are generally white, with a vertical band of red, and with a few animal figures. Women wear many necklaces of bright beads, and braid their hair into two braids, which end with tapes of various colors,— brown, red, green, maroon, and black. These braids are brought together over the head and knotted in place. We secured no women for measure until we had practically completed the work with men, when they came with a rush, the whole twenty-five at once, dressed in their best clothing, and insisted that the work must be done inside the school-house, out of sight, instead of on the street, where we had operated on the men. We had no opportunity to see any of the popular *danzas*, in some of which, we were told, songs were sung in the Tepehua language, but we did see examples of the little *teponastls*, or drums, used on these occasions; they are made from a round block, perhaps ten inches long and three inches in diameter; these are hollowed out below, so that two thin lips only are left above, which, when struck, give out far more musical tones than one might expect. The two nights that we were at Huehuetla, we saw men and women fishing in the stream; carrying blazing torches in their left hands, they waded out into the water and watched to see the dark bodies of the fish against the pebbly bottom of the stream; in the right hand they carried a *machete*, about a foot in length, with which they stabbed the fish, rarely missing.

We were now ready for the last tribe of the season, the Totonacs of Pantepec. Pantepec is in the district of Huachinango, and we had no order from the *jefe*; Don Valentino, the *presidente* of Huehuetla, said, however, that the *presidente* of Pantepec was his friend, and that he would give us a letter of introduction, which would serve all purposes. As we were to return by Huehuetla, we left the busts which we had made, and all but our most necessary baggage, at Don Pablo's house. Though we started at ten, we took the journey slowly, photographing and hunting birds. The road was a trail in a ravine, with all the beautiful scenery with which we now were so familiar. At one point we saw a curious phenomenon. The cliff rose vertically from the water's edge, at a place where the stream made a right angle; this cliff consisted of almost horizontal strata of varying hardness, so that some of the layers were worn a little more than others, leaving these projecting. In the space between these projecting layers, round river-pebbles, from the size of hen's eggs up to the size of a man's fist, were firmly wedged, so that it was with difficulty that they could be dislodged. Not a few, but hundreds of the pebbles, were thus wedged, so regularly and firmly that we could not believe the work to be that of nature, but suspected human hands. We learned, however, that nature really had done the work, on the occasion of a flood, the result of a cloud-burst, which swept into the valley two or three years before. At several places in this stream, we saw groups of from two or three to ten or twelve Totonac indians, who were fishing with little nets. Our trail led back and forth across this stream many times, and before we reached Pantepec we had made thirty-nine crossings. From our last crossing, we climbed a steep ascent, passing the little village of Tenasco, and found ourselves at Pantepec. We rode at once to the town-house, and were told that the *presidente* was sleeping; we went then to his house, where we were informed that he could not be disturbed. We left word that we must see him as soon as possible, and that he would find us at the *municipio*. Nearly three hours passed before he put in his appearance. Inasmuch as we had seen this man's *jefe*, and he knew our errand, we told the *secretario* to send a message for us to him at Huachinango. We carefully wrote out the message for forwarding, in which we told the *jefe*, that we had waited three hours for attention from the town officials, and asked how much longer we should put up with delay. We never heard his answer, but in less than ten minutes, the *presidente*, covered with perspiration, was waiting for our orders and every policeman or the force was ready for our bidding. The message he received from the *jefe* must have been vigorous, for not only was everything done for our comfort, but work was rushed. During the next day we measured ninety-eight men, photographed twelve subjects, and made moulds for all our five busts — an unparalleled day's labor. We were fortunate in one respect — that the men had been summoned that day for public labor. So far as men were concerned, they gave no difficulty as subjects. With the women it was different, and full half a day was taken in getting together our twenty-five types; not but what there were plenty of them, for our second day at Pantepec was market-day, and the *plaza* was gay with women, but they did not wish to be measured, and the whole town force, from *presidente* to the meanest *topil*, was afraid to meddle with them; at first, too, we had none but the most wretched cases, women broken down and worn out with years of labor. When nearly half our number had passed through our hands, and all presented this same unsatisfactory type, we were forced to make a sharp remonstrance, and only so did we get fair samples of young and middle-aged women.

At Pantepec the centre of the town is *mestizo*; the indians consist of Otomis, of whom there are thirty households, and Totonacs forming the bulk of the population. It is easy to distinguish the women of the two tribes by the difference in dress. The *quichiquemils* are particularly picturesque. Both are more heavily loaded with embroidery than any indian garments we had ever seen, but the styles of the two decorations are completely different. The *quichiquemils* of the Otomis are smaller and completely covered with red and black embroidery; those of the Totonacs are much larger, and portions of the white foundations may still be seen, notwithstanding the heavy patterns in brilliant colors — red, green, yellow and blue. Mothers put babies onto one side, with their little legs astride a hip, and then tie them firmly in place with an *ayate*, or carry-cloth, of cotton, thus leaving their hands free for work or other burdens. If we had difficulty measuring the Totonac women, we had still greater difficulty in photographing satisfactory groups of them. Neither pleadings nor bribes on our part, orders nor threats on the part of the officials, had much influence.

Pantepec is a large town, situated near the edge of the great mountain mass, and looking across a valley, which is backed by what appears to be a flat-topped, straight-edged, table mountain. The houses of the town are scattered over a considerable area upon the slope. The walls are of poles, heavily daubed with mud which is neatly and smoothly laid on. The corners of this mud covering are rounded, instead of angular, as usual elsewhere. The thatch is heavy and firm, and squarely cut along its lower edge, where it projects far beyond the walls. The *plaza* is above the town-house, and is extremely ugly; a kiosk, which certainly can lay no claim to beauty, stands in the centre; ugly shacks, used as *tiendas*, border a part of it along the main road. Striking, at this time, in the village were the *colorin* trees, some of which occurred in almost every enclosure; they were in bloom, and had long, slender, flaming-red, cigarette-shaped flowers, which appeared before the leaves, from trunks that were gnarled and brown and almost branchless. Many popular *danzas* are celebrated here, but none was taking place during our stay. San Gregorio, the town of paper-making, is not far from Pantepec, and large quantities of the bark paper are beaten in the little village of Ixcoyotla, which belongs to this *municipio*. Asking an old Otomi whether he knew about this paper, he answered us, with great cunning, that we probably knew as much of it as he did. He finally condescended to state that the *muñecos* of it were used in curing disease; that anyone who has a disease secures one of these *muñecos* and applies it to the diseased part. The *presidente* insisted

Totonac Women; Pantepec

that this paper was not made from *jonote*, but from *uli*, and that formerly it was much used in making strong and durable belts.

In starting back the next morning, we went down a different slope from the one by which we had come, with the result that we had to cross the stream five times more than before, making the full forty-four crossings, of which we had been warned by Culin while we were at Huehuetla. We made our way leisurely, stopped when we pleased, and at one point noticed a cave, which we had not seen before, just across the stream, at a point where it was at its deepest. The cave was so near the water's edge, that it could only be approached from the stream. The boys swam across and entered it to see if perchance they might find some of the paper figures used in *brujeria*. They found little of interest within; the walls and rocks were marked with crosses, and on the floor were hundreds of little sticks cut to various lengths. We were glad, indeed, to reach Don Pablo's house, to eat his good supper, and to occupy his good beds. Before we went to bed, Doña Panchita suggested that we ought to see certain *muñecos* kept by a man named Diego, and used as idols by the village. Accordingly, she sent orders that the man should bring his *muñecos* to the house for us to see. To this request, he returned the proper reply, that he would not do so; that they would be offended; that they were not toys to be carried about at the nod and beck of everyone. This greatly increased our interest, and we arranged for a trip to his house. We first sent a messenger forward, with word that we were coming, and ordered him to stay there to see that Diego did not run away or hide the idols. After supper, Doña Panchita, our company, Mr. and Mrs. Culin, and one or two others, picked our way by moonlight across the stepping-stones and foot-bridge, up a trail by coffee groves along a purling brook-side. We were soon at the house, and after some hesitation, Diego led us to the Holy of Holies. The *muñecos* were kept in a little house, which contained an altar built of boards, with fresh flowers for decoration. At the back of the altar, against the wall, were prints of Christian saints; on the altar were censers and an open bundle of *copal*. Two wooden boxes were at the right end of the altar, against the wall. These contained *muñecos* which, for some time, Diego hesitated to produce. Finally he took out an idol of rather fine-grained, brownish-gray stone; the head was large and infantile, with the Mongolian cast of countenance; its badly shaped and scrawny arms were raised so as to bring the hands together on the chest; the body was shapeless. This figure was clad in a suit of unbleached cotton, much too long and slender for it, and the arms of the *camisa*, and the legs of the *calzones* hung limp. When we had duly admired this figure, a second was produced — a pottery female-head, fairly shaped, with no body to speak of; this had glass earrings fastened in the ears. Next, a small headless figure was brought out; it was old, though probably made after the Conquest, and we agreed that it represented a *padre*. Next was a simple pottery head. Last was a figure, with small head and pointed cap, made apparently of pottery; the body had been pieced out to disproportionate length with wood, and ended in a pair of wooden feet; this was dressed in black velvet, and wore a black hat. These, Diego asserted, were all he had. After having expressed our delight with them, and our regret that we had not known what we were to see, that we might have brought with us some fine white *copal* as incense for these gods, we set them up in a straight line on the edge of the altar to make a flashlight picture. As we left, we gave Diego two *reales* to spend for the benefit of his gods. After we left, we were assured that he had finer ones of black stone, which he dresses in red, but we were content with the ones we had seen. These figures are particularly used on September 16th, San Miguel's day. They are also used at sowing-time, at harvest, and at the first cutting of sugar-cane. On these occasions, incense and candles are burned, the idols are taken in the hands, and to the sound of music, worshippers move the figures, causing them to dance. Pleased with this, they give good rains to the faithful worshippers. When there is too much rain, they go in procession to the river, playing music and dancing dolls; when arrived, they peg down many *ayates* and sacks, made for the purpose, into the water against the flow. These are dams, to stay the flood. On the other hand, when there is drought, a procession carries the idols to a cave, where a feast is given and a dance, with wands of flowers carried in the hands, indulged in.

Though the price for animals from Huehuetla to Las Tortugas was exorbitant, we had agreed to pay it — but told the man that, if he left later than six, it should be cut two dollars. It was long after eight before they appeared, and then it was only our own animals that were ready. We were forced to leave the packing to be done by the man himself without direction; we ourselves hurried along the trail, hardly stopping at San Bartolo on the way, arriving at Tenango at 4:15. Our animals were fagged, and we were soaked to the skin, having travelled through *nublina* most of the afternoon. Don Pablo received us with his usual courtesy, and had arranged for us to sleep at the same house, where we had been before. At bed-time, our man with the mules had not appeared, and we had received most contradictory and discouraging statements regarding him. He had started at nine with two mules and left half our stuff for another day; he had been seen at the river near San Bartolo with two mules heavily loaded, unable to proceed; he had concluded to stop at San Bartolo for the night, to push on to Tenango the next day, and reach Las Tortugas on the third. Dissatisfied and uncertain, we went to bed; still, we determined to leave at five, and so gave orders to our *mozo*. We rose at 4:15 and the horses were ready before five. Contradictory stories were again told us regarding our animals. Some said the man had passed with them at five o'clock; others that he had not yet come; others that he had spent the night at Santa Maria. Our foot *mozo* did not come, and sending the rest ahead, I waited for him. Hardly had they started, when Ramon galloped back to announce that the man was in town, that he had three animals and was nearly ready to leave. As he, himself, had told us that he must leave Tenango at three in order to reach Las Tortugas in time for the train, this was not reassuring. Ramon hastened on with the party. At six the *mozo* appeared and started at once. In a few minutes we passed our *arriero* who was packing, but not ready to start. I urged him to hasten, but did not wait. Mist had settled during the night, but it was now rising, and we could see the scenery, which, in wildness and beauty, was almost the equal of anything in Mexico, though with a character quite its own. Our trail ran along the side of a precipice; to our left rose great cliffs presenting almost vertical faces of smooth rock; the summits were jagged, and suggested that the mass consisted of stratified rocks tilted up on end. Just as we left town, two narrow and lofty parallel rocks suggested a gate-way. Further down, a mass was worn out into a sharp column, a little separated from the rock mass behind. On the right, was the precipice, ever abrupt, and sometimes the almost vertical bank of a yawning chasm. After an hour and a half over the fairly good road, we came to a grand ascent. It was magnificent, though difficult. In some spots the road was muddy, and at others

View at Pantepec

it was a series of rough stone steps; at still others, it was the unmodified bed of a mountain torrent. As we followed up this gorge, side-gorges joined it, in which we glimpsed pretty cascades, pits worn by little falls, trees, the trunks of which were covered with thick sheets of green moss, quantities of tree-ferns blighted by the late frost, cliffs, and wild forms of rock, in wonderful variety. At last I reached the summit and overtook Manuel, whose horse was completely fagged, and who had been forced to drop behind; for some time we saw the others before us, but somewhere they took a different trail, and we saw them no more. After a considerable descent, we made our final but easy rise. From here we were on a level road, which constantly improved until near Mepetec, while beyond it, we came to a true cart-road. From here a fine view presented itself, over a forest of pine trees to the clean brown plain so typical of Hidalgo, swept, as we soon found, by the equally typical Hidalgo wind. We rode rapidly from the *herreria* of the Trinidad to Metepec, and then to Las Tortugas, where we arrived at 11:40, having been five hours and a half upon the road. To our surprise, Louis and Ramon were not there. Having waited some time, as it was almost the hour for the train, we ordered dinner for two, but before we had begun to eat the others appeared. They had taken a short road, which did not go by Metepec, and travelled slowly that we might overtake them. After a good meal, we waited for our man with the pack animals. Meantime the train was preparing, and we watched it, realizing that if we missed it, we had a day of dust and scorching sun and heavy wind before us. The train's crew made all ready, the cry of "*Vamonos*" was given, and we settled down in desperation to await our tardy man. An hour after the train left, he arrived, received his fee less the two dollars, and started homeward. Twenty-three hours later we took the train, and our season's work was done.

CHAPTER XXI

IN THE HUAXTECA

(1901)

THE scenery on the Tampico branch was at its best, as there had been recent rains, and everything was fresh and green. At Tampico, we resisted the attractions of the hotels "where Americans always stop," and went to the unpretentious Pan Cardo. Here we were comfortably located, and early the next morning tried to define our plans. We were in uncertainty as to what towns we should visit in order to examine the Huaxtecs. The ancient Huaxtecs were among the most interesting of Mexican tribes. They are a northern offshoot of that great family, of which the Maya of Yucatan is the type. The linguistic relationship is evident upon the most careless comparison. The ancient area occupied by the Huaxtecs was near the Gulf of Mexico, and on both sides of the Panuco River, near the mouth of which some of their important centres were located. To-day Mexicans divide the Huaxteca into two parts,— the Huaxteca Veracruzana and the Huaxteca Potosina — the former in the state of Vera Cruz, the latter in the state of San Luis Potosi. At first, we thought to visit the latter, but the difficulty of reaching it was presented so forcibly, and the ease of reaching the Huaxteca Veracruzana so emphasized, that we determined upon the latter, and selected the town of Ozuluama for our central point. We could go by canoes across the river to Pueblo Viejo, where we could secure horses for the further journey. We were led to believe that it would be easy to make the trip in a single day. We had arranged for a canoe over night. It belonged in Pueblo Viejo, and it was to come over early in the morning; we were at the wharf at six, ready to start, but no canoe was in sight. Not only so, but a norther was blowing, and comforters, lounging on the wharf assured us that no canoe would come from Pueblo Viejo until the storm ceased, which would not be for twenty-four hours. We were loath to believe this information, and brought all our baggage from the various storing-places, where we had left it, out onto the wharf. Time passed; the norther continued, and no canoe from Pueblo Viejo came. Thinking that it might be possible to secure a canoe from here to Pueblo Viejo, we dickered with a boatman at the wharf. We had agreed to pay for the canoe ordered $1.00 for the journey, which was something more than the regular price. The man with whom we now were talking declared that he would not take us across for less than $3.50. We were on the point of yielding to necessity, when a rival appeared and offered to do the work for $2.50. Such is human perversity that we now insisted that he must go for $2.00, which he finally agreed to do. Hurrying away to get his canoe, he soon appeared, and our hearts sank. The man who had demanded $3.50 had a large, well-built boat, which should stand any wind and water. The man whom we had engaged had a canoe so narrow, low, and small that we doubted his ability to perform his contract; however, he assured us that all would be well, and showed himself so skilful in packing our stuff into his boat, that we ourselves embarked, and started down the little lagoon in his canoe. So long as we remained in this narrow, sheltered stream, all was well; but when he poled from its mouth out to the open river, we found it a different matter. More than this, we saw two or three canoes dancing over the white caps, and managed with great difficulty, although not loaded. The courage of our boatman was a little dashed; he suggested that we leave Ramon, Louis, and Manuel on an old scow standing on the bank and fast going to ruin, while he poled myself and the luggage over, after which he would return for my companions. This seemed good sense, and the boys were left behind. It was interesting to see the skill with which the man handled our rather awkward craft, loaded at it was almost to the water's edge. He had no motive power but his long pole. We did not ship a single drop of water, and at last entered the quiet, broad, canal-like lagoon on the other side of the river. A moment more, and we were unloading our luggage onto the shore. To do this, we were forced to wade through mud up to the knees. But at last all was safe, and with his empty canoe, our boatman started merrily back for his other passengers. When they arrived, only a few minutes were necessary for reloading the canoe, and we started up the lagoon. Little side lagoons opened frequently into the one through which we passed. At their mouths were V-shaped weirs of stakes, driven into the bottom and wattled together with flexible twigs. These were open at the mouth, and in the openings were set dip-nets, which could be lowered into the water. Just now, with the heavy norther blowing, thousands of *camaron* (shrimps) were driven into the nets, and at each one we saw fishermen busily occupied. The lagoon abounded in water-birds of many kinds, and hardly had we entered it, when Louis shot a pretty, small white heron.

Believing that the owner of animals to whom we had been referred was demanding too high a price for his horses and mules, we decided to see what the town authorities would do for us, and went to the *municipio*. The *presidente* told us, with delight, that the *jefe politico* of Ozuluama was there with his family, rusticating, and at once summoned him to meet us. He was a gentlemanly fellow, who told us that the price demanded was regular, but advised us to travel in a different way. "Here," he said, "you can get a large canoe; starting now, you can travel all night; reaching La Llave in the early morning, you can get horses and go the seven leagues remaining comfortably. Take a little something to eat before you start, and carry something for the way." This seemed an opportunity for a new experience, and, though the price was little, if any, less than we were asked to pay for animals, we decided to try it. Arrangements were begun at once, breakfast ordered, and a light lunch prepared for carrying. Meantime, the *jefe* told us that there were few indians in Ozuluama, but that in Citlaltepec we would find abundance. He gave us orders to his *secretario*, who represented him during his absence, and bade us god-speed. We left at one o'clock, in a great canoe, a heavy, timber-framed boat, propelled by long poles, by oars in quiet and deep water, and by a clumsy sail. A framework of poles, covered with matting, roofed over the middle of the boat, and a piece of matting was spread upon the floor. Hanging blankets to shelter ourselves from the heavy wind yet blowing, we busied ourselves variously, the boys skinning birds which they had shot, and I making up my various notes. The lagoon which we now entered was a large stretch of open water. We raised our sail, and made easy work. Having crossed the large lagoon, we entered the mouth of what probably would be considered a fair-sized river, which at first was closely bordered by a tangle of trees and vines, and presented a truly tropical appearance. Palms were abundant, and, here and there, one of unusual size towered high above the rest. The other trees were densely hung with long gray moss. Now and then, we disturbed alligators along the banks, and we were told that snakes were abundant in the grass. The quantity of water-birds was astonishing — great and small white herons, large blue herons, little blue herons, the curious, dark wry-necks, and ducks by thousands. The positions and attitudes of these long-necked and long-legged birds, in the water and on the trees, were curious and striking. The boys kept busy shooting and skinning birds all the afternoon. In the evening, the men built a fire with charcoal in a tin-lined box in the end of the canoe, and toasted *tortillas* and made coffee. The awning was scarcely large enough to cover the whole party comfortably, when we lay down to sleep, but we wrapped up in blankets and spread mats for beds. We suffered intensely with the cold, sleeping little. At five o'clock our boat came to a stop along the bank, and at six it was light enough to disembark and explore. Climbing up a little bank of clay, we found ourselves on a flat meadow, covered with grass and weeds, through which narrow trails ran to a few scattered palm-thatched huts. With a letter from the *jefe*, we called at Señora Mora's house. This lady was a widow, whose husband had but lately died; she was well to do, and promised to supply us with animals after we should have had our breakfast. This was long preparing, but at last good coffee, fine *enchiladas* and cheese were served, and, after eating heartily, we found six animals ready for us. When we asked for our account, the good lady replied that the bill was $2.00. It was plain that she had made no charge for either breakfast or animals, but only something for the boys whom she sent along to bring back the beasts. At about eleven, we started on what was called seven leagues, but what was certainly the longest nine leagues we had travelled for a long time. We had excellent horses that kept up a steady jog. Still, it was after five when we reached Ozuluama. The journey was for the most part over a *llano*, thicket-covered and sprinkled, here and there, with groves of palm; the soil was dark clay, which in spots, wet by recent rains, was hard travelling for the animals. We caught sight of the town, prettily located upon a hill-slope, about an hour before we reached it. From it, we looked out over an extensive stretch of dark green plains, broken, here and there, by little wooded hillocks, none of them so large as that upon which Ozuluama itself is situated. Riding to the town-house, the *secretario* was at once sent for. He ordered supper, and put a comfortable room, behind the office, at our disposal. On the back porch, just at our door, was chained a tiger-cat. It belonged to the *jefe*, and was a favorite with his little children, but since they had been gone, it had been teased until it had developed an ugly disposition. It was a beautiful little creature, graceful in form and elegantly spotted. But it snarled and strove to get at everyone who came near it. The *secretario* at once told us that Citlaltepec was not the point we ought to aim for, as it was purely Aztec; our best plan was to go to Tamalin, where we would find one congregation of Huaxtecs. From there, if we needed further subjects, we might go to Tancoco, although it did not belong to this district, but to that of Tuxpan. In the course of our conversation, I was reminded that Ozuluama is the home of Alejandro Marcelo, a full-blooded Huaxtec, who once published a book upon the Huaxtec language. Expressing an interest in meeting this man, he was sent for. He is far older than I had realized, celebrating his 74th birthday that very week. He was a man of unusual intelligence and most gentle manner. At nine o'clock next morning, supplied with new animals, we started for Tamalin, said to be thirteen leagues distant. We were well mounted, and the journey was much like that of the preceding day. For three hours we were impressed with the loneliness of the road; no people were to be seen anywhere. Here and there, set far back from the road, were country houses. The road itself was an extremely wide one, cut through a woods, which consisted for the most part of low and scrubby trees, with scattered clumps of palm trees here and there. Usually the trail was single, but where we came on mud patches, many little trails were distributed over the whole breadth of the road. Here and there, where there were particularly bad spots, into which our horses would have sunk knee-deep, we were forced to take trails back among the trees. While the earlier part of the journey was through rolling country, we came at noon into a true plain, though wooded. We found many cross-roads, broad and straight, cut through the woods, and were impressed by the great number of dry *barrancas* into which we had to descend, and out of which we had to climb. Most of these were actually dry, but many of them contained a dirty pool of stagnant water. At many places, the road was bordered with plants, the leaves of which somewhat resembled those of the pineapple. They were light green in color, narrow and long-pointed at the upper end, and spiny along the sides. This plant, named *guamara*, bears spikes of yellow fruits which are pointed at the upper end, but in color, size, texture, structure and taste reminded us of podophyllum, though it leaves a prickly sensation in the mouth, much like that produced by fresh pineapples. There were also many trees bearing little limes or lemons, of which we gathered abundance for making lemonade. At two o'clock our man pointed out a ranch-house near the road, in front of which two men sat eating, and told us we could procure food and drink there if we wished, and that we had plenty of time for stopping. We found the men at the table to be the parish priest of Tantima and his servant. The priest informed us that Tamalin was three and three-fourths leagues away, while Tantima was four. The road for the greater part of the distance to the two places was the same. We had an interesting conversation with the good priest, and for the first time we met the curious prejudice, which exists throughout this portion of the Huaxteca, against the Huaxtecs, and in favor of the Aztecs. We were kept waiting some little time for our dinner, but by three o'clock were again upon our way. Just as we started, we crossed the first true stream which we had met, but during the balance of the journey we crossed one or two others. Soon, leaving the main road, we bore off to the left, and found several bad spots of stiff black mud, into which our poor animals sank frightfully. After five o'clock we saw, from the slope on which we were, for we had left the *llano* and were again in rolling country, a little village, and higher and further to the left, a second. The first of these was Gutierrez Zamora, which is Huaxtec, with a few Mexican families living at one side; the second was our destination, Tamalin. We passed through Gutierrez at six, and reached Tamalin at seven.

The *alcalde* of the village was not there; in fact, we suspect that he but rarely is. The *secretario*, likewise, was absent. We finally prevailed upon his brother to help us to find an indian girl to cook our meals, and a room in the *secretario's* house. In this room there was but a single bed and our helper thought me very particular in demanding that *petates* should be brought as beds for my companions. He assured us that, when he traveled, he slept upon the floor, without *petates*. It was long after 10 o'clock before we had supper and secured a resting-place. We had planned to push out from here the following morning; no sign, however, of our baggage had appeared, and we were forced to spend two days at Tamalin waiting for its coming. Here, too, we found that there were no Huaxtecs, the town being, so far as it was indian, purely Aztec. We decided, therefore, to try Tancoco, returning, if need be, to Gutierrez.

Both Gutierrez and Tancoco were in the district of Tuxpan. Fortunately, we still carried our last year's letter from the governor of Vera Cruz to serve us with the local authorities, as it would be most inconvenient to go to Tuxpan for orders. Seeing that it was impossible to leave that day, I walked in the afternoon to Tantima to visit the priest. Between the two towns rises a fine, high rock hill. The ascent from Tamalin was in three slopes, with short levels between; the crest was but a few yards wide; the descent to Tantima was abrupt and short. From the summit we looked down upon the pretty, level, enclosed valley occupied by a rather regular town, built about a large plaza which, the day being a market day, was gay with booths and people. I met almost the whole population of Tamalin on my way over, as they returned from market. All the men were drunk; some were so helpless that they sprawled upon the road, while others were being helped by their more sober comrades. I reached the plaza just thirty-seven minutes after leaving Tamalin, and at once telegraphed to Ozuluama about the baggage. When I inquired for the priest's house, the telegraph operator informed me that the *padre* had told him all about us and our errand and that he would accompany me to the *curato*. Crossing the square, we found the *padre* living in a comfortable place, close by the great, pretentious, stone church. We were warmly welcomed, and orders were at once given for coffee. The Aztec servant hastened to bring some, piping hot, and was quite abashed at being sharply reproved for offering it directly to me. No, indeed, a gentlemen so distinguished was not to be thus served; the table was moved up before my chair, a clean cloth spread, sweet cakes were sent for, a glass of fresh milk placed, and then the coffee was set upon the table. Thus, in solitary grandeur, I sat and ate and drank, while the priest and operator took their cups of coffee in their hands. Though we had ordered horses for the following morning, the baggage had not come, and we waited all the day. Strolling around the village, we found it a pretty place, through which ran a fine stream, separating the houses into groups or clusters. It is a true Aztec town, and the houses are well-constructed. Several houses are set irregularly within a single enclosure; the walls are built of poles set upright, but these are so heavily daubed with a mixture of mud and chopped straw that they are strong and durable. In applying this daub, the hand is used, and a simple block of wood of rectangular form, with a projecting edge extending midway of the upper side, is used as a trowel for spreading it, and giving it a smooth finish. The thatchings are thick, and project far beyond the walls; they are of palm, and neatly cut at the edges; a cresting, thin, but evenly placed and firmly pegged down, projects over the ridge, down either slope, and its edges form the only break in the smooth surface. Many of the houses had *temascals*, differing considerably from those of Puebla and Tlaxcala. They are rectangular; the walls are built of poles, set upright, close together, and strengthened by being lashed to a horizontal timber set midway of their height. The roof is a round vault or arch of poles set lengthwise. The whole is neatly plastered over with a mixture of mud and chopped straw, and in the front a cross is worked in the clay mixture, to insure good fortune. The women here wove cotton in the usual indian fashion, but few wore the old dress, and those few were mostly aged. We noticed quantities of pottery here, and throughout the Huaxteca, but none of it is local in manufacture. Most of it has come from the two towns, Huejutla, an Aztec town, and Panuco. We were forced to spend a third night at Tamalin. The *secretario* had been at home for two days and had fairly done his duty; still, our animals were late when we were ready to start the following morning, and we were not off until 9:30. It was a steady climb, over a long series of ascents, until we reached a crest from which Tancoco could be seen. We made a long descent and then a little upward climb to the town, which is notable for its cleanliness and the industry and cleanness of its inhabitants. The town is situated upon a little hill, from which one looks out on a sea of green forests, with little rocky hillocks covered with trees rising from it, here and there, like wooded islands. Between us and Tamalin rose a semi-circle of ridges, sweeping from us off to the left and forward in the distance. In front, near the top of this curve of ridges, two leagues distant, lay Amatlan, clear and impressive, from this point. Riding up to the little town-house, which had a portico enclosed by a neat railing and supplied with pine benches, we dismounted, and, with some doubt as to its reception, presented our old letter. The *secretario* was an intelligent *mestizo* from Tuxpan. He sent at once for the *alcalde*, who was a good-natured, little Huaxtec, of pure blood, thoroughly dependent upon his subordinate officer. We were promised everything. The school-house, remarkably clean, was put at our disposal, and a messenger was sent to notify an old woman named Guadelupe that she was to prepare our meals. Before four o'clock, work was under way, and during the two days that we remained, there were no difficulties. The houses of the town are somewhat like those of Tamalin, but less well built. The single industry is the weaving of hats from palm. On the house-roofs, and on the ground before the houses, palm was drying. Some of the work was extremely delicate, and the four grades of hats sell for from four pesos upward. Men, women and children are all occupied in the manufacture, and as they sit in their houses or at the door of an evening, or as they walk through the village on errands, their hands are

View at Tancoco

ever busily occupied with the plaiting. There is absolutely nothing characteristic in dress, both men and women dressing like *mestizos* in the important cities of the Republic. Almost every one wears shoes; women, those with high French heels. A resident tailor makes the bulk of the clothing for the more particular men of the town. In our school-room we were supplied with good kerosene lamps, an experience almost unique. Few, if any, of the houses in the village were without the same mode of light. Many, if not all, of the women had sewing-machines.

We were more than ever impressed with the anomalous condition of these people in their own land. They were the cleanest, most industrious, best dressed and most progressive indians whom we had seen in any part of Mexico; but in the Huaxteca, the land which bears their name, they are being crowded by the less progressive Aztecs. *Mestizos* and Aztecs both speak of them with contempt, and treat them like dogs. As for their language, it is neglected and despised; while many of them know both Spanish and Aztec, neither *mestizo* nor Aztec considers it worth while to know a word of Huaxtec. While we had no trouble with the men, we began to feel that the women would fail us. It was after five o'clock, the last day of our stay, before a single one appeared. Then they came in a body, accompanied by the full town force, and each with her husband as a guard, to our quarters. They were dressed in their best calico, muslin, silk and satin, with laces and artificial flowers, earrings, necklaces, and with shoes the heels of which measured from thirty to thirty-five millimeters. They were perfumed; their hair was heavily oiled with odorous greases. Each shook hands with our whole party, greeted us politely, and sat down on the long school-benches, waiting for her turn for measurement. Notwithstanding this rather oppressively lady-like mode of procedure, we were assured by old Guadelupe that our errand and work in the town had caused much terror and doubt, the women particularly feeling sure that it boded ill. It was said that they recalled the fact that years ago certain of their old men predicted that strangers would eventually come to the village, who would bewitch the people and destroy the town. It was commonly believed that we were now fulfilling this prediction.

The physical type of the Huaxtecs seems to be well marked. A peculiar gray tint underlies the brown color of the skin. The head is short, broad, and curiously compressed behind; the eyes are wide apart, and frequently oblique; the mouth is large, with thick but not projecting lips.

We had planned to leave about the middle of the afternoon, and at 3:50 the best animals we have ever had were ready for our use. A magnificent horse, the special pride of the *alcalde* himself, was put at my disposal. When we came to settle for the animals, all payment was refused, their use being the voluntary offering of the town officials. The animals made nothing of the journey, and within an hour and a half we had again reached Tamalin.

We found that Aztec town as disagreeable as ever. Solemn promises had been made that various *danzas* should be ready for us, and that there should be no delay regarding animals. Of course, we found nothing doing. The only satisfactory memory connected with the town is our cook, Porfiria. She was a master hand, and with training, should make a reputation and a fortune. A pure indian, we would rather eat at her table than at that of any half-breed cook in all that section. She always had quantities of food, and no two meals were alike. Unless we expressly ordered something we had had before, it is doubtful whether she would have repeated a single dish. Her *enchiladas*, seasoned with cheese and onions, were the best we ever had, and after the first experience, we insisted on having them at every meal. Her masterpieces were in simple maize. Her *tortillas* were good, but *tortillas* one finds everywhere; she served *cocoles*, *chavacanes*, and *pemol*. *Cocoles* are round, flat biscuits or cakes of maize, a couple of inches across and half an inch in diameter; they contain shortening, and when served hot, are delicious. *Chavacanes* are thin, flat square crackers of corn-meal with shortening and eggs; they are good even when cold, but are best when hot from the griddle. *Pemol* is a corn-cake, crumbly, sweet, and baked; it contains sugar and shortening, and is made up into the form of rather large cakes, shaped like horse-collars.

As the result of vigorous remonstrance, the *secretario* really had the *danza* of *los Negros* at his house that night. Music was furnished by *pito* and *huehuetl*. The two performers, one representing a Spaniard and the other a negro, were masked. The action was lively, and the dialogue vociferous — both players frequently talking at once. The dance was kept up until nearly ten o'clock, after which, as we planned an early start, we were soon in bed. Just as we were dropping off to sleep, we heard the whistling and roaring of the norther outside, and the cold air found its way through every crack into our room. From our house the musicians and the dancers had gone to the *syndico's*, where they stayed some time; but, between one and two in the morning, they came back to our house and played in the room next to ours, with the door wide open. Our interest was not great enough to lead us forth again. Finally they left, but at four o'clock the musicians, now quite drunk, appeared again, and for a long time the *secretario*, his lady, and the school-master, danced in lonely grandeur up and down the room.

Don Leandro, the *secretario*, had promised to accompany us the following morning as far as San Geronimo. We had decided to go on horseback to Paso Real, a little distance beyond San Geronimo, and there take boat for Tampico. When morning came, we expressed surprise over Don Leandro's charging rent, in addition to the rather large price which we had already paid for beds. This seemed to hurt his sensitive feelings, with the result that we started without his company. The ride was monotonous, over a road which made few ascents or descents, and presented little of variety or interest. Little green hills bordered the road on either side, and on many of them were ranch-houses, some of rather good construction. In a little stream over which we passed, we saw a great idol's head, of stone, a foot or more across, and well made. San Geronimo we found to be the comfortable country-house of the *alcalde* of Tamalin and all the ranches among which we had made our journey. It was a fine old place, with high airy rooms, good verandas, and as old-fashioned tiled roof. Our journey had been hot, and we found a fine breeze blowing through the house. The *alcalde* knew all about our errand and was ready to be helpful. He was a tall, slender, mild-mannered and polite *mestizo*. After we had eaten, he rode with us to Paso Real to arrange about a boat and point out various objects of interest on the way. *Chapapote*, from which chewing gum is made, is an important product here, and among those interested in it as a business is an American dentist. We saw many birds, among which doves were conspicuous; the *alcalde* says that six or eight species occur here, the different kinds singing at different seasons; one of them had a peculiarly sad and mournful song, and is heard in the early morning. Another bird, the *primavera*, seems to be like our mocking-bird, imitating the notes and cries of many other birds and animals. At two places we passed black lines of foraging ants, and he told us that insects, frogs, toads, and even snakes, encountered by these lines, are helpless, being promptly overcome and devoured. Arrived at Paso Real, the *alcalde* arranged for our boat. He told us that loaded boats require three days for making the journey to Tampico, but that ours, being empty, would probably go through in twenty-four hours. The boat he arranged for had been partly loaded, but its owner had agreed to unload in order to receive us. As a favor to him, we consented to permit five or six not large boxes to go along. Having ordered supper for us at the house upon the summit from which the road descended to Paso Real, the *alcalde* left us. Supper was slow, but at last was over. Our baggage had already been carried to the boat, and we strolled down to take our passage. Less room was left for us than we had expected the boxes would leave, but it was dark and we raised no question. We waited an impatient hour for our canoemen to take their supper, being almost devoured by mosquitoes, but at last were off at nine o'clock. Our force consisted of two men and a little lad. It was with difficulty that two could be accommodated beneath the awning, and Manuel and I took our places outside. For my own part, sleep was impossible. Now that we were in motion, the mosquitoes ceased to trouble us. The stream was narrow, and on account of the curves, we were forced to move slowly. We floated out under and beneath bamboos, which hung far over the water and outlined themselves like lace-work against the sky. At first, there was moonlight. Later, the moon set, but the stars were brilliant. The early morning was cold, and a heavy dew dampened everything outside the awning. During the day our men stopped on every pretext to rest and sleep, and whenever we came to a considerable stretch of water, any sign of storm or cloud was heralded. Just before daybreak, we had reached the beginning of the first large lagoon. Here our sail was hoisted, though it was of little use, while we poled along near shore, following all the long curves. Our first stop, on account of a norther, was exciting; from the anxiety of the men, we expected to be instantly upset. We ran into the mouth of a little stream and lay to, and the men were almost instantly asleep. Our party went out exploring; our landing place was a heap of shells, whether artificial or natural I am not sure; the place was a favorite spot with hunters of caimans, or alligators, and we found numbers of almost complete skeletons and skulls lying on the banks. The boys picked up quantities of scales and teeth, and it was interesting to see how the new conical teeth grow up under the hollows of the old ones. We killed a duck or two for supper. One or two large caimans were seen, as we strolled along. Finally, I insisted upon the men starting again. We were traversing a system of great lagoons which opened one into another. Poling was our only mode of progress. That night Manuel and I occupied the shelter. When we rose, we found the great lagoon, through which we were then passing, quite different in its character from those preceding it. Thickets of mangroves bordered the shore; the display of aerial roots was interesting, and here we were able to examine the curious smooth tips of the roots which are to penetrate the soft mud bottom. We landed at one place to get wood and to catch a glimpse of the sea, whose roaring we had for hours heard. We left our boat in the lagoon, and walked a short distance over sand dunes, thickly grown with trees, to the beach, which only appeared in sight when we reached the top of the last dune. It was a gently sloping sandy stretch, upon which a fine surf was beating. There were no pebbles save bits of water-worn coral and shell. Quantities of sea-gulls were flying about and flocks of little snipe ran down over the retreating surf, catching

Our Canoe for Sixty Hours; The Lagoons

Mangrove Roots

food, turning and running rapidly in before the coming wave. A single shot into the flock killed thirty-one of the little creatures, which later in the day supplied us an excellent meal. From this lagoon of mangroves, we finally entered the great lagoon of La Riviera, which pretty town we passed a little before three o'clock. From here we knew that, by hiring horses, we could reach Tampico in two hours; had we really known what lay before us, we would have done so. Having passed La Riviera, we entered a narrow canal, bordered for the most part with tall, flat rushes and a great grass much like our wild rice. Here again we saw large herons and great kingfishers; the boys had repeatedly tried to shoot one of the latter birds, but with no success; finally, one was seen standing on the branch of a tree hanging over the stream; this one was shot, and when we picked it up, we found it to be curiously distorted, the breast being strangely swollen. When skinned, this swelling proved to be due to a fish which the bird had eaten, and which was almost as large as itself. Weighted with this heavy burden, it is no wonder that the bird had been shot so easily. At dusk we found ourselves at a landing-place, where we left the boxes, which turned out to be eight in number, each of which weighed one hundred and twenty-five pounds. They contained *chapapote*. Our men had talked much of *the* canal, to which, for some time, we had been looking forward. At this landing, arrangements were made for helping us through the canal, a little canoe being despatched after us, to help unload us. When we reached the canal, narrow, shallow and straight, cut for the most part through the solid rock, the moon was shining brightly. Our great canoe was soon aground, and whole party, seven in number, climbed out into the water to push and pull. We dislodged it soon, but shortly came to a complete standstill. Here for the first time, we realized the cargo which we carried, which before had been carefully covered so that we really were in ignorance of it. Eighty half-dozen cakes of sugar were unloaded into the little canoe, which paddled away. We waited, noting with regret that the falling water, probably due to tide, was fixing our canoe more and more firmly in the mud. Finally, the little canoe came back, taking another eighty half-dozen cakes of sugar on board. Our canoe having been thus lightened, we made another effort to move it, and, after many struggles and groans, finally found ourselves in deeper water, embarked, and poled off. Having reached the place upon the bank where the canoe loads had been left, we stopped to freight again. To our surprise, we found here once more the eight boxes of *chapapote*, which, apparently, had been carted across. We were now able to calculate the load which our "empty" canoe, hired at thirty pesos, in order to take us quickly through to Tampico, was carrying:

120 dozen cakes of *panela*, of 2 lbs.	2,880 lbs.
8 boxes *chapapote*, of 125 lbs	1,000 lbs.
6 sacks of beans, of 100 lbs	600 lbs.
Total	4,480 lbs.

In other words, we had been crowded and delayed by more than two tons of cargo. Perhaps, had we been actually alone in the boat, it might have made its journey in the twenty-four hours promised, instead of the sixty of accomplishment. It was nine o'clock when we were again aboard, and we made the boatman travel all night long. At the stroke of half-past-three we heard the bells of Tampico, and drew up along the waterside-landing of that city. For two full hours we lay there, listening to the buyers bartering with the boatmen for their load of maize, *frijol* and *panela* untill daylight, when we gave orders to unload.

CHAPTER XXII

IN MAYA LAND

(1901)

WE had planned to go from Tampico to Chiapas, and from there to Yucatan, where we were to finish our work for the season. We found, however, that there was no certainty in regard to a boat for Coatzacoalcos, while the Benito Juarez was about to sail for Progreso the next day. Not to lose time, we decided to do our Yucatan work first, and to let Chiapas wait until later. We were busy that day making arrangements for departure, and in the afternoon hired a canoe to take our stuff from the wharf to the boat, which was standing out in the river, beyond Doña Cecilia. There was a brisk wind against us, and we almost arrived too late to have our luggage taken aboard. The next morning, we took the first train to Doña Cecilia, and were on board the boat at nine o'clock. We had been told that the sailing would take place at ten, but, on arrival, found that they were waiting for cattle which were being brought across country. One hundred and twenty head were to make our chief cargo, and they were expected at six a. m. Nothing, however, was to be seen of them in any direction. We had taken breakfast, and it was almost twelve o'clock before the first signs of the animals were to be seen. Meantime, at eleven, a norther appeared, and we were informed that it would be impossible to leave short of twenty-four hours. Besides our company, there were three first-class passengers — a sort of German-Austrian baron and his lady, and a contractor, who was taking a force of hands to

Yucatan for farm labor. Eighty-three of these hands were our third-class passengers; they had been picked up all along the line of the Tampico Branch of the Central Railway, and few of them realized the hardships and trials which lay before them. We were assured that more than half of them would surely die before the end of their first year in Yucatan. As we could not leave until the norther passed, it was decided not to take the cattle on board until next day. Thus we spent a day as prisoners on the boat, standing in the river. In the morning the water was still rough and the wind heavy, but at 9:30 the loading of the animals began. They were brought out on a barge, about one-half of the whole number to a load; tackle was rigged and the creatures were lifted by ropes looped around their horns. The first few were lifted singly, but after that, two at once. While it sounds brutal, it is really a most convenient method, and the animals, though startled, do not seem to be injured in the least, nor indulge in much kicking. By 11:40 all were loaded and we were ready for our start. We had to wait until the customs-house inspector should come on board to discharge us, and this was not done until half-past one. We sailed out, between the jetties, at two o'clock, and found the Gulf rough, and a high wind, which continued through most of our voyage. The smell from the cattle was disagreeable, and between it and the roughness, all were seasick before the first afternoon was over.

Captain Irvine is the youngest captain of the Ward Line, being but twenty-six years of age. He has followed the sea since he was thirteen years old. A Nova Scotian by birth, he has sailed this coast for some little time, and is a competent official, doing his utmost for the pleasure and convenience of his passengers. The journey was uneventful. There was some excitement among the third-class passengers, many of whom were drunk and quarrelsome. The first evening, two of them were fighting, with the result that the head of one was split open and had to be dressed by the captain. When we had been some forty-eight or fifty hours at sea, we found ourselves off the Campeche banks, in quieter water. Those who had suffered from sickness were again quite themselves. It was 4:30 Sunday morning, February 3, after we had been almost three days and three nights at sea, and four days on the boat, that the Progreso light was sighted, and not long after we came to anchor. We waited from six o'clock until almost ten for lighters and the doctor. After he had made his inspection, we piled off with all our baggage onto a little steamer, which charged three dollars, each passenger, for taking us to the pier, which was close by, and to which our own boat could easily have run. This, however, was but the beginning of Yucatecan troubles. When we found ourselves on the wharf, the customs officials insisted upon our going to the general office for inspection, on account of the character and amount of our luggage. Arrived there, we found that we had no clearing papers for our stuff, and forty dollars duty was required for material which had already paid duty in entering Mexico, and which had only gone from one Mexican port to another, as baggage. In vain we argued and attempted to explain matters. The officials advised us to bring the American consul and have him straighten matters; but his office was shut, as it was Sunday. Meantime, we saw the train, which we had expected to take at 11:30, leave for Merida, and at twelve o'clock the customs-house offices were closed, and we were forced to leave the business for another day. Fortunately, there are two railroads from Progreso to Merida, and we were able to take an afternoon train over the narrow-gauge line for the capital city. The station was an enormous, wooden, barn-like structure; the cars were weather-beaten and dilapidated to a degree — except the first-class car, which was in fair condition. Passengers were gathering, but no particular signs of the starting of a train were evident. Boys at the station were selling slabs of pudding, squares of sponge cake soaked with red liquor, pieces of *papaya*, cups of sweetened boiled rice, and oranges. The oranges were unexpectedly high in price, two selling for a *medio*; the seller pares off the yellow skins and cuts them squarely in two before selling; the buyer eats merely the pulp, throwing the white skin away. As train-time neared, interesting incidents occurred. The ticket-agent was drunk and picked a quarrel with a decent, harmless-looking indian; the conductor dressed in the waiting-room, putting on a clean shirt and taking off his old one, at the same time talking to us about our baggage-checks. A fine horse, frisky and active, was loaded into the same baggage-freight car with our goods. The bells were rung as signals, and the station locked; the whole management — ticket-agent, conductor and baggagemen — then got upon the train and we were off. At one of the stations the ticket-agent took his horse out from the car, and riding off into the country, we saw no more of him.

The country through which we were running was just as I had imagined it. Though it was supposed to be the cold season, the day was frightfully hot, and everyone was suffering. The country was level and covered with a growth of scrub. There was, however, more color in the gray landscape than I had expected. Besides the grays of many shades — dusty trees, foliage, bark and branches — there were greens and yellows, both of foliage and flowers, and here and there, a little red. But everywhere there was the flat land, the gray limestone, the low scrub, the dust and dryness, and the blazing sun. There were many palm trees — chiefly cocoanut — on the country-places, and there were fields of hennequin, though neither so extensive

Loading Cattle; Doña Cecilia

Mayas, Returning from Work; Santa Maria

nor well-kept as I had anticipated. It resembles the maguey, though the leaves are not so broad, nor do they grow from the ground; the hennequin leaves are long, narrow, sharp-pointed, and rather thickly set upon a woody stalk that grows upright to a height of several feet. The leaves are trimmed off, from season to season, leaving the bare stalk, showing the leaf-scar. The upper leaves continue to grow. In places we noticed a curious mode of protecting trees by rings of limestone rock built around them; many of these trees appear to grow from an elevated, circular earth mass. At Conkal, the great stone church magnificently represented the olden time, but it bore two lightning rods and was accompanied by two wind-mills of American manufacture. Everywhere, in fact, the American wind-mill is in evidence. One can but wish that the poor users of the old *cenotes* might come to life, and, for a little time, enjoy the work of the winds in their behalf. Everywhere we saw plenty of Maya indians and heard something of the old language. All travellers to Yucatan comment on the universal cleanness of the population; notable in the indians, this marks equally well the *mestizos*, whites and negroes. They are not only clean, but all are well dressed. Men wear low, round-crowned, broad-brimmed palm hats; trousers are rarely of the tight-fitting Mexican kind; indians who work at heavy labor protect their clean white shirts and drawers with a strip of stuff, like ticking, wrapped about them. Women wear two white garments, both ample, hanging from the neck, bordered with black or colored bands. They generally wear long necklaces or rosaries, the beads of which are spaced with gold coins, and a cross of gold or a medal of the same material hangs at the bottom. Women of middle age are usually stout, and march with quite a stately tread.

Merida itself is much larger and better built than we

had expected. Many of the houses, especially on the outskirts, are elliptical in section, and have walls of small stones closely set in mud plaster. In the center of the town the houses are covered with painted plaster and are in the usual Latin-American style. Great numbers of quaint little coaches, with a single horse, were waiting at the station. As we walked up to the center of the town, we found but few places open, practically nothing but barber-shops and drug-stores. Of both of these, however, there were a surprising number.

Having been directed to the Hotel Concordia, we were disappointed when the old lady in charge stated that she had no rooms, and directed us across the way to the Hotel de Mexico. As we had arranged for the delivery of our stuff, we did not care to look elsewhere, and therefore inspected the rooms in this hotel. To reach them, we went through a barber-shop into a narrow *patio*, and, mounting some rickety stairs, found our quarters, which were filthy, vile-smelling, hot and uncared for. Yet for these choice quarters, with two beds in each of two rooms, leaving no space practically between, we were expected to pay four dollars. Upon remonstrating with the proprietor at the price demanded, he cooly said, "Oh, yes, everything here costs high; but there is money to pay it with." This really stated the fact. Conditions in Merida are the most abnormal of any place which I have visited. Owing to the war in the Philippines, and interference with the trade in hemp, the fiber of the hennequin is in great demand, and money is plentiful. At good restaurants each plate costs thirty cents, instead of ten or twelve, as in the City of Mexico itself. No coach will cross the street for less than fifty cents; for a cooling drink, such as in the capital city would cost three cents, one here pays twelve. The shortest street-car line charges ten cents; and everything else is in proportion. What the hotel-keeper said, about there being money to pay these frightful prices, was equally true. We paid *cargadors* four times, draymen three times, more than we have ever done in any other part of Mexico. In the restaurants we saw *cargadors* calling for plates at thirty cents, boot-blacks eating ices at one *real*, newsboys riding in coaches, and other astonishing sights. In the plaza, good music is played on Sunday nights, and every one is out in all his finery; fruits, sweetmeats, refreshing drinks, are hawked everywhere, and are much indulged in; under the corridors are little tables, where ices, iced milk and drinks are served. At the hotel we passed a night of horror, suffering from the heat, dust, ill-placed lights, mosquitoes and other insects. Leaving my companions I went the following morning to Progreso to attend to the unlucky baggage. For variety, I took the broad-gauge road, but found little difference in the country through which we passed. The number of windmills was astonishing, and most of them were Chicago æromotors. At one station a great crowd of pure indians got off and on the train. The American consul at Progreso is too much interested in archæology to be found at his office, but his Mexican vice-consul was present. To him our difficulty was explained, and on his advice we deposited the forty dollars demanded for duty, and signed various documents of remonstrance, upon which we paid almost four dollars more for stamps. We were then permitted to take out enough plates for immediate use, leaving the balance in Progreso until we should be ready for our return journey.

Acting on the advice of the vice-consul, we changed quarters in Merida from the Hotel de Mexico, to the Moromuzo, kept by an American who had been many years in the country, and where, though we paid even more for rooms, we had some comfort. By industrious search, we found a Chinese restaurant, where prices were not high and service quite as good as in the aristocratic place where we had dined before. The day before we called at the palace, hoping to see the governor, though it was Sunday. He was out of town, and we were asked to call the following day. Accordingly, in the afternoon, after returning from Progreso, I repeated my call but was told that the governor had gone out of town again and that I should come the following day. The third day, again presenting myself at the office, I learned that it was a holiday and that the governor would not be at the palace; the secretary recommended that I try to see him at his house. To his house I went, and sending in my card and my letters from the Federal authorities was surprised, after having been kept waiting in the corridor, to be informed that the governor would not see me, and that I should call at the palace, the next day, in the afternoon, at two o'clock. Sending back a polite message that we had waited three whole days to see his excellency, and that our time was limited, my surprise was still greater at receiving the tart reply that he had stated when he would see me. We spent the balance of day and all the morning of the next, looking about the town.

Having failed in my visit to Governor Canton, I took a street-car to Itzimna to see the bishop, to ask him for a letter to his clergy. The well-known Bisdop Ancona had lately died, and the new incumbent was a young man from the interior of Mexico, who had been here but a few months. He had been ill through the whole period of his residence, and seemed frail and weak. He received me in the kindest way, and after reading the letters I presented, asked whether I had not been in Puebla at a certain time two years before; on my replying in the affirmative, he remarked that he had met me at the palace of the bishop of Puebla and had then learned of my work and studies. He gave me an excellent letter to his clergy, and as I left, with much feeling, he urged me to be careful of my health and that of my companions while we were in the country. When he came from Puebla, only a few months before, he brought three companions with him, all of whom had died of yellow fever. He told me that, though this was not the season for that dread disease, cases of it had already broken out in the city; at the same time he stated that more than eight hundred cases of small-pox were reported in Merida, and that many of them were of the most virulent. Sunday we had walked through dust ankle-deep upon the roads; Tuesday and Wednesday it was with difficulty that we could cross the streets, which were filled with mud, and, part of the time, with muddy water a foot and more in depth. This is a frequent occurrence, and foot-passengers who desire to cross the street are often forced to hire a coach for that purpose. As one walks the street, he runs constant risk of being splashed with mud and water from passing vehicles and street-cars. During the four days we spent in Merida we met several persons interested in literary lines, and visited a number of institutions, among which the most interesting was the Museo Yucateco, of which Señor Gamboa Guzman is in charge. It is by no means what it should be, or what, with but small outlay, it might be. But it contains interesting things in archæology, in local history, and in zoology. It is of special interest to Americans because Le Plongeon was interested in its foundation and early development.

An old gentleman, clerk in the diocesan offices, advised us to visit Tekax and Peto for our study. The governor had set the hour of two for our reception. Merely to see when he would come, we seated ourselves in the garden of the plaza, so that we could watch the entrance to the palace. Two came, but no governor. At 2:30 several gentlemen were waiting near the office door. At three no governor had arrived. At five minutes past three, we noticed that hum of excitement and expectation which usually heralds some great event, and looking down the street, saw the governor pompously approaching. As he passed, hats were removed and profound salutations given. Waiting until he had entered the office, we walked up to the reception room, where we found ten or twelve gentlemen waiting audience. The great man himself had disappeared into an office which opened onto this reception-room, but the door of which was not closed. All waited patiently; from time to time the usher-secretary crept noiselessly to the office door and peeked through the key-hole to see whether the executive was ready. Finally, at 3:35 the word was given, and the privilege of the first audience was granted to myself. During these days of waiting — something which has never occurred with any of the many governors of states in Mexico upon whom I have called — I had expressed my surprise to a gentleman of wealth and prominence in the city, at the governor's compelling me to wait for audience. With some feeling, this gentleman replied, "But, sir, you are fortunate; you are a stranger, and bring letters from cabinet officials; many of the best gentlemen in this city have been kept waiting months in order to see Governor Canton in regard to business of the highest consequence to themselves and to the public." I will do the governor justice by saying that he listened with apparent interest to my statement, and that he gave orders that the letters which I wished, to local authorities, should be prepared without delay. Thanking him, I withdrew, and by five o'clock the secretary handed me the desired documents; we had lost four days. Early the following morning, as no *cargadors* were at hand, our little company resolved itself into a band of carriers and we took our baggage and equipment to the Peto station. The securing of tickets and the checking of baggage was quite an undertaking, and if the train had started at the time announced, we should have missed it; however, we were in good season, and left something less than an hour late. The country through which we passed was an improvement upon what we had seen before. The trees were greener, and many flowers were in bloom. From the train, we saw a group of pyramids at one point, and an isolated pyramid at another. Some of the indian towns through which we passed, with curious Maya names, were interesting. So, too, were the vendors at the station. Hot tamales, "*pura masa*" (pure dough), as Manuel said, slippery and soapy in feeling and consistency, done up in banana leaves and carefully tied, seemed to be the favorite goods; far better were split *tortillas* with beans inside and cheese outside; beautiful red bananas and plump smooth yellow ones were offered in quantity. We lost an hour at the station where trains met, reaching Tekax at eleven. We walked up to the hot *plaza*, where we found the town offices closed, and had difficulty in even leaving our stuff with the police. At a restaurant we had a fair breakfast, for which we paid a peso each person. As there were no signs of the town officials, we dropped into the *curato* to see the priest, to whom we presented the bishop's letter. He was a Spaniard, who had been in this country only a few months, and despises it heartily. He was sitting at table with two young men, who had accompanied him from Spain, and who love Yucatan no better than he. He greeted us most heartily, and was interested in our plan of work. He sent at once for the judge of the *registro civil*, who could tell us many curious things about the indians, and, as soon as the old man came, the good priest ordered chocolate to be served. We chatted for some time, when, seeing that the *jefe's* office was open, I suggested that I had better go to present my letters. The *cura* and the judge at once began to abuse that official roundly for his sins of commission, and particularly for those of omission, and told me that I should have him summoned; that it was much better than to trouble myself by going to his office, where I had already been twice in vain; it was but right that he should attend to business; he ought to be in his office when visitors came to see him. Accordingly a messenger was sent and the *jefe* summoned.

He seemed a rather nice young fellow, and was much impressed by the letter from his governor; he expressed himself as ready and anxious to serve us in every way, and made arrangements for us to begin work in the town-house, where, before dark, we had taken fifteen sets of measurements. This was a capital beginning, but the next two days our work fell flat. It was necessary to keep constantly at the *jefe*, and it soon became plain that he was making no great effort to secure subjects for us, on the assumption that we had better wait until Sunday, when there would be plenty of people without trouble to the police.

It was useless to urge effort, and we spent the time talking with the old judge in regard to the habits and superstitions of the indians and in walking with the judge of *primera instancia* up to the ridge which overlooked the town, and which was crowned by a little *hermita*. The population of Yucatan is still, for the most part, pure indian of Maya blood and speech. The former importance of this people is well known; they had made the greatest progress of any North American population, and the ruins of their old towns have often been described. They built temples and public buildings of stone and with elaborate carved decorations; they ornamented walls with stucco, often worked into remarkable figures; they cast copper and gold; they hived bees, and used both wax and honey in religious ceremonial. They spun and wove cotton, which they dyed with brilliant colors; they had a system of writing which, while largely pictorial, contained some phonetic elements. They are still a vital people, more than holding their own in the present population, and forcing their native language upon the white invaders. Nominally good Catholics, a great deal of old superstition still survives, and they have many interesting practices and beliefs. The cura presented me a *ke'esh* of gold, which he took from the church, where it had been left by a worshipper. It is a little votive figure crudely made, commonly of silver; the word means "exchange," and such figures are given by the indians to their saint or to the Virgin in exchange for themselves, after some sickness or danger.

The ridge overlooking the town is of limestone, and is covered with a handsome growth of trees and grass. The terrace on which the *hermita* is built is flat and cleared; it is reached by a gently graded ascent, with a flight of wide and easy steps, now much neglected. The little building is dismantled, though there is some talk of reconstructing it. Behind it is a well of vile and stagnant water, which is reputed to cure disease. From the ridge a pretty view of Tekax is to be had, bedded in a green sheet of trees. The town is regularly laid out, and presents little of interest, though the two-storied *portales* and the odd three-storied house of Señor Duarte attract attention. There are also many high, square, ventilated shafts, or towers, of distilleries. From the terrace where we stood, in the days of the last great insurrection, the indians swept down upon the town and are said to have killed 2,500 of the people, including men, women and children.

The school-teacher of the town is a man of varied attainments, being also a photographer, watch-maker, medical-adviser, chemist, and so forth. His house is full of scientific instruments — a really good camera, a fine aneroid barometer, several thermometers, including self-registering maximum and minimum, etc., etc. All seem excellent in quality, but I could not learn that he makes any use of them, except the camera. The *cura* and the judge deride his possession of the instruments, doubting whether he knows how to use them. They assert that he has an apparatus for projection, for which he paid 1000 pesos, which has never yet been unpacked. When we called on him he showed us, by his hygrometer, that the air was very humid, though the temperature was at 86° Fahr., and told us, what probably is true, that in this heavy, hot weather, every wound and bruise, however trifling, is likely to become serious. In illustration of this fact, the *cura* mentioned that his Spanish carpenter, who merely bruised his leg against the table, has suffered frightfully for three months, having now an ugly sore several inches across, that makes walking difficult. Great care is necessary with any injury that breaks or bruises the skin. We ourselves had already experienced the fact that insect-bites became ugly open sores that showed no signs of healing; as a fact, none of us succeeded in curing such for several weeks after leaving Yucatan. In the afternoon, the priest, the judge of *primera instancia* and myself took a coach to ride out to a neighboring *hacienda*, where there was a great sugar-mill, Louis accompanying us on horseback. Our road ran alongside the ridge and consisted of red limestone-clay. It was fairly good, though dry and dusty, and closely bordered with the usual Yucatecan scrub. The ridge, along which we were coursing, is the single elevation in the peninsula; beginning in northeastern Yucatan, it runs diagonally toward the southwest, ending near Campeche. It is generally covered with a dense growth of forest, unless artificial clearings have been made. Covies of birds, like quail, were seen here and there, along the road, and at one point a handsome green snake, a yard or more in length, glided across the way. Snakes are said to be common, and among them several are venomous — the rattlesnake, the coral-snake, and most dreaded of all, a little dark serpent a foot or so in length, with an enormous head, whose bite is said to be immediately fatal. There are also many tree-snakes, as thick as a man's arm. In the forest, mountain-lions are rare, but "tigers" are common. We found Santa Maria to be an extensive *hacienda*, and the sugar-mill was a large structure, well supplied with modern machinery, and turning out a large amount of product. We saw a few of the indian hands, went through the factory, and were shown through the owner's house, which has beautiful running water and baths, though there is little furniture, and nothing of what we would consider decoration. It was after dark before we started to town, and when we got there we found two wedding parties waiting for the padre's services.

The promised crowd filled the market Sunday, and our work went finely. Between the town officials and the priest, subjects were constantly supplied. Among the indians who presented themselves for measurement was old Manuel, sacristan from Xaya; he is a *h'men*, and we had hoped that he would show us the method of using the *sastun*, or divining crystal. He is a full-blood, and neither in face nor manner shows the least emotion. Automatic in movement, he is quiet and phlegmatic in manner; having assumed the usual indian pose for rest, a squat position in which no part of the body except the feet rests upon the ground, or any support, he sat quietly, with the movement of scarcely a muscle, for hours at a time. He sang for us the invocation to the winds of the four quarters, which they use in the ceremony of planting time. Though he is frequently employed to say the "milpa mass" and to conjure, he claims that he never learned how to use the *sastun*, but told us that another *h'men* in his village knew it well.

One of the *padre's* companions has been ill ever since he came to Yucatan; Sunday he suffered so greatly that a doctor was sent for in haste. Nothing was told us as to what his trouble might be, but personally I suspected that he had the small-pox. In connection with his illness, we learned for the first time that another companion of the priest, brought from Spain, died in the room I was occupying, less than two weeks before, from yellow fever. We had known that one of his companions had died of yellow fever, but supposed it was some months earlier. Toward evening the priest was sent for by a neighbor, who needed the last service. On the *padre's* return, we learned that this person was believed to be dying from *vomito*. For a moment we were in doubt what was best to do, especially as the police had told us that the *padre* had permitted no fumigation of his premises after his comrade's death, simply sprinkling holy water about the place. That night the young man in the next room suffered greatly, and I could not help but wonder what ailed him. However, I decided that what danger there might be from the disease we had already risked, and as we expected to remain but one or two more days, it seemed hardly worth while to make a change. Monday we planned a visit to San Juan and Xaya. The horses had been ordered for five o'clock, but mass had been said, chocolate taken, and all was ready, long before they appeared. Six, seven, eight all passed, and at last, at nine, only three animals appeared. This decided us to leave Ramon behind to pack the busts which we had made, while the others of the party, with the *padre*, mounted on his own horse, should make the journey. A foot *mozo* carried the camera. The road was of the usual kind, and was marked at every quarter league with a little cross of wood set into a pile of stones

Maya Dance; San Juan

The H'men with His Sastun; San Juan

and bearing the words, De Tekax —— L. As we passed La Trinidad we noticed great tanks of water for irrigation before the house, and tall trees with their bare, gray roots running over and enveloping the piles of stones on which they had been planted. There were no other plantations or villages until just before the ninth cross — two and a quarter leagues — we came to the hennequin plantation of San Juan. The mayor domo was delighted to see the *padre* and greeted us warmly, taking us at once to the great house. We rode between long lines of orange trees, loaded with sweet and juicy fruits, and were soon sitting in the cool and delightful hallway. It is impossible to say how many dozens of those oranges four of us ate, but we were urged to make away with all we could, as the daily gathering is something more than five thousand. Soon an elaborate breakfast was ready for us, but before we ate we took a drink of fresh milk from cocoanuts cut expressly for us. We had salmon, eggs, meat-stew, beans, tortillas, and wine. But the mayor domo expressed his regret that he did not know we were coming, as he would gladly have killed a little pig for us. As dessert a great dish of fresh *papaya* cut up into squares and soaking in its own juice, was served. Sitting in the cool corridor, after a good breakfast, and looking out over a beautiful country, with promises that all the subjects necessary for measurement should be supplied, the idea of riding on to Xaya lost attractiveness, and we sent a foot-messenger with an order to the town authorities to send the *h'men* with his *sastuns* without delay to see us.

This was our first opportunity to see the industry of hennequin, which is the chief product of this *hacienda*. The leaves, after cutting, are brought from the field tied up in bundles. These are opened, and the leaves are fed into a revolving, endless double chain, which carries them on iron arms upward and dumps them onto a table, where three men receive them and feed them into the stripper. This consists of a round table, into the inner, excavated, circular face of which a round knife with dull edge fits closely, though at only one place at once; the leaves, fed between the table and knife, are held firmly by them at about one-third their length. The projecting two-thirds of the leaves hang downward; as the table revolves the leaves thus held are carried to a vertical revolving rasp which strips out the flesh, leaving the fibre masses hanging. These taken out from between the table and the knife are fed again to a second revolving table which holds the masses of fibre, leaving the unstripped portion of the leaves exposed to a second rasp, which strips it. The hanks of fibre are dropped from the second table onto a horizontal wooden bar, where they are rapidly sorted over by a man who throws inferior and spotted bunches to one side. The whole operation is rapid and beautiful. The fresh fibre is then hung over bars, in the southern wind, to dry, after which it is baled in presses for shipment.

We had no trouble in completing the measurement of subjects from the indian hands on the place, and made portraits and photographs of native dancers. In the afternoon the *h'men* appeared. He was an extremely clean and neat indian of forty-five, and carried at his side a little sack, within which, carefully wrapped up in a handkerchief, were his *sastuns*. There were five in all; three were small round balls of glass, broken from the stoppers of perfume bottles; one was somewhat barrel-shaped and of bluish color, while the other, the largest of all, was rather long, fancifully formed, and with facets ground out upon it; it was yellowish in tint. The two latter were apparently from toilet bottles. Telling him that I was anxious to learn about something which had been stolen from me, I asked what was necessary in the way of preparation. He demanded a candle and

Maya House; San Juan

aguardiente. A great taper of yellow wax and a bottle of spirits were supplied. Taking these in his hand, he entered the little chapel of the *hacienda*, considering it a good place for conjuring. He piously kissed the altar tables and the bases of the crucifixes and saints; then picking out a dark corner he opened his cloth, took out his glasses, lighted the candle and squatted for his operation. Taking one of the crystal balls between his fingers, he held it between the flame and his eye and looked intently into it, as if seeking something. One after another, the five crystals were carefully examined. Finally, laying the last aside, he shook his head. He could see nothing, nothing whatever, that interested the gentleman, unless indeed sickness; this he pointed out in one of the little balls; redness, fever. Being urged to try again, after an interval he got down to real business; he took the *aguardiente*, dipped the crystals into the liquor, repeating formulas as he did so, and again made the test, but with no better result. He could see nothing, absolutely nothing, of stolen property; there was nothing in the crystal of interest to the gentleman, except fever; that there was, he was certain. This practice of divining by means of crystals is a survival from the old pagan days. It is probable that there is no indian town of any size in Yucatan where some *h'men* does not make use of it.

We had now finished our work with Maya indians, except the measurement of a few women and the making of a single bust. Upon rather strong representation to the *jefe*, a desperate effort was made by the policemen and the women were secured. Among the village police-force, one man had attracted our particular attention, as representing a type of face, quite common among the Mayas, which we have called the serpent-face. It is round and broad, with retreating chin and receding forehead, and with curious, widely-separated, expressionless eyes. We had already measured and photographed the subject, but, because he was a policeman and had been useful, we thought we would not subject him to the operation of bust-making. Seeing, however, that no other equally good subject had presented itself, we decided to make his bust, and told him so. To our surprise he refused. The *jefe*, for once, acted promptly and without hesitation issued an absolute order that the man's bust should be made. The order had no effect. The officials scolded, threatened, but Modesto Kan was immovable. The *jefe* ordered that he should be thrown into jail, which order was promptly obeyed, but all to no purpose. Our subject said we might whip him, fine him, keep him in jail, or kill him, but he would not have his bust made. Hours passed, and neither remonstrance nor threats on the part of the *jefe* or ourselves were of the least avail. On my last interview with him, I found him lying on a mat with so high a fever that I dared not urge the matter further, and we desisted from our efforts to secure him. It was the only subject among 3,000 indians, with whom we failed to carry out our work.

A story which the old judge had told us had its influence in my permitting this subject to escape. These Mayas often die for spite, or because they have made up their mind to do so. Don Manuel at one time was summoned by a rich indian with whom he was well acquainted. The man was not old, and had land, good houses, many head of cattle, much maize, and many fowls. He had three children, and owned the houses near his own in which they lived. Everything was prospering with him. Yet the message to the judge was that he should come at once to hear this indian's last words. With a companion he hastened to the house, and found the man in his hammock, dressed in his best clothes, waiting for them. He seemed in perfect health. When they accosted him, he told them he was about to make his will, and say his last words. They told him that a man in health had a perfect right to make his will, but remonstrated with him for saying that he was about to speak his last words. He insisted, however, that he was about to die. In vain they argued with him; he had had his dream. He gave to one child, house, animals, corn, poultry; to the second, similar gifts; to the third, the same. Then, having bidden them all farewell, he lay down in his hammock, took no food or drink, spoke to no one, and in six days was dead. Such cases are not uncommon among Maya indians of pure blood.

When we reached home that night we found Ramon unwell. Next day, the last of our stay at Tekax he was suffering with fever. He had done no work while we were absent the day before, and all the packing and doing-up of plaster fell upon the others of the party. As for him, he collapsed so completely that it scared me. The ordinary *mestizo* has no power of resistance; no matter how trifling the disease, he suffers frightfully and looks for momentary dissolution. It was plain from the first moment that Ramon believed that he had the yellow fever; instead of trying to keep at work or occupying himself with something which would distract his attention, he withdrew into the least-aired corner of a hot room and threw himself onto heap of rugs and blankets, in which he almost smothered himself, cut off from every breath of fresh air. In vain we urged him to exert himself; in the middle of the afternoon we took him to the doctor, who assured us that the case was in no way serious — at the worst nothing more than a light attack of malaria. In the afternoon the *jefe*, neglecting the *padre*, invited the judge of *primera instancia* and myself to accompany him upon a little expedition to the neighboring Cave of the Fifth of May. We went in a coach, taking Louis, who sat with the driver, as photographer; on the way, we visited the town cemetery, which we found a dreary place, with no effort at adornment and with an air of general neglect. We passed a number of places where they were boiling sugar, and at one we stopped to see the mode of dipping calabashes for *dulces*; the fruits are gourd-like, but have considerable soft pulp within the thin, hard crust; several holes are bored through the external shell and the calabashes, slung by strings into groups at the end of a pole, are dipped into the boiling sap or syrup; the dipping is done two or even three times, and the clusters are removed and allowed to drip and dry between dips. The loose flesh is soaked through with the syrup, making a rich, sweet mass, much used for desserts. Finally, we turned into another place where sugar was being made, and found it the cleanest and neatest of its kind. Here we sampled little cakes of clean brown sugar, and were treated with similar cakes in which peanuts and squash-pips were embedded, making a delicious confection. We were here supplied with a clean, fresh *jicara* cup, and, walking along the path a few rods, ascended slightly to the mouth of the cave, which was far handsomer than we had expected. The limestone of Yucatan abounds in caves and subterranean water-courses, especially near the base of the ridge already mentioned. The mouth of the cavern was fringed with ferns and other vegetation. A flight of rustic steps led down to the nearly level floor of red cave-earth. The light from outside entered sufficiently to show the greater portion of the cave. The rock walls, opposite the opening, were brilliantly green with some minute growth; from the floor rose a heap of stone upon the top of which was set an *olla* of large size to catch the water dripping from the roof; it was full of most beautifully clear, cool water, which we dipped out with our *jicara* and drank. At two or three other places on the

Freshly-dipped Calabashes; near Tekax

The Coach that Carried Us to the Station; Tekax

floor, and on projections from the side walls of the cave, were other *ollas*, or broken water-troughs of stone, for catching water. Lighting our candles we went behind a pendant veil of thick stalagmite. At some spots hummocks of snow-white crystalline matter, with a reticulated surface, had been deposited by dripping water. A few great masses of stalagmite rose from the floor, and there were some columns of the same material. On returning from the cavern, nothing would do but we must breakfast with the *jefe*, which we did, in state, though at our usual boarding-house.

The three great industries about Tekax are sugar, hennequin, and liquor. Father Juan insisted that we should visit one of the local distilleries, of which there are fourteen in Tekax. Sugar, ground with water into a thick syrup, is drawn off from the mill into great vats, where it is permitted to ferment; it is then taken into the still, where it is heated and vaporized, and the vapor carried up into high towers for condensation. These three-storied, square, wooden towers, with ventilator-shafts, re one of the characteristic features of the town.

Padre Juan insisted on supplying a coach for our leaving, in the morning. This coach, like those at Merida, was an extremely small affair, for a single horse. Under any circumstances it would scarcely carry three persons, without luggage, besides the driver. When it is remembered that our party, (consisting of four), the stout *padre*, four satchels, measuring-rod, tin pan and blankets, made up the load, it can be easily appreciated that the little coach was full. We rode slowly, and the poor, creaking vehicle threatened to fall to pieces every moment, but we reached the station safely. It was scarcely ten when we arrived at Merida and took our old quarters at the Moromuzo. Our invalid at once lay down, and neither threats nor bribes would move him; he looked as if he suffered, but he insisted on doing so; going to the nearest drug store we described his symptoms to the apothecary, who assured us that the case could not be serious, and supplied a remedy which was rapid and energetic in its action, though our sick man insisted that he was not improved.

We were now but waiting for notice of a vessel sailing from Progreso for Coatzacoalcos. Writing, errands, visits, filled up the time, but it was dreary waiting. The muddy streets, the heavy, moist, fetid air, the outrageous prices, the mosquitoes — all combined to make a disagreeable experience. We worried through three days, and still no announcement of a boat. In a visit made to the bishop, to tell him of our kind reception in Tekax and to make inquiry regarding books printed in the Maya, we were again warned by the prelate to be most careful of our health; that day, he told us, two of our countrymen, working at the electric-light plant, had been stricken with yellow fever and would surely die. The second day we were in town the boys met Don Poncio, one of the Spanish comrades of the *padre* at Tekax, who, with another of the household, had run away, leaving the good priest alone, as the young fellow who had been ill in the room next ours developed a full case of yellow fever the day we left, and was dead before night.

One day we went to a *cenote* for a bath. Passing through a house into a rather pretty garden, we came to a stairway, partly natural and partly cut in the solid rock, which we descended; we found ourselves in a natural cave, with a pool of blue, transparent water. A paved platform surrounded one side of the cave, and near its rear edge was a bench of masonry, which was continued along the side of the pool by a similar bench, cut partly from the living rock. The water was so clear that we could see, by the light coming from above, to its very bottom, and could detect little black fishes, like bull-heads, against the sand and pebbles. The pool was irregular in shape, so that a portion of it was out of sight behind the rock-wall, beyond which we found that there was a paved floor and benching similar to that in the portion which we had entered. We had a delightful and refreshing swim in this underground pool, but it was noticeable that, after we came out into the air, there was no evaporation of water from the body, and towels were absolutely necessary for drying. Such *cenotes* are found in many parts of Yucatan, and form the regular bathing-places, and are often the only natural supplies of drinking-water. Of streams above ground there are practically none in the whole peninsula.

The last day of our stay in Merida we saw the *xtoles*. These are bands of indian dancers who go from house to house during the carnival season; they are dressed in costumes which reproduce some features of the ancient indian dress. In the little company which we saw were fifteen dancers, including the standard-bearer; all were males, but half of them were dressed like females and took the part of such. The male dancers wore the usual white *camisa* and drawers, but these had a red stripe down the side of the leg; jingling hawk-bells of tin or brass were attached to various parts of their dress; a red belt encircled the waist; all wore sandals. The "female" dancers wore white dresses of the usual sort, with decorated borders at the arm and neck; also necklaces of gold beads and gold chains with pendants. Two of the dancers were little children, but the rest appeared to be young men up to about thirty-five years of age. All wore crowns upon the head; these consisted of a circlet of tin, from which rose two curved strips, which intersected over the middle of the head; from the circlet rose four feathers — either natural or made of tin. Two of the crowns of special size, with real feathers, marked the king and queen. Under the crowns, covering the top of the head and hanging down from the shoulders, were gay handkerchiefs of red or blue. All the dancers were masked. The men wore bandoliers of cotton, worked with bright designs representing animals, birds and geometrical forms; the square ends of these were hung with marine shells. In their hands, the dancers carried curious rattles and fans, which they used in making graceful movements as they danced. The handle of the fan consisted of the leg and foot of a turkey, while the body was composed of the brilliant and beautifully spotted feathers of the ocellated turkey, a bird peculiar to Yucatan and the adjacent country. There were two musicians, one with a long *pito*, or fife, and the other with a *huehuetl* or drum, which he struck with his hand. Hanging to the side of the drum near the top was a turtle-shell, upon which the drummer beat, from time to time, with a deer's horn. A standard was carried by the company, which bore a representation of the sun, with dancers and a serpent; the pole by which it was carried was surmounted with a tin disk representing the sun's face. The music was apparently of indian origin and the words of the song were Maya. The dancing itself was graceful and accompanied by many curious movements. Mr. Thompson, our American consul to Yucatan, believes this dance is ancient, and thinks he has found representations of it painted on the walls of ancient ruins at Chichen Itza.

Merida prides itself upon its carnival, which, it claims, ranks third, — Venice and New Orleans alone surpassing it. It was admitted that the celebration of this year was far below that of others. The cause of this dullness was generally stated to be the great amount of sickness prevalent in the city. However that may be, it certainly was a tame affair. On the 15th two processions took place, one in the

The Xtoles; Merida

The Xtoles; Merida

morning, the other in the afternoon; these were arranged by two clubs of young people, and each desired to surpass the other. We saw that of the afternoon, and found it not particularly interesting. A number of private carriages, drawn up in line, passed through the streets; within were gentlemen, ladies and children, but few of them wore masks, or were otherwise notable; besides these, in the procession, were five allegorical cars. One represented a gilded boat containing pretty girls; it was arranged to seem to rise and fall upon a billowy sea. A second float represented the well-known ancient statue, the Chacmool; an indian, in the attitude of the figure mentioned, held an *olla* upon his breast, while one or two others stood near him as guards or companions. The most attractive float was loaded with the products of Yucatan, and a group of figures symbolizing its industries and interests. Upon the fourth, a female figure stood erect in a chariot drawn by lions. The fifth was comic, and represented marriage in public and private — a vulgar couple indulging in affectionate display before a partition, and in a conjugal quarrel behind it. These floats were scattered at intervals through the procession, which was of no great length.

By this time Ramon had suffered violent agonies, and had become so weak that assistance was needed when he walked. The second day in Merida we had sent for a competent physician, who assured us that nothing was the matter excepting an unimportant attack of bilious fever, and that with a day or two of treatment he should be entirely recovered. On his second visit he was much irritated, as the young man had not made the promised improvement, and assured us that there was no cause for his collapse. During our first visit to Merida, in hunting through the city for Protestants — a practice in which he invariably indulged whenever we reached a town of consequence —

Ramon had happened on an interesting little man who represents the American Bible Society in this district. By name Fernandez, this gentleman was born in Argentina, educated in Spain, and has served as colporteur in the states of Chiapas, Tabasco and Yucatan for upwards of a dozen years. He was stout, active, and vivacious; he claimed to have been in every town in Chiapas, and gave us much advice regarding our journey to that state; he called upon us several times during our stay, and shared the general disgust over our sick man, who, he assured us, had nothing serious the matter, and only needed to arouse himself to throw off the bilious attack from which he suffered. On the streets we met the baron who had been with us on our voyage from Tampico. He told us that after one day in Merida, he and his lady decided that they preferred Progreso, and were stopping there, going down upon the day-train when they wished to visit Merida. He also warned us that we need never expect to see the forty dollars which we had advanced through the vice-consul, as whatever disposition should be made of our complaint regarding customs charges by the government, no such money was ever known to leave his hands. Following events entirely confirmed this gentleman's dire prophecy; neither Mr. Thompson nor Señor Solis have paid the least attention to communications regarding the matter sent after our return to our own country. It is little likely that the Mexican government refused to refund the payment; but we shall probably never know.

The remarks of the baron suggested a new line of action. Why longer wait in Merida for our boat? Progreso is cleaner, cooler, enjoys a sea breeze, and gives as good living for less than half the price we were paying. For comfort, for the benefit of our sick man, for the advantage of our pocket, we would be better off at Progreso than in Merida. While there were cases of smallpox in the little seaport, there were none of yellow fever. In every way it looked attractive, and on Monday morning we left, and found ourselves, before noon, comfortably located in the curious little hotel, La Estrella de Oro, in Progreso. To be sure, our rooms were mere stalls, being separated from each other by board partitions scarcely eight feet in height, and without ceiling, so that it was impossible to escape the conversation in neighboring rooms at night. The table, however, was excellent, and the price, compared with what we had been paying, economy itself. Having seen my companions comfortably located, I returned to Merida, where there was still some business demanding attention. This time I found a room in the Hotel Concordia, which was the most comfortable I enjoyed in Merida, although the price of $4 for the mere room was high. The day before, we had seen the Battle of Flowers of the carnival. No flowers figured in it; it consisted of a long procession of carriages, mostly private and mostly good; they were filled with well-dressed young people, of whom few were masked; all were supplied with confetti, which was thrown in handfuls by those in the carriages upon those in carriages going in the other direction, for the procession was double. Usually, girls and ladies threw at men and boys, who reciprocated the compliment; the ladies had their hair loose and flowing, and wore no hats; so that in a little time it was filled with the brilliant bits of paper. Everyone, also, had long strips of colored paper, rolled up like ribbons, which were now and then launched, either with no direct aim or at some person; as these strips unrolled they trailed prettily in the air, and everyone caught at the trailing streamers. Crowds of poor children chased along, beside and behind the carriages, catching at the showers of bits of paper, and at the long streamers, which they kept, or, in turn, hurled at passers. The balconies of all the better houses were filled with people, as were the seats and raised platform fronting the town-house, and those in the balconies and on the seats rained down paper upon those in the carriages. Many children in the balconies were masked, and wore grotesque costumes, but few grown persons were so decked out. While pretty and characteristic, the Battle of Flowers disappointed us, lacking the life and "abandon" which one usually associates with the idea of carnival. It was all reserved, and respectable, and unenthusiastic. The only persons who really seemed to enjoy it were the poor children, with their loads of bright paper and long streamers. Monday afternoon, the most striking function of the carnival, so far seen, took place. This was an enormous procession of vehicles; private carriages, with elaborate equipment, were filled with finely-dressed gentlemen and ladies; common rented coaches were in line, and some of them were loaded to their full capacity with common people — four, five, or even six, in one; in one were four brawny, young *cargadors;* in another an old grandmother, her two daughters, and some grandchildren, pure indians, rode complacently, enjoying the admiration which they knew their best clothes must attract; in some of the fine private coaches, no one but indian nurses or favored servants rode. Even here, few of the parties were really dashing, lively or beautiful. The whole thing was constrained, artificial and sedate. An occasional group seemed to really enjoy the occasion. One bony horse dragged an ancient buggy or cart, which might well be that of some country doctor, and in it was the gentleman himself, commonly dressed, but with a whole family of little people, who were bubbling over with enjoyment. Another happy party was that of a common carter, who had his own dray in the line, with his children, neatly but commonly dressed, as its only occupants; in two or three carriages were maskers, though none of them appeared funny; one

Carnival at Progreso

Carnival at Progreso

drayman's cart had been hired by a crowd of loud and boisterous youngsters, who performed all kinds of pranks and bawled nonsensical remarks to the crowd.

My chief errand was to see the leader of the *xtoles*, to purchase from him some of the objects which they had used in their dance. Just as I was starting, at evening, for the address he had given me, I met Señor Fernandez in the plaza, and he agreed to accompany me to the place. We went some little distance on the street-car, and, dismounting at the corner of a narrow lane, were about to start through it, when someone touched my companion on the arm, and greeted him. He recognized the owner of the little shop before which we stood. Heartily invited to enter the *tienda*, we did so and stated the object of our quest. The shopkeeper at once said that we must have a lantern, as the road was dark, and ordered his clerk to accompany us with one, for which we were truly thankful. We came, finally, to the house where Don Gregorio, the leader of the dancers, lived. Fernandez was friendly and voluble, greeting every company of girls and women that we met, or who were at the house, as "*lindas*," and passing compliments. He was, however, uneasy, continually glancing around and asking repeatedly when Don Gregorio would appear. The dancers were still absent, but expected every moment; in fact, we could hear their music in the distance. When, finally, they did appear, their leader, who was very drunk, insisted that he could not treat in the matter until after the next day, which would be the culmination of the carnival, and their chief day for dancing. The instant that we received this answer, Fernandez seized the lantern, which the clerk had left, and, grasping me by the arm, we started off at breakneck pace. As we almost rushed down the stony road, he looked furtively to right and left, and told me that there were, no doubt, persons in the neighborhood who had recognized him, and said that, more than once, in this very neighborhood, he had been stoned when selling bibles, and that any moment we ran our chances of a night attack. Apparently, however, people were too much excited over carnival to waste their time in baiting Protestants, and we heard no whizzing missiles, and soon, reaching the corner shop, left the lantern, and went home. There had been doubt as to whether trains would run the following day, Tuesday, on account of carnival. I found, however, that the train on which I had counted, leaving at seven in the morning, went as usual, though it was the only train of the day for Progreso. My companions were delighted to see me, and I found our sick man sure that death was imminent; to tell the truth, he was constantly spitting black blood, which oozed from his gums, and which gave me more concern than any of his previous symptoms. We found the carnival at Progreso more natural and unpretentious, but also far more lively and amusing, than anything in Merida. To be sure, some of the performances bordered on the indecent, but on the whole, it was jolly, and scarcely gave cause for Manuel's pious ejaculation that there were many *abusos*. Groups of men and boys went through the streets decked with ribbons and flowers, and with their faces painted or daubed; many carried handfuls of flour, or of blue paint, which they dashed into the faces or over the clean clothes of those they met; bands of maskers danced through the streets; companies of almost naked boys, daubed with colors, played *toro* with one who was inside a frame of wood. One man, completely naked, painted grotesquely, pranced through the streets on all fours; young fellows, dressed in women's clothes, with faces masked or painted, wandered about singly, addressing persons on the street in a high falsetto voice with all sorts of woeful stories or absurd questions. Very pretty was a company of trained dancers, — with a standard, leader, music, and fancy costume, — each of whom carried two staves in his hands; these performed a variety of graceful movements, and sung a song in Spanish; this was interestingly like the song of the *xtoles*, and the movements were almost precisely theirs. In the evening, we attended the *baile de los mestizos* — dance of the *mestizos*, where the elite of the little city was gathered, and the place was crowded. Very little of it was enough, for while the music and dancing were all right, the heat, the tobacco-smoke, and the perfume, were overpowering.

To our joy, on Wednesday, the "Hidalgo" appeared, bound for Coatzacoalcos. All day Thursday we waited for it to unload its cargo, and on Friday morning, we loaded into a little sail-boat at the wharf, which we hired for a price far below what the regular steamer would have charged to take us to our vessel. The luggage had been weighed and valued, and an imposing bill of lading, and an official document, had been made out, to prevent our paying duty a third time when we should reach our port. At 10:30 we were on the "Hidalgo," ready for leaving. It is the crankiest steamer on the Ward Line, and dirty in the extreme. The table is incomparably bad. The one redeeming feature is that the first-class cabins are good, and on the upper deck, where they receive abundance of fresh air; there were plenty of seats for everyone to sit upon the deck, a thing which was not true of the "Benito Juarez." Of other first-class passengers, there were two harmless Yucatecan gentlemen — one of whom was seasick all the voyage, — and two Americans, brothers, one from St. Louis, Mo., and the other from Springfield, Ill. The captain of our vessel was a Norwegian, the first officer was a Mexican, the chief engineer an American, the purser a low-German, the chief steward an Oaxaca indian, and the cook a Filipino.

Never was I so glad to reach a resting-place, never so relieved, as when we got our baggage and our sick man safely on board. As to the latter, he at once lay down, and, practically, was not on his feet during the voyage. We had expected to make the run in thirty hours, but were hindered by rough weather, catching portions of two northers; the second was so bad that, when almost in sight of our destination, we were forced to put to sea again, and lost many hours of time and miles of distance. On the morning of the third day, however, we had dropped anchor, and on looking from the cabins at five, caught sight of Coatzacoalcos; but it was not the Coatzacoalcos of 1896. Prodigious changes had taken place. The Pearson Company, having taken possession of the railroad, had made great improvements; their pretentious general-offices, located at the wharf, had recently been completed; the railroad station had been improved; the old shack, where we slept in 1896, had been torn down, and a construction track occupied its place; on the little rise behind, a pretty and large hotel had been erected; on the higher land, to the right, a line of well-built houses, making some pretension to architectural effect, had been constructed. It was only after landing, and walking through the older portions of the town, that any familiar scenes were recognized. Though we were ready to land at five, and wished to catch the train at seven, we were forced to wait for the official inspection, and saw the longed-for train — and there would be no other for two days — pull out before our eyes. Finally, at nine o'clock, we were permitted to land. To my surprise, my shipping document was called for, but, being produced, we were subjected to no difficulty. The balance of the day was spent in wandering about the village, meeting former acquaintances, attending to odds and ends of shipment, and strolling on the familiar beach, which was still covered with scurrying crabs and sprinkled with white "sand dollars." During the night, a terrific norther blew, and the next day, cold, dull gray, rainy, kept us indoors. By this time, the purser of the "Hidalgo," who had himself had yellow fever, and said he was familiar with it, had convinced us that Ramon really had had a slight touch of that dread disease, but having passed his tenth day of sickness, was destined to recover, and would be no serious menace to other people.

CHAPTER XXIII

OX-CART EXPERIENCES

(1901)

ON the following morning, at seven, we took the railroad train, and at five at night had reached Tehuantepec, and were pleasantly located in our old hotel, the Europa. On February 28, we visited the market, called at the house of the *jefe politico* for a letter to the town authorities of Huilotepec, and visited Dr. Castle, whom we found much the same as ever. We failed to find the *jefe* at his office, though we went there several times, but found him sitting in a *tienda* much the worse for drinking. He was charmed to see us, embraced us warmly, and told us that his thoughts had frequently been with us since our former sojourn in his district. New supplies of wine, and, on the appearance of certain ladies, of champagne, were ordered in witness of his satisfaction. In regard to our desires, he was delighted to learn that Louis was shooting birds, declaring that we were just in time; that he had a damnable order from Mexico to send on skins of all the birds of his district for the National Museum, and that he had not known what to do in the matter; we must prepare them; if we did so, willingly, we should be handsomely paid; but if not, he would be compelled to force us. The jail was ready, and men die easily in Southern Mexico. With this, he made some suggestions that it was easy for a person to be officially reported as accidentally killed, or dead from *vomito*. He insisted that we should not go alone to Huilotepec, but that he himself would accompany us

Manuel and an Ignana; Tehuantepec

Market Women; San Blas

and make sure that everything was done according to our wishes. All these dire threats and great promises were completely forgotten on the following day, when we sallied forth alone.

In the *jefe's* office we learned that during the past year not only Coatzacoalcos, but Tehuantepec, had suffered frightfully from yellow fever. Of course, the disease is no rarity on the Gulf coast, though it was never worse than in the last season; but in Tehuantepec, and on the Pacific coast, it is a thing so rare as to be almost unknown. So true is this, that, when it was first reported from this district, the federal government did not believe the story, and sent a commission to investigate. We learned that the commission arrived at evening, and, finding two persons dead in their black vomit on the street, made no further investigation, but started for Mexico on the following train. The spread of the disease to the west coast is generally attributed, and no doubt correctly, to the railroad. The disease was particularly fatal, in both places, to Americans and Englishmen, and it was whispered that 90 per cent of the employes of the new railroad management succumbed. The chief clerk in the *jefe's* office told us that, while many cases occurred here, no pure indians were taken, and that none of the *mestizos* who were affected died — the mortality being confined to the foreigners.

Dr. Castle had moved, but his place was as interesting as ever. For pets, he had three hairless dogs, a *mapachtl*, two macaws, two parrots, and a lot of doves, one of which he had taught tricks. He was much interested in cactuses, and had established a garden in which he planned to have all the species of the district. We had purchased some iguanas in the market, and Louis had been skinning them. The Doctor said that there were three species of iguanas in the district, the largest being green, changing to orange or gray, and its flesh not being eaten, as it is too sweet; the second species is of medium size, and gray or black in color; the third is rarer, smaller, and is striped lengthwise; it lives among the rocks near the coast. The two last species are both eaten, and are often sold in market. Here we learned, by a casual remark which Manuel dropped on seeing the ugliest of the hairless dogs, that these are believed, not only here, but in Puebla, and no doubt elsewhere through the Republic, to cure rheumatism. In order to effect a cure, the dog must sleep for three nights with the patient, and the uglier the dog the more certain the cure. Through Dr. Castle, we also learned that the Zapotec indians hereabouts, have many songs, of which the *sandunga* is a great favorite. Questioning an indian friend of mine, we afterwards learned that there are many of these pieces of music which are held to be truly indian. The words are largely Zapotec; Spanish words are scattered through the song, and the sentiment is largely borrowed. Most of the songs are love-songs, and they abound in metaphorical expressions. Our little trip to Huilotepec was for the purpose of photographing the curious and interesting *mapa* belonging to the village. We rode out over the hot and dusty river-bed road, arriving at noon. Sending for the *agente* and *secretario*, we ordered breakfast and made known our errand. Though it plainly was not to their taste, the *mapa* was brought out for our inspection. It is painted on a piece of coarse cotton cloth, of native weaving, in three colors — blue, red and black. The places around Huilotepec are indicated by their ancient hieroglyphs. Several personages of the ancient time are represented in the conventional manner commonly used in Zapotec writings before the Conquest. After eating, we placed the *mapa* against the wall, wrote out a description of it, and photographed it. Dismay now filled the soul of the *agente*, and the one *principal* whom he had summoned for advice. They talked long and earnestly with me about the *mapa*, and begged me to assure the *jefe* that it was no good; that it was not *autorizado*; that it was *mudo*. To quiet their fears, I was compelled to write a letter to that effect to be delivered to the *jefe;* if it ever came to hand, he certainly found it incomprehensible. Mrs. Seler, in her book, describes the trouble that they had in seeing this *mapa*, and the interest which their examination of it aroused. Dr. Castle told us that, several years ago, he accompanied a Mr. Werner and a priest to Huilotepec to see the *mapa*, and, if possible, to secure a picture of it. For a long time they were unable to secure a glimpse of the old document, and it was only when the priest assured the indians that the doctor was an American engineer, who had been commissioned to survey the line in dispute between the village and the Juaves, that they were allowed to see it. Before permission was then given, a general meeting of the *principales* was held, and none of the guests were permitted to touch the document. Mr. Werner made an exposure, which he sent to the States for development; it was lost or destroyed. It is thus possible that ours is the only picture of it in existence.

We had been told that a coach went regularly from San Geronimo to Tuxtla Gutierrez, making the journey in two days. This seemed too good to be true, and no one at Tehuantepec knew anything of such an arrangement, but we took the train the following morning for San Geronimo, hoping to get off without delay. All that the traveller sees upon descending from the train is the station, the place of Señor Espindola, and the little Hotel Europa. To our surprise, we found that our baggage had not yet come from Coatzacoalcos, although we had seen it loaded on the train ourselves. Still worse, we were informed that frequently fifteen days were consumed in transportation of freight from that point hither, and that we had no right to expect it so promptly. Inquiry regarding the coach revealed the fact that no such vehicle existed. Six hard days of horseback riding would be necessary for the journey, and, though Ramon admitted himself to be much better, he was too weak for such an undertaking. This had had its influence in determining us to go by coach in the first place. When in doubt as to what we should do, Señor Espindola suggested that the journey could be made by ox-cart in ten or eleven days. Though this seemed slow, it was better than to run risks with our invalid, and we determined to journey in that fashion as soon as our luggage should appear.

The station is situated on a somewhat elevated plain, constantly swept by heavy winds. While we were there, this wind was hot, and loaded with dust. In the afternoon, we walked through the indian town, which extends over a considerable area. The houses are rectangular, with adobe walls, mostly whitewashed, and with steep, pitched roofs. We met a funeral procession in the road, with the usual band in front. The coffin open, so as to show the child, was carried on the shoulders of several men. The mother, in contortions of real or simulated grief, was supported by two women, and the mourners brought up the rear, wailing now and then. Among the mourners was a woman who suffered from black *pinto*, notably developed. The principal industry of the town is pottery. The clay, which is of a greyish-black color, is stiff and hard, and is first broken up with a mallet. When worked into a stiff paste, it is built by hand into great *ollas* and plates, one and a half or two feet in diameter. These *ollas* we saw at many houses, and sometimes they were lashed to carts, plainly for bringing water from the stream. A single *olla* thus lashed, practically filled a fair-sized cart.

The little hotel at the station is a new venture, and

Drying Pottery; San Geronimo

Cart and Olla; San Geronimo

deserves complete success. At few places in Mexico have we found meals so good and cheap. In the evening, more from curiosity than expectation, we watched the train come from the east, and to our surprise and satisfaction, found our luggage. We had really made up our minds that we must spend some days in waiting; on the whole, the quiet and comfort of the little tavern would not have been unpleasant; but we hastened at once to Señor Espindola, and urged him to make instant arrangements for our leaving in the morning. To this he replied that no *carretero* would be likely to start on Sunday, and that we would have to wait until the following day. Matters turned out better than anticipated, and before nine, the following morning, our arrangements had been made. Two *carretas* were hired, at twenty-eight pesos each, to make the journey; our driver agreed that, without counting that day, he could get us to Tuxtla in eight days; in order to encourage him, we promised to pay five pesos extra for each *carreta*, in case we reached the city of Tuxtla on Monday the 11th. His name was Eustasio; he was a good-natured little Zapotec, from Juchitan originally, but living now at Guviño, Union Hidalgo. He warned us that, for the first day, we would have to put up with some discomfort, but that, upon reaching his home, he would fit us out magnificently. He promised to start at four that afternoon, and we were ready; of course, he was not, nor was he at five; so we went back to the hotel for a last good supper, and finally at 5:50 started. There were four teams and carts in the company, loaded with freight for Hidalgo. The night was clear, with a fine moon. The road was over heavy sand. Sometimes we walked in the moonlight, passing Ixtaltepec at 8:30, and reaching Espinal at ten, where we lost three-quarters of an hour in loading freight. From there all went well, until a-quarter-of-two in the morning, when we were passing through a country covered with scrub timber. Here we constantly met many carts heavily loaded; the road was narrow, and several times collisions, due to the falling asleep of one or other of the *carreteros*, were narrowly escaped. Finally, one really did take place, between our second cart and a heavily loaded one going in the other direction. The axle of our cart was broken, and the vehicle totally disabled. Two hours and a quarter were consumed in making repairs and in reloading. Here, for the first time, we were impressed with two characteristics in our driver: first, his ability to swear, surpassing anything that we had ever heard; second, his astonishing skill and ingenuity in repairing any accident or break, which happened on the road. Before our journey was over, we learned that both these qualities are common to his profession. It was four o'clock in the morning before we were again upon our way. All hope of reaching Union Hidalgo at the promised hour disappeared. Before sunrise, we had turned into the hot, dusty, broad, straight high-road, which, after my journey of 1896, I had devoutly hoped never to see again. Just as the sun rose, we took quite a walk, killing some parrots, *calandrias*, and *chacalaccas* as we walked. They said that *javali* — peccaries, — were common there. The day was blisteringly hot, long before we reached Union Hidalgo; hot, hungry and sleepy, we reached our carter's home, a little before ten in the morning. The *carreta* in which we were travelling was here far ahead, and after we had rested half-an-hour or more, Manuel, hot and perspiring, appeared, and reported that the disabled cart had broken down again, and that the other two were delayed by a sick animal. All came straggling in later. We had planned to leave here toward evening, travelling all Monday night; but hardly had we rested a little, and eaten dinner, when Eustasio announced that we should spend the night here, and not leave until the following

The Drunkard's Exchange; Union Hidalgo

Before Reaching Union Hidalgo

afternoon. He said the animals were hot and tired from travelling in the daytime, and that to push on would defeat our plans. He swore that, unless God decreed otherwise, we should reach Tuxtla Gutierrez by the promised date. There was nothing for it but submission, though we would gladly have chosen a more interesting town than Union Hidalgo for a stay of almost two days. When evening came, I took my bed of poles out into the open air, into the space between two houses; Ramon lay down upon a loaded *carreta*, also out of doors, while Louis and Manuel took possession of hammocks in one of the houses. It was a cloudless night, with brilliant moon. The air soon grew cool. After midnight, I was aroused by the most frightful yelling, and opening my eyes, I saw a barefooted, bareheaded indian yelling out the most frightful imprecations and oaths. At first I thought that he was insulting some one in the house, but both the houses were fast closed. Ramon, completely wrapped in his blanket, could attract no notice, and I did not believe that I had been observed, nor that I was addressed. For quite ten minutes the crazy drunkard stood there in the moonlight, bawling out a frightful torrent of abuse, invective, and profanity, with an occasional "*Viva Mexico! Muere Guatemala!*" patriotically thrown in. At last he disappeared, but for a long time could be heard howling, as he went from house to house. Believing that it might be well to be prepared for intruders, I arose and pulled a stake from one of the carts, and laid it at my side, upon the bed. But I was soon fast asleep again. Awaking at five, I found myself so cold, and the dew so heavy, that I dressed, and wrapped my blanket around me, and sat up, waiting for daylight. At 5:30 our drunken friend passed again, somewhat less voluble, but still vociferous. He was absolutely crazed with drink, and through the day several times made his appearance, and always with a torrent of abuse and profanity which made one's blood run cold. Before the day was well begun, a second person, almost as drunk, but far more quiet, a nice-looking old man, began making similar visits about the village. The two drunkards, differing in age and build, differed also in dress, but on the occasion of one of their visits, they were taken with the crazy notion of exchanging clothes, and proceeded to undress, making the exchange, and re-clothing themselves in garments ridiculously non-fitting — all with the utmost gravity and unsteadiness. During the day, our *carretas* were being prepared. Apologizing for the inconvenience of the preceding day, Eustasio proposed to fix our cart "as fine as a church." He put a decent cover over it, and laid our sacks of plaster on the floor. Upon this, he spread a layer of corn-stalks, and over them, a new and clean *petate*. To be sure, the space left above was low for comfort, and we were horrified when we saw him loading up the second one, not only with the balance of our luggage, but high with maize, fodder, and great nets of ears of corn, to feed the animals. We had supposed that two persons and part of the luggage would go in each of the carts, and never thought of carrying food enough to last four oxen eight days. Crowding four people into our *carreta* made it impossible to lie down in comfort. Still, such is the custom of the country, and we submitted. During the day we heard a woman crying in a house. Upon investigating, we found that she was the wife of a *carretero* who had been injured on the road, and for whom a *carreta* had been sent. Shortly afterward, they brought the poor fellow into town, amid weeping and lamenting. When they took him from the *carreta* in which he had been brought, he was supported by two men and helped into the house, where he was laid upon a hammock. He groaned with pain, and a crowd of curious villagers pressed into the room.

It was easy to locate four broken ribs behind, and he complained of great internal bleeding. It seemed that he had started to climb up onto his moving cart in the usual way, and the stake which he had seized broke, letting him fall to the ground under the wheel of the heavily-loaded cart, which passed over his body.

Finally, all was ready, and at about five in the evening we started. Packed like sardines in a box, we were most uncomfortable. Personally, I did not try to sleep, neither lying down, nor closing my eyes. Shortly after leaving town, we crossed a running stream, and from the other side went over a piece of corduroy, upon which we jounced and jolted. Soon after, we descended into a little gully, from which our team had difficulty in drawing us. The baggage-cart had a more serious time; the team made several attempts to drag it up the slope, but failed, even though our whole company, by pushing and bracing, encouraging and howling, aided. There was a real element of danger in such help, the slipping animals and the back-sliding cart constantly threatening to fall upon the pushers. Finally, the cart was propped upon the slope, and its own team removed; our team, which was heavier and stronger, was then hitched on, but it was only with a hard tug, and with heavy pushing, that success was gained, and the cart reached the summit of the slope. We crossed a fine marsh of salt water, quite like the lagoon at San Mateo del Mar, and were told that we were not far from the Juave town of San Dionisio. From here, the country, was, for a distance, an open plain. With the moonlight, the night was almost as bright as day; cold winds swept sheets of sand and dust over us. At one o'clock, we happened upon a cluster of six or eight carts, drawn up for rest, and the company of travellers were warming themselves at little fires, or cooking a late supper. We learned that this gypsy-like group was a *compania comica*, a comic theatre troupe, who had been playing at Tuxtla, and were now on their way to Juchitan. We never before realized that such travelling of ox-carts as we were now experiencing was a regular matter, and that the carter's trade is a real business. At two o'clock, we stopped to repack our loads, but were shortly on the way again. After the sun rose, we were in misery; the road was deep with dust, and we were grimy, hot, and choking. When the cross that marks the beginning of the land belonging to Ixhuatlan was pointed out, we were delighted, but it was still a long ride before we crossed the little stream and rode into the villlage.

Ixhuatlan is like all the Zapotec towns of this district, but less clean, on account of its lying in the midst of dust, instead of sand. Our carts drew up in a little grove, a regular resting-place for carting companies, where more than fifteen were already taking their daytime rest. Having ordered breakfast, we hastened to the stream, where all enjoyed a bath and cleansing. Coffee, bread, *tortillas*, eggs, and brandied peaches, made a good impression, and we ordered our buxom young Zapotec cook, who was a hustler, to have an equally good dinner ready at 2:30. We set this hour, believing that she would be late, but she was more than prompt, and called us at two to a chicken dinner. It was interesting to watch the *carreteros* in the grove. The scenes of starting and arriving, packing and unpacking, chaffing and quarreling, were all interesting. In the lagoons of Vera Cruz, our boatmen applied the term *jornada* to a straight stretch across a lagoon made at one poling; here among the *carreteros*, the word *jornada* means the run made from resting-place to resting-place. In neither case is strict attention paid to the original meaning of the word, a day's journey. Ixhuatlan is a made town; a paternal government, disturbed over the no progress of the pure Juaves in their seaside towns, set aside the ground on which this town now rests, and moved a village of Juaves to the spot. High hopes were expressed for the success of the experiment; now, however, the town is not a Juave town. It is true, that a few families of that people still remain, but for the most part, the Juaves have drifted back to the shore, and resumed their fishing, shrimp-catching and salt-making, while the expansive Zapotecs have crowded in, and practically make up the population of the place. Between dinner and our starting, we wandered about the village, dropping into the various houses in search of relics. As elsewhere, we were impressed with the independent bearing and freeness of the Zapotec woman. She talks with everyone, on any subject, shrewdly. She loves to chaff, and is willing to take sarcasm, as freely as she gives it. In one house we had a specially interesting time, being shown a lot of things. The woman had some broken pottery figures of ancient times, but also produced some interesting crude affairs of modern make from Juchitan. These were figures of men and women — the latter generally carrying babies in indian fashion — of horses and other animals. As works of art, they make no pretension, but they are stained with native colors, and are used as gifts at New Year's by the common people. Here we saw the making of baked *tortillas*, and sampled some hot from the oven. Such *tortillas* are called *tortillas del horno* — oven *tortillas*. Flat *tortillas*, about the size of a fruit-plate, are fashioned in the usual way; a great *olla* is sunk in the ground until its mouth is level with the surface. This is kept covered by a *comal*, or a smaller *olla*, and a good hot fire of coals is kept burning within. When the *tortillas* have been shaped, they are stuck on the hot *olla*, being pressed against the sides, to which they adhere, and are left to bake. In baking, the edges curl up so that the cake, instead of being flat, is saucer-shaped. They are crisp and good. Leaving at four, we continued on the hot, deep, dusty road, but saw interesting plants and animals along the way. There were fine displays of the parasitic fig, from examples where the parasite was just beginning to embrace its victim, through cases where it had surrounded the tree with a fine network of its own material, to those where the original tree-trunk was entirely imbedded in the great continuous gray investing trunk of the parasite, now larger than its host. Some trees bore bunches of pale-purple flowers of tubular form, which fell easily from the calyx, and dotted the ground along the roadside. Other trees appeared as if covered with veils of little purplish-red flowers hung over them. Others were a mass of golden bloom, the flowers being about the size of cherry blossoms. A few trees, yet leafless, showed large, brilliant white flowers at the tips of rather slender branches. At Ixhuatlan, we saw the first monkey's comb of the trip. This orange-yellow flower, growing in clusters so curiously shaped as to suggest the name, is among the most characteristic, from this point on through Chiapas into Guatemala. There were but few birds, but among them were macaws and toucans. Eustasio said that in the season, when certain berry-bearing trees are in full fruit, the latter may be seen by hundreds.

When night had really fallen, I unwisely sat in front with the driver, to prevent his sleeping, and to keep the animals moving. Both drivers had a way of dozing off, utterly regardless of the movements of the animals or the dangers of the road. Carts going in opposite directions must often depend absolutely upon the oxen for their chance of escaping collisions or being thrown over precipices. Frequently the animals themselves stop, and the whole company is at a standstill until the driver wakes up. In this *jornada*, we had planned to reach La Frontera, the border of the state of Chiapas, at which place we had been promised we should arrive at 8:30 in the morning. Everything had gone well, and we were just about to reach the place, where it was planned to repack for the last time; it was just daylight, and Eustasio was congratulating us upon our prompt arrival; we drove to the brink of a dry stream, on the other side of which was our resting-place; just at that instant, we heard the other driver cry out; we stopped, and found that the baggage-cart was overturned. This dashed all hopes. There was unhitching, unloading, the making of a new axle, and reloading. It was plain that we could not reach La Frontera. While the men were putting things to rights, we strolled up the dry stream-bed to a shanty, where Eustasio told us we could breakfast. There was a well there, with fresh water, and the shanty, for the refreshment of travellers, consisted of nothing but a little shelter of poles. Here, however, we found baked *tortillas*, *atole*, and hard meat; the breakfast for four persons, cost twenty-five centavos, equal to ten cents American money. Through the day, birds were hunted and skinned, reading and writing carried on, until at half-past-three in the afternoon we were again ready for movement. The road was now sandy, and not dusty, the sand being produced by the decomposition of crystalline rocks. Mounting to a high *llano*, we shot a pair of curious birds, which looked like water-birds, but were living in a dry place and were able to run with great speed. They were of the size of a hen, and had a long beak, long legs and four flat though not webbed toes. At the end of this high *llano*, we passed the Hacienda of Agua Blanca, a property belonging to the *jefe* of Juchitan. From here, we descended rapidly over a poor road, coming out at nine onto the straight road from Tapanatepec, at this point four leagues behind us. From here on, the whole road was familiar to me. La Frontera was just ahead, and, arriving there at 10 o'clock, we spent an hour. Before us rose a massive mountain, the ascent of which seemed appalling. We could see a white line of road zigzagging up its side, and well remembered Governor Leon's pride in having constructed a cart-road against great natural difficulties. Thirty or forty ox-teams had gathered here, either ready to make the ascent, or resting, after having come down the mountain. Having gotten breath and courage, we started at about eleven. The road had suffered during the five years since I last passed over it, but was still an excellent work of engineering. As we mounted, zigzagging constantly, the magnificent view over the valley widened; each new turn increased its beauty. My companions were asleep, and had had so little rest recently, that I hated to disturb them for the view. When, however, we were two-thirds up the slope, they awakened, and were as delighted as myself. We all got out, and walked for a considerable distance. An astonishing number of little streams and pools of fresh water burst forth from the rocks, and cut across the road or flowed along its sides. Finally, we reached the summit, and began the descent. This had made no impression on me when I went over it on horseback, but travelling in an ox-cart was a different matter, and I shall never again forget it. It was less abrupt than the ascent — less of vertical zigzag, and more of long steady windings. It also was excavated in the solid rock. It was badly neglected, and the cart jolted, and threatened every instant to upset us, or leap into the gulf. Coming out into a more level district, we passed Paraje and Dolores, reaching Carizal at five, where we stopped for the day. This is a regular resting place for *carreteros*, and there were plenty of carts there for the day.

As soon as the oxen were unyoked, I turned out my companions and lay down in the cart, trying to get an hour's sleep before the sun should rise, as I had not closed my eyes since leaving Union Hidalgo two days before. I was asleep at once, but in less than an hour was awakened by the assaults of swarms of minute black-flies, whose stings were dreadful. The rest of the company suffered in the same way, so we all got up and went to work. A group of *carreteros* breakfasting, invited me to eat with them — hard *tortillas*, *atole* and salted meat, formed a much better breakfast than we got, a little later, at the house upon the hill where travellers eat their meals. At this house they had a little parrot which was very tame, and also a *chacalacca*, which had been hatched by a domestic hen from a captured egg. This bird is more slender and graceful than a hen, but our landlord informed us that its eggs are much larger than those of the common fowl, and much used for food. Both this bird and the little parrot regularly fly off with flocks of their wild fellows, but always come back afterward to the house. This was a most interesting example of an intermediate stage between true wildness and domescation. There was little doing throughout the day. Heat, black-flies, and sunlight all made it impossible to sleep; but we took a bath in the running brook, and skinned some birds, and tasted *posole* for the first time. *Posole* is a mixture of pounded or ground corn and sugar, of a yellow or brownish color, much like grape-nuts. It may be eaten dry, but is much more commonly mixed with water. The indian dips up a *jicara* full of clear spring water, and then, taking a handful of *posole* from his pouch, kneads it up until a rather thick, light-yellow liquid results, which is drunk, and is refreshing and satisfying.

Almost all the *carreteros* at this camp were Juchitecos. They were great, strong fellows, and almost all of them wore the old-fashioned indian breech-clout of red cotton under their drawers or trousers. When they were working at their carts, greasing the wheels, or making repairs, they were apt to lay by all their clothing but this simple piece of cloth, and their dark-brown bodies, finely muscled, hard and tough, presented handsome pictures. The little fellows who accompanied them, up to the age of twelve, usually ran about with no article of clothing save their little breech-clouts and white cotton shirts. In the early afternoon, serious work began, and everywhere we saw these men patching coverings, greasing wheels, readjusting cargoes, feeding and watering their animals, harnessing, and making other preparations for leaving. During the idle portion of the day, dice were in evidence, and Eustasio was fascinated with the game. The stakes, of course, were small, but he kept at it persistently until he had lost five pesos, when, with forcible words, he gave up. I am sure the dice were loaded, but I am equally sure, from all I know of Eustasio, that the next time he makes that journey, he will have some loaded dice himself. Setting out at 3:30, we were at the head of a long line of cars, and were soon making another steady zigzag to ever greater heights than those before climbed. According to the official *itinerario*, the distance from Dolores to San Miguel is five leagues; we had left Dolores a league behind in arriving at Carizal, and we naturally assumed that four leagues would bring us to San Miguel. Eustasio, however, who never under-estimated, claimed that it would take constant travelling until eight in the morning to reach Los Pinos, which is still this side of San Miguel. This is a fair example of the inaccuracy of figures published by the government. As I looked behind at the long line of carts, some of which were empty, and able to journey at good speed, the desire took possession of me to hire one, at least for a short distance, in the hope of getting a little sleep. Looking over the line, to make my choice, I had just selected one, and was about to broach my plan, when its driver ran the vehicle into the branches of a tree, which projected over the road, and tore away his awning. The idea was unaffected by this accident, however, and picking out a cart, which had a thick layer of corn-husks piled in it, promising a comfortable bed, I arranged my bargain with the owner, and deserted my party, betaking myself to my private car. Having no load, we pushed ahead and, stretching myself at full length upon the heap of corn-husks, I was soon asleep. It was my purpose to disembark at Los Pinos, but we had passed that place long before I awoke, and were in sight of San Miguel when I opened my eyes. It was too early for breakfast, so I concluded to ride along to Macuilapa, where my carter turned off into another road. It was just eight when we arrived, and I thought of my companions as probably just reaching Los Pinos. Starting from there at three in the afternoon, they should overtake me at seven. So I took possession of the great country-house, sitting in the corridor all day long. The house is a long, large, single-storied building, with heavy tiled-roof; the store-houses, sheds and other out-houses, with the adobe huts belonging to the workmen, surround a somewhat regular area. The view, however, in front of the house is uninterrupted, and looks off into a narrow valley, bounded prettily by hills. The house has a wide brick-paved corridor. Near it was an interesting ancient stone carving. The rock was coarsely crystalline, and gray, or olive-gray in color. It had been battered into the bold, simple outline of a frog, crouched for leaping; the head had an almost human face, with a single central tooth projecting from the lower jaw. The work was in low relief, and looked as if the ancient workman had taken a natural boulder, and beaten with his hammer-stone only sufficiently to bring out the details. The stone measured perhaps four feet in length, three feet in breadth, and two feet in thickness. It was found in the mountains near, and, from the marks upon it, seems to have been embedded in the soil half way up the legs. Probably, when first made, it was placed so that the feet were even with the ground surface, but the accumulation of vegetable soil since has been considerable. The Hacienda of Macuilapa manufactures sugar and raises indigo, quantities of the seed of which were being cleaned when I was there. The owner of the place is a man of means, but the meals served were of a mean and frugal kind. Everyone made dire prophecies about the time of possible arrival of my companions, and the period necessary for our further journey to Tuxtla Gutierrez. I had not expected my companions before seven, and after these dismal forebodings, gave up that expectation. To my surprise, they appeared, in good health and spirits, at five o'clock, though with exciting tales of peril and suffering. After a meal together, we again mounted in the old fashion, and were on our way. The air was fresh and cool, and at 9:30 the moon rose, giving perfect light. The road was high and sandy, with occasional small ascents and descents. At eleven, we stopped to rest, I agreeing to wake them all at midnight; at one o'clock I was awakened by our *carretero* raising the tongue of the wagon! We passed La Razon at three. As one of the oxen, which had been somewhat lame, was now in bad condition, we all dismounted, half-a-league before we reached Zapote, and walked the rest of the way. The Hacienda of Zapote is really almost a town. There are two *fincas*, belonging to two brothers. Their fine large houses, the outbuildings, and the clusters of adobe huts for the workmen, make an imposing appearance. We stopped at the first group of buildings, which stands a little lower than the other. Arriving at six, we spent the whole day at this place; the meals at the great house were excellent and cheap. In the afternoon we heard marimba-playing; the instrument

A Day Rest; the Carizal

Marimba-Playing; Hacienda de Zapote

was called *la golondrina* and cost the owner forty-three pesos. The players were carefully trained, being four brothers. The youngest of them was not more than fourteen years old, but he put much expression and spirit into his playing. It was the first time that any of the party, but myself, had heard this instrument, and all were delighted at its brilliant, quick, and pleasing music. We left at 3:45 in the afternoon, but our ailing animal was worse than ever, and Eustasio ran ahead, trying to secure others at different ranches. He had had no success when, after a rough ride of several hours, we drew up at Jiquipilas, where we waited until the morning. We planned to secure new animals, to leave at dawn, and to reach Tuxtla after a twenty-four hour ride. We laid down and slept, waking at five, but finding no sign of animals. We breakfasted at seven, and a little later the new oxen appeared. There were two yokes of rather light animals. Leaving our sick beast, and driving the other three along with us, the new animals were put to the loads, and at eight o'clock we started. I failed to recognize Rancho Disengaño, but having passed it, we found ourselves at the bottom of the much-dreaded, last important climb of the journey. The little team dragging the passenger cart was inefficient and unruly; tiring of them, I dismounted and went ahead on foot. For a time I drove the unyoked cattle, but a stubborn one wandering into the brush, I gave up the job, and left poor Louis, who had just overtaken me, to chase him. He had hard work, through tangled brush, here and there, up and down, until at last the animal was once more upon the road. The boy was hot, tired, and loaded with *pinolillos*. These insects had been in evidence for a long time back. They are exceedingly small ticks, which fix their claws firmly in the flesh, and cause intolerable itching. Keeping in the road, the traveller is little likely to be troubled by them; but walking through grass, or among leafy plants, is dangerous. Having climbed a portion of our great ascent, we found ourselves at Agua Bendita. It was not as beautiful as on the occasion of my other visit; the projecting ledge of rock had little water dripping, and in the round catch-basins, which formerly were filled with fresh, clear water, there was scarcely any; on account of the unusual dryness, the ferns were wilted, and there was little of that beauty and freshness which so delighted me before. Eustasio said that he had never seen the spot so dry in all his many journeys. Nor were there orchids blooming on the great tree near; nor any of the little toucans which had been so attractive in 1896. As we stood, seeking for these well-remembered things, we heard curious cries rising from the valley. At first, I thought it was indians wailing for the dead; then, that it was a band of pilgrims singing. But it turned out to be a company of cowboys, bringing cattle up for shipment to Tabasco. Some rode ahead, and, with loud but not unmusical cries, invited and urged the animals and their drivers to follow. The beasts were divided into three bands, thirty or forty in a band, each of which had its mounted drivers. The animals were lively, and we were warned that they were *muy bravo*. Manuel had taken the task of driving our loose cattle, and was fearful that he would be overtaken, asserting that the cowboys had said that he must keep on, as they could not pass him with their animals. When he came up to where we were, we put a quick end to his folly, driving our three oxen to the outer edge of the road, where Louis and he stood guard over them, while I crept up on the cliff to avoid scaring the animals that were coming. It took much driving, urging, and coaxing on the part of the cowboys to get the first two or three to pass us, but after they had led the way, the others followed with a rush.

Agua Bendita

Moving the Great Stone; Agua Bendita

Presently our passenger-cart came along, with both teams of oxen hitched to it; the new animals had proved too light to drag their proper loads, so the freight-cart had been left behind, and the full force employed in dragging the first cart up the hill. Just beyond this spot, we found a gang of indians, under a superintendent, prying off an immense rock mass that had fallen from the cliff above onto the road, with the intention of dumping it over the wall into the abyss. It would have been a sight to have seen it plunge, but we had no time to wait, so simply stopped a few minutes to see the method of moving the immense mass with pole pries. Our cart had gone ahead, so we finished the ascent on foot, and having gained the summit, walked a short distance on the high plateau to Petapa, where the cart and *carretero*, Manuel and Ramon, were waiting. Before we arrived, we met our men going back with the four oxen for the freight-cart. We had supper at the ranch, and waited, until at six o'clock everything was ready. Here we sent back the two yokes of animals which we had brought from Jiquipilas, and secured a fine, strong beast to make up our number, and started. We did not stop to grease the wheels, for lack of time. It was dark, and the first part of the journey was uncertain and difficult; coming out on to the Llano Grande, we found things easy, though here and there were stony places, where we jolted fearfully. At 10:30, we had passed La Cienega, and our ungreased wheels were not only an annoyance, but, Eustasio suggested, a source of danger, as they might take fire. So, at 11:30, we stopped to grease them. As the axles and wheels were then too hot for grease to be safely applied, we lay down while they should cool. Probably in less than five minutes, we were all asleep, and no one moved until, waking with a start and looking at my watch, I found it two in the morning. We hastily applied grease, without removing the wheels, and hurried onward, passing Sabino Perez, Yerba Santa, and Sabinal. Here, the errors in our *itinerario*, and in our driver's guessing at distances, were curiously emphasized. We had a rather heavy descent, for some distance, over a limestone hill called Santo Domingo. Nowhere do I know of any road which, under the best of circumstances, seems as long as the last stretch before Tuxtla Gutierrez. This we had noticed on our earlier journey, when we were mounted on horseback. Present conditions were not likely to diminish the impression. At last, at 11:30 in the morning of March 12, we reached the capital city of the State of Chiapas, and were taken by our *carretero* to the little old Hotel Mexico, kept by Paco, where we met a hearty welcome and, for several days, made up for the hardships of our journey in the way of eating.

CHAPTER XXIV

AT TUXTLA GUTIERREZ

(1901)

WE knew that Governor Pimentel was not at home, having met him in Coalzacoalcos, where we had presented our official letters, and had received from him a communication to his Lieutenant-Governor, Lopez. Having spent the afternoon in settling and cleaning, I called in the evening upon Governor Lopez and explained my needs. After chatting a little time together, he inquired whether I had not made the steamboat journey from Coalzacoalcos to Vera Cruz in March, 1896, and, upon my answering in the affirmative, told me that we had been fellow-travellers on that occasion. He promised that there should be no delay, and madc an appointment with me for the morning. I then called on Don Conrado Palacios, who lived directly opposite our little tavern, and who claimed that he recognized me the moment I dismounted from our cart this morning. He is still photographer, but for three years of the time since last we met has been living in the State of Vera Cruz, and but lately returned to Tuxtla. In the morning, Governor Lopez supplied the letters for my further journey, and summoned the *jefe politico* and the *presidente* of the city and gave them personal orders that they were to assist, in every way, my work at Tuxtla, among the Zoques. The *jefe* himself took charge of my arrangements, put his office at my disposition for a workshop, and the work began at once. Contrary to my usual experience, we had less difficulty in securing female subjects here than male. The male indians of Tuxtla are, in large part, employed in contract labor on *fincas* at a distance from the town. According to their contract, they are not subject to the order of local authorities, and may not be summoned without permission of their employers, or a pecuniary settlement with them. The first day, more than half the women were measured, and the second day, the rest. As is well known the women of Tehuantepec are famous for their beauty. It is not so well known that rivalry exists between them and the women of Tuxtla in this matter. This rivalry had been called to our attention on our preceding visit, and we found that it had in no wise abated. Personally, we saw no comparison between the two sets of women, the Tehuantepecanas being far superior. Eustasio, however, ungallantly and unpatriotically declared that he thought the women of Tuxtla the handsomer; however, we suspect that Eustasio would find the women of any town he might be in, the champions in beauty for the time being. Their dress is picturesque. The *enagua* is made of two strips of dark blue cloth, sewed together, side by side, with a fancy stitching of colored silks. The free borders are also decorated with similar stitching, and the ends of the strip, which is usually more than two yards in length, sewn together with similarly decorative needlework. In fastening this garment about the body, no belt is used. The open bag is gathered in about the waist, the surplus is folded into pleats in front and the overlap, at the upper edge, is so tucked in as to hold the garment tightly in place, and at the same time form a pouch, or pocket, in which small articles are carried. The little *huipil*, worn upon the upper body, is of thin, white cotton cloth, native-woven, but a neat and pretty stuff; there are no sleeves, and the neck-opening and arm-slits are bordered with pleated strips of cotton, worked with black embroidery. A larger

Zoque Mode of Carrying Babies;
Tuxtla Gutierrez

Fat, Rich, and Pinta; Tuxtla Gutierrez

huipil is regularly carried, but we never saw it in use; practically, it never is worn. If put in place, it would form a garment for the body, with the neck-opening and sleeves bordered with lace, and the lower edge reaching to the knees. The woman carries this garment with her, folding it into a sort of pad, which she places on her head, letting it hang down upon the back and shoulders. Upon this cushion, the woman carries a great bowl, made from the rind of a sort of squash or pumpkin, in which she brings her stuff to market. These vessels are a specialty of the neighborhood, being made at Chiapa; they are richly decorated with a lacquer finish, of bright color. In carrying a baby, the child is placed against one side of the body, with its little legs astride, one in front and one behind, and then lashed in place by a strip of cloth, which is knotted over the woman's opposite shoulder. Almost every Zoque woman is asymmetrical, from this mode of carrying babies, one shoulder being much higher than the other. Among the subjects measured, was a woman notable in several ways. She was the fattest indian woman we had ever seen; she was the richest of her kind, and not only were her garments beautiful in work and decoration, but she was gorgeous with necklaces, bristling with gold coins and crosses; more than this, she was a capital case of purple *pinta*. The disease is common among the indians of the town, and, while both the red and white forms are found, purple seems to be the common type. Sometimes the face looks as if powder-burned, the purple blotch appearing as if in scattered specks; at other times, the purple spots are continuous, and the skin seems raised and pitted.

It appears that the adjusting of family quarrels and disputes between friends are among the duties of the *jefe*. In the office that day, a quarrel was settled involving two young men related by blood and by comradeship; a woman and a man of middle age were also interested; the quarrel had been a serious one, involving assaults, ambushes, and shootings. The *jefe* first summoned each of the four persons singly, going over the whole matter with each one; the more intelligent of the two combatants was first to be reasoned with; then the woman was called in and he and she were left together in the office. For a long time, they would not even speak to each other. Finding this condition, the *jefe* reasoned with them, and warned them that they must come to some conclusion, after which he left them to themselves again. At first they would not speak, but finally held a conversation, and came to an understanding; the old man was then called in and made to talk the matter over with the two, who had already been in conference. Lastly, the more belligerent youth was summoned, the *jefe* remaining in the room with the whole party. At first he would not speak, but finally his pride and anger gave way, and he shook hands with his cousin, and the whole party left, after promising the *jefe* that the past should be forgotten.

The first afternoon that we were working, a curious couple came to the *jefe's* office. The woman was not unattractive, though rather bold and hard in bearing. She was dark, pretentiously made-up, and rather elegantly dressed. The gentleman was a quiet, handsome fellow, dressed in sober black. When they sailed in, I supposed they were the *jefe's* personal friends. Sitting down, they showed interest in my work, and the lady in a rather strident voice, but with much composure, addressed us in English. Her knowledge of our language, however, proved to be extremely limited, being confined to such expressions as "How are you, sir?" "I am very well," "Yes, sir," "No, sir," and "I know New York." She was a mystery to the town, where she was commonly called "the Turkish lady."

Zoque Women; Tuxtla Gutierrez

The Indian Alcaldes; Tuxtla Gutierrez

This nickname, her limited knowledge of English, and her boasted acquaintance with New York, aroused the question, in my mind, whether she might not have been an oriental dancer. She, herself, told us that she was born in South America, and referred to Caracas, as if it were a place with which she was familiar. The *jefe* was extremely polite in his dealings with these people, and, as soon as they were seated, rang his bell for glasses, and we all drank the lady's health in cognac. The fact was, that these two persons were prisoners; they had come here within a few days, and had the city for a prison; as they had made no effort to leave the town, their movements were not interfered with, but if they had attempted to step outside the city limits, they would have been shot without a word of warning. The *jefe* himself did not know who they were, nor what crime they had committed; nor did he know how long they would remain in his custody; they had come a weary journey, as he put it, "along the Cordillera;" they had been passed from hand to hand, from one *jefe* to another; when the order came, he was to start them on their journey to the *jefe* of the next district. Of the many stories told regarding them, a few will serve as samples. She was said to be the wife of a wealthy merchant of Campeche, from whom she had eloped with her companion, carrying away $150,000. According to another view, they were connected with an important band of forgers and robbers, who had been carrying on extensive operations. The most minutely detailed story, however, was that she had been the mistress and favorite of Francisco Canton, Governor of the State of Yucatan; that, pleased with a younger and handsomer man, she had stolen $7,000 from His Excellency, and attempted an elopement; that, captured, they were being sent as prisoners, nominally to Mexico. Whether any of these stories had a basis of fact, we cannot say, but from remarks the prisoners themselves made to us, we feel sure that the centre of their trouble was Merida, and that, in some way, they had offended the pompous governor. At all events, it is likely that, long before these words are written, both have met their death upon the road. It is a common thing for prisoners, passing along the Cordillera, to be shot "while attempting to escape from their guard."

The *jefe politico* of this district is a man of education, and professional ability; he is a physician, trained in the City of Mexico; he is ingenious in mechanics, and has devised a number of instruments and inventions of a scientific kind. He had been but a short time in this district, having come from Tonala, where he has a *finca*. He entertained us at his house, while we were there, and showed us every assistance. It is plain, however, that he found us a white elephant upon his hands. Not that his willingness was lacking, but where should he find one hundred indian men? We pestered him almost to death for subjects, when at last his *secretario* suggested the district jail. This was a veritable inspiration. There they were sure we would have no difficulty in finding the remainder of our hundred. To the jail we went, but out of seventy-five prisoners fully half were Tzotzils from Chamula and not Zoques. More than half of the remainder were not indian, but *mestizos*. In fact, out of the total number, only a baker's dozen served our purpose. When we again presented ourselves, the following morning, for subjects, the poor man was in genuine desperation. But again his assistant made a shrewd suggestion. Yesterday we were at the jail; to-day we should go to the *cuartel*, and measure the soldiers. There were two hundred there, and this would more than see us through. The *jefe* himself accompanied us to the barracks and introduced us to the colonel, leaving orders that we should be supplied with every aid, and went off happy, in the sense of a bad job well done. But out of the two hundred soldiers in the barracks, just ten turned out to be Zoques of pure blood. And long before the day was over, we were again clamoring at the *jefe's* house for thirty-six more subjects. To tell the truth, we doubted his ability to secure them, and, in order to lose no time, started our goods and plaster by *carreta* for San Cristobal. Still, while it was plain that he did not know where to look for help, the good man assured us that we should have our thirty-six subjects the next morning. Meantime, he sent officials with us to visit certain indian houses which we desired to examine, and arranged that we should see a certain characteristic indian dance at his house, at four o'clock that afternoon.

Tuxtla Gutierrez is a capital city. It is also a busy commercial centre. Of course, the population is for the most part *mestizo*, and not indian. We had been surprised at finding so many indians in the city as there were. We were yet more surprised to find to what extent the houses of the city, though admirably built, were truly indian in style, presenting many points of interest. The walls of the "god-house" were heavy and substantial, smoothly daubed with mud, neatly plastered and often adorned with colored decorations. The "cook-house," slighter and less well-built, was made of poles daubed with mud, and rough with heavy thatching. The granary was elevated above the ground, and sheltered with its own neat thatching.

In the afternoon, at four o'clock, we betook ourselves to the *jefe's* house to see the dance. At Tuxtla, there are two town governments, that of the *mestizos* and that of the indians. The indian officials — "*alcaldes indios*" — are recognizable by their dress, which is a survival of the ancient indian dress of the district. Their *camisa*, broad hat, and leather breeches, are characteristic. Around the head, under the hat, they wear a red cloth, and those who have served as indian *alcaldes* continue to wear this head-cloth after their official service ends. These indian officials had been commissioned to bring together the dancers, and make all necessary arrangements. The colonel, the prisoners of state, and one or two other guests were present. The leader of the dance was gaily dressed, in a pair of wide drawers with lace about the legs below the knee, a pair of overdrawers made of bright-colored handkerchiefs, and a helmet or cap of bright-red stuff from which rose a crest of macaw feathers, tipped with tufts of cotton. On his back, he bore a kind of pouch, the upper edge of which was bordered with a line of macaw feathers. In his hand, he carried a wooden war-axe. A pretty little girl, dressed in a Guatemaltec *enagua*, wore a fancy head-dress, and, in her hand, bore a *jicara*, which was filled with pink carnival flowers. These two dancers faced each other and in dancing moved slowly back and forth, and from one foot to the other; the only other dancers were two men, one of whom was dressed as, and took the part of, a woman. This couple danced in much the same way, but with greater freedom than the chief persons, and at times circled around them. The music consisted of a violin and native *pito* or pipe, and a drum of the *huehuetl* type,— cut from a single cylindrical block, but with skin stretched over both ends instead of one.

I was surprised the following morning when thirty-six subjects were produced; we knew that, for the moment, the building operations of the government palace were discontinued, and we suspected that all the work done by indians in Tuxtla was likewise temporarily ceased. When the last one had passed under the instruments, the *jefe* heaved a sigh, rang his bell for glasses, and the event was celebrated by a final draught of cognac.

The man with whom we had expected to arrange for

Zoque Dancers; Tuxtla Gutierrez

Tzendals from Tenejapa; Cold Hands

animals had promised to come to the hotel at seven. He came not then, nor at half-past, nor at eight, nor at nine. When we sent an inquiry, he made the cool reply, that it was now too late to arrange matters; that he would see us at eight the following morning. Furious at his failure, we ourselves went with the boy from the hotel at ten o'clock to his house, but could not get him even to open the door. "To-morrow! To-morrow!" was his cry. Desperate, we went, although it was now almost midnight, to another *arriero*, who, after some dickering, agreed to leave at eight the following morning, charging a price something more than fifty per cent above the usual rate. Of course he was behindhand, but we actually set out at nine.

CHAPTER XXV

TZOTZILS AND TZENDALS

(1901)

WE started out over the hot and dusty road, passing here and there through cuts of the white earth, which is used by the women of Chiapa in their lacquer-work. We soon reached the river, and, leaving our animals behind, to cool before swimming them across, embarked with a dozen other passengers, and all our baggage, in one of the great canoes, which we by no means filled. Landing on the other side, with an hour to wait, we walked down stream, and took a fine bath in the fresh cold, clear, deep water. Just below where we were bathing, some indians had exploded a dynamite cartridge, killing a quantity of fish, and the surface was immediately spotted with their white, upturned bellies. A canoe-load of four men put out to gather the fish, as soon as the shot was fired. Just as they reached the spot, and were leaning over the boat to catch them, the canoe overturned, and all the men were floundering in the water, up to their necks, and the canoe was rapidly drifting down the stream. The fish they get here are quite large, and seem to be a kind of cat-fish. Strolling back to our landing-place, we were interested in the lively scenes there being enacted. Under little arbors of leafy boughs, women were washing clothing; crowds of children, of both sexes, were playing on the sand or splashing in the water; half-a-dozen great canoes were dragged up on the bank, and amid these a group of little brown fellows, from ten to fourteen years of age, were swimming; here

Zoque Compadres Greeting; Tuxtla Gutierrez

Our Ferry-Boat; Chiapa

and there, a man or woman squatted in the shallow water, dipped water over their bare bodies with *jicaras*. Now and then the great ferry-boat, loaded with passengers and with animals swimming alongside, made its crossing. Presently our seven animals were swum across, and, after a moment's drying, were repacked and saddled, and we were ready for our forward movement.

Chiapa was formerly the great town of the Chiapanecs, an indian tribe to whom tradition assigns past splendor, but who, to-day, are represented in three villages, Chiapa, Suchiapa, and Acala. They are much mixed with Spanish blood, and have largely forgotten their ancient language. It is, however, from them, that the modern state, Chiapas, received its name. Chiapa, itself, is a city of some size, situated on a terrace a little way from the river, with a ridge of hills rising behind it. The *plaza* is large, and in it stands a market-building. Near by is a picturesque old gothic fountain, built of brick. Market was almost over, but we were interested in seeing the quantities of pineapples and cacao beans there offered. To lose no time waiting for dinner, we bought bread and one or two large pineapples, which we ate under the shade of the trees in the *plaza*. The pineapples were delicious, being tender and exceedingly sweet; our *arriero* refused to eat any of them, asserting that they were barely fit to eat, lacking sweetness, and being prickly to the taste. The pineapples of Simojovel were to his liking; they are sugar-sweet, leaving no prickly sensation, and anyone can eat three whole ones at a sitting. After luncheon, we looked about for examples of lacquer-work. In one house, we found some small objects and wooden trays of indifferent workmanship. An old crone, badly affected with *pinto*, the mother of the young woman artist, showed us the wares. With her was the older sister of the lady-worker, who, after we had bought two of the trays, asked whence we came. Upon our telling her that Manuel was a native of Cordoba, and that I had come from the United States, without a word of warning she raised her hands, turned her eyes upward, and gave vent to a torrent of shrill, impassioned, apostrophe to her absent, artistic sister: "*A dios, hermana mia*, Anastasia Torres, to think that your art-products should penetrate to those distant lands, to those remote portions of the world, to be the wonder and admiration of foreign eyes. *A dios, hermana mia*, Anastasia Torres!" This she repeated several times, in a voice high enough to be heard a block or two away. Leaving her to continue her exclamations of joy and admiration over the fate of her sister's workmanship, we returned to the *plaza*, where, in a house near by, we found a considerable stock of better work, consisting of decorated bowls, cups, toy *jicaras*, gourd-rattles, etc. This brilliant work, characteristic of the town, is carried hundreds of miles into the States of Oaxaca, Tabasco, Vera Cruz, and into the Republic of Guatemala. At two o'clock we hurried from the town in the midst of terrific heat. As we rode out, over the dry and sandy road, we were impressed by the display of death; not only was there one cemetery, with its whitened walls and monuments, but at least three other burial places capped the little hillocks at the border of the town. One, particularly attracted attention, as it resembled an ancient terraced pyramid, with a flight of steps up one side.

From the foothills, we struck up the flank of the great mountain mass itself. Mounting higher and higher, a great panorama presented itself behind and below us, including the Chiapa valley, with the hills beyond it. It was, however, merely extensive, and not particularly beautiful or picturesque. As we followed the slope towards the crest, into the narrowing valley, the scene became bolder, until we were at the very edge of a mighty chasm, which yawned sheer at our side. Following it, we saw the gorge suddenly shallow hundreds of feet by a vast precipice of limestone rock rising from its bottom. Having passed this, we journeyed on up the cañon, lessened in grandeur, but still presenting pretty bits of scenery. Up to this point, limestone had prevailed, but from here on, we passed over various formations — heavy beds of sand or clay, lying upon conglomerates and shales. The road wound astonishingly, and at one point, coming out upon a hog's-back ridge, we found that we had actually made a loop, and stood directly above where we had been some time before. Near sunset, we reached the summit, and looked down upon the little town of Ixtapa, upon a high *llano* below, and seeming to be a half-hour's ride distant. Descending on to the *llano*, we found it intersected by deep and narrow gorges; following along the level, narrow ridge, surrounded by ravines on every side, except the one from which we had approached, we presently descended, along its flank, the bank of the deepest of these *barrancas*. The sun had set long before we reached the bottom, and through the darkness, we had to climb up over the steep dugway in the sandy clay to the village, which we reached at seven. The little room supplied us for a sleeping-place was clean and neat, the floor was strewn with fresh and fragrant pine-needles, and the wooden beds were supplied with *petates*. Leaving before eight, the following morning, we travelled through a beautiful cañon, with an abundant stream of whitish-blue water, tumbling in fine cascades among the rocks, and dashing now and then into deep pools of inky blackness. Having passed through it, our bridle-trail plunged abruptly downward. From it, we looked upon a neighboring slope, cut at three different levels, one above the other, for the cart-road. Passing next through a small cañon of little beauty, but where the air was heavy with an odor like vanilla, coming from sheets of pale-purple or violet flowers, on trees of eight or ten feet in height, we reached San Sebastian, where we found our *carretero*, whom we supposed to have reached San Cristobal the day before. Rating him soundly, and threatening dire consequences from his delay, we resumed our journey. We were also worried over our *mozo*, who started from Chiapa at noon, the day before, with our photographic instruments, and whom we had not seen since, although there were several places where we would gladly have taken views. From here, for a long distance, the road was a hard, steep climb, over limestone in great variety — solid limestone, tufaceous stuff, concretionary coatings, satin spar, and calcite crystals. Having passed a small pueblo, or large *finca*, lying in a little plain below us, we looked down upon Zinacantan. The descent was quickly made, and passing through the village, without stopping, we made a long, slow, ascent before catching sight of our destination, San Cristobal. It made a fine appearance, lying on a little terrace at the base of hills, at the very end of the valley. Its churches and public buildings are so situated as to make the most impression; on account of its length and narrowness, the town appears much larger than it really is. We entered at one end, and then, practically, paralleled our trail through it to the centre, where we stopped at the Hotel Progreso, at 3:30 in the afternoon. We went to the palace, and made arrangements so promptly that we could have begun work immediately, if the *carretero* and *mozo* had not been behind. As it was, we waited until next day, and were warned by the *secretario* at the *jefatura* that there would not be enough light for work before nine o'clock. In the evening, we called on Padre Sanchez, well known for his study of the native languages, and the works he had written regarding them. He is a large man, well-built, of

The Jail; San Cristobal

Tzotzil Musicians in San Cristobal Jail

attractive appearance, and of genial manner. He has been *cura* in various indian towns among the Chamulas, and he loves the indians, and is regarded as a friend by them. We were prepared for a cold night, and had it, though no heavy frost formed, as had done the night before. In one day's journey, the traveller finds towns, in this neighborhood, with totally different climates. Here woolen garments are necessary, and in towns like Chamula and Cancuc the indians find the heaviest ones comfortable. Our rating of the *carretero* had an effect both prompt and dire; when we left him, he hastened to hire carriers to bring in the more important part of our load; these, he insisted, should travel all night, and at eight o clock we found them at the hotel. In the darkness they had stumbled, and our loads had fallen. Whole boxes of unused plates were wrecked, and, still worse, many of our choicest negatives were broken. At nine o'clock the missing *mozo* appeared with the instruments; it is customary for our carrier to keep up with the company, as we have frequent need of taking views upon the journey; this was almost the only instance, in the hundreds of leagues that we have travelled on horseback, over mountain roads, where our carrier had failed to keep alongside of the animals, or make the same time in journeying that we mounted travellers did.

Though there had been an early mist, there was no lack of sunshine, even before seven. Still, we did not go to the palace until nine o'clock, the hour set. San Cristobal was formerly the capital of the state, and its public buildings are more pretentious than usual in *cabeceras*. The place in which we did our work was a building of two stories, filling one side of the plaza. We worked in the broad corridor of the second story, outside of the *secretario's* office, from which our subjects, mostly indians who had come to pay school-taxes, were sent to us for measurement. The market-place of San Cristobal is characteristically indian. Not only do the two chief tribes which frequent it — Tzotzils and Tzendals — differ in dress, but even the different villages of each wear characteristic garments. The Tzotzil of Chamula differs from his brother of Huixtan and San Bartolome; the Tzendal women of Tenejapa, Cancuc and San Andres may be quickly recognized by difference in dress.

Most interesting are the Tzotzils of Chamula. Though looked upon by the *mestizos* of San Cristobal as mere brutes and savages, they are notably industrious. They weave heavy, woolen blankets and *chamaras*; they are skilled carpenters, making plain furniture of every kind; they are musicians, and manufacture quantities of harps, guitars, and violins; they braid straw, and make hats of palm; they are excellent leather-dressers, and give a black stain and polish to heavy leather, which is unequalled by the work of their white neighbors. Men wear lower garments of cotton, and heavy black woolen over-garments, which are gathered at the waist with woolen girdles. They wear broad-brimmed, low-crowned hats, of their own braiding, which they adorn with long, streaming, red and green ribbons. Their sandals are supplied with heel-guards of black leather, the height of which indicates the wealth or consequence of the wearer. These indians of Chamula have a love of liberty and desire for independence. The most serious outbreak of recent times was theirs in 1868, when, under the influence of the young woman, Checheb, they attempted to restore the native government, the indian life, and the old-time religion. Temples were erected to the ancient gods, whose inspired priestess the young woman claimed to be; but three hundred years of Christianity had accustomed them to the idea of a Christ crucified; an indian Christ was necessary, not one from the hated in-

Tzotzils; Huixtan

Tzotzil Woman; Chamula

vading race; accordingly, a little indian lad, the nephew of the priestess, was crucified, to become a saviour for their race. Their plans involved the killing of every white and *mestizo* in all the country; in reality, more than one hundred men, women, and children, in the *fincas* and little towns, were killed; San Cristobal, then the capital city, suffered a veritable panic, and it took the entire force of the whole state to restore order.

The Tzendals of Tenejapa are picturesque in the extreme. Their dark skin, their long black hair, completely covering and concealing the ears, their coarse features, and the black and white striped *chamaras* of wool — which they buy from the weavers of Chamula — form a striking combination. They do but little weaving, their chief industry being the raising and selling of fruits. Most of the men carry a little sack, netted from strong fibre, slung at one side. Among other trifling possessions in it, is generally a little gourd filled with a green powder, which they call *mai*, or *pelico*. It consists chiefly of tobacco, with a mixture of lime and chili, and is chewed, no doubt, for stimulating properties — to remove the weariness of the road, and "to strengthen the teeth," as some say.

When we had exhausted the stock of those who came to pay their taxes, it was suggested that we would find good subjects in the jail. This occupied what was once a fine old convent, built around a large open court, and connected with the church, which, judging from its elaborately carved façade, must have been beautiful. On presenting our credentials to the officials, an order was given, and all the pure-blood indians, one hundred at least, were lined up before us for inspection. There were Tzotzils from Chamula, and Tzendals from Tenejapa, and among them many excellent faces, showing the pure types, finely developed. Having made our inspection, and indicated those whom we should use, we looked about the prison. The prisoners were housed in the old rooms of the monastery, each of which was large enough for six or eight persons. In these rooms, each prisoner had his personal possessions — good clothing, tools, cherished articles, instruments of music. Those who cared to do so, were permitted to work at such things as they could do, and the product of their labor was sold for their benefit. Some braided palm into long strips, to make up into hats; others plaited straw into elaborate, decorative cords or bands for hats; some wove *pita* into pouches; some dressed leather. Almost all were busily employed. Freedom of conversation and visiting was permitted, and there was no particular hardship in the matter of imprisonment, except the inability to go outside. We were impressed with the fact that, in appearance and manner, few, if any, of these indian prisoners, particularly the Chamulas, showed any signs of criminal tendencies. In fact, they were as clean, as frank, as docile, as intelligent, as any persons we might find in Mexico. A little curious to know the charges on which they had been committed, we inquired, and discovered that some had fifteen or twenty points against them, among which were such trifling charges as murder, manslaughter, arson, rape, and highway robbery. We thought best not to inquire too closely, but it is doubtful, whether any of the subjects here incarcerated under these long and dreadful lists of charges, are guilty of anything except insurrection — a final struggle for freedom.

There were various signs of the approach of Holy Week, and the landlady at our hotel, and her various helpers, were busy manufacturing incense for that occasion. This was made in sticks, as thick as the thumb, and six or eight inches in length, of a black color. Besides copal, leaves and other materials from various kinds of odorous plants were em-

Position of Rest; Tzendals, Tenezapa

Tzotzils from Huixtan

ployed in its fabrication; the incense thus made is really fragrant, and it would be interesting to know whether it is, in part at least, of indian origin. In three days we had completed our examination of the men, but not a woman had been produced for examination. On the fourth day, we reiterated our demands to the authorities, and Don Murcio, the janitor or messenger, who had been put subject to our order, was almost frantic. He declared that to secure the women we needed would tax every power of the government; that they refused to come; that his mere appearance in the market caused a scattering. Finally, we told him, that if he would provide twenty-five Chamula women, we would get the Tzendals in their villages, as we passed through them. Encouraged, by having one-half of our demand abated, he made another visit to the market. Soon we heard excited voices, and a moment later Don Murcio came rushing up the stairs with both arms filled with black *chamaras*. It is the custom of the indian women, when they come to market, and settle down with wares to sell, to fold their heavier garments and lay them on the ground beside them. Don Murcio had gathered up the first of these he came to, and fled with them to the government palace, while the crowd of angry women, chasing along behind, expressed their feelings vigorously. Putting the garments out of reach, the women were told by the officials, that each would receive back her property as soon as the strangers made their desired measurements. While we were dealing with the first cluster, Don Murcio sallied forth, and returned once more with garments and women. In this way, the work proceeded, until the final lot were in our hands. Not to unnecessarily increase their terrors, we had refrained from photographing, until the final company had been secured. We had told the officials of our plan, and as these later ones were measured, they were told that they must wait for their garments until the last one was measured, and until the gentleman had done some other work. When all had been measured, it was explained to the six of seven in the group, that they were to go down into the *patio*, where a picture would be taken of the company. That they might be properly prepared for the picture, their garments were returned. Suspecting no treachery, Don Murcio led the way, and one of two police officers accompanied the forward part of the procession, while Louis brought up the rear, in expectation of making the portrait. All went well until the first two or three had entered the *patio*, when the rest suddenly balked, and started to run out onto the street. Hearing the confusion, I started down and caught one of the women as she neared the doorway, while Louis held another, and each of the police officers, and Don Murcio, seized a prisoner. So violent, however, were the struggles, and so loud the outcries of the woman whom I held, that I released her, which was the unintended signal for each of the other guards to do the same, and our group vanished and all thought of gathering a second was given up in desperation.

The morning had thus passed; animals for the further journey had been ordered for ten o'clock, and were really ready a little before three. For once, however, *we* were not prepared. It was our custom to pack the busts in petroleum boxes; these boxes, each holding a five-gallon can of oil, are of just the size to take a single bust, and they are so thin and light, yet at the same time, so well constructed, that they served our purpose admirably. In small indian towns, they are frequently unobtainable, but in the places where *mestizos* live, it had been always easy to procure them, at prices varying from ten to twenty-five cents each. In a town the size of San Cristobal, it should be easy to get them; to our surprise, we found that they had been in such demand, for carrying purposes by public

TZOTZIL BROTHERS; CHAMULA

TZENDAL FATHER AND SON; TENEJAPA

workmen, that the supply was small and the price outrageous. We had left the securing of the boxes and the packing of the busts to our plaster-worker, and, though we knew he had had difficulty, imagined that he had secured all needed, and that the busts would be all ready. Diligent search, however, had secured but two boxes, and ridiculous prices had been demanded for those. All of us took to the streets, visiting stores and private houses, and at last five boxes were secured, though they were a dilapidated lot, with bad covers. For these we paid an average of sixty-two cents each. Realizing the time and labor necessary for securing boxes, stuff for packing, and for the work of putting up the busts, we dismissed our horsemen, and arranged for leaving the next morning. In fact, night had fallen before our work was done. Leaving a little before eight, we had a magnificent mountain ride. For a league or more, we rose steadily over a cart-road; keeping at a high altitude, and, with but little of ups and downs, we journeyed through fine pine forests, with oaks mingled, here and there, among the pines. We met quantities of Chamula and Tencjapa indians on their way to market. The Chamulas carried chairs, loads of well-tanned skins, and sacks full of little, round wooden boxes, well and neatly made, while the Tenejapes were loaded with nets of oranges, *limas*, and *ahuacates*. We were sorry to leave the village of Chamula to one side, but lack of time forbade our visiting it. It was amusing to note the terror of our *arriero* on the road. Until we passed Cancuc, he was constantly expecting attack from the dreadful indians of Chamula, Tenejapa, and Cancuc, telling us that such attacks might be expected at any time, but particularly in the early morning and in the dusk of evening. What indians we met were most gentle, and answered our salutations with apparent kindness. After a long journey on the high, smooth road, we finally began descending into a pretty valley, and soon saw the great town of Tenejapa, below us, on a space almost as level as a floor, neatly laid out, and still decked with the arches erected for a recent fiesta. The *agente* of the town had been warned of our coming, by telephone from the *jefatura*, and received us warmly, a little before one o'clock, giving us a large and comfortable room in the municipal building, supplied with chairs and benches, and a table, though without beds or mats. We were here delayed by the slowness of the old man, who had been furnished at San Cristobal for carrying our instruments. By three o'clock, all was ready, and the twenty-five women were summoned. They gave no kind of trouble, and by six o'clock the work was done. Women here braid their hair in two braids, which are wrapped about closely with cords, making them look like red ropes; these are then wound around the head and picturesquely fastened. The *huipils* of cotton are short, and decorated with scattered designs, worked in color, and loosely arranged in transverse bands. Belts are of wool, red in color, and broad, but not long. Over their shoulders the women wear, particularly in cool weather, a red and blue striped cotton shawl or wrap. The red worn — whether in belts, wraps, or hair-strings — is all of one shade, a dull crimson-red. As night fell, dozens of little bonfires were lighted in the plaza, made from cobwork piles of fat-pine. People were already gathering from other pueblos for market, and many of them slept through the night in the open market-place. The band played a mournful piece, repeatedly, during the evening, and some rockets were fired — no doubt, the tailing-off of the late fiesta.

Market had begun in the morning, as we prepared to leave, but the great plaza was not more than half-full, and there was little that was characteristic. Noteworthy, how-

Close of Market, Tenejapa

ever, were the great loaves of salt made at Ixtapa; about the size of old-fashioned sugar-loaves, they were shaped in rush-mats, and showed the marks of the matting on their surface; saws were used to cut off pieces for purchasers. The *agente* said that it was not good, being mixed with earth or sand. He, himself, came from the neighborhood of Tapachula, where quantities of salt are made from the lagoon water. The salt-water and the salt-soaked earth from the bottom of the lagoon are put into vats and leached, and the resulting saline is boiled in ovens, each of which contains an *olla*. The industry is conducted by *ladinos*, as well as indians, but the salt is poor.

It was 8:45 when we started, and almost immediately we began a hard climb over limestone, giving a severe test to our poor animals. At the summit we found a group of indian carriers, who, as usual, stopped at the pass to rest and look upon the landscape. The view was really beautiful, the little town lying in a curious, level valley, which was encircled by an abrupt slope, and which had been excavated from an almost level plateau. For some time, we followed this high level, but finally plunged down into a deep gully, where our road passed away to the left in a dry gorge, while to the right, the valley deepened abruptly by a great vertical wall. When we reached the point of sudden deepening, in the gorge below, we saw water, bursting in volume from the cliff's base. Dismounting from our horses, and climbing down, we found a magnificent arch of limestone over the emerging stream, the water of which was fresh and cold, and clear as crystal. The shallow portion of the valley marks the ancient level of the stream. In some past time, the stream had sunk, cutting a subterranean channel under its old bed, which was left high and dry. The deep part of the valley may be due to the falling of the roof of rock above the subterranean stream. Following up the ancient valley, we presently turned into one of its old tributary gorges, coming out into a country well-wooded with pines and oaks. The whole country hereabouts is composed of monoclines, all the crests presenting one long, gentle slope, with rocks dipping with the slope, and one abrupt short slope, cutting the strata. The roads, for the most part, follow along the edge of these monoclines, making them unsually long, though easy. The rocks over which we passed were an olive shaly-sandstone, with notable concentric weathering, limestone, and here and there, red sandstone, abundantly green-spotted. Indians, everywhere, were burning over fields, preparatory to planting, while the day was clear, the smoke rose in clouds, and at many places we suffered from these field fires. Twice we passed a point just as the flames leaped from one side of the road to the other, and rode between two lines of blaze. The fire, burning green branches and stalks, caused thousands of loud explosions, like the rattle of musketry.

Long before we were near it, we caught sight of Cancuc, the beautiful, perched upon its lofty crest. In San Cristobal, our journey had been matter of conversation among the *mestizos* and many and dire predictions had been made. "Ah, yes, it is easy for these gentlemen to do this work here in the *cabecera*, but let them get to Tenejapa, and Cancuc — there it will be another matter; they will be killed upon the journey; if they reach Cancuc, they will never leave the town alive." The town is built on the edge of a ridge, which drops in both directions, leaving barely room for the placing of houses. From it, we looked out in every direction over a magnificent landscape. Cancuc is famous for the insurrection of 1712. Curiously, like the outbreak at Chamula in 1868, it was due to the visions and religious influence of a girl. Maria Candaleria was the centre and impulse of the whole movement. Dr. Brinton has thrown

Tzendal Man and Wife; Tenejapa

Tzendals; Tenejapa

the incident, which abounded in picturesque details, and which caused the Spanish government great difficulty, into a little drama, which bears the name of the inspired priestess.

We were now within the district of my friend Valencia. Two years ago, when we passed through the country of the Mixes, he was the *jefe politico* of the District of Yautepec; he had been transferred to this state and this district, with his *cabecera* at Ocosingo. That town lay far from our course, and we had written Señor Valencia, that we planned to pass through his district, but had not time to visit the *cabecera*. We named the towns through which we planned to pass, and begged him to send orders directly to the local authorities, instead of trying to communicate with us. This he had done promptly, and during our stay in his district, everything was done for us without delay. The *agente* at Cancuc is a new official, but a man of sense, and sympathy for the indians, among whom he lives. We arrived at half-past three and had our *mozo* been on time, might have done some work. The *agente* showed us the historic picture in the old church; it is the portrait of a clergyman, whose influence did much to quell the insurrection in 1713. More interesting to us than the old picture, were groups of indians, kneeling and praying. When they knelt, they touched their foreheads and faces to the ground, which they saluted with a kiss. Having assumed the attitude of prayer, they were oblivious to all around them, and, curiously, their prayers were in the native language. The town-house was placed at the disposition of our party, but the *agente's* bed, in his own house, was given to me. As I sat writing at the table in his room, the whole town government — a dozen or so in number — stalked in. Most of them wore the heavy black *chamaras* made by the Chamula indians. These were so long that they almost swept the ground. The faces of the men were dark and wild, and their hair hung in great black shocks down upon their shoulders and backs. In their hands they held their long official staves. Advancing to the table where I sat, in the order of their rank, they saluted me, kissing my hand; arranging themselves in a half-circle before my table, the *presidente* placed before me a bowl filled with eggs, each wrapped in corn-husks, while the first *alcalde* deposited a cloth filled with a high pile of hot *tortillas;* a speech was made in Tzendal, which was translated by the second official, in which they told me that they appreciated our visit; it gave them pleasure that such important persons should come from such a distance to investigate the life and manners of their humble town; they trusted that our errand might be entirely to our wishes, and that, in leaving, we might bear with us a pleasant memory. They begged us to accept the poor presents they had brought, while they assured us that, in them, we had our thousand most obedient servants. And this in Cancuc — the town where we were to have met our death! At night, the fires on a hundred hills around us made a magnificent display, forming all sorts of fantastic combinations and outlines. In the evening, the son of the *agente*, who had been to Tenango with a friend, came home in great excitement. He was a lively young fellow of eighteen years. At the river-crossing, where they arrived at five in the evening, a black cow, standing in the river, scared their horses so that they could not make them cross; the boy emptied his revolver at the animal, but with no effect; it was clearly a *vaca bruja* — witch cow; an hour and a half was lost before they succeeded in getting their horses past with a rush.

The morning was spent in making pictures. While still in Yucatan, we heard about the music of Cancuc, and among our views was one of the musicians. These are three in number, and they head processions at fiestas; the drum, like that we saw at Tuxtla, is cylindrical, with two

The Town Government; Cancuc

heads; the *pito* is the usual reed whistle; the *tortuga*, a large turtle-shell, was brought from Palenque; it is hung by a belt to the player, and is beaten on the lower side with two leg-bones of a deer. The Cancuc dress is simple. Men wear the breech-clout, and, when they carry burdens, little else; at other times, they wear short, cotton trousers which hardly reach the knees. The chief garment is a *camisa*, of native cotton, with a colored stitching at the neck and along the seam where the two edges join; this *camisa* is of such length that, when girded, it hangs just to, or a little below, the lower edge of the trouser leg. The belts are home-woven, but are made of cotton which is bought already dyed a brilliant red or yellow. Women wear woolen belts made by Chamulas; their *enaguas* are plain, dull blue in color; their *huipils* are a dirty white, with a minimum of colored stitching. The chief industry at Cancuc is raising pigs for market.

At 1:15 we started from the town, and rode down the crest of long, gently-sloping ridges, which seemed interminable. The rock over which we passed was red sandstone, mottled and streaked with green, red shale, and occasional patches of conglomerate. Crossing a little stream by a pretty bridge, we made an abrupt ascent, and soon saw the little town, Cuaquitepec, at the base of the opposite hill.

We met many indians carrying great ovoidal jars which were made at Tenango, and which are chiefly used for carrying *chicha*. This is a fermented drink, made from the sap of sugar-cane, and is much used throughout this state and the adjoining parts of Central America. We inquired of a girl who carried such a vessel, what she had, and asked to try it. She gave us a sip in a wee gourd-vessel, holding less than a wine-glass. Knowing nothing of the price of *chicha*, we gave her six centavos, with which she seemed well satisfied. A little later, deciding to test the drink again, we stopped a man, who had a vessel of it, and again were given the little cup. On stating that we wished a centavo's worth, we were much surprised to have him fill a great *jicara* for the price mentioned. It seems the little vessel is carried only for sampling, and that a sale is made only after the purchaser has approved the quality.

Reaching Cuaquitepec at five, we rode up to the town-house, that the authorities might know that we had passed. The place is small and dwindling; there are relatively many *ladinos*, and few indians. They were expecting us, and seemed disappointed at our refusal to stop. The shell of the old church, almost ready to fall, suggested past magnificence. The little modern structure, at its side, is suited to the present needs. We were vexed at the wanton sacrifice of a great tree, which had stood near the town-house, but whose giant trunk was prostrate, and stripped of its branches. A man on foot showed us the road beyond the town, and it was moonlight before we reached Citala, where we planned to sleep. Of the town itself, we know nothing. The old church is decaying, but in its best days must have been magnificent. The *presidente* was absent, but his wife, an active, bustling intelligent *ladino*, expected us, and did everything possible for our comfort. Eggs, beans, *tortillas* and coffee made up the supper. A room, containing a bed for me, and *petates* on the floor for my companions, was waiting. When a light was struck more than a dozen great cockroaches were seen running over the wall, none of them less than two inches and a half in length, and of the most brilliant orange and dark brown. In the morning, a fine chicken breakfast was promptly ready, and the woman had summoned a *cargador* to be ready for our starting. She said that in this town there is a considerable indian population, and that these Tzendals are tall and strongly-built, in comparison with those of Cuaquitepec, and other neighboring

Indian Carriers Resting

Driving Pigs, near Cancuc

towns. She regretted that we could not wait until her husband came, as she had sent him word of our arrival, and was expecting him. We assured her that she had done everything which he could possibly have done, had he been present, and that we should, with pleasure, report our satisfaction to the *jefe*.

The *cargador* whom she supplied, was a comfort, after the wretched sluggards whom we had lately had. With our instruments upon his shoulders, he trotted, like a faithful dog, directly at our side, from start to finish, never showing the least weariness or sense of burden. Both foot *mozos* and *arrieros* through this district carry a mass of *posole* with them on a journey. Unlike that which Eustasio and his Zapotec companions carried, the mass here is pure corn, white and moist, being kept wrapped in fresh banana leaves; at every brookside, a *jicara* of fresh water is dipped, and a handful of *posole* is squeezed up in it till thoroughly mixed, when it is drunk. It tastes a little sour, and is refreshing. At 11:15, we passed the bridge over the stream on which Chilon is built, and a moment later drew up at the town-house. Here we regretted that our serious work with the Tzendals was done. We were received royally, and told that our house was ready. This was really so, a pretty little house of three good rooms having been cleaned and prepared for our use. We lay down and napped until the good dinner, which had been started when we had first been seen upon the road, and some time before we reached the village, was ready. Sitting on the porch of our little house, and looking out over bushes, full of roses, in the garden before us, we rested until the greatest heat of the day was past, when we started, and pushed on over the three leagues that lay between us and Yajalon, where we arrived at near sunset. The town is large, and, in great part, indian. The women dressed more gaily than in any other Tzendal town which we have seen; their *huipils* were decorated with a mass of bright designs, worked in colored wools or silk. Here we saw our first Chol, a carrier, passing through the village with his load; in order to make a start upon our final tribe, we had him halted, to take his measurements and picture. At this town, we stopped at a sort of boarding-house, or traveller's-rest, close by the town-house, kept by a widow with several children. We impressed upon this good woman the necessity of having breakfast without fail at five o'clock, as we wished to make an early start, stopping at Hidalgo for work during the hotter portion of the day, and pressing on to Tumbala at night. The poor creature kept me awake all night, making her preparations for the meal, which was to be a masterpiece of culinary art, and at four o'clock routed us all out with the report that breakfast was waiting on the table. It was a turkey-breakfast, too.

CHAPTER XXVI

CHOLS

(1901)

OF course, after such a start, we were delayed in getting the animals ready for the journey, and the sun had been up full half an hour when we left. It was a short ride to Hidalgo, which lies prettily in a small, flat valley, on a good-sized stream. We were doubtful about our reception, for Yajalon was the last town in Valencia's district, and we had no documents to present to the town officials, until we should reach El Salto, the *cabecera*, except our general letter from Governor Lopez. It is true that the *presidente* of Yajalon, at our request, had telephoned Hidalgo that we came highly recommended, and that everything possible must be done for our assistance. The *agente* was an old man, suffering from headache, who showed but listless interest in our work. In a general way, he gave us his endorsement, and we, therefore, took the management into our own hands. He had kept the people in town, so that we had subjects, though fewer than we had hoped. We measured twenty-seven men, and there were really no more in the town, the rest being away on *fincas*. The men gave us no trouble, but the women were another matter. Several times we issued orders that they be brought to the town-house for measurement, and each time, after an effort to obey our orders, we were told that they would not come. "Very good," said I, "if they will not come, it is plain that we must go and measure them in their houses." Accompanied by the town government, we started on our rounds. The first house was tightly closed, and no reply was made to our demands for entrance. The second was the same; one might imagine that it had been deserted for weeks. At the third, the door was opened, and within, an aged woman, ugly, bent, decrepit. Here we measured. The next house, and the next, and the next, were shut. And then another open house contained another veritable hag. Passing several other houses, tightly closed, we found a third old woman, and I saw that we were destined to secure nothing but decrepit hags, as representatives of the fair sex. At the next closed house, I stopped, and turning to an official, who spoke Spanish, said, "I am tired of these closed houses; who owns this house?" His name was given, and I wrote it down. "Very well," said I, "I shall recommend to the *jefe* of the district, when I reach El Salto, that he be made to pay a fine of five pesos." At this, the town officials gasped, but we walked to the next house, which was also closed. "Who owns this house?" And down went a second name. By the time I had three names of owners of closed houses on my paper, the officials held a hasty whispered consultation; then coming to me, they begged me to excuse them for a moment, as the *secretario* would accompany me upon my round, and they would soon rejoin us. With this, they disappeared, and we entered another old woman's house. When we emerged, a wonderful change had taken place; every house in the village had its door wide open, and in the doorway were to be seen anywhere from one to three or four ladies of all ages. From this time on, there was no lack of women, and the twenty-five were promptly measured.

We had picked out our subjects for modeling before we started on our rounds to measure women; and had left Ramon in charge of that part of our work, staying only long enough to see him make the mould of the first subject.

This was an indian, named Juan, the first *alcalde* of the village. We had carefully explained the operation to our subjects; we had described in detail the sensations and emotions connected with the thing, and thought we had the subjects well prepared. When Juan began, he seemed to have good courage, but we told a young fellow, who sat near and understood Spanish, that he should tell the man certain encouraging things which we repeated to him. The translation was promptly done, and we were therefore much surprised to see our subject's confidence gradually give way to terror. While we were applying the first mould, he began to sob and cry like a child; this was, however, nothing compared with the abject terror and sorrow which he displayed while we were making the face-mould. The tears flowed from his eyes; he sobbed, cried aloud, and we could see the thumping of his heart against his chest. We had never had a subject who took the matter so hardly. When the operation was completed, we learned the cause of all this trouble. Our interpreter turned out to be a joker, and, while we were telling him encouraging remarks, with which to soothe the subject, he was saying, "Now you will die; pretty soon you will not be able to breathe any more; you will be dead and buried before to-morrow; your poor widow will no doubt feel badly, but probably she will find another quite as good as you." We had always realized the possibility of such misinterpretations, but, so far as we know, this was the only time that our interpreter ever played us false.

On our return from measuring the women, we found that Ramon had made no progress. The three subjects, whom we had selected and left in his charge, under strenuous orders, had taken fright at Juan's experience and fled. We lost two hours in hunting them and bringing them in; and we should not have succeeded then, had it not been for

Juan's assistance. He seemed to feel that, having undergone the operation, it might ease his position, and decrease possible danger, if he had companions in misery. Finally, at 4:30, long after the hour we had set, we left for Tumbala. We secured six *cargadors* — one each for the four moulds, one for the instruments, and one for the remaining plaster,—as our pack-animals had long since passed. Five of them were left to follow at their leisure, on condition that they reach Tumbala early the next morning, but the sixth, a wee old man, who had helped us woman-hunting, went with us, by his own request, to carry the instruments. He was so small that we did not believe he could carry the burden, but he made no sort of trouble about it, trotting along most happily. We had been told that the road was *pura subida* — pure ascent — and so we found it. We were soon in the tropical forest of the Chinantla, and the land of the Mixes, with begonias, tree-ferns, bromelias, and orchids. Here and there, were bad bits of road, deep mud, slippery stones, irregular limestone masses. It was dark before we reached Tumbala, and although there was a moon, the mists were so dense that it did little good. Arriving at 6:45, we found the town a wretched place, with a worthless and nerveless *agente*. This was once the largest of the Chol towns, and we had thought to do the bulk of our work there. It is fortunate, indeed, that we stopped at Hidalgo, because Tumbala is now completely ruined by the contract-labor system, which has sent its men all through the country onto *fincas*. The *agente* would probably have done nothing for us, but his little daughter, much impressed by our letter from the governor, took an active interest in our welfare, promised to prepare a dinner, and decided him to give us sleeping-quarters in a store-room in the building. He thawed a little after we had eaten, but spoke discouragingly regarding the possibility of work-

The Toro; Frame and Bearer; El Triunfo

Playing Toro; El Triunfo

ing there. He said we would do well to go to El Triunfo; that it would take two days to find indians and bring them to the town; that there were no animals, nothing to eat, no conveniences in Tumbala, in all of which he probably was quite correct. Our *arrieros* had contracted only to this point from San Cristobal. We urged them to make the further journey, and offered them a price much above the regular, but they wanted to be back in San Cristobal for Holy Week, and assured us that the roads ahead were the worst that could be imagined, and that they ran the risk of killing all their animals if they went with us.

As we were on the road, a little before we reached Tumbala, we found a company of indian boys making camp for the night. Calling to us, they said that Don Enrique had told them if they saw us on the road, to say that we should keep straight on to El Triunfo, as he had a message for us. We had never heard of Don Enrique, and thought there was some error, but after supper, the *agente* handed us a letter which had come that afternoon from the gentleman in question. In it we read: "Sir: Mr. Ellsworth, of the Rio Michol Rubber Co., Salto, asked me by telephone to tell you that he will be waiting for you the 4th of April in La Cruzada, and hopes that you will kindly accompany Mrs. Ellsworth as far as Mexico, and that, in case she would not find a steamer in Frontera, he is going to charter one. Hoping to see you here in Triunfo, and waiting for an answer to La Cruzada, I remain, Yours truly, H. Rau." This was a gleam of light amid our dark affairs. There we were, with all our baggage and instruments, but without carriers, deserted by our *arrieros*, and with no opportunity in Tumbala to secure new animals or helpers; it was like the voice of a friend, to receive this English letter from El Triunfo, and we felt that, if worst came to worst, Don Enrique might help us out.

The room in which we slept was filled with stored stuff and two tables. On one of these I made my bed, while my companions spread a large *petate* on the floor, and our little indian carrier put down a small one for himself, as he declared he should not leave us until morning. He had a good supper, and in a fit of generosity, presented Louis with what was left of his package of *posole*. With much enthusiasm, he told us of an "animal" which he had seen and tried to catch upon the road. From his description, it appeared to be an armadillo. Before he lay down on his *petate*, he kissed my hand, wished me a good night's rest, and asked my good-night blessing He was happy in possession of a *real's* worth of *aguardiente*, from which, at intervals during the night, he drank. Early in the morning, he opened the door, and, looking out, crossed himself, and repeated his morning prayer. He then came to *Tatita* (little father) to receive his morning's blessing, and hoped that I had passed a good night in slumber. He then brought me a *jicara* of cool, fresh water, after which he urged me to take a sip from his dear bottle. Going outside a little time, he returned with two roses, heavy with dew and very fragrant, and gave them to me as if they were a gift for kings. Very soon, however, his potations got the better of him, and bidding us a fond farewell, he started for Hidalgo.

It was my day of fever, and I spent the greater portion of the morning on my hard bed, getting up from time to time to try to move the *agente* to procure an animal, on which I might make the journey to El Triunfo. Finally, in despair, after difficulty in securing a foot-messenger, I sent a letter to Don Enrique, asking him to send an animal for my use. During the afternoon, a fine mule and a letter came from El Triunfo. "Sir: The boy brought me your letter, and I send you a good mule for yourself, so we shall talk all the rest when you shall get here. If you need more pack-mules I will send them afterwards, as soon as you tell me how many you need. Hoping to see you this afternoon, I remain, Yours very truly, Henry Rau." The road was down hill, and there were but two or three bad spots. I rode through tropical forests, the whole distance, with high trees, bound together with a mass of vines, and loaded with parasitic or ærial plants. Here and there, rose the largest tree-ferns I have ever seen. I was not in the best mood, however, for enjoying the journey, and the hour-and-a-quarter seemed like much more. The great coffee *finca* of El Triunfo occupied an irregular valley, the slopes of which were covered with thousands of coffee-trees, with their magnificent dark green leaves and sweet-scented, white flowers. Three hundred and fifty thousand trees made up the plantation, which was one of two owned and managed by Señor Rau. The house was large, and rather pretentious, two stories in height, with buildings for cleaning, packing and storing coffee on the same terrace, and with a veritable village of houses for the indian workmen down below. I received a warm reception from the Señor and his household, who have established here a veritable bit of Germany in tropical America. Not only was I myself cared for, but I was urged to make no haste in going further, as no steamer would go from La Cruzada before the 4th, and it would be easy to reach that place in twenty-four hours. So, for several days the hospitable plantation-house was my home. Great lines of mules were constantly going from here, through to El Salto and La Cruzada, with loads of coffee, and coming back with provisions, and the many supplies necessary for an establishment of this importance. When the next *mulada* should appear, animals would be sent to Tumbala for my companions and the luggage. Curiously, none came for two whole days — a very unusual occurrence — and the boys remained prisoners in that dreary town for all that time. For my own part, I was thankful to reach a place where a comfortable bed and certain meals were to be counted on. My fever left me, but the following morning I found myself suffering from swollen jaws; every tooth was loose and sore, and it was difficult to chew even the flesh of bananas; this difficulty I had lately suffered, whenever in the moist mountain district of Pennsylvania, and I feared that there would be no relief until I was permanently out of the district of forest-grown mountains. Nor was I mistaken, for ten days passed, and we had reached the dry central tableand of Mexico, before my suffering ended. One day, while we were on the *finca*, considerable excitement was caused by one of the indians working in the field being bitten by a poisonous serpent. The man was brought at once to the house, and remedies were applied which prevented serious results, although his leg swelled badly. The serpent was killed, and measured about five feet in length, having much the general appearance of a rattlesnake, but with no rattles. Don Enrique says that the most dangerous snake in this district is a little creature more brightly colored, with a smaller head, which is less markedly flat, and with smaller fangs; he showed us one of these, not more than a foot in length, from whose bite a man on the plantation, a year before, had died. In telling us of this event, he gave us a suggestion of the working of the contract-labor system; the man who died owed one hundred and forty pesos of work — almost three years of labor; the *jefe*, indeed, had sent the son to work out the debt, but the young man soon ran away, and the most diligent effort to recapture him had failed.

Perhaps two hundred persons lived as workmen on the *finca* of El Triunfo. They were, of course, all indians, and

Chol Women; La Trinidad

were about evenly divided between Tzendals and Chols; it was impossible to gather them for measurement till Sunday, when they all came to the house and the store. It was a day of amusement and recreation for the laborers, a day when all of them — men, women, children — drank quantities of liquor. It was interesting to watch them as they came up to the store to make their little purchases for the week. All were in their best clothing, and family groups presented many interesting scenes. On Sundays and fiestas, they play *toro* — one man creeping into a framework of light canes covered with leather, meant to represent a bull, while others play the part of bull-fighters. The Chols present a well-marked type. They are short, broad-headed and dark-skinned; their noses are among the most aquiline in Mexico. Men, especially those of Tumbala, have a characteristic mode of cropping the hair; that on the back of the head is cut close, leaving the hair of the forward third of the head longer. The men are almost immediately recognized, wherever met, by the characteristic *camisa*, made of white cotton, vertically striped with narrow lines of pink, which is woven in the Chol towns, and does not appear to be used by other indians.

The doors of the hospitable home at El Triunfo are ever open, and a day rarely passes without some traveller seeking shelter and entertainment. Spaniards, Mexicans, Germans, Englishmen, Americans, all are welcome, and during the few days of our stay, the house was never free of other visitors. Among these was Stanton Morrison, famous in Yale's football team in '92; he now lives in this district, and has a coffee *finca* four hours' ride away.

Finally, at 10:10 Tuesday morning, April 2d, having completed all our work, we started from El Triunfo for our last ride of the season. We could easily have gone, starting in the early morning, to El Salto before night; as it was, Don Enrique planned a different method. We had good animals, which he had loaned us, or for which he had arranged for us with the muleteers. At two o'clock we reached La Trinidad, where he had promised that we should eat the finest meal in the State of Chiapas. We found a complete surprise. Trinidad is little more than a *finca*, or *rancho*, but it has an *agente*, and quite a population of Chol indians. The *agente* was a decent-looking fellow, active and ambitious; he talks a little English, and is something of an amateur photographer. His house of poles and mud presented no notable external features, but within, it was supplied with furniture so varied and abundant as is rare in any part of Mexico. Chairs, rockers, tables, cupboards, washstands, all were there; and beds, real beds, which for cleanness were marvels. As soon as we entered the house, fresh water and clean towels were brought. On the tables were vases of fresh-gathered flowers, in quantities, and beautifully arranged. The visible service for all this elegance, and for the meals, were two little indian girls not more than six or eight years old, neatly dressed, and an indian boy of the same size and cleanness. The invisible helpers were buxom indian girls, well-dressed and clean, but who never came into the room where we were, leaving all carrying, setting of tables, and serving, in the hands of these three little servants. There was, indeed, one other person in the household — a beautiful girl, slender and refined, whose relation to the master I do not know, but who was treated by him as if she were a veritable queen, or some lovely flower in the wilderness. Here we rested, ate and slept in comfort, and here, when morning came, we paid a bill which ordinarily would have seemed large; however, if one finds beautiful flowers in the wilderness, he must expect to pay. It was worth while paying to enjoy the best sleep, in the best bed, that one had had for months.

A Chol Family; La Trinidad

Chols; La Trinidad

The *agente* rode with us in the morning quite a league upon our road, to a place which he was clearing for a *milpa*. We had heard so much of the horrors of the road to El Salto, that we were prepared for the worst. It was not an abrupt descent, as we had expected, but for the most part level, over black mud. There were a few ups and downs, and there was one limestone hill with tree-ferns and begonias, and all that that implies. Much of the way we had a drizzling rain, and everywhere the air was hot and heavy. After four hours' riding, we stopped at ten to eat a breakfast which we had brought with us, and then rode through to El Salto, where we arrived at 12:30. This is the *cabecera* of the district, and the *jefe* could not understand why we should continue on our journey, as the steamer would not leave until the following day. Don Enrique, however, had urged us not to stop at El Salto, where he insisted the risk from yellow fever was great. He advised us to go on to La Cruzada, where he had a house and an agent, and where, he told us, we could arrange for sleeping and eating as comfortably, and far more safely, than in the town. The distance was short, but the place, in truth, was dreary. The landing was at the bottom of a little slope, at the upper edge of which stood Don Enrique's place, the storehouse of the steamship company, the house and barnyard of the manager of the mule trains, and one or two unattractive huts. When we arrived, we found that the mayor domo had that day resigned, and left the place, going to El Salto; before he left, he quarreled with the cook, and she had gone off in high dudgeon. Two young employes, left behind, advised us to return to El Salto until the time of embarkation. We, however, had left El Salto behind us, and had our luggage with us, and were little inclined to retrace our steps. After some grumbling, we were supplied with beds, but told that the food problem was impossible. After much wheedling, coaxing, bribing, and threatening, a woman in one of the huts promised to cook something for us, and we had nothing more to do but wait, until the steamer should be ready. The chief excitement of the day was when the mule trains were driven in, towards evening. With them came a swarm of mosquitoes, which absolutely darkened the air. Fortunately they did not stay, but after an hour and a half of troubling, disappeared as suddenly as they arrived. The river had fallen to that degree that it was impossible for our steamer, the Mariscal, to come up to La Cruzada, and we learned that it was anchored about a league down the river. A flatboat, poled by indians, came up to the landing, ready to receive cargo and passengers, and to transfer them to the steamer. In the morning, the loading of the flatboat and the getting ready for departure, took all our thought. At ten o'clock Mr. and Mrs. Ellsworth, with their baby and two servants, appeared in small canoes, which had been poled by indians from the plantation, several hours' journey up the Michol River. At the last moment, Mr. Ellsworth had decided to accompany his party to the city. When everything was loaded, quite promptly, at twelve o'clock, the flatboat pushed out from its moorings. Mr. Ellsworth's little launch was standing at the landing, and he invited me to ride in it, with him and Mrs. Ellsworth and the baby, to the steamer. We started off right proudly in the Miriam, but, alas, pride goes before destruction, and we had hardly left the heavy flatboat a little behind us, when our machinery broke down, and we had to wait until the clumsy scow overtook us, when we became common passengers again, and drifted down the stream to the Mariscal, passing the Lumeha plantation, an American enterprise.

The Mariscal itself was a little steamer, too small for the passengers and freight it had to carry. It had no beds nor cabin; it was dirty and crowded; it had not food enough to

Chols Resting; La Trinidad

feed the first-class passengers, who paid twenty-five pesos each for their short journey. There was, indeed, no other class of passengers, only one grade of tickets being sold. When complaints were made of the accommodations, or lack of all accommodations, the *agente*, who was on the vessel with us, expressed surprise, and seemed profoundly hurt. The stream is full of curves and bends, is broad, and notably uniform in breadth; it has considerable current, and is bordered closely by the tropical forest, except where little clearings have been made for *fincas*. Formerly, caimans, or alligators, were common, but they have become rare, through the diligent hunting to which they have been subjected for supplying skins. Two days are usually taken in the journey to Frontera, though it is not a fifteen hours' run. Mr. Ellsworth arranged for our going directly through, so that, except one stop at a midway station, we made a continuous journey, and drew up at Frontera at 9:50 in the morning.

It is a mean little town, but far cleaner than Coatzacoalcos. Real grass grows there, and the little plaza is almost a lawn. Last year, when yellow fever was so terrible at Coatzacoalcos, and when, even at El Salto, there were forty cases, there were none here. The town is hot, and during the two days we spent there, our chief effort was to keep cool. The steamer, Mexico, appeared upon the 6th, planning to leave the same day. A norther came, however, and rendered the bar impassable. In the morning, Easter Sunday, the wind had fallen somewhat. We saw the little celebration at the church, and, learning that the boat was likely to leave at noon, went aboard. At one we started. Sailing down the river, we soon found ourselves between the piers, and the moment of test had come. At the first thump of the keel upon the sand, we doubted whether we should pass the bar; still we kept along with steam full on and the bow headed seaward; nine times we struck the sandy bottom, but then found ourselves in deeper water, and were again upon the Gulf. The Mexico was just as dirty, the food was just as bad, and the crew just as unaccommodating, as in 1896, when we had our first experience of her. Rather than lie in the stuffy cabin, I took my blanket out on deck, and rolled up there for the night. Room was plenty, as there were only a score of passengers. When we woke, the boat was standing in the harbor of Coatzacoalcos, and we landed to eat a breakfast at the hotel. Through the day, we wandered about town, but were again upon the vessel at four o'clock. We now numbered about a hundred passengers, and everything was crowded. In the company was a comic theatre troupe. The day before, a number of the passengers had been seasick; on this occasion, three-fourths were suffering, and the decks were a disgusting spectacle. Still, fresh air was there, and again I made my bed on deck. In the middle of the night, having moved slightly, I felt a sharp and sudden pain in my right temple, exactly as if I had rolled upon a sharp, hot tack. I had my jacket for a pillow, and thought at first that there really was a tack in one of the pockets, and sought, but in vain, to find it. Lying down to sleep again, I presently moved my hand over the blanket on the deck, and suddenly, again, I felt the sharp, burning prick, this time in my thumb. Certain that it could not be a tack this time, I brought my hand down forcibly, and, rising, saw by the moonlight that I had killed a large, black scorpion. For two hours the stings felt like fire, but by morning had ceased to pain me; then I found two or three of the other passengers suffering from similar stings, and reached the conclusion that the Mexico was swarming with the creatures. At dawn, we sighted Vera Cruz, and were soon in the harbor, standing at anchor; at eight o'clock, we stood upon the wharf, and our journeys in Indian Mexico were ended.

Indian Hut; Santa Anita

Guadalupe; December 12

CHAPTER XXVII

CONCLUSION

BUT it was not necessary to go to distant Oaxaca and Chiapas to find Mexican indians. On the border of the capital city lie Santa Anita, Iztacalco, Mexicalcingo, Ixtapalapa, and a quantity of other villages and towns, where one may still find Aztec indians of pure blood, sometimes speaking the old language, sometimes wearing characteristic dress, and maintaining, to the present, many ancient practices and customs. At Santa Anita, for example, one may eat *juiles* and *tamales*, catch a glimpse of indian weddings, and delight his eyes with the fresh beauty of the *chinampas*, — wonderful spots of verdure and flowers — the floating gardens of the ancient Aztecs. Half an hour, or less, in the tram-car takes the traveller to Guadalupe, which may be called the heart of Indian Mexico. There, on the rock of Tepeyac, the Virgin appeared to Juan Diego; there, in the churches, dedicated in honor of that apparition, thousands of indians, from leagues around, gather yearly. On December 12, in the crowded streets of Guadalupe, groups, fantastically garbed as indians, dance in the Virgin's honor, and in their songs and dances, modern though they be, can be found suggestions of the olden time. Now and then, one may witness, what I saw in December, 1895 — a group of indian pilgrims from a distant town, singing and dancing to the Virgin, within the great church itself. And near the high altar, where thick glass plates are set into the floor, letting a dim light into the crypts below, one may see crowds of indians rubbing the smooth surface with their diseased parts to effect a cure. On the streets of the capital city, one daily sees bands of pure Otomis in rags and filth, bringing their loads of charcoal and of corn to market. Their ugly dark faces, their strange native dress, their harsh language, make on the stranger an impression not easily forgotten.

Reliable figures are wanting as to the number of pure Mexican indians. If the population of the Republic be estimated at fifteen millions, it should be safe to say that five millions of this number are indians of pure blood, speaking their old language, keeping alive much of the ancient life and thought. In some parts of Mexico, it almost seems as if what white-blood once existed is now breeding out. The indian of Mexico is conservative; he does not want contact with a larger world; his village suffices for his needs; he is ready to pay taxes for the sake of being let alone, to live in peace, after the way his fathers lived. In his bosom there is still hatred of the white man and the *mestizo*, and distrust of every stranger. The Chamula outbreak in 1868, and the Maya war just ended, are examples of this smouldering hatred. Mexico has a serious problem in its Indians; the solution of the problem has been attempted in various ways, according to whether the population dealt with was Totonac, Yaqui, Maya: it is no small task, to build a nation out of an indian population.

Soon after the publication of my "Indians of Southern Mexico," I had the pleasure of presenting a copy of the book to President Diaz, and of looking through its pictures with him. When we came to the general view of Yodocono, and its little lake, tears stood in the old man's eyes as he said, "Sir, that was my mother's birthplace, and in her honor I have established, at my own expense, two schools, one for boys, and one for girls." Looking at the round huts of Chicahuastla, he shivered, and remarked: "Ah, sir, but it is cold in Chicahuastla." I replied, "Your Excellency, I see that you have been in Chicahuastla." When he saw the Zapotec types, from the District of Tehuantepec, he said: "They are fine large fellows; they make good soldiers; when I was Governor of Oaxaca, I had a body-guard of them." He then told me of the six orphan boys who, in memory of his body-guard, he had adopted and educated; he told me with pride of the success which the five who still live had made, and of the positions they were filling. When he reached the portrait of the little Mixtec, carrying a sack of corn, who, with pride, had told me, in answer to my question, that his name was Porfirio Diaz, the President of the Republic looked long and earnestly at the picture, and I noticed that, when we turned the pages, his finger marked the spot where the likeness of his name-sake was, and, when the book was finished, before closing it, he turned back again, and looked at the little fellow's face. At the first Otomi portrait, he had said: "Ah, sir, but my schools will change the Otomis."

It would be pleasant to have faith in President Diaz' solution of the Otomi problem, but to me it seems doubtful. Of course, I recall with pleasure my visit to the boys' school at San Nicolas Panotla. It was interesting to see those little Tlaxcalan fellows solve problems in alligation and percentage, in bonds and mortgages; but it is doubtful whether any of them, in actual life, will have to deal with blending coffees, or with selling bonds, and cutting coupons. Still, from such indian towns great men have come in the past, and great men will come in the future. Benito Juarez, who laid the foundations on which Diaz has so magnificently built, was a pure-blood Zapotec. From the Aztecs, the Tlaxcalans, Mixtecs, Zapotecs and Mayas, we may hope much in the future. They were races of achievement in the past, and the monuments of their achievement still remain.

But that the Otomi, the Triqui, or the Mixe, should be made over by the schools is doubtful. Personally, I feel that the prosperity of Mexico rests more upon the indian blood than on any other element of national power. That schools will do much to train the more gifted tribes perhaps is true. But there are indians, and indians, in Mexico.

GLOSSARY OF SPANISH AND INDIAN WORDS

abusos. abuses, disturbances.
adios. adieu, good-bye.
agente. agent.
agua. water.
agua bendita. blessed water.
agua miel. lit. honey water, the unfermented juice of the maguey.
aguardiente. a spirituous liquor.
aguas frescas. refreshing drinks.
ahuacate. a fruit, the alligator pear.
aje, or axe. an insect; a greasy mass, yielding a lacquer-like lustre.
alcalde. a town judge.
arbol. tree.
arriero. a convoyer of loaded mules or horses.
atole. a corn gruel.
autorizada. authorized, having authority.
axolotl. a water salamander, with peculiar life-history.
ayatl, or ayate. a carry-cloth.
barranca. a gorge, or gully.
bruja. witch.
brujeria. witch-craft.
burro. ass.
cabecera. the head-town of a district.
cafe. coffee.
caiman. a reptile much like an alligator.
camaron. shrimp.
camisa. shirt.
cantera, cantero. a water-jar, or pitcher.
cargador. carrier.
carreta. cart.
carretero. a carter.
cascaron. an eggshell filled with bits of cut paper.
catalan. a wine, named from a Spanish town.

cenote. a cave with water.
centavo. a coin, the one-hundredth part of a peso; a cent.
chac mool. a stone figure, found at Chichen Itza, Yucatan.
chalupa. a boat-shaped crust with meat or vegetables in it.
chamara. a blanket for wearing.
champurrado. a mixture, as of atole and chocolate.
chapapote. chewing-gum.
chicha. an intoxicant made from sugar-cane.
chicle. chewing-gum.
chinampa. "floating garden," a garden patch.
chirimiya. a shrill musical instrument, somewhat like a fife or flageolet.
chirimoya. the custard-apple.
cigarro. cigarette.
cincalotl, cincalote. granary.
clarin. a bird, with clear note.
cochero. coachman.
colorin. a tree.
comiteco. a spirits made at Comitan.
Conquista. Conquest.
copal. a gum, much used as incense.
coro. loft.
corral. an enclosure for animals.
costumbre. custom.
coton, cotones. a man's upper garment, a sort of poncho.
cuartel. barracks.
cuezcomatl, cuezcomate. granary.
cura. parish priest.
curato. parish house.
danza. dance.
doctrina. doctrine, catechism.
don. Mr., used only when the Christian name of a person is spoken.
dulce. sweet, sweetmeat.
dulcero. maker or seller of sweets.
dulceria. sweetmeat factory.
enagua. woman's skirt.
enchilada. a fried tortilla with chili and cheese.
feria. fair.
fiesta. festival.
finca. farm, plantation.
firma. signature.

fiscal. fiscal officer.
frijol, frijoles. bean, beans.
golondrina. swallow.
gramatica. grammar.
gringo. somewhat derisive term applied to foreigners, especially Americans.
guardia. guard.
hacienda. a country-place.
haciendado, haciendero. the owner of an hacienda.
hennequin. a plant producing fibre, sisal hemp.
hermita. a retired shrine.
herreria. smithy, forge, ironworks.
h'men. conjuror.
huehuetes. the old ones.
huehuetl, huehuete. the ancient upright drum.
huerfano. orphan.
huipil, huipili. a woman's waist garment.
huipilili. a woman's waist garment, worn under the huipil.
idioma. idiom, language.
incomunicado. solitary, not allowed communication.
itinerario. itinerary.
itztli. obsidian.
ixtli. fibre from the maguey and cactus.
jacal. a hut.
jarabe. a popular dance.
jicara. a gourd-cup, or vessel.
jonote. a tree.
jornada. a day's march.
juez, judge.
ke'esh. a votive figure.
ladino. a mestizo, a person not Indian.
ladron, ladrones. thief, thieves.
liana. vine.
licenciado. lawyer.
lima. a fruit, somewhat like an insipid orange.
lindas. pretty (girls).
llano. a grassy plain.
machete. a large knife.
maestro. teacher, a master in any trade.
maguey. a plant, the century plant or agave, yielding pulque.

mai, pelico. tobacco, mixed with chili and lime.
malacatl, malacate. spindle-whorl.
malinche. malinche.
mamey. a fruit, orange flesh and brown exterior.
manta. cotton-cloth, a woman's dress.
mañana. to-morrow.
mapachtl. a small animal, perhaps the raccoon or badger.
mapaho. beating-sticks, for cleaning cotton.
mayores. chiefs, village elders, police.
medio. six centavos.
meson. a house for travellers.
mescal. a spirits, made from an agave.
mestizo. a person of mixed blood.
metate. stone upon which corn is ground.
milagro. miracle.
milpa. cornfield.
mogote. a mound or tumulus.
mole. a stew, highly seasoned with chili.
mole prieto. black mole.
moral. a tree, mulberry.
mozo. a young man, a servant.
mudo. mute, dumb.
mulada. a mule train.
muñeco. doll, figure.
municipio. town, town-government, town-house.
nacimiento. an arrangement of figures and grotto-work, made at Christmastide.
nada. nothing.
nagual. conjuror.
negrito. (diminutive) negro.
nublina. mist, fog.
ocote. pine-tree, splinter of pine.
otro. other.
padre. father, priest.
padrecito. priest.
pais. country, esp. one's native town.
panela. sugar in cake or loaf.
papaya. a fruit.
pastorela. a drama relative to the Nativity.
pastores. shepherds.

patio. inside court of house.
pelico, mai. tobacco, with chili and lime.
peso. a money denomination, one hundred centavos, one dollar.
petate. mat.
pinolillo. a species of tick.
pinto. a disease, spotted skin.
pita. a fibre.
pitero. a fifer.
pito. fife.
plaza. town square.
portales. a building with corridor in front.
posol, posole. corn prepared to carry on journey, for mixing with water.
prefecto. prefect.
presidente. president.
principales. principal men, councillors.
pueblito. small pueblo, village.
pulque. an intoxicant, made from maguey sap.
quichiquemil. a woman's upper garment.
rancho. a country-place.
ranchito. a small ranch.
rebozo. a woman's garment, a wrap or light shawl.
regidor. alderman.
remedio. remedy.
sangre. blood.
santo, santito. saint.
señor. sir, gentleman.
señora. madam, lady.
señorita. Miss, young woman.
serape. a blanket, for wearing.
sindico. recorder.
soltero. an unmarried man.
sombrero. hat.
subida. ascent.
tabla. board.
tamales. dumplings of corn-meal.
tambour. drum.
tatita. papa.
tepache. a fermented drink.
teponastl, teponaste. the ancient horizontal drum.
tienda. store, shop.

tierra caliente. hot country.
tigre. tiger, jaguar.
tinaja. water-jar.
topil. a messenger or police.
toro. bull.
tortillas. corn-cakes, cooked on a griddle.
tortuga. turtle.
tsupakwa. dart-thrower.
ule. rubber.
vaca. cow.
vamonos. come on, we are going.
viejos. old.
vomito. yellow fever.
xalama. a tree.
xtol, xtoles. a dancer, or dancers (see Merida, narrative).
zacate, sacate. hay, fodder.

ITINERARY

The expedition of 1896 was preliminary. We went by rail from the City of Mexico to Oaxaca, capital of the state of the same name. Thence, we journeyed by horse through the states of Oaxaca and Chiapas, to the city of Guatemala, entering the Republic of Guatemala at Nenton. The return journey was made by rail to the Pacific port of San Jose, steamer to Salina Cruz, rail to Coatzacoalcos, steamer to Vera Cruz, and rail to the City of Mexico. Only the portion of this journey between Oaxaca and Nenton is here described, the rest not lying in Indian Mexico. The City of Mexico was headquarters for the work in 1897-98. A trip was made by rail from there to Dos Rios, to measure and photograph the Otomis of Huixquilucan, in the state of Mexico. Thence we went to Patzcuaro by rail, and studied the Tarascans in the villages about Lake Patzcuaro, visiting these by canoe-trips. We then made a trip on horseback to Uruapan (then without rail connection), returning by some important indian towns. After returning to Mexico, we visited the states of Tlaxcala and Puebla. In and around the City of Tlaxcala, we secured our Tlaxcalan subjects. At Cuauhtlantzinco, we worked upon Aztecs. Our experiences at this large town of Puebla are not described, as Bandelier has already rendered the place familiar, and we ourselves have written of it elsewhere. With these two peoples, we made our first essays at bust-making. After returning to Mexico, we went by rail, on the Guadalajara branch of the Mexican Central, to Negrete. From there, by coach (there being then no railroad) to Zamora. Thence, we struck, on horseback, through the Tarascan territory, across to Patzcuaro. On the way, we secured our full series of Tarascan busts, at the Once Pueblos. By rail, we went from Patzcuaro to Dos Rios, to secure our lacking busts of Otomis at Huixquilucan. In the second field expedition, January to March 1899, we worked entirely in the state of Oaxaca. At first a trip was made, by horse, from Oaxaca into the Mixteca Alta, where Mixtecs and Triquis were studied. Again starting from Oaxaca, we traveled over our old trails of 1896, through the mountains to Tehuantepec, returning by the high-road in common use. Zapotecs were studied at Mitla and Tehuantepec, and the Mixes, Juaves, and Chontals in various towns and villages. The season's work closed by our study, at and near Cuicatlan, of the Cuicatecs. At this town, too, we began to work upon Chinantecs. In the third field expedition, during the early months of 1900, we visited seven populations, making our regular study upon six of them. To fill a week that would otherwise have been lost, we made a pedestrian trip through the interesting indian towns on the slopes of Malintzi. Then, from Cuicatlan as a center, we made two journeys — one to San Juan Zautla and San Pedro Soochiapan, to examine Chinantecs; the other to Coixtlahuaca, for seeing Chochos. From Cuicatlan, we struck north by rail to San Antonio, and, by coach to Teotitlan del Camino and by horse beyond, penetrated to the great Mazatec town of Huauhtla. Chinantecs, Chochos, and Mazatecs are tribes of Oaxaca. Leaving that state, we traveled by rail to Tulancingo. From there, by coach and on horseback, we visited Otomi, Aztec, Tepehua and Totonac towns in the states of Puebla and Hidalgo. With the field season of 1901, our work in Indian Mexico ended. It was pursued in three separated areas. From the City of Mexico, we went by rail to Tampico. From that point, a journey by canoe and horse enabled us to see the Huaxtecs of the state of Vera Cruz. Returning to Tampico, a trip by steamer across the gulf brought us to Yucatan. Progreso and Merida were visited, and our work was done upon the Mayas living near the town of Tekax. A second trip on the gulf brought us to Coatzacoalcos, whence the railroad was used to Tehuantepec and San Geronimo. From the latter point, an ox-cart journey of ten nights, across the states of Oaxaca and Chiapas, brought us to Tuxtla Gutierrez. By horse we continued through Chiapas to El Salto, where we took steamer for Frontera. From there, by steamer to Vera Cruz and then by rail, we traveled to the City of Mexico. Zoques, Tzotzils, Tzendals, and Chols were studied in this portion of the journey.

APPENDIX

STARR IN OLD MEXICO

OAXACA, Mexico, March 1.— Prof. Frederick Starr, of the University of Chicago, is deep in the midst of his savages. He is manipulating primitive town governments, wielding the authority of federal and state governments, county police, and that of the clergy as well. He is threatening, cajoling, clapping in jail, when necessary, and in general conquering his series of strange nations. I found him doing all this, and more, in a little native village fifty miles from the city of Oaxaca, Feb. 2nd. The fat little man was complete master of the Zapotec town of Mitla, far distant from the end of the last of the railroads, a town famous for its ruins. He bustled about like a captain in a war haste, dressed in a massive Indian sombrero, from which a white string floated picturesquely behind, a necktie of slim, dusty black, which seemed not to have been unknotted for many a day, a shirt less immaculate than the one he may wear at the entertainment shortly to be given him in London, and no coat. The professor's trousers are not Indian. They are farm trousers, of an original type, with double seat for the saddle.

The professor's blood was up. A grand native feast — in which drunken dances, bull-fights, and a state of accumulated irresponsibility are the rule — had delayed him three days. The Indians could no more be measured and "busted"— as the professor calls the making of plaster casts — than could the liquor they had drunk. After three days of pleading, threatening, and berating, in which orders from every government and church official in the country, from lowest to highest, had failed, Prof. Starr seized the black-bearded and wiry president of the town council, the chief potentate of the reeling set, called him a drunken scoundrel, threatened in deep seriousness to imprison every man in the town, and finally won his point — but not until the feast was done. When feasts are over, the people are kindly, suave, gracious.

Then the professor corralled those he wanted. He was to measure for scientific purposes 100 of the Indians, in the order in which they chanced to present themselves. After such wheedling as it must have taken infinite practice to acquire — pattings of the Zapotec back, hugging of the men, chucking the children, with elaborate explanations — the thing "took" and the people fell into the spirit of it. The jail was the only accessible building, and was strangely empty. It was of adobe, a jail of one room, with a dirt floor. There were no windows, only the single barred door.

From every cane-walled, thatched, tropical hut that helps to make the irregular cluster around the central plaza and its adjoining bull ring they came, if not to be measured, to see. They were driven by the highest of the town authorities — for every element of the population waited on the bidding of the little sugar-tongued professor from the north — one by one into the jail, and the rest curiously watched. The measuring was done without undressing, but the "busting" was the point of chief interest. Five representative specimens had been carefully selected for this purpose. They were won slowly, by the glitter of 75 cents of Mexican silver. In some towns, only 50 cents was required, and in others, $1. The smirking Indian, with his wildness hidden away, or only peeping from his eye, entered. He disrobed with no shame. He was put flat on the floor, face down, on a little piece of matting. At this stage some objected. Then the Anglo-Saxon was down on the floor, wheedling, talking such sweetness as can be spoken without silliness only in the Spanish tongue.

The victim finally consents. Then the Mexican plaster worker, who has followed the caravan from its start, goes to work. He makes a cast of the back of the head and shoulders, and the Indian is turned over, face up. Another cast of the breast and neck and chin is made, and yet another of the front half of the head and the face, with little tubes for breathing sticking through it. The Indian has grunted, snorted, laughed and squirmed, but he has been made to understand that he must be still. That great 75 cents is held always over him, and the thing is accomplished.

During all the process, the crowd of Indians about and in the jail was eager-eyed and astonished. The women wear odd woolen, blanket-like skirts of red or black, folded in two great plaits down the front. The dress does not reach the ankles, and the feet are bare. They carry the baby on the back, wound in the rebozo, with its bare legs straddling her and sticking out. The men wear a sandal quite different from the ordinary Mexican footgear.

Of the 100 that were to be measured, Jose was one. Jose was of a better family, a character in the town, and proud. He rebelled. This breach of the professor's authority could not be allowed. Jose was summoned by the president of the town, the honeyed, affable "Señor Presidente," the same who had been called the drunken scoundrel, now accommodating, a true and emotional friend. Jose sent a thousand excuses, and finally defiance.

"That man," cried the professor, showing his writ of authority from the *jefe politico* of the district, "I order to be arrested."

Jose did not flee. He was found next morning in the bull ring riding a bull. He was arrested by the Chicagoan's orders, and taken to jail. He was peremptorily ordered by the professor to appear for the measurement. He escaped, and again defied the powers. He was again caught, and it was explained to him by the president that this man of might from the beyond had sworn to drag Jose with him all the way across this wild country slowly to Tehuantepec, thence back to the city of Oaxaca, where the state authorities would deal most painfully with him. And this, indeed, in mighty manner and impressively, had the "man from the beyond" sworn to do. Jose came and was measured, and I afterward saw him calling to the professor to come and take a jolly drink out of the gourd he was shaking at him, in the manner of a comrade.

In the afternoon, the work being done, the civilities and sugared conduct must be continued, with a view to future visits. The professor wanted to enter the church, which, though modern, stands in the middle of one of the mysterious ruins. The church was locked, and the mayor-domo not to be found.

"But I must photograph a strange picture you have in there."

"The mayor-domo is drunk, at your service, my most excellent friend," replied the president, sympathetically. "I am sorry, but he got under the influence three days ago at the beginning of the feast, and he has slept ever since. Ah, the mayor-domo is sleeping now, my excellent friend, and he has the keys."

"You shall send a boy into the tower to ring the bell and wake the mayor-domo," cried the professor.

The crowd sat on the stone steps, the bell was pealed, and at last the church was opened, and the picture photographed.

The procession then moved to the top of an ancient pyramid, in which tombs have been opened, and bones and gold ornaments found. The professor dashed through all the tunnels, with the government after him, before mounting to the top. On top a strange conversation was held between the professor and the president and secretary. They appealed to this northern man, who seemed to have all earthly authority back of him, to grant them one longed-for boon. Would he not please speak, when he returned to the capital, to the minister of encouragement, that he send them a brass band! They wanted to welcome northern visitors to the ruins with modern music.

"You have great power. You need but to ask of those in Mexico and the band will come. Most beloved friend, oh, most excellent professor from the far north, give to us a brass band!" And the professor promised to speak to Minister Leal about it. Then, too, the beastly state government was dragging some of their precious ruins away to put in a museum. Would the professor please have the kindness to stop this? The professor promised to do what he could, and he was hugged and blessed and patted by the simple people.

Prof. Starr began his ethnological studies to westward of Oaxaca. Mitla is eastward. In the west, he visited two tribes — the Mixtecas and the Triquis. The latter are a branch of the former, but much different, living in round bamboo huts, surprisingly like those of some African tribes. He secured two excellent casts of the Triquis, and three of the Mixtecas. He intended to take five of each tribe he visited, but his plaster failed to arrive. He studies the languages, also, as he goes, and finds many varying dialects, from each of which he secures a test vocabulary of 200 words. He is now approaching the Mixes, the "cannibals." All the City of Mexico papers laugh at the idea of his encountering the slightest danger, and the professor himself scoffs at it. He believes some of the Mixes have, within forty years, eaten human flesh, but he says he is certain they are harmless now.

CHARLES F. EMBREE.

[From *The Chicago Record:* March 24, 1899.]

THE PURPLE SPOT ON MAYA BABIES

WHEN I was in Yucatan in 1901 the parish priest of Texax told me that it was said that every pure blood Maya Indian has a violet or purple spot on his back, in the sacral region. He stated that this spot was called by the native name, uits, "bread," and that it was vulgar or insulting to make reference to it. I at once examined three Mayas of pure blood — a boy of ten years and two adult males — but found no trace of such a spot. I concluded that the presence of the spot might be an infantile character, as it is among the Japanese, but at that time I had no opportunity to examine Maya babies.

Dr. Baelz, a German physician, who has spent many years in Japan, long ago called attention to the existence of such spots on Japanese infants. The spots described by him were of a blue or purple color, were located upon the back (especially in the sacral region), and were variable in form and size. They were temporary, disappearing at from two to eight years of age. The occurrence of these infantile color blotches was so common in Japan as to be almost characteristic of the race.

In time, other students reported similar spots on other Asiatic babies, and on non-Asiatic babies of Mongolian or Mongoliod peoples. Chinese, Annamese, Coreans, Greenland Eskimos, and some Malays are now known to have such spots. Sacral spots have also been reported among Samoans and Hawaiians.

Practically, all these people belong to the great yellow race, as defined by De Quatrefages, and are, if not pure representatives of that race, mixed bloods, in part, of it. Baelz and some other writers have, therefore, gone so far as to consider the purple sacral spot a mark peculiar to that race, and to believe its occurrence proof of Mongolian origin. They have asked whether the spot occurs among American Indians, and would consider its occurrence evidence of an Asiatic origin for our native tribes. Satisfactory observations had not been made. Baelz himself found two cases among Vancouver Island Indians.

In my recent trip to Mexico I planned to look for this spot among several Indian tribes. Out of six populations that I expected to visit I really saw but two — the Aztecs and the Mayas. I do not believe that the sacral spot exists among Aztecs. I made no search, because Aztec friends, who would be sure to know, all agreed in denying its occurrence. Among the Mayas, the case is different. In the little Maya town of Palenque I examined all the pure blood babies. The back of the first little creature bared for my inspection bore a clearly defined, dark blue-purple spot, just where it might be expected. The spot was almost two inches wide and nearly three-fourths of an inch high. The child was a boy of eight months. A brother, two years old, showed no trace of the spot, but the mother says it was formerly well defined.

Every one of the seven pure Maya babies, below ten months old, in the town was purple-spotted. A pair of boy twins, two months old, were marked in precisely the same place with pale blue-purple spots, of the same size and form. In one boy of ten months the spot seemed to be disappearing and was represented by three ill-defined and separated blotches. In the village, there were three babies of suitable age, but of mixed — Spanish-Maya — blood; no one of these showed any trace of the colored spot. We may say, then, that in Palenque every Maya baby below ten months of age was sacral spotted, and that no Mestizo baby was.

Does this prove that the Mayas are Asiatics by ancestry? The daily press asserts that I make that claim; it is mistaken. I am free to say I don't know what to do with my spotted Maya babies. I presume that Baelz will cousin them with his little Japanese.

FREDERICK STARR.

From *The Chicago Tribune:* January 11, 1903.

INDEX